Psychology
Is
Social

READINGS AND CONVERSATIONS IN SOCIAL PSYCHOLOGY

Psychology Is Social

Fourth Edition

Edward Krupat

*Massachusetts College of Pharmacy
and Allied Health Sciences*

 LONGMAN

An Imprint of Addison Wesley Longman, Inc.

New York • Reading, Massachusetts • Menlo Park, California • Harlow, England
Don Mills, Ontario • Sydney • Mexico City • Madrid • Amsterdam

In memory of my mother

⌒

Acquisitions Editor: Eric Stano
Project Editor: Cyndy Taylor
Cover Design: Nancy Danahy
Text Design: Paris Typesetting, Inc.
Electronic Page Makeup: Paris Typesetting, Inc.
Printer and Binder: Maple Press
Cover Printer: Maple Press

Please visit our website at http://longman.awl.com

ISBN: 0-321-04035-X

2345678910—MA—010099

Contents

Preface to the Fourth Edition

Each time I revise *Psychology is Social,* two challenges present themselves. The first is, how can I retain the features of the book that past users have liked? Which specific selections should I keep, and how can I find new articles for the book that past users will like just as much as the old ones? The second is, what can I do that is new? What little wrinkles can I add to attract first-time readers, and what can I do to make the book more inviting for those who are new to it?

The answers to both of these questions, however, are pretty much the same. First and foremost, I have retained contents from the third edition and selected articles for the fourth based on their readability. Some topics are inherently more interesting than others, but even the most interesting topic can seem deadly boring and the most engaging research impossible to understand unless the writer is doing his or her job. So, once again, I have gone out looking for serious social psychology explained at a high level, but written in a straightforward and engaging manner. For instance, two new selections, Scott Stossel's *Atlantic Monthly* piece on violence in the media and Robert Sternberg's description of his triangular theory of love, make important and conceptually complex points while using language that is simple and examples that are accessible to all.

Beyond this I have tried to focus on three themes that I believe are consistent with the state of the field today. First is an interest in diversity. Social psychologists have finally discovered that many of the phenomena we study and the findings we report are culturally based and that the way in which Americans process information, socialize children, and respond to social pressures are not necessarily universal. To respond to this growing interest in the section on self, for example, I have included a part of the highly respected and much-cited article by Hazel Markus and Shinobu Kitayama on culture and the self dealing with the distinction between the independent and interdependent self. Under social influence, I have selected part of a chapter from *Social Psychology Across Cultures* discussing conformity and independence as they vary from country to country.

Second, I think the field is interested in rediscovering some of its roots, reflected in the desire for students to read some of its classic studies in the original. To satisfy this interest I have selected articles containing two of the most cited pieces of research in the field. First is the classic experiment by Leon Festinger & Merrill Carlsmith, one of the defining studies in testing dissonance theory, written clearly and directly. The second is a description of the diffusion-of-responsibility helping model written by Bibb Latane & John Darley (originally in the first edition of the book, and now resurrected for the fourth). Both of these offer students a chance to see how the original theories were stated and tested, allowing and encouraging them to compare the current state of knowledge with the research that served as the building blocks for what followed.

A third theme is an interest in field research, research that tests important concepts and theories beyond the laboratory and has strong external validity. Once fueled by a debate about experimental *versus* field research, basic *versus* applied, social psychology finally seems to have found respect for experimental *and* field studies, applied *and* basic interests. Two examples of important non-experimental research included for the first time in this edition are the work of Shelley Taylor and Gayle Dakof in testing the role of social support for cancer patients, and the research of Mark Snyder and Allen Omoto on identifying the motivations for volunteering to work with AIDS patients.

In short, I hope that the new edition reflects the field of social psychology as it exists today, with room for old and new, applied and basic, experimental and field. In creating this new edition, I want to thank Claude Steele, Richard Moreland, and Caryl Rusbult, each of whom offered wonderful insights and important personal reflections about their respective areas of study in my conversations with them. One of the greatest pleasures I get from revising this book is the opportunity to chat with

leaders in the field, to learn something new from them, and to pass their ideas and reflections along to others. At Addison Wesley Longman, Eric Stano deserves much gratitude for encouraging me to revise the book, and Tim Roberts has helped get the work done, coordinating many different tasks and solving problems with much good cheer. I owe special thanks to Richard Smith, a wonderful friend and colleague, who offered many valuable comments on the field and how to improve the book to fit it. And in addition I want to thank Kenneth Bordens, Samuel Juni, Janet Sigal, and Yvonne Wells for their highly useful comments on what they have liked about the book in the past and what it might look like in the future. On the home front, my wife Barbara deserves, as usual, more credit than I usually remember to give her. The work would be impossible without support at the office and at home, and I am truly grateful to my friends and colleagues for large amounts at the former and to my wife for an endless supply at the latter.

Ed Krupat
Boston, MA

Social Psychology: An Introduction

In order to get a sense of just what social psychology *is,* first it is necessary to deal with some common misconceptions and see just what social psychology *is not.* When I meet someone and I am asked what I do for a living, the simple statement "I'm a social psychologist" usually causes nothing but trouble and confusion. Either I get a blank stare or I receive a response that embodies the misunderstandings people have about social psychology.

The most common reaction is, "Oh, so where is your practice?" revealing a common misconception that all of psychology is *clinical* or *abnormal* psychology. When I answer that I don't have a practice, that I teach and do research, people are often confused because they associate psychology with the study of abnormal behavior and the practice of psychotherapy. The niche that social psychologists have carved out for themselves is unique in that social psychologists study *normal* rather than abnormal processes, they consider the *whole* individual rather than merely reaction times or learning curves, and they believe that behavior is determined by the manner in which the individual sees and makes sense of the world. In short, social psychologists do research that attempts to understand and explain everyday social behavior, the ways in which people interact and influence one another. So while I don't "have a practice," the practice of social psychology can still be useful and helpful to people in many ways.

The second reaction to the statement "I'm a social psychologist" is "Oh, how nice. You're a sociologist. I have a cousin who's a sociologist too." No matter how many times I try to say, "No, not a sociologist. A social psychologist," the answer comes back, "Sociologist, social psychologist. Big deal, no difference."

The point, of course, is that there are considerable differences. One key issue

1

that distinguishes many sociologists from their psychologically oriented colleagues is that sociologists tend to study people at what is known as the aggregate level. Sociological explanations often tend to lose the individual, to submerge the individual in a consideration of group classifications, social structures, and patterns of social organization. Social psychologists in no way deny the powerful effects of culture, religion, and social class on behavior. Yet their interest is not in looking at the class structure itself. Instead, social psychologists focus on the individual and how he or she contributes to, perceives, and is affected by these larger entities.

B = f(P,E)

Although the focus may be different, social psychology does share one key element with sociology. This is a recognition that the individual's behavior is critically determined by what is happening outside the individual in his or her environment. Referred to as *situationalism,* this focus on the role of *external* variables actually sets social psychology apart from many other areas of psychology that deal with *internal* determinants of behavior, such as personality, motivation, drives, and needs.

We can ask: Which are more important, psychological (internal) or sociological (external) variables? Historically, many psychologists and sociologists have spent a great deal of time and energy debating the relative importance of internal versus external influences as if the answer had to be one or the other. Kurt Lewin, who many recognize as the single most important voice in social psychology, made this debate seem trivial in generating a simple but highly sensible formula. It reads:

$$B = f(P,E)$$

Translated, Lewin has said that "Behavior is a function of the person and the environment." He has told us that we will find useful but incomplete answers if we only look inside the individual for answers, just as we will find good but equally incomplete answers if we only look to the person's environment. We must therefore look within *and* without, recognizing that it is the combination or interaction of these factors that determines how and why people behave as they do. In essence, we could say that social psychology's true contribution is not simply giving a situationist look to psychology, but in going beyond that by embracing the perspective of "interactionism."

An Example: Suicide. Let us make this point more concrete by taking a social phenomenon, suicide, and seeing how it has been explained by some classic sociological and psychological thinkers. Emile Durkheim, the French sociologist, looked at the sociocultural factors that he believed determined suicide rates. He investigated records of suicide in different historical periods and in different countries and found that people in various social classes and religious categories living under certain political conditions were more likely to commit suicide than others (Durkheim 1897). However, while he made it clear that social conditions do affect suicide rates, Durkheim did not fully provide the "why" of suicide. Although social conditions can make certain groups feel more involved than others, Durkheim cannot tell us why, under identical social conditions, some people did commit suicide while others did not, or even why some committed suicide while others committed homicide. His approach leaves out the individual and the subjective impact of the situation on the person. He can explain why suicide rates differ in various groups, not how the individuals within those groups perceived their conditions and reacted to them.

In direct contrast to a purely sociological explanation of suicide, we have the purely psychological. It is different, but also lacking in certain respects. The classic Freudian explanation of suicide is that it represents a case of aggression turned against the self. Some of the personal characteristics associated with suicide are extreme depression, a lack of good interpersonal relationships, and the feeling of being a burden to others. This approach has just what the other does not—a personal description of the feelings and perceptions of the suicidal person—but it lacks what the sociological one has.

Emphasizing the role of internal factors such as personality and emotion tends to ignore the complex social forces acting on the person. While some people may feel depressed and contemplate suicide, social forces and complex social norms may influence whether the suicide will actually be carried out and even how. For instance, in World War II those Japanese pilots who flew kamikaze missions felt that they died with honor for their cause, yet the thought of flying a kamikaze mission seemed bizarre to American pilots. The difference was in the norms and values of the two societies. Therefore, to truly understand a phenomenon such as suicide, we need to understand the manner in which both internal and external factors interact.

Some Practical and Research Examples. Applying the interactionist approach to a more mundane example, imagine that you were working for an advertising agency attempting to develop a campaign to sell auto insurance. Should you expose people to ads that reassure and calm them, like the Allstate commercials that tell consumers they are "in good hands" if they buy that brand of insurance? Or would it be better to shake them up by showing them scenes from gruesome auto accidents, reminding them that your insurance company will take care of their families if they should die?

The question of "high fear" versus "low fear" only asks half of the interactionist question: what kind of situation or environment should we expose people to? The other half of the $B = f(P,E)$ equation suggests that the outcome should also depend on the nature of the people involved. After many studies with conflicting results on the effects of low versus high fear campaigns, researchers began to look into the interaction of fear and personality. In a classic study in which Irving Janis and Seymour Feshback (1954) tried to get people to change their toothbrushing habits, for instance, the researchers discovered that subjects who were high in anxiety responded well to low fear, but were overwhelmed when presented with a powerful fear-inducing campaign. However, people who were low in anxiety were able to cope with the high fear message and responded slightly better to that than the low fear message.

More recently, social psychological health researchers have proposed that hospital patients should benefit from being given more information before they undergo threatening procedures such as surgery. Although attempts to provide a more information-filled environment have been generally successful, for some patients information seems to do more harm thatn good. Reminding us of the interaction of person and environment, Suzanne Miller and Charles Mangan (1983) found that people who typically cope with stress by focusing on their problems benefitted greatly from being provided with information; however, those whose coping style was characterized by denial were actually better off when they received less information.

$B = f(P,E)$ helps us understand why some students choose to go to huge mega-universities while others select small colleges, and why some people thrive in urban settings while others want to be as far away from a city as they can be. Many years ago when I was a graduate student, I got a summer job as a research assistant in New York City. During the course of the summer, I overheard a famous social psychologist complaining about the lack of resources he was being provided with. Aware of his fame, I suggested that he could probably have any position he wanted, and I even had the audacity to recruit him personally to the school I was attending, the University of Michigan. He thanked me and declined to even consider it, saying, "If I ever had the choice between a so-so position in a great city and a great position in a smaller town, I would always opt for the city." Having related this story over the years, I find that some students would agree, but many others would give just the opposite answer. Although I have no idea what Lewin would have answered for himself, I do know that, in order to predict how satisfied people in general would be with their homes and jobs, we would tell you that you had to know about *both* the people and their environment.

BASIC AND APPLIED RESEARCH

As we have noted, social psychology's response to the person/environment debate, which many people phrased as an "either/or" question, is to say *both*. Another parallel debate has been the so-called "basic/applied" question. Should researchers direct their attention toward basic (or pure) research, whose goal is the development and testing of knowledge and theories? Or should they be focused on the applied side, becoming involved in problem solving and the search for solutions to important social issues?

The answer given by social psychology once again is that this is not an either/or situation; these two interests are not mutually exclusive. Good theories should be testable in and applicable to the real world, and they should help us find solutions to important matters. The real world is the perfect context to test and refine our theories to see if they hold up when exposed to the complexities of life. In a similar vein, good applications and effective interventions need to be based on solid theory. Without important theoretical bases for developing solutions, we wander from one problem to the next without an effective framework. To cite Kurt Lewin once again, "There is nothing so practical as a good theory" (Lewin 1951, p. 169).

After going from one extreme to the other on the basic/applied question, modern social psychology finally seems to be maturing and thereby reflecting and honoring Lewin's words. Once, basic and applied researchers looked down upon one another and had little contact. Then the two camps made an uneasy peace and began to interact and show grudging respect for one another's contributions. But today the basic/applied split shows signs of slowly disappearing. Some of the field's most respected basic researchers are among its most active problem solvers. And those who are looking to prevent the spread of AIDS, who are involved in reforming the legal system, and who are combating discrimination are actively working from and testing new theories as they develop interventions and offer advice and solutions.

A NOTE ABOUT THE BOOK

This book is divided into ten sections, each reflecting a major area of interest in social psychology. Each section begins with a "conversation" with a social psychologist who is highly respected in that area. Social psychology is all about people, why they act, how they think, what they do—and the conversations demonstrate that, behind all of this research, real people exist. In these conversations I have asked them to explain what their ideas or theories are, how they came up with them, and even how they came to be interested in their topic in the first place. The conversations are unrehearsed and free-flowing, and they are meant to make academic subjects come alive by offering readers a glimpse into the thinking of those people whose names we see in the textbooks.

The articles in the book, usually about three to a section, have been chosen to represent a number of types and viewpoints. They come from popular sources and texts as well as academic journals, but my primary concern in selecting each of them has been readability. In research papers in particular, I have edited the "Results" sections in those instances where the statistical discussions were too complex and technical. In short, I have made every attempt to make this book, to use a phrase that has become a cliché in just a few short years, "user-friendly."

So I invite students to read, to learn, even to *enjoy* as you discover what social psychologists have discovered about you and me, about the nature and causes of everyday social interaction.

References

Durkheim, E. (1987). *Le suicide: Etude de Sociologie.* (Trans. *Suicide: A Study in Sociology.*) Paris: Alcan.

Janis, I. and Freshbach, S. (1954). Personality differences associated with responsiveness to fear-arousing communications. *Journal of Personality, 23,* 154–166.

Lewin, K. (1951). Problems of research in social psychology. In D. Cartwright (Ed.), *Field Theory in Social Science: Selected Theoretical Papers.* Westport, CT: Greenwood.

Miller, S. M. and Mangan, C. E. (1983). Interacting effects of information and coping style in adapting to gynecologic stress: Should the doctor tell all? *Journal of Personality and Social Psychology, 45,* 223–236.

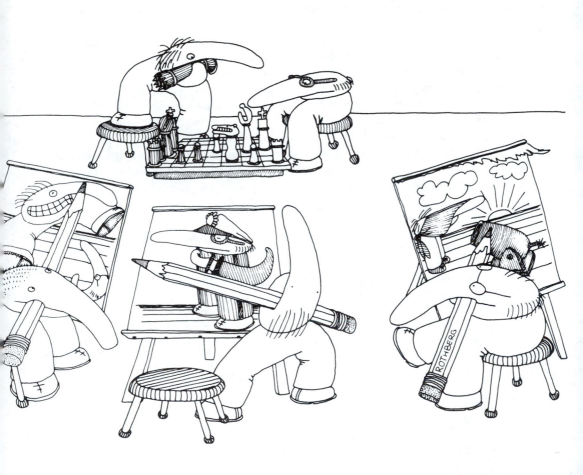

Social Cognition: Making Sense of the World

An emphasis on social cognition dominates modern day social psychology. This focus on how we think about people and situations is not just an important subfield in itself, but serves as the framework for much current research and intervention throughout the field of social psychology.

Susan Fiske, Professor of Psychology at the University of Massachusetts at Amherst, is one of the most respected people in this field. Her book, *Social Cognition,* coauthored with Shelley Taylor, is regarded as a uniquely clear and complete presentation of this broad area. Moreover, her recent involvement as an expert witness has helped to further illuminate the ways in which research evidence can be used in judicial proceedings. In our conversation, Prof. Fiske explains the different ways in which we have conceived of people as thinkers and how the manner in which we think about others can affect our everyday lives. Moving us beyond the laboratory, she tells how social cognition has branched out into law, medicine, and politics.

A CONVERSATION WITH SUSAN FISKE

Krupat: *If we are going to talk about the field known as social cognition, perhaps you could start out by telling me what it is all about?*

Fiske: The simplest answer is that it deals with how people think about other people and themselves and how they come to some kind of coherent understanding of each other. Sometimes what I tell people on airplanes is it's about how people form first impressions of strangers. That's not quite right, but on airplanes it's an effective conversation-stopper when necessary.

Krupat: *In psychology we have a broad area known as cognition. What is social about social cognition?*

Fiske: There have been endless debates about that. I think at its core social cognition is social on the target end—it is concerned with people thinking about people, as opposed to people thinking about nonperson objects. On the other end it's about the impact of the social situation and social factors on people's thinking. A lot of the most recent work has looked at people's interaction goals, at people actually dealing with each other and forming strategies or tactics for interaction. So we could say it is about "thinking for doing" in a social setting.

Krupat: *To pick up on your earlier point, how much of a difference does it make if the object of your perception is a person rather than a thing?*

Fiske: When you're thinking about another person or perceiving another person, that's a mutual process. The person is relevant to you. So if you're looking at your new roommate or the person next to you in a lecture, you're not just looking at a chair or a sculpture. How the person is dressed, the expression on the person's face, and how that person responds to you are all important in a way that's simply not true for objects.

Krupat: *Another way that I have heard this area described involves the person as an information processor. How is that similar to or different from what we have been talking about?*

Fiske: That was a perspective used early on, but the computer metaphor is fading from favor as people are finding it too narrow and too oriented towards sequentia, A-leads-to-B-leads-to-C kinds of processes. There are too many things that happen simultaneously, too many things related to emotions, feelings, and behavior.

Krupat: *Regardless of the metaphor we choose, how good would you say that we are at this business of social thinking and reasoning?*

Fiske: We have a lot of very adaptive ways of thinking socially because we do it so much and because it is so vital to us. We do go astray under certain circumstances, but I think it is fair to say that most of the time, people are good enough at perceiving each other and at making sense of each other. Still, it is also true that we are prone to a lot of very specific kinds of errors which get us into trouble in various situations. One of the most common kinds of errors is a bias toward explaining other people's behavior in terms of their unique personality instead of explaining it in terms of the situation or circumstances surrounding them. This is known as the fundamental attribution error. Another kind of cognitive bias has to do with stereotyping people, seeing them as members of some group-based category rather than as unique individuals.

Krupat: *You said that these can get us into trouble. How so?*

Fiske: Take the fundamental attribution error. That gets you into trouble if you assume that other people are highly predictable based on a particular personality or disposition that you have identified in them. If they are actually responding to situational pressures instead, then you are going to be wrong about what the person is going to do, feel, and think. The same thing is true of stereotypes. To the extent you rely on the person's category to make sense of the person when he or she is a unique individual with a lot of characteristics besides that category membership, you are not going to know how to deal with this person effectively. In both cases you are coming up with simplistic models of what other people are about, and it interferes with your ability to predict and control events.

Krupat: *Do these kinds of biases actually get us into trouble?*

Fiske: In the majority of your interactions, you can't deal with people as totally unique individuals. So having good enough perceptions of group membership or personality probably gets you through a lot of daily interactions. Even if they're wrong, most of these decisions may not have too many consequences for you. But if that person is somebody's boss, then it's not a good enough decision. I would argue that people are very pragmatic about this. When it matters to them, when they're motivated, then they're more careful or at least try to be more careful, and as a result they think more about the other person. If it is important to be accurate in this situation, then people will engage in more complex thought processes, which gives them at least the possibility of being more accurate. It all depends on motivation. It's as simple as that.

Krupat: *So we can be careful if we want to exert the effort. It's just that we are not always motivated to do so. Is that what you are saying?*

Fiske: There are two broad-brush strategies to describe our thinking about other people, although I should say that this is really a continuum and not a dichotomy. One extreme is to go with fairly automatic first impressions, with the first thing that you find out about people. I have talked about this in terms of "category-based processes," and other people have talked about "automatic processes." At the other end, an alternative way of making sense of people which is much more thoughtful and takes a lot more information in usually builds a sort of coherent story or a portrait about the person, taking all the pieces of information together. In the attitude literature, that is called "systematic processing" or "central processing," and in the person perception literature, "individuating" or "piecemeal processing."

Krupat: *This sounds a lot like the debate I have heard between seeing the person as a "naive scientist" versus a "cognitive miser."*

Fiske: In the late sixties and early seventies, the approach that dominated this area was to look at people as if they were scientists carefully gathering information and combining it in some kind of rational manner in order to come out with considered, thoughtful conclusions. The problem was that people weren't doing that much of the time. And that's where the cognitive miser idea came in. According to this, people have meager cognitive resources compared to the complicated environment that's out there. So in order to deal with the booming, buzzing confusion, people have to be economical about the use of their cognitive resources; so they take a lot of shortcuts. And that was kind of a second wave of social cognition research. The current wave of social cognition research takes that a step further and says that we can be more careful when we are motivated to be. So the term that we've come up with for that is "motivated tactician." This reflects the pragmatic orientation that people have towards having to interact and think about each other in order to decide how to deal effectively with them. It says that people have a number of different cognitive strategies or tactics available to them and that they choose among these, depending on what their goals are in a situation.

Krupat: *Are we learning things from the field of social cognition that go beyond some of the things that we already knew from the broader field of cognition?*

Fiske: Yes. For example, in research on attention, basic research in cognition has found that people pay attention to things that are novel. When you take that over to people, you have to define novelty more broadly, in ways that include people who are novel in a particular circumstance. In a regular college classroom, somebody who is seven feet tall is definitely novel, but not on a basketball team. Or how about the only woman in a group of men or the only black in a group of whites? Research on novelty in social situations has led to the idea that a novel stimulus person looms large in people's thinking and seems to have had a lot of impact. You wouldn't necessarily find that if you're just thinking about objects, because the objects are not interacting.

Krupat: *Are there any equivalent kinds of things in the study of memory, for instance?*

Fiske: Within person memory research, researchers have been interested in the differences in how people form impressions and remember things about others. You might think that if I gave you a list of personality traits, you would remember them best if you were told simply to memorize them. But in fact that's not true. People remember them best when they are trying to form an impression of a person who has all of those traits. What is interesting about that—and you couldn't have found that within nonsocial cognition research—is that it's because people are constructing a theory of the person.

Krupat: *But is it always good to construct a theory of a person? Wouldn't it be possible to have such a strong theory about someone that you virtually assure that your expectancies will end up being confirmed—what has been known as a self-fulfilling prophecy?*

Fiske: As you say, when you get into actual interactions, these theories or expectancies can create behavior in the other person. You might ask questions and seek information that confirms your prior ideas. In terms of the courtroom, you can certainly see these effects where people's expectancies or leading questions asked by attorneys lead to biases in what people report, for instance, in eyewitness testimony. An interesting finding, by the way, is that people's confidence and certainty in what they are reporting is totally uncorrelated with their accuracy.

Krupat: *I know that you have been personally involved in a couple of important trials as an expert witness, and we seem to see many social cognition researchers involved in a range of social causes and issues. Are more and more laboratory scientists poking their noses into practical arenas these days?*

Fiske: There are a number of us who are interested in stereotypes and stereotyping. There are other people who are interested in how people's health beliefs get formed and how they cope with major negative life events. Other people study advertising and how social cognition influences consumers. Still others study what social cognition can tell us about how people deal with political information and how candidates get packaged. The variety of applications is staggering.

Krupat: *So you believe that we can really have an impact and make a difference with the knowledge we generate?*

Fiske: Social psychology seems to hold an attraction for people who are interested in making the world a better place, but who want to do it as scientists. One thing that interested me in the two legal cases you mentioned was that when you examine a real world problem, like a perfectly qualified person not getting promoted in a firm or the effects of pornography on sexual harassment, and try to analyze it in terms of what social cognition researchers know, it's possible to come up with some pretty concrete insights about the situation. Moreover, it's convincing to people outside the field. Our explanations are much less speculative than other kinds of psychological explanations, and they are very credible to people in the media, people in the courtroom, and people in politics. You can actually make the world a better place by studying and understanding this and then exporting it to people who have a use for it. To me, that's the encouraging part, and that's what's fun about it.

Susan Fiske
Shelley Taylor

Cognition in Social Psychology

In this selection, Fiske and Taylor explain what it means to take a cognitive approach in social psychology and how the perception of *things* is different from the perception of *people*. As briefly explored in the preceding conversation, Fiske and Taylor consider the different ways in which social psychologists have characterized people as thinkers: naive scientist (careful and systematic); cognitive miser (taker of shortcuts that can mislead); and motivated tactician (careful or sloppy, depending on one's goals and situation).

In contrast to experimental psychology, social psychology has consistently leaned on cognitive concepts, even when most psychology was behaviorist. Social psychology has always been cognitive in at least three ways. First, since Lewin, social psychologists have decided that social behavior is more usefully understood as a function of people's perceptions of their world, rather than as a function of objective descriptions of their stimulus environment (Manis, 1977; Zajonc, 1980a). For example, an objective reward, like money or praise, that people perceive as a bribe or as flattery, will influence them differently than a reward they perceive as without manipulative intent. What predicts their reaction, then, is their perception, not simply the giver's actions.

Other people can influence a person's actions without even being present, which is the ultimate reliance on perceptions to the exclusion of objective stimuli. Thus, someone may react to a proffered bribe or to flattery by imagining the reactions of others ("What would my mother say?" "What will my friends think?"). Of course, such thoughts are the person's own fantasies, having, perhaps, a tenuous connection to objective reality. Thus, the *causes* of social behavior are doubly cognitive: our perceptions of others actually present and our imagination of their presence both predict behavior (cf. G. W. Allport, 1954).

Social psychologists view not only causes but also the end *result* of social perception and interaction in heavily cognitive terms, and this is a second way in which social psychology has always been cognitive. Thought often comes before feeling and behaving as the main reaction that social researchers measure. A person may worry about a bribe (thought), hate the idea (feeling) and reject it (behavior), but social psychologists often mainly ask: "What do you think about it?" Even when they focus on behavior and feelings, their questions are often, "What do you intend to do?" and "How would you label your feeling?" These arguably are not behavior and feelings, but cognitions about them. Thus, social psychological causes are largely cognitive, and the results are largely cognitive.

A third way in which social psychology has always been cognitive is that the person in-between the presumed cause and the result is viewed as a *thinking organism;* this view contrasts with viewing the person as an emotional organism or a mindless automaton (Manis, 1977). Many social psychological theories paint a portrait of the typical person as reasoning (perhaps badly), before acting. In attempting to deal with complex human problems, as social psychology always has, complex mental processes seem essential. How else can one account for stereotyping and prejudice, propaganda and persuasion, altruism and aggression, and more? It is hard to imagine where a narrowly behaviorist theory would even begin. A strict stimulus-response (S-R) theory does not include the thinking organism that seems essential to account for such problems. In several senses, then, social psychology contrasts with strict S-R theories in its reliance on S-O-R theories that include stimulus, organism, and response. Consequently, the thinker, who comes in-between stimulus and response, has always been paramount in social psychology.

The social thinker has taken many guises in recent decades of research. These guises describe the various roles of cognition in social psychology. Besides the varied roles of cognition, motivation has played different roles in the view of the social thinker. Keeping in mind these two components, cognition and motivation, we can identify four general views of the thinker in social psychology: consistency seeker, naive scientist, cognitive miser, and motivated tactician.

The first view emerged from the massive quantities of work on attitude change after World War II. In the later 1950s, several theories were proposed, all sharing some crucial basic assumptions. The consistency theories, as they were called, viewed people as *consistency seekers* motivated by perceived discrepancies among their cognitions (e.g., Festinger, 1957; Heider, 1958; see Abelson et al., 1968, for an overview). For example, if David knows he is on a diet and knows that he has just eaten a hot fudge sundae, he must do some thinking to bring those two cognitions into line.

Two points are crucial. First, these theories relied on perceived inconsistency, which places cognitive activity in a central role. For example, if would-be dieters can convince themselves that one splurge will not matter, eating a sundae is not inconsistent for them. Objective inconsistency, then, is not important. Subjective inconsistency—among various cognitions or among feelings and cognitions—is central to these theories. Actual inconsistency that is not perceived as such does not yield psychological inconsistency.

Second, once inconsistency *is* perceived, the person is presumed to feel uncomfortable (a negative drive state) and to be motivated to reduce the inconsistency. Reducing the aversive drive state is a pleasant relief, rewarding in itself. This sort of motivational model is called a drive reduction model. Less formally, the sundae-consuming dieter will not be free from anxiety until he manufactures some excuse. Hence, consistency theories posit that people change their attitudes and beliefs for motivational reasons, because of unmet needs for consistency. In sum, motivation and cognition both were central to the consistency theories.

Ironically, as they proliferated, consistency theories ceased to dominate the field, partly because the variants on a theme became indistinguishable. Moreover, it was difficult to predict what a person would perceive as inconsistent and to what degree, and which route to resolving inconsistency a person would take. Finally, people do in fact tolerate a fair amount of inconsistency, so the motivation to avoid it—as an overriding principle—was called into doubt (cf. Kiesler, Collins, & Miller, 1969).

Research in social cognition began in the early 1970s, and with it two new models of the thinker emerged. Cognition and motivation played rather different roles in these two models, compared to the roles they played in the consistency seeker model. In both new models, motivation is secondary in importance to cognition. At present, however, a brief look is useful.

The first new model within the framework of social cognition research is the *naive scientist,* a model of how people uncover the causes of behavior. Attribution theories concern how people explain their own and the other people's behavior; they came to the forefront of research in early 1970s. Attribution theories describe people's causal analyses of, or attributions about, the social world. For example, an attribution can address whether someone's behavior seems to be caused by the external situation or by the person's internal disposition. If you want to know why your acquaintance Bruce snapped at you one morning, it would be important to decide if there were mitigating circumstances (his girlfriend left him; you just backed into his car) or if he has an irritable disposition (he always behaves this way and to everyone).

Attribution theorists at first assumed that people are fairly rational in distinguishing among various potential causes. In part, this was a purposeful theoretical strategy designed to push a rational view of people as far as possible, in order to discover its shortcomings. The theories started with the working hypothesis that, given enough time, people resemble naive scientists, who will gather all the relevant data and arrive at the most logical conclusion. In this view, you would think about your friend's behavior in a variety of settings, and carefully weigh the evidence for a situational cause, or a dispositional cause, of his behavior. Thus, the role of cognition in the naive scientist model is as an outcome of fairly rational analysis.

If you are wrong about why Bruce was irritable, the early theories would have viewed your error as emotion-based departure from the normal process or as a simple error in available information. For example, if you attribute Bruce's unpleasant behavior to his irritable disposition, it may be because you are motivated to avoid the idea that he is angry at you. Hence, errors arise, mainly as interference from nonrational motivations. In the early attribution theories, motivation enters mainly as a potential qualification on the usual process.

Unfortunately, people are not always so careful. On an everyday basis, people often make attributions in a relatively thoughtless fashion. The cognitive system can be illustrated by such trivial problems as trying to keep a credit card number, an area code, and a telephone number in your head as you dial, or by more serious problems such as working poorly when you are distracted. The impact of cognitive limitations shows up in social inferences, too. To illustrate, in deciding why Bruce was irritable, you may seize on the easiest explanation rather than the most accurate one. Rather than asking Bruce whether there is something disturbing him, you may simply label him as unpleasant, without giving it much thought. Quite often, people simply are not very thorough.

Hence, the third general view of the thinker (and the second major type of model in social cognition research), comes under the rubric of a *descriptive* model; what people actually do, rather than what they should do. One name for this is the *cognitive miser* model (S. E. Taylor, 1981). The idea is that people are limited in their capacity to process information, so they take shortcuts whenever they can. People adopt strategies that simplify complex problems; the strategies may not be normatively correct or produce normatively correct answers, but they emphasize efficiency. The capacity-limited thinker searches for rapid adequate solutions, rather than slow accurate solutions. Consequently, errors and biases stem from inherent features of the cognitive miser model, which is silent on the issue of motivations or feelings of any sort. The role of cognition is central to the cognitive miser view, and the role of motivation has vanished almost entirely, with isolated exceptions.

As the cognitive miser viewpoint has matured, the importance of motivations and emotions has again become evident. Having developed considerable sophistication about people's cognitive processes, researchers are beginning to appreciate anew the interesting and important influences of motivation on cognition. With growing emphasis on motivated social cognition (Showers & Cantor, 1985), researchers are returning to old problems with new perspectives gained from studying social cognition. The emerging view of the social perceiver, then, might best be termed the *motivated tactician,* a fully engaged thinker who has multiple cognitive strategies available and chooses among them based on goals, motives, and needs. Sometimes the motivated tactician chooses wisely, in the interest of adaptability and accuracy, and sometimes the motivated tactician chooses defensively, in the interest of speed or self-esteem. Thus, views of the social thinker are coming full cycle, back to appreciating the importance of motivation, but with increased sophistication about cognitive structure and process.

In summary, social psychology has always been cognitive in the broad sense of positing important steps that intervene between observable stimulus and observable response. One early major set of theories viewed people as consistency seekers, and motivation played a central role in driving the whole system. With the rise of social cognition research, new views have emerged. In one major wave of research, psychologists view people as naive scientists. These psychologists see motivation mainly as a source of error. In another recent view, psychologists see people as cognitive misers and locate errors in the inherent limitations of the cognitive system, saying almost nothing about motivation. Finally, motivational influences on cognition reemerge in a revitalized view of the thinker as a motivated tactician.

PEOPLE ARE NOT THINGS

As one reviews research on social cognition, the analogy between the perception of things and the perception of people becomes increasingly clear. The argument is made repeatedly: the principles that describe how people think in general also describe how people think about people. Many theories of social cognition have developed in ways that undeniably build on fundamental cognitive principles, as we will see. Nevertheless, borrowing such principles, we must consider fundamental differences when applying them to cognition about people. After all, cognitive psychology is relatively more concerned with the processing of information about inanimate objects and abstract concepts, whereas social psychology is more concerned with the processing of information about people and social experience.

At this point, the reader who is new to social cognition research already may be saying, "Wait, you can't tell me that the way I think about mental arithmetic or about my coffee cup has anything to do with the way I think about my friends." The wisdom or folly of applying the principles of object perception to the perception of people has been debated for some time (Heider, 1958; Higgins, Kuiper, & Olson, 1981; Krauss, 1981; Schneider et al., 1979; Tagiuri & Petrullo, 1958). Some of the important differences between people and things include the following:

- People intentionally influence the environment; they attempt to control it for their own purposes. Objects, of course, are not intentional causal agents.
- People perceive back; as you are busy forming impressions of them, they are doing the same to you. Social cognition is mutual cognition.
- Social cognition implicates the self, because the target is judging you, because the target may provide you with information about yourself, and because the target is more similar to you than any object could be.
- A social stimulus may change upon being the target of cognition. People worry about how they come across, and may adjust their appearance or behavior accordingly; coffee cups, obviously, do not.
- People's traits are nonobservable attributes that are vital to thinking about them. An object's nonobservable attributes are somewhat less crucial. Both a person and a cup can be fragile, but that inferred characteristic is both less important and more directly seen in the cup.
- People change over time and circumstances more than objects typically do. This can make cognitions rapidly obsolete or unreliable.
- The accuracy of one's cognitions about people is harder to check than the accuracy of one's cognitions about objects. Even psychologists have a hard time agreeing on whether a given person is extroverted, sensitive, or honest, but most ordinary people easily could test whether a given cup is heat-resistant, fragile, or leaky.
- People are unavoidably complex. One cannot study cognitions about people without making numerous choices to simplify. The researcher has to simplify a social stimulus without eliminating much of the inherent richness of the target.
- Because people are so complex, because they have traits and intents hidden from view, and because they affect us in ways objects do not, social cognition automatically involves social explanation. It is more important for an ordinary person to explain why a person is fragile than to explain why a cup is.

For these reasons, social cognitive psychology will never be a literal translation of cognitive psychology. It profits from theories and methods adapted to new uses, but the social world provides perspectives and challenges that are dramatic, if not unique, features of thinking about other people and oneself.

References

Abelson, R. P., Aronson E., McGuire, W. J., Newcomb, T. M., Rosenberg, M. J., & Tannenbaum, P. H. (Eds.) (1968). *Theories of cognitive consistency: A sourcebook.* Chicago: Rand McNally.

Allport, G. W. (1958). *The nature of prejudice.* Reading, MA: Addison-Wesley.

Festinger, L. (1957). *A theory of cognitive dissonance.* Palo Alto, CA: Stanford University Press.

Heider, F. (1958). *The psychology of interpersonal relations.* New York: Wiley.

Higgins, E. T., Kuiper, N. A., & Olson, J. M. (1981). Social Cognition: A need to get personal. In E. T. Higgins, C. P. Herman, & M. P. Zanna (Eds.), *Social cognition: The Ontario Symposium* (Vol. 1, pp. 395–429). Hillsdale, NJ: Erlbaum.

Kiesler, C. A., Collins, D. E., & Miller, N. (1969). *Attitude change: A critical analysis of theoretical approaches.* New York: Wiley.

Krauss, R. M. (1981). Impression formation, impression management, and non-verbal behaviors. In E. T. Higgins, C. P. Herman, & M. P. Zanna (Eds.), *Social cognition: The Ontario Symposium* (Vol. 1, pp. 323–341). Hillsdale, NJ: Erlbaum.

Manis, M. (1977). Cognitive social psychology. *Personality and Social Psychology Bulletin, 3,* 550–556.

Schneider, D. J., Hastorf, A. H., & Ellsworth, P. C. (1979). *Person perception.* Reading, MA: Addison-Wesley.

Tagiuri, R., & Petrullo, L. (Eds.) (1958). *Person perception and interpersonal behavior.* Palo Alto, CA: Stanford University Press.

Showers, C., & Cantor, N. (1985). Social cognition: A look at motivated strategies. In M. R. Rosenzweig, & L. W. Porter (Eds.), *Annual Review of Psychology* (Vol. 36, pp. 275–305). Palo Alto, CA: Annual Reviews.

Taylor, S. E. (1981). A categorization approach to stereotyping. In D. L. Hamilton (Ed.), *Cognitive processes in stereotyping and integroup behavior* (pp. 88–114). Hillsdale, NJ: Erlbaum.

Zajonc, R. B. (1980). Cognition and social cognition: A historical perceptive. In L. Festinger (Ed.), *Retrospections on social psychology* (pp. 180–204). New York: Oxford University Press.

Albert H. Hastorf
Hadley Cantril

They Saw a Game—A Case Study

In this classic study of a football game between Princeton and Dartmouth, Hastorf and Cantril demonstrate one of the most fundamental ideas in all of social psychology: No two people ever "see" exactly the same event or person because each one sees it through his or her own unique cognitive filter. The authors tell us that in effect two different games were going on that day—one as seen by the Dartmouth fans and one as seen by those from Princeton. To be more technically accurate, there were probably as many different games being seen as there were people in the stands.

On a brisk Saturday afternoon, November 23, 1951, the Dartmouth Football team played Princeton in Princeton's Palmer Stadium. It was the last game of the season for both teams, and of rather special significance because the Princeton team had won all its games so far and one of its players, Kazmaier, was receiving All-American mention, had just appeared as the cover man on *Time* magazine, and was playing his last game.

A few minutes after the opening kick-off, it became apparent that the game was going to be a rough one. The referees were kept busy blowing their whistles and penalizing both sides. In the second quarter, Princeton's star left the game with a broken nose. In the third quarter, a Dartmouth player was taken off the field with a broken leg. Tempers flared both during and after the game. The official statistics of the game, which Princeton won, showed that Dartmouth was penalized 70 yards, Princeton 25, not counting more than a few plays in which both sides were penalized.

Needless to say, accusations soon began to fly. The game immediately became a matter of concern to players, students, coaches, and the administrative officials of the two institutions, as well as to alumni and the general public, who had not seen the game but had become sensitive to the problem of big-time football through the recent exposures of subsidized players, commercialism, etc. Discussion of the game continued for several weeks.

One of the factors contributing to the extended discussion of the game was the extensive space given to it by both campus and metropolitan newspapers. An indication of the fervor with which the discussions were carried on is shown by a few excerpts from the campus dailies.

Social Cognition: Making Sense of the World | **19**

For example, on November 27 (four days after the game), the *Daily Princeton-ian* (Princeton's student newspaper) said:

> This observer has never seen quite such a disgusting exhibition of so-called "sport." Both teams were guilty but the blame must be laid primarily on Dartmouth's doorstep. Princeton, obviously the better team, had no reason to rough up Dartmouth. Looking at the situation rationally, we don't see why the Indians should make a deliberate attempt to cripple Dick Kazmaier or any other Princeton player. The Dartmouth psychology, however, is not rational itself.

The November 30th edition of the *Princeton Alumni Weekly* said:

> But certain memories of what occurred will not be easily erased. Into the record books will go in indelible fashion the fact that the last game of Dick Kazmaier's career was cut short by more than half when he was forced out with a broken nose and a mild concussion, sustained from a tackle that came well after he had thrown a pass.
>   This second-period development was followed by a third-quarter outbreak of roughness that was climaxed when a Dartmouth player deliberately kicked Brad Glass in the ribs while the latter was on his back. Throughout the often unpleasant afternoon, there was undeniable evidence that the losers' tactics were the result of an actual style of play, and reports on other games they have played this season substantiate this.

Dartmouth students were "seeing" an entirely different version of the game through the editorial eyes of the *Dartmouth* (Dartmouth's undergraduate newspaper). For example, on November 27, the *Dartmouth* said:

> However, the Dartmouth-Princeton game set the stage for the other type of dirty football. A type which may be termed as an unjustifiable accusation.
>   Dick Kazmaier was injured early in the game. Kazmaier was the star, an All-American. Other stars have been injured before, but Kazmaier had been built to represent a Princeton idol. When an idol is hurt there is only one recourse—the tag of dirty football. So what did the Tiger Coach Charley Caldwell do? He announced to the world that the Big Green had been out to extinguish the Princeton star. His purpose was achieved. After this incident, Caldwell instilled the old see-what-they-did-go-get-them attitude into his players. His talk got results. Gene Howard and Jim Miller were both injured. Both had dropped back to pass, had passed, and were standing unprotected in the backfield. Result: one bad leg and one leg broken.
>   The game was rough and did get a bit out of hand in the third quarter. Yet most of the roughing penalties were called against Princeton, while Dartmouth received more of the illegal-use-of-the-hands variety.

On November 28 the *Dartmouth* said:

> Dick Kazmaier of Princeton admittedly is an unusually able football player. Many Dartmouth men traveled to Princeton, not expecting to win—only hoping to see an All-American in action. Dick Kazmaier was hurt in the second period, and played only a token part in the remainder of the game. For this, spectators were sorry.

But there were no such feelings for Dick Kazmaier's health. Medical authorities have confirmed that as a relatively unprotected passing and running star in a contact sport, he is quite liable to injury. Also, his particular injuries—a broken nose and slight concussion—were no more serious than is experienced almost any day in any football practice, where there is no more serious stake than playing the following Saturday. Up to the Princeton game, Dartmouth players suffered about 10 known nose fractures and face injuries, not to mention several slight concussions. Did Princeton players feel so badly about losing their star? They shouldn't have. During the past undefeated campaign they stopped several individual stars by a concentrated effort, including such mainstays as Frank Hauff of Navy, Glenn Adams of Pennsylvania and Rocco Calvo of Cornell. In other words, the same brand of football condemned by the *Prince*—that of stopping the big man—is practiced quite successfully by the Tigers.

Basically, then, there was disagreement as to what had happened during the "game." Hence we took the opportunity presented by the occasion to make a "real life" study of a perceptual problem.[1]

PROCEDURE

Two steps were involved in gathering data. The first consisted of answers to a questionnaire designed to get reactions to the game and to learn something of the climate of opinion in each institution. This questionnaire was administered a week after the game to both Dartmouth and Princeton undergraduates who were taking introductory and intermediate psychology courses.

The second step consisted of showing the same motion picture of the game to a sample of undergraduates in each school and having them check on another questionnaire, as they watched the film, any infraction of the rules they saw and whether these infractions were "mild" or "flagrant."[2] At Dartmouth, members of two fraternities were asked to view the film on December 6; at Princeton, members of two undergraduate clubs saw the film early in January.

The answers to both questionnaires were carefully coded and transferred to punch cards.

---

[1]We are not concerned here with the problem of guilt or responsibility for infractions, and nothing here implies any judgment as to who was to blame.

[2]The film shown was kindly loaned for the purpose of the experiment by the Dartmouth College Athletic Council. It should be pointed out that a movie of a football game follows the ball, is thus selective, and omits a good deal of the total action on the field. Also, of course, in viewing only a film of the game, the possibilities of participation as spectator are greatly limited.

RESULTS

Table 1.1 shows the questions which received different replies from the two student populations on the first questionnaire.

Questions asking if the students had friends on the team, if they had ever played football themselves, if they felt they knew the rules of the game well, etc., showed no differences in either school and no relation to answers given to other questions. This is not surprising since the students in both schools come from essentially the same type of educational, economic, and ethnic background.

Summarizing the data of Tables 1.1 and 1.2, we find a marked contrast between the two student groups.

Nearly all *Princeton* students judged the game as "rough and dirty"—not one of them thought it "clean and fair." And almost nine-tenths of them thought the other side started the rough play. By and large, they felt that the charges they understood were being made were true; most of them felt the charges were made in order to avoid similar situations in the future.

When Princeton students looked at the movie of the game, they saw the Dartmouth team make over twice as many infractions as their own team and the Dartmouth team make over twice as many infractions as were seen by Dartmouth students. When Princeton students judged these infractions as "flagrant" or "mild," the ratio was about two "flagrant" to one "mild" on the Dartmouth team, and about one "flagrant" to three "mild" on the Princeton team.

As for the *Dartmouth* students, while the plurality of answers fell in the "rough and dirty" category, over one-tenth thought the game was "clean and fair" and over a third introduced their own category of "rough and fair" to describe the action. Although a third of the Dartmouth students felt that Dartmouth was to blame for starting the rough play, the majority of Dartmouth students thought both sides were to blame. By and large, Dartmouth men felt that the charges they understood were being made were not true, and most of them thought the reason for the charges was Princeton's concern for its football star.

When Dartmouth students looked at the movie of the game, they saw both teams make about the same number of infractions, and their own team make only half the number of infractions the Princeton students saw them make. The ratio of "flagrant" to "mild" infractions was about one to one when Dartmouth students judged the Dartmouth team, and about one "flagrant" to two "mild" when Dartmouth students judged infractions made by the Princeton team.

It should be noted that Dartmouth and Princeton students were thinking of different charges in judging their validity and in assigning reasons as to why the charges were made. It should also be noted that whether or not students were spectators of the game in the stadium made little difference in their responses.

INTERPRETATION: THE NATURE OF A SOCIAL EVENT

It seems clear that the "game" actually was many different games and that each version of the events that transpired was just as "real" to a particular person as other

TABLE 1.1   Data From First Questionnaire

Question	Dartmouth students (N = 163) %	Princeton students (N = 161) %
1. Did you happen to see the actual game between Dartmouth and Princeton in Palmer Stadium this year?		
Yes	33	71
No	67	29
2. Have you seen a movie of the game or seen it on television?		
Yes, movie	33	2
Yes, television	0	1
No, neither	67	97
3. (Asked of those who answered "yes" to either or both of above questions.) From your observations of what went on at the game, do you believe the game was clean and fairly played, or that it was unnecessarily rough and dirty?		
Clean and fair	6	0
Rough and dirty	24	69
Rough and fair*	25	2
No answer	45	29
4. (Asked of those who answered "no" on both of the first questions.) From what you have heard and read about the game, do you feel it was clean and fairly played, or that it was unnecessarily rough and dirty?		
Clean and fair	7	0
Rough and dirty	18	24
Rough and fair*	14	1
Don't know	6	4
No answer	55	71
(Combined answers to questions 3 and 4 above)		
Clean and fair	13	0
Rough and dirty	42	93
Rough and fair	39	3
Don't know	6	4
5. From what you saw in the game or the movies, or from what you might have read, which team do you feel started the rough play?		
Dartmouth started it	36	86
Princeton started it	2	0
Both started it	53	11
Neither	6	1
No answer	3	2
6. What is your understanding of the charges being made?**		
Dartmouth tried to get Kazmaier	71	47
Dartmouth intentionally dirty	52	44
Dartmouth unnecessarily rough	8	35
7. Do you feel there is any truth to these charges?		
Yes	10	55
No	57	4
Partly	29	35
Don't know	4	6
8. Why do you think the charges were made?		
Injury to Princeton star	70	23
To prevent repetition	2	46
No answer	28	31

*This answer was not included on the checklist but was written in by the percentage of students indicated.

**Replies do not add to 100% since more than one charge could be given.

TABLE 1.2 Data From Second Questionnaire Checked While Seeing Film

		Total number of infractions checked against	
Group	*N*	Dartmouth team Mean	Princeton team Mean
Dartmouth students	48	4.3	4.4
Princeton students	49	9.8	4.2

versions were to other people. A consideration of the experiential phenomena that constitute a "football game" for the spectator may help us to account for the results obtained and illustrate something of the nature of any social event.

Like any other complex social occurrence, a "football game" consists of a whole host of happenings. Many different events are occurring simultaneously. Furthermore, each happening is a link in a chain of happenings, so that one follows another in sequence. The "football game," as well as other complex social situations, consists of a whole matrix of events. In the game situation, this matrix of events consists of the actions of all of the players, the behavior of the referees and linesmen, and the action on the sidelines, in the grandstands, over the loudspeaker, etc.

Of crucial importance is the fact that an "occurrence" on the football field or in any other social situation does not become an experiential "event" unless and until some significance is given to it: an "occurrence" becomes an *"event"* only when the happening has significance. And a happening generally has significance only if it re-activates learned significances already registered in what we have called a person's assumptive form-world (Cantril, 1950).

Hence, the particular occurrences that different people experienced in the foot-ball game were a limited series of events from the total matrix of events *potentially* available to them. People experienced those occurrences that reactivated signifi-cances they brought to the occasion; they failed to experience those occurrences which did not reactivate past significances.

In this particular study, one of the most interesting examples of this phenome-non was a telegram sent to an officer of Dartmouth College by a member of a Dart-mouth alumni group in the Midwest. He had viewed the film which had been shipped to his alumni group from Princeton after its use with Princeton students, who saw, as we noted, an average of over nine infractions by Dartmouth players during the game. The alumnus, who couldn't see the infractions he had heard publi-cized, wired:

> Preview of Princeton movies indicates considerable cutting of important part please wire explanation and possibly air mail missing part before showing scheduled for January 25 we have splicing equipment.

The "same" sensory impingements emanating from the football field, transmit-ted through the visual mechanism to the brain, also obviously gave rise to different experiences in different people. The significances assumed by different happenings for different people depend in large part on the purposes people bring to the occasion and the assumptions they have of the purposes and probable behavior of other people involved.

In brief, the data here indicate that there is no such "thing" as a "game" existing "out there" in its own right which people merely "observe." The "game" "exists" for a person and is experienced by him only in so far as certain happenings have significances in terms of his purpose. Out of all of the occurrences going on in the environment, a person selects those that have some significance for him from his own egocentric position in the total matrix.

Obviously in the case of a football game, the value of the experience of watching the game is enhanced if the purpose of "your" team is accomplished, that is, if the happening of the desired consequence is experienced, i.e., if your team wins. But the value attribute of the experience can, of course, be spoiled if the desire to win crowds out behavior we value and have come to call sportsmanlike.

The sharing of significances provides the links except for which a "social" event would not be experienced and would not exist for anyone.

A "football game" would be impossible except for the rules of the game which we bring to the situation and which enable us to share with others the significances of various happenings. These rules make possible a certain repeatability of events such as first downs, touchdowns, etc. If a person is unfamiliar with the rules of the game, the behavior he sees lacks repeatability and consistent significance, and hence "doesn't make sense."

Only because there is the possibility of repetition is there the possibility that a happening has a significance. For example, the balls used in games are designed to give a high degree of repeatability. While a football is about the only ball used in games which is not a sphere, the shape of the modern football has apparently evolved in order to achieve a higher degree of accuracy and speed in forward passing then would be obtained with a spherical ball, thus increasing the repeatability of an important phase of the game.

The rules of a football game, like laws, rituals, customs, and mores, are registered and preserved forms of sequential significances enabling people to share the significances of occurrences. The sharing of sequential significances which have value for us provides the links that operationally make social events possible. They are analogous to the forces of attraction that hold parts of an atom together, keeping each part from following its individual, independent course.

From this point of view it is inaccurate and misleading to say that different people have different "attitudes" concerning the same "thing." For the "thing" simply is *not* the same for different people whether the "thing" is a football game, a presidential candidate, Communism, or spinach. We do not simply "react to" a happening or to some impingement from the environment in a determined way (except in behavior that has become reflexive or habitual). We behave according to what we bring to the occasion, and what each of us brings to the occasion is more or less unique. And except for these significances which we bring to the occasion, the happenings around us would be meaningless occurrences, would be "inconsequential."

From the transactional view, an attitude is not a predisposition to react in a certain way to an occurrence or stimulus "out there" that exists in its own right with certain fixed characteristics which we "color" according to our predisposition (Kilpatrick, 1952). That is, a subject does not simply "react to" an "object." An attitude would rather seem to be a complex of registered significances reactivated by some stimulus which assumes its own particular significance for us in terms of our purposes. That is, the object as experienced would not exist for us except for the reactivated aspects of the form-world which provide particular significance to the hieroglyphics of sensory impingements.

References

Cantril, H. (1950) *The "why" of man's experience.* New York: Macmillan.

Kilpatrick, F. P. (Ed.), (1952) *Human behavior from the transactional point of view.* Hanover, N.H.: Institute for Associated Research.

Richard R. Lau
Dan Russell

Attributions in the Sports Pages

Many laboratory studies have been designed to study the way in which we explain how things happen. But Lau and Russell have studied how we make causal attributions by checking the sports pages—by seeing how players and coaches explain how they won or lost games. Their findings are consistent with those from other settings, that athletes tend to make dispositional attributions (we're an awfully good team) for success, but situational attributions (they were certainly lucky) for failures. In addition to other interesting findings testing theoretical predictions, Lau and Russell point out that using methods such as this (referred to as the use of archival records) can bring many advantages, and that many of the possible problems of this approach can often be overcome.

An important motivator of human thought is the desire to understand the determinants of behavior. Like the psychologist, the average person is assumed to test "causal theories" concerning the reasons behind his or her own actions and the actions of other people. Such causal knowledge is highly adaptive, yielding an understanding of (and consequently the ability to predict and control) many situations in which they find themselves.

The desire to achieve an understanding of the causes of human behavior has always been considered the chief motivation underlying the attribution process (e.g., Jones & Davis, 1965; Kelley, 1967, 1971). Rather than studying attributions in important human situations, however, most attribution research has asked some captive population (typically college undergraduates) to give causal explanations for their own or some other person's behavior in hypothetical or fairly trivial situations. Therefore, the type of attributions that can be made (and even whether or not to make attributions at all) is generally determined by the experimenter.

But how relevant are the results of such laboratory-based experiments to real-world settings in which attributions occur? Causal explanations that are made in the course of everyday human interaction may serve purposes beyond understanding the determinants of behavior. For instance, Kelley's research has led him to ask, "What if the person learns and is motivated to make attributions not for some abstract understanding of the world, but rather, to explain his own actions and to attempt to control the actions of his close associates?" (Orvis, Kelley, & Butler, 1976, p. 379; see also Kelley, Note 1). Certainly, attributions serve a variety of motivations, and the determinants or consequences of the attribution process could be very different when attributions are serving different purposes. It is therefore important to explore the generality of the findings from laboratory-based attribution research in real-world settings.

The sports pages are a natural setting where explanations for behavior are frequently given by players, coaches, and sportswriters. There are several good reasons why the sports pages are an excellent site to study the attribution process. First, the typical laboratory experiment gathers attributions on forced-choice, closed-ended scales. In the sports pages, on the other hand, the players, coaches, and sportswriters have a much greater range of possible responses available to them. They are, of course, constrained by plausibility and the norms or conventions of that setting, but certainly the scope of possible explanations is much greater in such free responses than is usually the case in the laboratory.

Second, athletic events are highly involving. Avid sports fans "live and die" with their teams every game, and players and coaches are even more involved. They spend a great deal of time, energy, joy, and suffering to win games. Moreover, a string of bad performances could possibly cost professional athletes or coaches their jobs. Such high levels of involvement are rarely achieved in the laboratory.

The current study examined explanations for the outcomes of sporting events given in the sports pages. The actual explanations were coded for attributional content. Using these data, several important questions in the attribution area were addressed.

A good deal of research has documented the tendency to make internal attributions for success and external attributions for failure. A recent controversy concerns whether this tendency (often called "hedonic biases") reflects a motivational bias or not (see reviews by Bradley, 1978; and Snyder, Stephan, & Rosenfield, 1978). A motivational interpretation of hedonic bias is consistent with the notion that attributions frequently serve self-presentational purposes. Such a motivational interpretation predicts that the general tendency for success to be attributed internally and failure to be attributed externally should increase with the ego-involvement of the attributor, a prediction that has been tested in other investigations of hedonic bias (Harvey, Arkin, Gleason, & Johnson, 1974; MIller & Norman, 1975; Snyder, Stephan, & Rosenfield, 1976). In the present context, a motivational hypothesis would predict that coaches and players would show a greater tendency to attribute success internally and failure externally, in comparison with sportswriters, since the former should be more ego-involved with the outcome.

Miller and Ross (1975) contend that most support for a motivational or self-enhancement interpretation of hedonic bias has come from fairly trivial experiments, and they see the case as far from proven. As an alternative, Miller and Ross offer a nonmotivational explanation for the phenomenon. They argue that people typically expect and intend to succeed; hence, success is attributed internally, and unexpected and unintended failures are attributed externally. For instance, Feather and Simon (1971a, 1971b) found that unexpected success or failure was more likely to be attributed to external factors than was expected success or failure. In the current investigation, this nonmotivational explanation would predict that expected success should result in more internal attributions than unexpected success, whereas unexpected failure should result in more external attributions than expected failure. The ego-involvement of the attributor should be irrelevant.

There are several aspects of the setting being investigated here that could affect the motivational hypothesis. One is the fact that these attributions are given publicly, and there is an informal norm among athletes to be humble about their successful performances and to accept blame for their failures. This factor could mute evidence of a hedonic bias for players and coaches. On the other hand, the involvement of players and coaches in the outcome is much greater in this study than is true in most laboratory experiments, and this could accentuate a hedonic bias (if the motivational interpretation is correct). Evidence for or against a motivational bias in the current study must be considered in light of the above aspects of this setting.

A second question addressed in the current study concerns *when* attributions occur. Little research to date has directly investigated this question (Wong & Weiner, Note 2, is the only exception we know of). Indeed, the use of closed-ended rating scales to gather attribution data (as is typically done in attribution research) generally precludes the possibility of participants either simply not making causal attributions or varying the number of attributions made. Kelley (1971) has suggested that unexpected events will evoke cognitive processing by the individual. For example, if a bad team defeats a good one, a wide variety of explanations become plausible (such as weather, luck, very high motivation on the part of the underdog or low motivation for the favorite, injuries). But if the favorite wins as expected, the relative abilities of the two teams are clearly the most plausible explanation. Thus, unexpected events may prompt an "attributional search" (assuming the event is of some importance to the individual) in which the variety of explanations are tested both for their plausibility and for their satisfaction of the individual's needs and motives, so it is hypothesized that unexpected outcomes will lead to a greater number of causal attributions being made.

Finally, based on Weiner's (1974, 1979) attribution model, it is hypothesized that expected outcomes of games should result in stable causal explanations, irrespective of whether the outcome is successful or unsuccessful. On the one hand, this hypothesis seeks to replicate prior laboratory research supporting Weiner's model (e.g., Feather & Simon, 1971b; Frieze & Weiner, 1971; Weiner, Frieze, Kukla, Rest & Rosenbaum, 1971). But given that (a) the setting is so involving, (b) the explanations are coded from free responses, and (c) the attributions may be serving self-presentational purposes, the current situation is in many ways very different from the typical context in which Weiner's model has been tested.

METHOD

Procedure

Articles covering 33 major sporting events in eight daily newspapers during the fall of 1977 were analyzed for attributional content. These events included the six games of the World Series and a variety of college and professional football games. For the most part, articles from the city of one of the teams involved in the game were used, because only these articles were long enough to contain explanations for the results of the game. (Shorter articles about games of less interest to the readers of a newspaper are most often limited to descriptions of the game rather than including explanations for the outcome.) A total of 594 explanations from 107 articles were identified.

Eight advanced undergraduates collected the attributions. These students were all thoroughly trained to identify any explanations offered for the outcome of a game. They worked in pairs, with one member of each team serving as a "check" on his or her partner, to ensure that all explanations were recorded from each article.

Each explanation was written on one side of a 3 × 5 card. The game, newspaper, and source of attribution—player, coach, or sportswriter—were recorded on the back of the card. This procedure was designed to allow for "blind" coding of the attributions, although the source of the attribution was sometimes obvious from the explanation itself.

Coding

To test the hypotheses, it was necessary to code the causal explanations in terms of two causal dimensions: stability and locus of causality. These dimensions were coded directly from the attributional statements, based on the definitions of the two causal dimensions given by Weiner (1974). The following definitional criteria were used by the coders.

Stability. The stability of an attribution was defined temporally; an explanation was considered stable if it would predict the same outcome recurring in future games. Unstable attributions referred to factors that could vary over time, such as a great effort by a team or a bad call by an umpire or referee.

Locus of causality. For the locus of causality dimension, it was simply noted whether the attribution referred to something about one team or the other, or to the particular situation. For players and coaches, attributions referring to one's own team were categorized as internal, whereas attributions to the other team or to the particular situation were categorized as external. Likewise, attributions to the sportswriter's home team were categorized as internal, whereas attributions to the other team or to the situation were categorized as external.

The following examples illustrate the coding scheme. After the fourth game of the World Series, a game won by the Yankees (giving them a 3–1 lead in the series), Yankee manager Billy Martin said of Lou Piniella, the star of the game, "Piniella has done it all." This statement refers to something about the Yankees, and it was said by a Yankee, so it was coded as internal. The verb tense of the statement ("has done") suggests that Martin was not referring simply to the one game, but to the course of the entire season. Hence the statement also seems to refer to a stable attribute of the individual in question (ability or stable effort) and was coded as stable along the stable–unstable dimension. After the same game, Ron Cey, a member of the losing Dodgers, said, "I think we've hit the ball all right. But I think we're unlucky." This is clearly an attribution to bad luck, and was coded as external (circumstances) and unstable. The next two statements were made by Dodger manager Tommy Lasorda after the Dodgers had lost the last game of the series. "It took a great team to beat us, and the Yankees definitely are a great team." This is an attribution to the Yankees' ability, and as it was said by a Dodger, it was coded as external and stable. Finally, of Reggie Jackson's performance in the sixth game, Lasorda said, "You're supposed to keep the ball in on him. Well, we didn't." Here the attribution is something "we" did, something "we" presumably could have done better, but did not. Hence it was coded as internal and unstable.

Additional Measures

A further datum was recorded with each attribution. If there had been a clear favorite for a game, the result was categorized as expected or an unexpected, depending on the outcome. Games in which there had been no clear favorite were placed in a third category, regardless of outcome. Because the World Series is a series of games, it was difficult to say that there were clear expectancies for one of the teams to win any given game, although at the outset the Dodgers were expected to win most of the games. Football games are more discrete events, with teams usually meeting once or twice a season. Hence, only attributions taken from football games were used in analyses involving expectancies.

The odds established by Harrah's Reno Race Sportsbook as reported in the newspaper were used to determine favorites. If a team was favored by two points or less, however, the game was categorized as having "no clear favorite." In addition, if the result of a game was highly discrepant (more than 10 points) from the predicted outcome, even if the favorite still won, the result of the game was also categorized as unexpected. That is, if (a) the favorite lost the game, (b) a big favorite won by a very small margin, or (c) a slight favorite won by a very big margin, the result of the game was categorized as unexpected.

Finally, the number of attributions from each article and the length of each article in inches were recorded. The number of attributions per inch was used as a measure of the frequency of attributions in an article.

RESULTS

Hedonic Bias

The data were first analyzed for evidence of success–failure differences in the locus of causality. The percentage of internal and external attributions for winners and losers (combining the attributions of players, coaches, and sportswriters) were compared. As expected, clear evidence of a tendency to attribute success internally was found: 74.9% of the attributions from the perspective of the winning team were internal, while only 54.9% of the attributions from the losing team were internal.

TABLE 1.3 Test of the Motivational Bias Hypothesis

Attribution	Players and coaches		Sportswriters	
	Win	Loss	Win	Loss
Internal	80.3	52.8	66.5	57.1
External	19.7	47.2	31.5	42.9
n	132	144	111	140

Note: Figures are in percents.

Given this evidence of a success–failure difference in causal explanations, further analyses compared the motivational versus expectancy explanations for this difference. To test for a motivational basis for the success–failure difference in locus of attributions, the attributions of coaches and players were compared to those of sportswriters. A motivational explanation predicts that the success–failure difference in attributions will be greater for coaches and players in comparison with sportswriters, based on the greater ego-involvement of the former group with the outcome.

To test for this effect, the attributions made by players and coaches versus sportswriters for winning and losing outcomes were compared. The percentages are shown in Table 1.3. Players and coaches showed greater evidence of a motivational bias, making more internal attributions for success and fewer internal attributions for failure, relative to sportswriters. It should be pointed out, however, that the evidence for a motivational bias here is only relative, since for both winning and losing (and for players, coaches, and sportswriters), the majority of the attributions were internal.

A closer examination of Table 1.3 suggests that differences in attributing causality between players, coaches, and sportswriters occur chiefly after wins. Players and coaches are much more likely to attribute a good outcome to internal causes than are sportswriters, but only slightly less likely to attribute a bad outcome to themselves than are the writers. This finding is consistent with previous work that has found evidence of self-serving biases chiefly after success but not failure (see Miller & Ross, 1975).

The expectancy explanation proposes that expected events will be attributed internally, whereas unexpected outcomes will be attributed externally. Since players and coaches typically expect and intend to succeed, the argument goes, their successes are attributed internally. In the current data, there are games that a losing team should clearly expect to lose, as well as games that a winning team should clearly expect to win; both of these cases would be predicted to produce internal attributions. Cases in which the winning or losing outcomes are unexpected should, on the other hand, produce external attributions.

Table 1.4 presents the percentage of internal and external explanations for ex-

TABLE 1.4 Test of the Expectancy Hypothesis

Attribution	Winners		Losers	
	Expected	Unexpected	Expected	Unexpected
Internal	78.7	79.7	63.0	62.3
External	21.3	20.3	37.0	37.7
n	89	69	54	130

Note: Figures are in percents.

pected and unexpected outcomes separately from the perspective of winning and losing teams. Clearly, more internal attributions were made for wins than for losses, but just as clearly, expectancies did not mediate this effect. Expanding this analysis to compare the attributions of players and coaches to sportswriters provides no additional evidence for the importance of expectancies. All interactions involving expectancies and source of attribution (players and coaches or sportswriters) were nonsignificant.

Frequency of Causal Attributions

A second set of analyses concerned when the attributions occurred, with the number of attributions per inch of newsprint serving as an index of how frequently causal explanations were made for a particular game. It was predicted that unexpected outcomes would elicit a greater number of attributions, regardless of whether the outcome was a win or a loss. Because the number of attributions typically reported in each article differed between newspapers, the number of attributions per inch for each article was centered (by subtracting the mean) for the different newspapers separately, and then these centered measures were analyzed. The only significant effect found was for expected versus unexpected events, with unexpected outcomes eliciting a greater number of attributions per inch (see Table 1.5). Thus as hypothesized, unexpected outcomes produced a greater number of explanations.

TABLE 1.5 Frequency of Attributions as a Function of Expectedness of Outcome and Win–Loss

Outcome	Win	Loss
Expected	−.027	−.032
n	22	10
Unexpected	.036	.032
n	12	22

Note: Cell entries are a centered measure of the number of attributions per inch of newsprint. Negative entries indicate fewer attributions than average, positive entries indicate more attributions than average.

TABLE 1.6 Stability and Expectancies

Condition	Expected	Unexpected
Stable	37.8	29.0
Unstable	62.2	71.0
n	164	186

Note: Figures are in percents.

Expectancy and Stability

Finally, based on Weiner's (1974, 1979) attribution model, it was predicted that expected outcomes would elicit more stable causal attributions than unexpected outcomes. The relevant data are shown in Table 1.6. There was a tendency for this hypothesis to be supported. Also notable in Table 1.6 is the preponderance of unstable attributions. Fully two thirds of all attributions were coded as unstable. This indicates the strong preference for explanations involving effort (such as great concentration or making a spectacular play) on the part of their team or the other team by attributors. Other research has also indicated that effort is the most frequent attribution in achievement settings (e.g., Elig & Frieze, 1979).

DISCUSSION

The results from the current study support a variety of predictions from attribution research in a real-world setting. The empirically well-established success-versus-failure difference in the locus of causal attribution was found in the current context. The results supported a motivationally based explanation for this success–failure difference, in contrast to a nonmotivational explanation based on expectancies. Attributions were also found to be more frequent following unexpected outcomes, as predicted. Finally, some support was found for the prediction from Weiner's (1974, 1979) attribution model, that expected outcomes lead to more stable causal explanations.

The causal accounts gathered here were freely given by the attributors (although the attributions were sometimes given in response to "why" questions from the sportswriters) and were less constrained in form and content than those generated in laboratory settings. The causal attributions made by the attributors were also very public, and may therefore serve more to justify performance (by the athletes and coaches) or to justify predictions for a specific game (by the sportswriters) than to reach an abstract causal understanding of the events.

This raises a question concerning whether these public statements differ from the private explanations made by the attributors. Do the causal attributions collected in the present study reflect the attributions "really" made by the players, coaches, and sportswriters? Although we have no means of assessing private attributions, the answer to this question is most certainly *no* in some instances and *yes* in others. For example, norms concerning social behavior (e.g, humility or bravado) may affect the public explanations offered by the attributor, but not the private ones really believed. On the other hand, one could argue that the attributor, to maintain consistency, brings his or her private attributions in line with his other public statements.

The only research we know of that addresses this question of public and private attributions found only one instance in which the two differed. Folkes (1978) examined the differences between the public explanations given by people when refusing a date and the actual (private) reasons for their refusal. Her findings indicate that only when the real reason for the refusal had something to do with internal characteristics of the person being rejected (e.g., he or she was physically unattractive) did people give some other (external) public explanation for their refusal. Folkes' subjects did not "lead on" the person being rejected by inaccurately communicating the permanence (stability) of their rejection, however.

Do possible differences between public and private attributions (about which we can only speculate) make our findings irrelevant to previous attribution research? As mentioned above, research conducted by Kelley and his colleagues (Orvis, Kelley, & Butler, 1976) has suggested that the attribution process may often serve impression management or self-presentational purposes. Attributions as *justifications* rather than as *explanations* for behavior may be more prevalent in highly involving real-world settings such as the present one. The relevance of the present study to previous research lies in extending the findings of laboratory-based investigations to a situation in which public attributions are quite possibly serving self-presentational purposes.

The present study supported a motivational basis for the success–failure differences in the locus of causal attribution over an explanation relying on expectancies. As noted above, however, more internal attributions were made for both success *and* failure, although the frequency of internal explanations was much higher for success. Miller and Ross (1975) have argued that evidence for a self-serving bias in attributions requires evidence of both internal causal ascriptions for success (self-enhancing attributions) and external ascriptions for failure (self-protective attributions). The present results do not provide evidence for a self-protective bias.

One could argue, however, that the typical or base-rate attribution for sports performance in general is internal and that any self-protective or self-enhancing attributional bias must influence this modal attribution. The work of Weiner (1974, 1979) and others on causal explanations in achievement contexts has found that explanations for achievement outcomes are typically internal for both success and failure (see also Scanlon & Passer, Note 3). Any attributional bias must operate within the context in which attributions are being made, and the effect of the bias will always be relative to the modal attribution for this situation. Placing self-serving biases in this perspective, it seems more reasonable, as Bradley (1978) suggests, to see both self-protective and self-enhancing biases as reflecting a general tendency to view oneself positively, and to consider the modal locus of causality used to explain events in the situation under study when predicting how an attributional bias will reveal itself.

Another issue we have addressed is the "when" of attribution. As was pointed out earlier, the sports pages are a real-world setting in which attributions frequently occur. The effect of one variable, whether the result of the game was expected or not, was found to have a significant influence on the prevalence of causal explana-tions. As a cautionary note on interpreting the finding that more attributions are made following unexpected events, we should note that the results most appropri-ately apply only to the sportswriters. They make as many attributions as they want in their stories. The sportswriters also serve as gatekeepers in that they decide which statements by players and coaches to print. The writers are of course limited by what the players and coaches say, but they certainly do not print every word uttered. Therefore, although there is every reason to expect players and coaches as well as sportswriters to make fewer attributions after expected events than after unexpected events, these data are most germane to the writers.

The current findings clearly demonstrate the usefulness of archival data to attri-bution research. It is possible, and we might argue more appropriate, to study the at-tribution process in natural settings. Such settings are almost always more involving than laboratory experiments, and questions of external validity are easily addressed.

Reference Notes

1. Kelley, H. H. *Recent research in causal attribution.* Address at the meeting of the West-ern Psychological Association, Los Angeles, April, 1976.
2. Wong, P. T. P., & Weiner, B. *When people ask why questions and the temporal course of the attribution process.* Unpublished manuscript, University of California, Los Angeles, 1979.
3. Scanlon, T. K., & Passer, M. W. *Self-serving biases in the competitive sport setting: An attributional dilemma.* Unpublished manuscript, University of California, Los Angeles, 1978.

References

Bishop Y. M. M., Fienberg, S. E., & Holland, P. W. *Discrete multivariate analysis: Theory and practice.* Cambridge: MIT Press, 1975.

Bradley, G. W. self-serving biases in the attribution process: A reexamination of the fact or fiction question. *Journal of Personality and Social Psychology,* 1978. *36,* 56–71

Cronbach, L. J., & Meehl, P. E. Construct validity in psychological tests. *Psychological Bul-letin,* 1955, *52.* 281–302.

Elig, T. W., & Frieze, I. H. A multi-dimensional scheme for coding and interpreting per-ceived causality for success and failure events: The Coding Scheme of Perceived Causality (CSPC). JSAS *Catalog of Selected Documents in Psychology,* 1975, *5,* 313.

Elig, T. W., & Frieze, I. H. Measuring causal attributions for success and failure. *Journal of Personality and Social Psychology,* 1979, *37,* 621–634.

Feather, N. T., & Simon, J. G. Attribution of responsibility and valence of success and failure in relation to initial confidence and task performance. *Journal of Personality and Social Psychology,* 1971, *18,* 172–188. (a).

Feather, N. T., & Simon, J. G. Causal attributions for success and failure in relation to expec-tations of success based upon selective or manipulative control. *Journal of Personality,* 1971, *39,* 527–541. (b).

Folkes, V. S. *Causal communication in the early stages of affiliative relationships.* Unpub-lished doctoral dissertation, University of California, Los Angeles, 1978.

Frieze, I. H., & Weiner, B. Cue utilization and attributional judgments for success and failure. *Journal of Personality,* 1971, *39,* 591–605.

Harvey, J. H., Arkin, R. M., Gleason, J. M., & Johnston, S. A. Effect of expected and observed outcome of an action on differential causal attributions of actor and observer. *Journal of Personality,* 1974, *42,* 62–77.

Iso-Ahola, S. Effects of self-enhancement and consistency on causal and trait attributions following success and failure in motor performance. *Research Quarterly,* 1977, *48,* 718–726

Jones, E. E., & Davis, K. E. From acts to dispositions: The attribution process in person perception. In L. Berkowitz (Ed.), *Advances in experimental social psychology* (Vol. 2). New York: Academic Press, 1965.

Kelley, H. H. Attribution theory in social psychology. In D. Levine (Ed.), *Nebraska Symposium on Motivation* (Vol. 15). Lincoln: University of Nebraska Press, 1967.

Kelley, H. H. Attribution in social interaction. In E. E. Jones et al. (Eds.), *Attribution: Perceiving the causes of behavior.* Morristown, N.J.: General Learning Press, 1971.

Miller, D. T., & Norman, S. A. Actor–observer differences in perceptions of effective control. *Journal of Personality and Social Psychology,* 1975, *31,* 503–515.

Miller, D. T., & Ross, M. Self-serving biases in the attribution of casualty: Fact or Fiction? *Psychological Bulletin,* 1975, *82,* 213–225.

Monson, T. C., & Snyder, M. Actors, observers, and the attribution process: Toward a reconceptualization. *Journal of Experimental Social Psychology,* 1977, *13,* 89–111

Orvis, B. R., Kelley, H. H., & Butler, D. Attributional conflict in young couples. In J. H. Harvey et al. (Eds.). *New directions in attribution research* (Vol. 1). Hillsdale, NJ: Erlbaum, 1976.

Ross, L. The intuitive psychologist and his shortcomings: Distortions in the attribution process. In L. Berkowitz (Ed.), *Advances in experimental social psychology* (Vol. 10). New York: Academic Press, 1977.

Ross, M., & Sicoly, F. Egocentric biases in availability and attribution. *Journal of Personality and Social Psychology,* 1979, *37,* 322–336.

Snyder, M. L., Stephan, W. G., & Rosenfield, D. Egotism and attribution. *Journal of Personality and Social Psychology,* 1976, *33,* 435–441.

Snyder, M. L., Stephan, W. G., & Rosenfield, D. Attributional egotism. In J. H. Harvey et al. (Eds.). *New directions in attribution research* (Vol. 2). Hillsdale, NJ: Erlbaum, 1978.

Weiner, B. Achievement motivation as conceptualized by an attribution theorist. In B. Weiner (Ed.), *Achievement motivation and attribution theory.* Morristown, NJ: General Learning Press, 1974.

Weiner, B. A theory of motivation for some classroom experiences. *Journal of Educational Psychology,* 1979, *71,* 3–25.

Weiner, B., Frieze, I., Kukla, L. R., Rest, S., & Rosenbaum, R. M. Perceiving the causes of success and failure. In E. E. Jones et al. (Eds.). *Attribution: Perceiving the causes of behavior.* Morristown, NJ: General Learning Press, 1971.

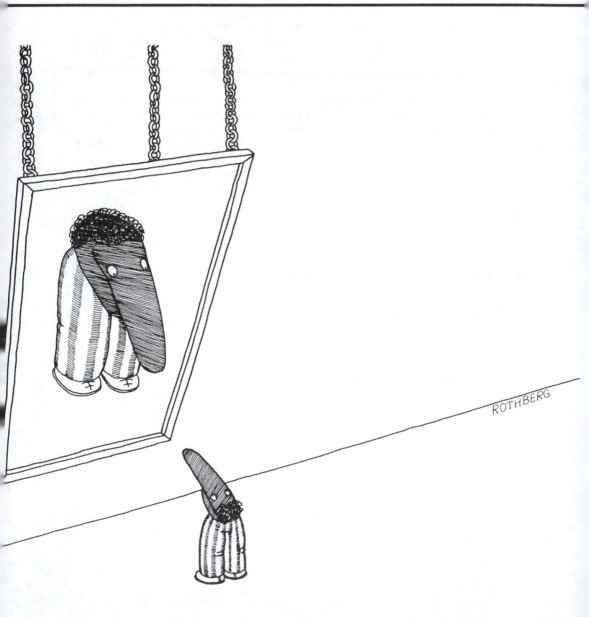

2

ROTHBERG

The Self: Who Am I?

When we ask the question, "Who am I?" we ask about the self, the most prized and personal possession a person can have. The study of the self has a checkered history. At times we have rejected it as being too private and too personal to be studied effectively, yet in recent years social psychologists have developed a passion for learning more about who we are and how we think about ourselves.

Jennifer Crocker, Professor or Psychology at the State University of New York at Buffalo and a past winner of the Gordon Allport Intergroup Relations Prize, has become one of the leading researchers in the study of the self-concept. Part of our conversation dealt with her current research concerning the disadvantaged and stigmatized, while other topics covered ranged from the ways in which we maintain and protect the self to a consideration of self in relation to culture. Her comments illustrate how important and complex the self is, yet how easy to understand and appreciate when it is explained clearly.

A CONVERSATION WITH JENNIFER CROCKER

Krupat: *Our everyday language is so full of worlds that start with self: self-esteem, self-conscious, and self-image. Given our "self-centered" focus, can you tell me just what the self is?*

Crocker: The concept is very broad. Some would say that it refers to all of the thoughts and feelings we have about ourselves, but that's a very loose definition. Other people would talk about the self as a mental representation. Someone like Hazel Markus would say that we have a representation of what we're like, what we could be like in the future, and what we've been like in the past. It's this mental representation, plus an evaluation of it, which constitutes the self or the self-concept.

Krupat: *Why is it that social psychologists seem to be interested at all in the self? It seems like it's a very individual concept rather than a social concept.*

Crocker: It might seem that way, but the way we think and feel about ourselves is extraordinarily influenced by our relationships with other people, and the self also has tremendous effects on how we relate to other people. It is a product of social interaction, and it influences our social interaction. There is a huge interplay, and it really is a very social or interpersonal phenomenon.

Krupat: *Where does the idea on self-esteem fit into this?*

Crocker: People think about self-esteem in different ways. One way to think about it is as a global sense of self-worth, sort of an overall self-evaluation of the form, "I am worthy of respect. I'm a worthwhile human being." There also can be domain-specific self-esteem, which is how good I am at athletics, at academics, at math, or at mechanical kinds of things.

Krupat: *I would assume that people must give differing weights to each specific domain, depending on what they're good at.*

Crocker: Right. William James said that self-esteem equals success divided by pretensions. What he was arguing is that your self-esteem depends on how good you are at what matters to you. People value certain things and devalue others. I'm not good at mechanical things, but that doesn't affect my self-esteem much at all, but I very much value academics, and how I do in that domain does affect my self-esteem a lot.

Krupat: *Do we value what we are good at, or do we work to get good at the things we value. Which is the chicken and which is the egg?*

Crocker: I think it goes both ways. Some things are very much valued by the culture and the subculture in which one grows up, and it's hard to fight your culture. This culture, for example, places a lot of importance on physical attractiveness. It's very hard to devalue that, although some people are able to do it. There also is pretty good evidence that people are able to more or less devalue certain domains. for example, when people learn that they compare badly to someone close to them, they'll often devalue that domain of achievement as a way of protecting their self-esteem and maintaining a positive view of themselves. People differ in how well they're able to do that and in what domains they do that, but they do devalue things that they don't do well in as a way of protecting their self-esteem.

Krupat: *It almost sounds as if life is simply a struggle to maintain, protect, and enhance self-esteem. How important is this as a human motive? Is it what makes us tick?*

Crocker: There certainly are people who would argue that the desire to maintain a positive view of the self is a fundamental motive. And there are a lot of different theoretical perspectives of why that might be the case. One is that low self-esteem simply feels bad. Low self-esteem is associated with negative emotions, feeling emotional pain, or being depressed. It may also be functional or adaptive to have high self-esteem. If we think we're worthwhile, if we think we're deserving, we may aspire to do more and may make more efforts to succeed. One of the things that complicates this notion of self-esteem as a universal human motive is that the form that self-esteem takes differs widely by culture. For example, people in the United States seem to be trying constantly to enhance their levels of esteem, and they show all kinds of biases and positive illusions about the self. Those kinds of things are either much weaker or nonexistent in many Asian cultures. It truly does raise questions about how universal a motive this really is.

Krupat: *You mean all these self words don't exist or don't take on the same significance in other parts of the world?*

Crocker: Not at all. The United States has been characterized as one of the most individualistic cultures in the world. People here are motivated to realize their individual potential and to enhance themselves. Many other cultures are much less concerned with the self and are much more concerned with relationships with other people. In Japan, for example, it has been argued that people can't even think about themselves without thinking about their relationships with the groups that they belong to. Instead of wanting to enhance themselves, to express their individual uniqueness, or to realize their individual potential, people are much more oriented toward fitting in and getting along with others, submerging themselves to the group, and facilitating their relationships with others.

Krupat: *We have talked a little about self in relationship to nationality, but we haven't talked much about it in relationship to matters such as race and gender.*

Crocker: That's one of the things that I'm especially interested in. One of the questions that's interested me is, "What are the effects of the social structure, the social hierarchy, on how people feel about themselves?" If you are in a group that's discriminated against, does that affect the way you feel about yourself? Shouldn't people who belong to groups that are discriminated against or are disadvantaged in society view themselves negatively? Amazingly, there is a good deal of evidence that members of groups that are stigmatized or subordinated do not show low self-esteem. In America, Blacks and Chicanos, for example, show self-esteem that is at least equal to and often higher than that of Whites.

Krupat: *How do you account for this?*

Crocker: There are a number of ways. One is that when people are discriminated against they learn not to value the things that they can't have. Women, for example, are seldom CEOs of big companies. Well, they may just decide that this is not really important. So one way to maintain self-esteem despite the fact that your group is doing badly is to say, "What my group doesn't get is not what really matters to me." Another way to protect self-esteem if you're in a disadvantaged or discriminated-against group is to compare yourself with people that are like you. So women or Blacks might say, "The comparisons that really matter to me are the people who are like me." When you compare yourself to people who are in the same boat, then you are going to be less focused on the fact that you are disadvantaged relative to other groups. Another way self-esteem is protected if your group is discriminated against is that, when negative things happen to you, you have an explanation for why they are happening. If you don't get the job, then you suspect that discrimination might be the reason why. That provides you with an explanation that's external to yourself. It's not me; it's something about the other person or something about the situation, something about the way society is structured. It doesn't reflect my own inadequacies; it reflects the way the world is or the way the other person is. And so it doesn't lower self-esteem.

Krupat: *That may protect self-esteem, but if you come to believe that effort won't be rewarded because of the way society is, then why should you work hard?*

Crocker: One of the things that may be critical in terms of whether groups that are discriminated against suffer from low self-esteem is whether they believe that their society is a meritocracy, a place where people get what they deserve. Do they believe that by working hard, having the right personal qualities, exerting effort, people can get success? Maintaining self-esteem for the stigmatized or the oppressed may require at some level rejecting the notion that the world is a fair place where people who deserve it succeed and people who don't deserve it don't succeed. The data on the beliefs of Black Americans suggest that they don't believe that this is a meritocracy nearly as much as white Americans do, but they also don't entirely reject that idea either.

Krupat: *Let's move on to questions of how we each know the self. Where does the issue of self-awareness fit into all this?*

Crocker: Some of the time we are really thinking about ourselves, conscious of ourselves, and reflecting on ourselves. But some of the time we are caught up in the situation and we're really not thinking or reflecting about the self. So our attention can be basically inner-directed or it can be outer-directed.

Krupat: *Does that vary from situation to situation, or are some people just more self-conscious than others?*

Crocker: Both. There is evidence that there are chronic tendencies to be high or low in self-consciousness. And there are also clearly situations that can elicit self-awareness or direct our attention toward ourselves. The one that's most studied is being in the presence of a mirror. When we see a reflection, this draws our attention to ourselves, it makes us think about ourselves. Other kinds of situations can do that: being in front of an audience or a camera, or being in any kind of situation that makes us aware of or reflects our attention back to ourselves as an object.

Krupat: *When teenagers say, "I'm always so self-conscious," the term has a negative connotation. Yet when I hear you talking about self-consciousness or self-awareness, it sounds as if it can be functional rather than dysfunctional.*

Crocker: I think it has both functional and dysfunctional aspects to it. On the positive side, people are much more likely to behave in ways that are consistent with their attitudes when they are self-conscious than when they are not. On the other hand, self-consciousness and self-awareness can often induce negative emotions in people. One of the things that self-awareness does is to lead us to compare ourselves to our ideal standard, which we often don't live up to. That is probably the aspect of self-consciousness that teenagers are often referring to.

Krupat: *To what extent do we each create and shape our own self-image, and to what extent would you say this happens to us passively?*

Crocker: I think both processes very much occur. I know that sounds like a wishy-washy answer, but I really think that both happen. Part of it depends upon how far back you go. My self-esteem may be genetically influenced, and it is also influenced by attachment patterns that developed in early childhood. Clearly, we are somewhat passive recipients of those early influences. At another level I think people are actively engaged in maintaining, defending, or protecting their self-concept. Bill Swann argues that what people are motivated to do is to verify whatever self-concept they happen to have. He believes that people who have positive self-views want that positive self-view reinforced, but that people who have negative self-views want to get that reinforced. In fact, these people actually seek out feedback about their negative attributes to reinforce these negative views of themselves.

Krupat: *I had thought in general that there is a bias toward a positive self-view.*

Crocker: Yes, but others have argued that this is not always the case. People very much want to have positive feedback about themselves. It feels good. But people differ in how believable they find that positive feedback. When people who start out with positive self-views get positive feedback from others, they find that information highly credible and they say, "That makes perfect sense to me." But people who start out with a negative self-view may find positive feedback difficult to accept because it is not consistent with how they see themselves. Even though they would like to believe it, they may not entirely trust it because it does not fit with what they think is true about themselves.

Krupat: *Up to now we have been talking about self as if there were only one "true" self, but that doesn't quite feel right to me. For in-*

stance, I would imagine that the self you might see on a first date might be a different self than you would see after six years of marriage.

Crocker: That's right. Regardless of what we really think about ourselves, we don't necessarily choose to present ourselves to other people in that way. On a date you try to appear charming. On a job interview you try to appear competent and intelligent.

Krupat: *But still we can ask, "Which is the 'real' you?"*

Crocker: The problem here is that the presented self is often very sincere. It may be that a part of me really is competent. I'm just giving you that piece of me in the job interview and not revealing the incompetent me. So it's not that what I present is entirely phony; it may just be that I am choosing to present the best of me in that situation. That is the *real* me, even if it's not the *whole* me.

William B. Swann, Jr.
J. Gregory Hixon
Chris De La Ronde

Embracing the Bitter "Truth": Negative Self-Concepts and Marital Commitment

In this article, Swann and his colleagues test and find support for an interesting position that he has taken concerning self-esteem. Believing that people want to find support for their existing self-concepts, Swann predicts that people will gravitate toward relationships in which their partners see them as they see themselves. Consistent with this, Swann finds that people with negative self-esteem were actually more committed to their spouses if those people thought *poorly* of them than if the spouses had a more positive opinion of them.

I flee who chases me, and chose who flees me.

—Ovid, ca. 8/1925, line 26

Over the years, everyone from poets and philosophers to grandmothers has noted that people love to be loved. In the last few decades, social scientists have documented this proposition so many times that it is now a bedrock assumption of most theories of social behavior (e.g., Berscheid, 1985). Surely, all other things being equal, rational people do not flee from loving partners in favor of indifferent ones. Or do they?

Recent theorizing has suggested that people want more than adoration from their relationship partners; they also want verification and confirmation of their self-concepts. This research suggests that if people with negative self-concepts truly look to their relationships for self-verification, they may shun partners who appraise them favorably and embrace those who appraise them unfavorably.

SELF-VERIFICATION PROCESSES AND
THE SEARCH FOR FEEDBACK THAT FITS

Self-verification theory (Swann, 1990) begins with the assumption that the key to successful social relations is the capacity for people to recognize how others perceive them (e.g., Cooley, 1902; Mead, 1934, 1934; Stryker, 1981). To this end, people note the reactions of others and use these reactions as a basis for inferring their own self-concepts. From this vantage point, self-concepts are cognitive distillations of past relationships.

Because self-concepts are abstracted from the reactions of others, they should allow people to predict how others will respond to them in the future. Recognizing this, people come to rely on stable self-concepts and view substantial self-concept change as a threat to intrapsychic and interpersonal functioning (for related accounts, see Aronson, 1968; Festinger, 1957; Lecky, 1945). Consider, for example, how a woman who perceives herself as socially inept might feel upon overhearing her husband characterize her as socially skilled. If she takes his comment seriously, she will probably find it thoroughly unsettling, as it challenges a long-standing belief about who she is and implies that she may not know herself after all. And if she does not know *herself,* what does she know?

Even if she lacked such existential concerns, she might still want her husband to recognize her social ineptitude for purely pragmatic or interpersonal reasons (e.g., Goffman, 1959). That is, as long as he recognizes her limitations, he will form modest expectations of her and their interactions will proceed smoothly. In contrast, should he form an inappropriately favorable impression, he might develop unrealistic expectations that she could not meet.

Both intrapsychic and interpersonal considerations may therefore motivate people to prefer self-verifying appraisals over self-discrepant ones. This reasoning leads to an unusual prediction: Although people with negative self-views may find that unfavorable evaluations frustrate their desire for praise, they may nevertheless seek such evaluations because they find them to be reassuring—particularly when they contemplate the intrapsychic and interpersonal anarchy that inappropriately favorable appraisals may bring. People with negative self-views may accordingly prefer relatively negative evaluations and relationship partners who provide such evaluations.

Although laboratory studies have shown that people with firmly held negative self-views prefer interaction partners who evaluate them unfavorably (e.g., Swann, Hixon, Stein-Seroussi, & Gilbert, 1990; Swann, Stein-Seroussi, & Giesler, in press; Swann, Wenzlaff, Krull, & Pelham, in press), no one knows whether or how this tendency influences people's choice of relationship partners outside the laboratory. Some theorists have argued that these findings are a product of idiosyncratic features of laboratory settings and would not generalize to naturally occurring situations (e.g, Raynor & McFarlin, 1986). To address this issue, we moved outside the laboratory to examine people's reactions to appraisals from persons with whom they were involved in ongoing relationships. In particular, we focused on the extent to which married persons with negative, moderate, or positive self-concepts seemed committed to spouses who appraised them relatively favorably or unfavorably.

SELF-VERIFICATION AT THE HORSE RANCH AND MALL

We recruited 95 married couples from a sample of patrons of a horse ranch (41 couples) and shopping mall (54 couples) in the central Texas area by offering them $5 apiece. Participants ranged in age from 19 to 78, with a mean of 32.1 years. Most participants were Caucasians (87.8%) and had at least some college education (91%). Spouses had known one another for an average of 9 years and had been married for an average of 6 years. Members of 3 couples misunderstood the instructions, and members of 6 other couples gave conflicting responses (e.g., reported having a different number of children); we accordingly deleted their data.

The experimenter seated the members of each couple at opposite ends of a long table so they could not discern one another's responses. After obtaining informed consent and assuring participants that their partners would never see their responses, the experimenter presented each participant with an identical questionnaire as part of an investigation of "the relation between personality and close relationships." In addition to the items described below, the questionnaire included items pertaining to the structure of self-knowledge, interpersonal accuracy, and related issues.

The measure of self-concepts was the short form of the Self-Attributes Questionnaire (SAQ; Pelham & Swann, 1989). The SAQ is a measure of a confederacy of five specific self-views central to self-worth: intellectual capability, physical attractiveness, athletic ability, social skills, and aptitude for arts and music. For each attribute, participants rated themselves relative to other people their own age and gender on graduated-interval scales ranging from 0 (bottom 5%) to 9 (top 5%).

After completing the self-ratings, participants filled out the principle index of partner appraisal: the sum of their ratings of their partners on the five SAQ attributes. As expected, spouses rated participants with moderate ($M = 32$) or positive ($M = 34$) self-views.

The measure of commitment focused on the participants' intentions, feelings, and actions regarding their relationships. On 9-point scales, participants responded to seven items tapping desire to remain in the relationship, plans to remain in the relationship, relationship satisfaction, time spent together, amount of talking, discussion

TABLE 2.1 Average Level of Marital Commitment by Self-concept and Spouse's Appraisal

Spouse's appraisal	Self-concept		
	Negative	Moderate	Positive
Unfavorable	52.4	52.8	52.0
Moderate	52.7	53.2	53.1
Favorable	43.8	53.8	58.7

Note: Higher values indicate more commitment.

of problems and worries, and disclosure of personal matters. Responses to these items were closely associated and were summed.

The means plotted in Table 2.1 suggest that people were committed to spouses who verified their self-concepts. Just as participants with positive self-concepts were more committed to their relationships insofar as their spouses thought well of them, participants with negative self-concepts were more committed to the extent that their spouses thought poorly of them. Those with moderate self-concepts were not influenced by the nature of their spouses' appraisals.

WHY PEOPLE WITH NEGATIVE SELF-VIEWS EMBRACED SPOUSES WHO DEROGATED THEM

Our most provocative finding was that people with negative self-views were more committed to spouses who appraised them unfavorably. To better understand this finding, we examined our participants' responses to several questions that they completed after the major measures. We found the following:

1. The more participants believed that their spouses' appraisals "made them feel that they really knew themselves" rather than "confused them" (summed over the five SAQ attributes), the more committed they were to the relationship.
2. There was no evidence that people were committed to partners who appraised them unfavorably because they thought such partners would help them improve themselves. In fact, participants with negative self-views were less confident that feedback from their spouses would help them improve themselves ($M = 6.56$) than were participants with moderate ($M = 7.28$) and positive ($M = 7.49$) self-views.
3. People with negative self-views were not especially committed to spouses who rated them negatively because they hoped to win their spouses over. Indeed, participants with negative self-views showed a marginally reliable tendency to be more committed to spouses to the extent that they expected their spouses' appraisals on the five SAQ attributes would worsen.
4. People with negative self-views did not commit themselves to spouses who rated them unfavorably because they took expressions of negativity as signs of perceptiveness.
5. Self-verification was not the exclusive province of women or men.

GENERAL DISCUSSION

In our investigation, married people with negative self-views responded in a remarkable fashion. Whereas participants with positive self-concepts displayed more commitment to spouses who evaluated them favorably than to spouses who evaluated them unfavorably, participants with negative self-views displayed more commitment to spouses who evaluated them *unfavorably* than to spouses who evaluated them favorably. Our findings therefore suggest that people embrace spouses who appraise them in a self-verifying manner, even if this means committing themselves to persons who think poorly of them. This tendency may have undesirable consequences, especially for people who want to improve their self-esteem. Such people may discover, for example, that they are unable to benefit from therapy because their spouses reinforce their negative self-concepts (for a related experiment, see Swann & Predmore, 1985).

Skeptics could, of course, note that our design was correlational and that it is thus hazardous to assume that the spouses' appraisals caused the level of commitment. Although we agree that caution is in order, we are reassured by the evidence we report that casts doubt on several alternative explanations of our effects and by the fact that recent laboratory research has yielded findings that parallel our own (see Swann, 1990, for a review). To us, a more troubling issue is the discrepancy between our findings and the voluminous literature indicating that people prefer favorable evaluations. One reason for this discrepancy may be that past researchers have typically examined participants' reactions to evaluations from complete strangers in laboratory settings. Clearly, it is one thing to express attraction for a stranger who offers an inappropriately favorable evaluation. It is quite another to pursue a relationship with such a person (e.g., Huston & Levinger, 1978), because doing so may invite the undesired intrapsychic and interpersonal consequences associated with discrepant feedback. Thus, for example, the same flattering remarks that seem harmless and pleasant when delivered by a stranger may seem disturbing and unsettling when delivered by someone who should know the person well.

Of course, some laboratory studies, including those we have conducted, *have* shown evidence of self-verification strivings. Why? Perhaps because we have focused on our participants' choice of feedback and interaction partners rather than on immediate, affective reactions to evaluations, as most past researchers have done. Recent research and theorizing (e.g., Swann, 1990; Swann et al., 1990) have suggested that when people with negative self-views first receive favorable evaluations, they are quite enamored with them; only after they have had time to compare such evaluations with their self-concepts has a preference for self-verifying evaluations emerged. Similarly, immediately after receiving unfavorable feedback, people with negative self-views report being distressed by it, yet shortly thereafter they go on to seek additional unfavorable feedback (e.g., Swann, Wenzlaff, Krull, & Pelham, in press)!

This research then, suggests that people with negative self-views are enveloped in a psychological cross fire between a desire for positive feedback and a desire for self-verifying feedback. For such persons, it seems that the warmth produced by favorable feedback is chilled by incredulity, and that the reassurance produced by negative feedback is tempered by sadness that the "truth" could not be more kind. Given this dilemma, it seems likely that people with negative self-concepts may seek unfavorable (self-verifying) evaluations in some contexts and positive appraisals in others (e.g., Swann, Hixon, & De La Ronde, 1991). When they do court unfavorable evaluations, however, it is not out of masochism, as it seems that they engage in such activities in spite of rather than because of the unhappiness that such appraisals foster.

References

Aronson, E. (1960). A theory of cognitive dissonance: A current perspective. In L. Berkowitz (Ed.), *Advances in experimental social psychology* (Vol. 4, pp. 1–34). New York: Academic Press.

Backman, C. W., & Secord, P. F. (1962). Liking, selective interaction, and misperception in congruent interpersonal relations. *Sociometry, 25,* 321–335.

Berscheid, E. (1985). Interpersonal attraction. In G. Lindzey & E. Aronson (Eds.), *Handbook of social psychology* (Vol. 2, pp. 413–484). New York: Random House.

Cooley, C. H. (1902). *Human nature and the social order.* New York: Scribner's.

Doherty, E. G., & Secord, P. F. (1971). Change of roommate and interpersonal congruency. *Representative Research in Social Psychology, 2,* 70–75.

Festinger, L. (1957). *A theory of cognitive dissonance.* Evanston, IL: Row, Peterson.

Goffman, E. (1959). *The presentation of self in everyday life.* New York: Anchor Books.

Huston, T. L., & Levinger, G. (1978). Interpersonal attraction and relationships. *Annual Review of Psychology, 29,* 115–156.

Kenny, D. A., & Judd, C. M. (1986). Consequences of violating the independence assumption in the analysis of variance. *Psychological Bulletin, 99,* 442–431.

Lecky, P. (1945). *Self-consistency: A theory of personality.* New York: Island Press.

Mead, G. H. (1934). *Mind, self and society.* Chicago: University of Chicago Press.

Ovid. (1925). *The Loves* (Book II) (J. Lewis May, Trans.). Burgay, England: John Lane The Bodley Head. (Original work published ca. 8).

Pelham, B. W., & Swann, W. B., Jr. (1989). From self-conceptions to self-worth: On the sources and structure of global self-esteem. *Journal of Personality and Social Psychology, 57,* 672–680.

Raynor, J. O., & McFarlin, D. B. (1986). Motivation and the self-system. In R. M. Sorrentino & E. T. Higgins (Eds.), *Motivation and cognition: Foundations of social behavior* (pp. 315–349). New York: Guilford Press.

Stryker, S. (1981). *Symbolic interactionism.* Menlo Park, CA: Benjamin/Cummings.

Swann, W. B., Jr. (1990). To be adored or to be known: The interplay of self-enhancement and self-verification. In R. M. Sorrentino & E. T. Higgins (Eds.), *Motivation and cognition* (Vol. 2, pp. 408–448). New York: Guilford Press.

Swann, W. B., Jr., Hixon, J. G., & De La Ronde, C. (1991). *Dating games and marital reality.* Manuscript submitted for publication.

Swann, W. B., Jr., Hixon, J. G., Stein-Seroussi, A., & Gilbert, D. T. (1990). The fleeting gleam of praise: Behavioral reactions to self-relevant feedback. *Journal of Personality and Social Psychology, 59,* 17–26.

Swann, W. B., Jr., & Predmore, S. C. (1985). Intimates as agents of social support: Sources of consolidation or despair? *Journal of Personality and Social Psychology, 49,* 1609–1617.

Swann, W. B., Jr., Stein-Seroussi, A., & Giesler, R. B. (in press). Why people self-verify. *Journal of Personality and Social Psychology.*

Swann, W. B., Jr., Wenzlaff, R. M., Krull, D. S., & Pelham, B. W. (in press). The allure of negative feedback: Self-verification strivings among depressed persons. *Journal of Abnormal Psychology.*

David G. Myers
Jack Ridl

Can We All Be Better Than Average?

Did you realize that 50% of the doctors in the United States graduated in the bottom half of their medical school classes? Of course they did—statistically that has to be so. But do you think that these very same people think of themselves as below average students or doctors? That is the question that Myers and Ridl pose in this brief, but thought-provoking article. Discussing what has been called the "self-serving bias," the authors point out that people process information about themselves in a manner that enhances their self-image, but that they are not as generous when thinking about others. Having learned of this effect and how common it is, it would be useful to consider instances where this bias serves a positive purpose (for instance, in helping people maintain self-esteem after failure) versus those where it might prove to be less appropriate (blaming others for one's own faults).

Harry is a better-than-average golfer; his wife, Jean, a better-than-average tennis player. Harry may spend more time searching in the rough than he does strolling the fairways, and Jean may have a serve that would bring down a weather balloon. Yet, ask Harry to comment on his golf game, or Jean on her serve, and both will bashfully admit: "Oh, I guess I'd have to say, 'better than average.' "

Believing ourselves better-than-average observers of the ways and wiles of human nature, we were not surprised to find in some recent studies evidence that average people see themselves as "better than average." Social psychology, it seems, is dusting off the old story of human pride. As William Saroyan put it: "Every man is a good man in a bad world—as he himself knows."

Many experiments disclose a self-serving bias in the way we perceive events. We explain our positive behavior in terms of our dispositions ("I helped that blind man because I am a considerate person") while we attribute nasty remarks or inconsiderate behavior to external factors ("I was angry because everything was going wrong"). This enables us to take credit for our good acts and find scapegoats for our bad.

People assigned the roles of teachers or therapists in experiments tend to take credit for any positive outcome, but blame failure on the person being helped. The pseudoclinician surmises, "I helped Mrs. X get better, but, despite all my help, Mr. Y got worse." Generally speaking, people attribute their successes mostly to ability and effort, but blame their failures on bad luck or other outside factors.

Games that combine skill and chance may be popular because they permit similar rationalizing. Winners at bridge, for example, can easily attribute their success to skill, while losers can mutter, "Four points, four lousy points was all I had, a king and a jack." Or when we win at a word game, for example, it is because of our verbal dexterity; when we lose; it is because "who could get anywhere with a q but no u?" In experiments that pit two or more people against others, winners usually take personal credit for their victories but hold their partners responsible when they lose, following a tradition established by Adam: "The woman whom thou gavest to be with me, she gave me the tree, and I did eat."

Even college professors—obviously, much better than average folk—are not immune. When we are frustrated in our attempts to write and publish, we blame the situation: "With these horrible teaching loads and inadequate resources, you can't be a productive scholar." When fortunate circumstances do enable us to publish, we are inclined to ignore them and take personal credit for our having overcome great difficulties.

Students are equally vain. Anthony Greenwald, a psychologist at Ohio State University, asked students who had just received their grades on an examination to judge how well the exam measured their knowledge. Students who did well typically saw the exam as a good measure of their competence, while students who did poorly felt it was a poor test of their knowledge. Faculty members must share the blame for the students' delusions about competence, for their grandiose self-perceptions are no doubt based, in part, on the recent trend toward grade-inflation. The C grade has gone the way of grammar. The lament uttered among today's students is not, "An F? I had better buckle down or try something else." Instead, one hears, "He gave me a B–? B–! C is average. At least, I'm better than average."

The self-serving bias would be less troubling if we were equally generous in our perception of others, but researchers have found that we are inclined to attribute others' failures to their dispositions. We often hear, or say, "It doesn't surprise me at all that John made those remarks. He's hostile. Personally, I can't stand such people." John may have made "those remarks" not because he is hostile, but because he despises corruption. The tendency to chastise John for his temper while excusing our own often leads to social conflict. Bill attributes Mary's actions to her nasty disposition, but sees his own toughness as "certainly reasonable, given the stress I'm under." Mary, of course, perceives the situation a being precisely the reverse.

No generalization has been more firmly established during the last two decades of social-psychological research than this: our attitudes both shape our behavior and are shaped by it. Every time we act, we amplify the idea underlying the act. For example, people who are induced by a researcher to say something they are unsure of will generally begin to believe their "little lies," especially if they feel they had some choice in what they said. Likewise, harming an innocent victim—by muttering a cutting comment or delivering electric shocks—typically leads aggressors to derogate their victims, thus justifying their own actions, at least to some extent. Such acts corrode the conscience of those who perform them; they soon become not people playing a part, but the part itself. Action and attitude feed one another, sometimes to the point of moral numbness.

The French psychologist Jean-Paul Codol conducted 20 experiments on the self-serving bias of the French, with people ranging from 12-year-olds to adults. The perceived superiority of the self was omnipresent, regardless of those involved or the experimental methods used. In one case, Codol had each person in a group of four give three estimates of the length of a rod. After they all had given their estimates, the experimenter measured the rod and announced its correct length. Rating their performances later, most individuals—regardless of their real accuracy—proclaimed themselves at or near the top of their group. In other experiments, Codol found that the more people admired a particular trait, such as honesty or creativity, the more likely they were to see themselves as more honest or creative than other people.

We can almost hear readers saying, "But, of course, those were Frenchmen, and you know the French!" The phenomenon is not uniquely French, however. Americans are just as likely to accept and recall more positive than negative information about themselves and to see themselves as better than average. Research indicates that, compared with ourselves, most of us see our friends, neighbors, coworkers, and classmates as a sorry lot. They are weaker ethically ("I was shocked to hear that Betty . . ."), more intolerant ("I admit I have my prejudices, but I couldn't believe it when Carl said . . ."), and less intelligent ("I'm no genius, mind you, but even a moron could . . ."). We even think our peers are likely to die sooner than we are. C. R. Snyder, a psychologist at the University of Kansas, reports that college students view themselves as likely to outlive by 10 years their actuarially predicted age of death. It has been said that Freud's favorite joke was about the man who told his wife, "If one of us should die first, I think I would go live in Paris."

You can demonstrate the self-serving bias for yourself, if you like. Have people anonymously compare themselves with others on a variety of socially desirable traits by filling in a blank: for example, "My hunch is that about ____% of the others in the group are more sympathetic than I am." You will find that the percentage is usually a modest one. Bias operates more freely in assessing attitudes and character traits, such as sympathy, responsibility, and considerateness, rather than in more objective matters, such as a person's income or height.

Consciously, at least, a "superiority complex" pervades most self-comparisons, although it may, in many cases, be merely a cover for deeper insecurities. But rarely are we willing to proclaim our perceived superiorities publicly, since we know that others (who harbor similar self-perceptions) are unlikely to be charmed.

Most of us, moreover, have already learned that self-put downs are a useful technique for eliciting "strokes" from others. We know that a remark like "Every time I see Carol in that beautiful dress, I wish I weren't so ordinary-looking" will elicit a comforting "Now Jane, don't say you're plain. You have gorgeous hair and your ponytail will soon be back in style."

Experiments conducted by psychologist Baruch Fischhoff and colleagues at Decision Research in Eugene, Oregon, indicate there is also a pervasive "intellectual conceit" to our judgments of our knowledge. We boast that we knew all along how a given experiment or historical event would turn out, despite the fact that, in many cases, the results were unexpected. Thus, we seldom feel surprised by the results of psychological research or of current events. "I knew the Yankees would win last year. I could have told you in July that they would pull it off."

Such statements are not lies, but self-deceptions that may be personally useful. Some sociobiologists have even suggested that self-deception may be a trait that has been bred into us through natural selection: cheaters, for example, may give a more convincing display of honesty if they believe in their honesty. Similarly, thinking positively about one's abilities and traits may provide the self-confidence conducive to success.

This egocentric bias is not always adaptive, however. In a series of nine experiments, Barry Schlenker, a psychologist at the University of Florida, showed how egocentric bias can disrupt a group of people working together on a task. After completing each task, the group was told whether or not it had been successful. The feedback was random, bearing no relation to how well or poorly the group had actually done.

Yet, in every study, the members of successful groups claimed more responsibility for the group's performance than did members of failing groups. The same self-congratulatory tendency surfaced when people evaluated their contributions to the group. Unless their self-conceit could be debunked by public exposure, most people presented themselves as contributing more to the group's success than others did when the results were good; few of them said they did less.

Such self-deception can cause trouble in a group by leading its members to expect greater-than-average rewards (pay or otherwise) when their organization does well, and less-than-average blame when it doesn't. If most individuals in a group believe they are underpaid and underappreciated, disharmony and envy are likely.

Michael Ross and Fiore Sicoly at the University of Waterloo, in Ontario, observed a similar phenomenon when only two people were involved. In one experiment, they interrupted conversing pairs in cafeterias and lounges and asked each person to estimate how much he or she had spoken during the conversation. Each reported having spoken, on the average, 59 percent of the time. In other studies, the investigators found that married persons usually saw themselves as taking more responsibility for activities such as cleaning the house and caring for the children than did their spouses. Ross and Sicoly believe that the bias is partly due to the greater ease with which we recall things *we* have done, compared with what we've seen others do. That we tend to remember our positively valued acts better than negatively valued ones suggests that there are self-serving motivations involved as well.

Such biased self-assessments can distort judgments in business as well, as psychologist Laurie Larwood of Claremont University has demonstrated. When corporation presidents predict more growth for their firms than for the competition, and production managers similarly overpredict performance, their overoptimism can be disastrous. If those who deal in the stock market or in commodities see their business intuition as superior to their competitors', they may be in for some rude awakenings.

Many educational administrators have the same biases. Although the number of college-age Americans will shrink nearly 25 percent between 1979 and the early 1990s, few college officials are making plans to deal with the probable decline in admissions. They figure, rightly, that even in a time of decline, not all colleges will shrink. And since their schools are better than average, they have little doubt that their institutions will be among the few that do not suffer.

We are vulnerable to the consequences of the self-serving bias. Larwood found that Los Angeles residents felt they were healthier than average and that the greater this perception, the less likely they were to avail themselves of a public inoculation program. She also surveyed homes in a Northeastern city and found that most people professed to be more concerned than others about assuring clean air and water and believed they used less electricity than other city residents. Average citizens were, self-proclaimed, better-than-average citizens. As Larwood observed, if most people "are merely the average persons that they must be statistically, but behave as though they are superior, their goals and expectations must inevitably conflict. Too much will be produced, not enough people will get inoculations, and each of us will continue to use our (more than) fair share of resources."

The better-than-average phenomenon affects our perception not only of ourselves, but also of our groups. Codol found, as have some American researchers, that people see their own groups as superior to other, comparable groups. The children in each of several school classrooms, for instance, were likely to see their class as surpassing others in desirable characteristics such as friendliness or cooperativeness. Psychologist Irving Janis of Yale University noted that one source of international conflict is the tendency of each side to believe in the moral superiority of its acts. Americans say that the United States builds missile bases near the Russian border in Turkey to protect the free world from communism, while the Soviet Union puts missiles in Cuba to threaten our security. The Soviets, of course, see the motivation behind the bases as exactly the opposite.

Modern research on self-serving perceptions confirms some ancient wisdom. The tragic flaw portrayed in Greek drama was *hubris,* or extreme pride. Like the subjects of our experiments, the Greek tragic figures did not self-consciously choose evil, but rather thought too highly of themselves (they were better than average), with consequent disaster. Human evil is described as such by its victims, not its perpetrators. Søren Kierkegaard lamented that becoming aware of our own sin is like trying to see our own eyeballs.

The true end of humility is not self-contempt (which still leaves people concerned with themselves). To paraphrase the English novelist and essayist C. S. Lewis, humility does not consist in handsome people trying to believe they are ugly, and clever people trying to believe they are fools. When we hear a Nobel laureate respond to an interviewer with, "Well, Ted, yes, I was surprised, pleased even, when I heard the news. Actually, I'd have to consider myself no more than a better-than-average nuclear bioorganic microecological physical chemist," we may wonder where that leaves those of us who have a hard time following a recipe for pound cake.

But when Muhammad Ali announced that he was the greatest, there was a sense in which his pronouncement did not violate the spirit of humility. False modesty can actually lead to an ironic pride in one's better-than-average humility. (Perhaps some readers are by now congratulating themselves on being unusually free of the inflated self-perception this article describes.)

True humility is more like self-forgetfulness than false modesty. It leaves people free to rejoice in their special talents and, with the same honesty, recognize their neighbor's. But the neighbor's talents and one's own are recognized as gifts and, like one's height, are not fit subjects for either inordinate pride or self-depreciation. Ali's self-preoccupation did violate this aspect of humility, for in that ideal state there is neither vain-glory nor false modesty, only honest self-acceptance.

As we have seen, true humility is a state not easily attained. The self-serving bias is the social psychologist's modern rendition of the forever underappreciated truth about human pride. "There is," said C. S. Lewis, "no fault which we are more unconscious of in ourselves. . . . If anyone would like to acquire humility, I can, I think, tell him the first step. The first step is to realize that one is proud. And a biggish step, too."

Hazel Rose Markus
Shinobu Kitayama

Culture and the Self: Implications for Cognition, Emotion, and Motivation

In this article, Hazel Markus and Shinobu Kitayama point out that people in different cultures often have distinctly different ways of construing the "self," which are a consequence of the ways in which they see their relationship to others. They point out that Americans are socialized to see themselves as independent of others, that U.S. culture encourages people to pay attention and call attention to the self. Americans therefore attempt to discover and express their unique personal attributes in their behavior with others. In contrast to the "independent self" that is typical of Americans, they point out that people in Asian cultures typically develop an "interdependent self" because their culture leads them to focus on the fundamental relatedness of individuals to one another. The emphasis here is on paying attention to others, to fitting in, and to maintaining harmonious relations. The authors develop these ideas by careful attention to anthropologiocal as well as psychological theories, and note how these differing cultural self-images have important consequences for our thoughts, feelings, and actions.

In America, "the squeaky wheel gets the grease." In Japan, "the nail that stands out gets pounded down." American parents who are trying to induce their children to eat their suppers are fond of saying "think of the starving kids in Ethiopia, and appreciate how lucky you are to be different from them." Japanese parents are likely to say "Think about the farmer who worked so hard to produce this rice for you; if you don't eat it, he will feel bad, for his efforts will have been in vain" (H. Yamada, February 16, 1989). A small Texas corporation seeking to elevate productivity told its employees to look in the mirror and say "I am beautiful" 100 times before coming to work each day. Employees of a Japanese supermarket that was recently opened in New Jersey were instructed to begin the day by holding hands and telling each other that "he" or "she is beautiful" ("A Japanese Supermarket," 1989).

Such anecdotes suggest that people in Japan and America may hold strikingly divergent construals of the self, others, the the interdependence of the two. The American examples stress attending to the self, the appreciation of one's difference from others, and the importance of asserting the self. The Japanese examples emphasize attending to and fitting in with others and the importance of harmonious interdependence with them. These construals of the self and others are tied to the implicit, normative tasks that various cultures hold for what people should be doing in their lives (cf. Cantor & Kihlstrom, 1987; Erikson, 1950; Veroff, 1983). Anthropologists and psychologists assume that such construals can influence, and in many cases determine, the very nature of individual experience (Chodorow, 1978; Dumont, 1970; Geertz, 1975; Gergen, 1968; Gilligan, 1982; Holland & Quinn, 1987; Lykes, 1985; Marsella, De Vos, & Hsu, 1985; Sampson, 1985, 1988, 1989; Shweder & LeVine, 1984; Smith, 1985; Triandis, 1989; Weisz, Rothbaum, & Blackburn, 1984; White & Kirkpatrick, 1985).

Despite the growing body of psychological and anthropological evidence that people hold divergent views about the self, most of what psychologists currently know about human nature is based on one particular view—the so-called Western view of the individual as an independent, self-contained, autonomous entity who (a) comprises a unique configuration of internal attributes (e.g., traits, abilities, motives, and values) and (b) behaves primarily as a consequence of these internal attributes (Geertz, 1975; Sampson, 1988, 1989; Sweder & LeVine, 1984). As a result of this monocultural approach to the self (see Kennedy, Scheier, & Rogers, 1984), psychologists' understanding of those phenomena that are linked in one way or another to the self may be unnecessarily restricted. (For some important exceptions, see Bond, 1986, 1988; Cousins, 1989; Fiske, in press; Maehr & Nicholls, 1980; Stevenson, Azuma, & Hakuta, 1986; Triandis, 1989; Bontempo, Villareal, Asai, & Lucca, 1988). In this article, we suggest that construals of the self, of others, and of the relationship between the self and others may be even more powerful than previously suggested and that their influence is clearly reflected in differences among cultures. In particular, we compare an *independent* view of the self with one other, very different view, an *interdependent* view. The independent view is most clearly exemplified in some sizable segment of American culture, as well as in many Western European cultures. The interdependent view is exemplified in Japanese culutre as well as in other Asian cultures. But it is also characteristic of African cultures, Latin-American cultures, and many southern European cultures. We delineate how these divergent views of the self—the independent and the interdependent—can have a systematic influence on various aspects of cognition, emotion, and motivation.

We suggest that for many cultures of the world, the Western notion of the self as an entity containing significant dispositional attributes, and as detached from context, is simply not an adequate description of selfhood. Rather, in many construals, the self is viewed as *inter*dependent with the surrounding context, and it is the "other" or the "self-in-relation-to-other" that is focal in individual experience. One general consequence of this divergence in self-construal is that when psychological processes (e.g., cognition, emotion, and motivation) explicitly, or even quite implicitly, implicate the self as a target or as a referent, the nature of these processes will vary according to the exact form or organization of self inherent in a given construal. With respect to cognition, for example, for those with interdependent selves, in contrast to those with independent selves, some aspects of knowledge representation and some of the processes involved in social and nonsocial thinking alike are influenced by a pervasive attentiveness to the relevant *others* in the social context. Thus, one's actions are more likely to be seen as situationally bound, and characterizations of the individual will include this context. Furthermore, for those with interdependent construals of the self, both the expression and the experience of emotions and motives may be significantly shaped and governed by a consideration of the reactions of others. Specifically, for example, some emotions, like anger, that derive from and promote an independent view of the self, may be less prevalent among those with interdependent selves, and self-serving motives may be replaced by what appear as other-serving motives. An examination of cultural variation in some aspects of cognition, emotion, and motivation will allow psychologists to ask exactly what is universal in these processes, and has the potential to provide some new insights for theories of these psychological processes.

The distinctions that we make between independent and interdependent construals must be regarded as general tendencies that may emerge when the members of the culture are considered as a whole. The prototypical American view of the self, for example, may prove to be most characteristic of White, middle-class men with a Western European ethnic background. It may be somewhat less descriptive of women in general, or of men and women from other ethnic groups or social classes. Moreover, we realize that there may well be important distinctions among those views we discuss as similar, and that there may be views of the self and others that cannot easily be classified as either independent or interdependent.

Our intention is not to catalog all types of self-construals, but rather to highlight a view of the self that is often assumed to be universal but that may be quite specific to some segments of Western culture. We argue that self-construals play a major role in regulating various psychological processes.

THE SELF: A DELICATE CATEGORY

Universal Aspects of the Self

In exploring the possibility of different types of self-construals, we begin with Hallowell's (1955) notion that people everywhere are likely to develop an understanding of themselves as physically distinct and separable from others. Head (1920), for example, claimed the existence of a universal schema of the body that provided one with an anchor in time and space. Similarly, Allport (1937) suggested that there must exist an aspect of personality that allows one, when awakening each morning, to be sure that he or she is the same person who went to sleep the night before. Most recently, Neisser (1988) referred to this aspect of self as the *ecological self*, which he defined as "the self as perceived with respect to the physical environment: 'I' am the person here in this place, engaged in this particular activity" (p. 3). Beyond a physical or ecological sense of self, each person probably has some awareness of internal activity, such as dreams, and of the continuous flow of thoughts and feelings, which are private to the extent that they cannot be directly known by others. The awareness of this unshared experience will lead the person to some sense of an inner, private self.

Divergent Aspects of the Self

Some understanding and some representation of the private, inner aspects of the self may well be universal, but many other aspects of the self may be quite specific to particular cultures. People are capable of believing an astonishing variety of things about themselves (cf. Heelas & Lock, 1981; Marsella et al., 1985; Shweder & LeVine, 1984; Triandis, 1989). The self can be construed, framed, or conceptually represented in multiple ways. A cross-cultural survey of the self lends support to Durkheim's (1912/1968) early notion that the category of the self is primarily the product of social factors, and to Mauss's (1938/1985) claim that as a social category, the self is a "delicate" one, subject to quite substantial, if not infinite, variation.

The exact content and structure of the inner self may differ considerably by culture. Furthermore, the nature of the outer or public self that derives from one's relations with other people and social institutions may also vary markedly by culture. And, as suggested by Triandis (1989), the significance assigned to the private, inner aspects versus the public, relational aspects in regulating behavior will vary accordingly. In fact, it may not be unreasonable to suppose, as did numerous earlier anthropologists (see Allen, 1985), that in some cultures, on certain occasions, the *individual,* in the sense of a set of significant inner attributes of the person, may cease to be the primary unit of consciousness. Instead, the sense of belongingness to a social relation may become so strong that it makes better sense to think of the *relationship* as a functional unit of conscious reflection.

The current analysis focuses on just one variation in what people in different cultures can come to believe about themselves. This one variation concerns what they believe about the relationship between the self and *others* and, especially, the degree to which they see themselves as *separate* from others or as *connected* with others. We suggest that the significance and the exact functional role that the person assigns to the other when defining the self depend on the culturally shared assumptions about the separation or connectedness between the self and others.

TWO CONSTRUALS OF THE SELF: INDEPENDENT AND INTERDEPENDENT

The Independent Construal

In many Western cultures, there is a faith in the inherent separateness of distinct persons. The normative imperative of this culture is to become independent from others and to discover and express one's unique attributes (Johnson, 1985; Marsella et al., 1985; J. G. Miller, 1988; Shweder & Bourne, 1984). Achieving the cultural goal of independence requires construing oneself as an individual whose behavior is organized and made meaningful primarily by reference to one's own internal repertoire of thoughts, feelings, and actions, rather than by reference to the thoughts, feelings, and actions of others. According to this construal of self, to borrow Geertz's (1975) often quoted phrase, the person is viewed as "a bounded, unique, more or less integrated motivational and cognitive universe, a dynamic center of awareness, emotion, judgment, and action organized into a distinctive whole and set contrastively both against other such wholes and against a social and natural background" (p. 48).

This view of the self derives from a belief in the wholeness and uniqueness of each person's configuration of internal attributes (Johnson, 1985; Sampson, 1985, 1988, 1989; Waterman, 1981). It gives rise to processes like "self-actualization," "realizing oneself," "expressing one's unique configuration of needs, rights, and capacities," or "developing one's distinct potential." The essential aspect of this view involves a conception of the self as an autonomous, independent person; we thus refer to it as the *independent, construal of the self.* Other similar labels include *individualist, egocentric, separate, autonomous, idiocentric,* and *self-contained.* We assume that, on average, relatively more individuals in Western cultures will hold this view than will individuals in non-Western cultures. Within a given culture, however, individuals will vary in the extent to which they are good cultural representatives and construe the self in the mandated way.

The independent self must, of course, be responsive to the social environment (Fiske, in press). This responsiveness, however, is fostered not so much for the sake of the responsiveness itself. Rather, social responsiveness often, if not always, derives from the need to strategically determine the best way to express or assert the internal attributes of the self. Others, or the social situation in general, are important, but primarily as standards of reflected appraisal, or as sources that can verify and affirm the inner core of the self.

The Western, independent view of the self is illustrated in Figure 2.1A. The large circle represents the self, and the smaller circles represent specific others. The Xs are representations of the various aspects of the self or the others. In some cases, the larger circle and the small circle intersect, and there is an X in the intersection. This refers to a representation of the self-in-relation-to-theirs or to a particular social relation (e.g., "I am very polite in front of my professor"). An X within the self circle but outside of the intersection represents an aspect of the self perceived to be relatively independent of specific others and, thus, invariant over time and context. These self-representations usually have as their referent some individual desire, preference, attribute, or ability (e.g., "I am creative"). For those with independent construals of the self, it is these inner attributes that are most significant in regulating behavior and that are assumed, both by the actor and by the observer alike, to be diagnostic of the actor. Such representations of the inner self are thus the most elaborated in memory and the most accessible when thinking of the self (as indicated by Xs in Figure 2.1A). They can be called *core conceptions, salient identities,* or *self-schemata* (e.g., Gergen, 1968; Markus, 1977; Stryker, 1986).

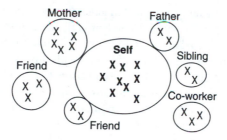

A. Independent View of Self

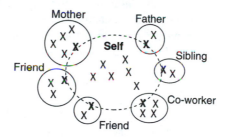

B. Inderpendent View of Self

FIGURE 2.1

Conceptual Representations of the Self. (A: Independent construal. B: Interdependent construal.)

The Interdependent Construal

In contrast, many non-Western cultures insist, in Kondo's (1982) terms, on the fundamental *connectedness* of human beings to each other. A normative imperative of these cultures is to maintain this interdependence among individuals (De Vos, 1985; Hsu, 1985; Miller, 1988; Shweder & Bourne, 1984). Experiencing interdependence entails seeing oneself as part of an encompassing social relationship and recognizing that one's behavior is determined, contingent on, and, to a large extent organized by what the actor perceives to be the thoughts, feelings, and actions of *others* in the relationship. The Japanese experience of the self, therefore, includes a sense of interdependence and of one's status as a participant in a larger social unit (Sampson, 1988). Within such a construal, the self becomes most meaningful and complete when it is cast in the appropriate social relationship. According to Lebra (1976) the Japanese are most fully human in the context of others.

This view of the self and the relationship between the self and others features the person not as separate from the social context but as more connected and less differentiated from others. People are motivated to find a way to fit in with relevant others, to fulfill and create obligation, and in general to become part of various inter-personal relationships. Unlike the independent self, the significant features of the self according to this construal are to be found in the interdependent and thus, in the more public components of the self. We therefore call this view the *interdependent construal of the self.* The same notion has been variously referred to, with somewhat different connotations, as *sociocentric, holistic, collective, allocentric, ensembled, constitutive, contextualist, connected,* and *relational.* As with the independent self, others are critical for social comparison and self-validation, yet in an interdependent formulation of the self, these others become an integral part of the setting, situation, or context to which the self is connected, fitted, and assimilated. The exact manner in which one achieves the task of connection, therefore, depends crucially on the na-ture of the context, particularly the others present in the context. Others thus partici-pate actively and continuously in the definition of the interdependent self.

The interdependent self also possesses and expresses a set of internal attributes, such as abilities, opinions, judgments, and personality characteristics. However, these internal attributes are understood as situation specific, and thus as sometimes elusive and unreliable. And, as such, they are unlikely to assume a powerful role in regulating overt behavior, especially if this behavior implicates significant others. In many domains of social life, one's opinions, abilities, and characteristics are as-signed only secondary roles—they must instead be constantly controlled and regu-lated to come to terms with the primary task of interdependence. Such voluntary control of the inner attributes constitutes the core of the cultural ideal of becoming mature. The understanding of one's autonomy as secondary to, and constrained by, the primary task of interdependence distinguishes interdependent selves from inde-pendent selves, for whom autonomy and its expression is often afforded primary significance. An independent behavior (e.g., asserting an opinion) exhibited by a person in an interdependent culture is likely to be based on the premise of underly-ing interdependence and thus may have a somewhat different significance than it has for a person from an independent culture.

The interdependent self is illustrated in Figure 2.1B. For those with interdepen-dent selves, the significant self-representations (the **X**s) are those in relationship to specific others. Interdependent selves certainly include representations of invariant personal attributes and abilities, and these representations can become phenomeno-logically quite salient, but in many circumstances they are less important in regulat-ing observable behavior and are not assumed to be particularly diagnostic of the self. Instead, the self-knowledge that guides behavior is of the self-in-relation to specific others in particular contexts. The fundamental units of the self-esteem, the core conceptions, or self-schemata are thus predicated on significant interpersonal relationships.

An interdependent self cannot be properly characterized as a bounded whole, for it changes structure with the nature of the particular social context. The uniqueness of such a self derives from the specific configuration of relationships that each person has developed. What is focal and objectified in an interdependent self, then, is not the inner self, but the *relationships* of the person to other actors (Hamaguchi, 1985).

The notion of an interdependent self is linked with a monistic philosophical tradition in which the person is thought to be of the same substance as the rest of nature (see Bond, 1986; Phillips, 1976; Roland, 1988; Sass, 1988). As a consequence, the relationship between the self and other, or between subject and object, is assumed to be much closer. Thus, many non-Western cultures insist on the inseparability of basic elements (Galtung, 1981), including self and other, and person and situation. In Chinese culture, for instance, there is an emphasis on synthesizing the constituent parts of any problem or situation into an integrated or harmonious whole (Moore, 1967; Northrop, 1946). Thus, persons are only parts that when separated from the larger social whole cannot be fully understood (Phillips, 1976; Schweder, 1984). Such a holistic view is in opposition to the Cartesian, dualistic tradition that characterizes Western thinking and in which the self is separated from the object and from the natural world.

Examples of the interdependent self. An interdependent view of the self is common to many of the otherwise highly diverse cultures of the world. Studies of the mainland Chinese, for example, summarized in a recent book by Bond (1986), show that even among the most rapidly modernizing segments of the Chinese population, there is a tendency for people to act primarily in accordance with the anticipated expectations of others and social norms rather than with internal wishes or personal attributes (Yang, 1981b). A premium is placed on emphasizing collective welfare and on showing a sympathetic concern for others. Throughout the studies of the Chinese reported by Bond, one can see the clear imprint of the Confucian emphasis on interrelatedness and kindness. According to Hsu (1985), the supreme Chinese virtue, *jen,* implies the person's capability to interact with fellow human beings in a sincere, polite, and decent fashion (see also Elvin, 1985).

Numerous other examples of cultures in which people are likely to have some version of an interdependent self can also be identified. For example, Triandis, Marin, Lisansky, and Betancourt (1984) have described the importance of *simpatico* among Hispanics. This quality refers to the ability to both respect and share others' feelings. In characterizing the psychology of Filipinos, Church (1987) described the importance that people attribute to smooth interpersonal relations and to being "agreeable even under difficult circumstances, sensitive to what others are feeling and willing to adjust one's behavior accordingly." Similarly, Weisz (in press) reported that Thais place a premium on self-effacement, humility, deference, and on trying to avoid disturbing others. Among the Japanese, it is similarly crucial not to disturb the *wa,* or the harmonious ebb and flow of interpersonal relations (see also Geertz, 1974, for characterizations of similar imperatives among the Balinese and Moroccans).

Beattie (1980) claimed that Africans are also extremely sensitive to the interdependencies among people and view the world and others in it as extensions of one another. The self is viewed not as a hedged closure but as an open field. Similarly, Marriott (1976) argued that Hindu conceptions assume that the self is an open entity that is given shape by the social context. In his insightful book, Katar (1978) described the Hindu's ideal of interpersonal fusion and how it is accompanied by a personal, cultural sense of hell, which is separation from others. In fact, Miller, Bersoff, and Harwood (1990), in a recent, carefully controlled study on moral reasoning, found that Indians regard responsiveness to the needs of others as an objective moral obligation to a far greater extent than do Americans. Although the self-systems of people from these cultures are markedly different in many other important respects, they appear to be alike in the greater value (when compared with Americans) that is attached to proper relations with others, and in the requirement to flexibly change one's own behavior in accordance with the nature of the relationship.

Even in American culture, there is a strong theme of interdependence that is reflected in the values and activities of many of its subcultures. Religious groups, such as the Quakers, explicitly value and promote interdependence, as do many small towns and rural communities (e.g., Bellah, Madsen, Sullivan, Swindler, & Tipton, 1985). Some notion of a more connected, ensembled, interdependent self, as opposed to a self-contained, independent self, is also being developed by several of what Sampson (1989) calls "postmodern" theorists. These theorists are questioning the sovereignty of the American view of the mature person as autonomous, self-determined, and unencumbered. They argue that psychology is currently dominated by a view of the person that does not adequately reflect the extent to which people everywhere are created by, constrained by, and responsive to their various interpersonal contexts (see Gergen & Gergen, 1988; Gilligan, 1982; Miller, 1986; Tajfel, 1984).

The role of the other in the interdependent self. In an interdependent view, in contrast to an independent view, others will be assigned much more importance, will carry more weight, and will be relatively focal in one's own behavior. There are several direct consequences of an interdependent construal of the self. First, relationships, rather than being means for realizing various individual goals, will often be ends in and of themselves. Although people everywhere must maintain some relatedness with others, an appreciation and a need for people will be more important for those with an interdependent self than for those with an independent self. Second, maintaining a connection to others will mean being constantly aware of others and focusing on their needs, desires, and goals. In some cases, the goals of others may become so focal in consciousness that the goals of others may be experienced as personal goals. In other cases, fulfilling one's own goals may be quite distinct from those of others, but meeting another's goals, needs, and desires will be a necessary requirement for satisfying one's own goals, needs, and desires. The assumption is that while promoting the goals of others, one's own goals will be attended to by the person with whom one is interdependent. Hence, people may actively work to fulfill the others' goals while passively monitoring the reciprocal contributions from these others for one's own goal-fulfillment. Yamagishi (1988), in fact, suggested that the Japanese feel extremely uncomfortable, much more so than Americans, when the opportunity for such passive monitoring of others' actions is denied.

From the standpoint of an independent, "self-ish" self, one might be led to romanticize the interdependent self, who is ever attuned to the concerns of others. Yet in many cases, responsive and cooperative actions are exercised only when there is a reasonable assurance of the "good-intentions" of others, namely their commitment to continue to engage in reciprocal interaction and mutual support. Clearly, interdependent selves do not attend to the needs, desires, and goals of *all* others. Attention to others is not indiscriminate; it is highly selective and will be most characteristic of relationships with "in-group" members. These are others with whom one shares a common fate, such as family members or members of the same lasting social group, such as the work group. Out-group members are typically treated quite differently and are unlikely to experience either the advantages or disadvantages of interdependence. Independent selves are also selective in their association with others but not to the extent of interdependent selves because much less of their behavior is directly contingent on the actions of others. Given the importance of others in constructing reality and regulating behavior, the in-group–out-group distinction is a vital one for interdependent selves, and the subjective boundary of one's "in-group" may tend to be narrower for the interdependent selves than for the independent selves (Triandis, 1989).

To illustrate the reciprocal nature of interaction among those with interdependent views, imagine that one has a friend over for lunch and has decided to make a sandwich for him. The conversation might be: "Hey, Tom, what do you want in your sandwich? I have turkey, salami, and cheese." Tom responds, "Oh, I like turkey." Note that the friend is given a choice because the host assumes that the friend has a right, if not a duty, to make a choice reflecting his inner attributes, such as preferences or desires. And the friend makes his choice exactly because of the belief in the same assumption. This script is "natural," however, only within the independent view of self. What would happen if the friend were a visitor from Japan? A likely response to the question "Hey, Tomio, what do you want?" would be a little moment of bewilderment and then a noncommital utterance like "I don't know." This happens because under the assumptions of an interdependent self, it is the responsibility of the host to be able to "read" the mind of the friend and offer what the host perceives to be the best for the friend. And the duty of the guest, on the other hand, is to receive the favor with grace and to be prepared to return the favor in the near future, if not right at the next moment. A likely, interdependent script for the same situation would be: "Hey, Tomio, I made you a turkey sandwich because I remember that last week you said you like turkey more than beef." And Tomio will respond, "Oh, thank you, I really like turkey."

The reciprocal interdependence with others that is the sign of the interdependent self seems to require constant engagement of what Mead (1934) meant by taking the role of the other. It involves the willingness and ability to feel and think what others are feeling and thinking, to absorb this information without being told, and then to help others satisfy their wishes and realize their goals. Maintaining connection requires inhibiting the "I" perspective and processing instead of the "thou" perspective (Hsu, 1981). The requirement is to "read" the other's mind and thus to know what the other is thinking or feeling. In contrast, with an independent self, it is the individual's responsibility to "say what's on one's mind" if one expects to be attended to or understood.

References

Allen, N. J. (1985). The category of the person: A reading of Mauss's last essay. In M. Carrithers, S. Collins, & S. Lukes (Eds.), *The category of the person: Anthropology, philosophy, history* (pp. 26–35). Cambridge, England: Cambridge University Press.

Allport, G. W. (1937). *Personality: A psychological interpretation.* New York: Holt.

Beattie, J. (1980). Representations of the self in traditional Africa. *Africa, 50,* 313–320.

Bellah, R. N., Madsen, R., Sullivan, W. M., Swidler, A., & Tipton, S. M. (1985). *Habits of the heart: Individualism and commitment in American life.* Berkeley, CA: University of California Press.

Bond, M. H. (1986). *The psychology of the Chinese people.* New York: Oxford University Press.

Bond, M. H. (Ed.). (1988). *The cross-cultural challenge to social psychology.* Beverly Hills, CA: Sage.

Cantor, N., & Kihlstrom, J. (1987). *Personality and social intelligence.* Englewood Cliffs, NJ: Prentice-Hall.

Chodorow, N. (1978). *The reproduction of mothering: Psychoanalysis and the sociology of gender.* Berkeley, CA: University of California Press.

Church, a. T. (1987). Personality research in a non-Western culture: The Philippines. *Psychological Bulletin, 102,* 272–292.

Cousins, S. (1989). Culture and selfhood in Japan and the U.S. *Journal of Personality and Social Psychology, 56,* 124–131.

De Vos, G. (1985). Dimensions of the self in Japanese culture. In A. Marsella, G. De Vos, & F. L. K. Hsu (Eds.), *Culture and self* (pp. 149–184). London: Tavistock.

Dumont, L. (1970). *Homo hierarchicus.* Chicago: University of Chicago Press.

Durkheim, E. (1968). *Les formes elementaires de la vie religieuse* [Basic forms of religious belief] (6th ed.). Paris: Presses Universitaires de France. (Original work published 1912)

Elvin, M. (1985). Between the earth and heaven: Conceptions of the self in China. In M. Carrithers, S. Collins, & S. Lukes (Eds.), *The category of the person: Anthropology, philosophy, history* (pp. 156–189). New York: Cambridge University Press.

Erikson, E. (1950). Identification as the basis for a theory of motivation. *American Psychological Review, 26,* 14–21.

Fiske, A. P. (in press). *Making up society: The four elementary relational structures.* New York: Free Press.

Galtung, J. (1981). Structure, culture, and intellectual style: An essay comparing Saxonic, Teutonic, Gallic and Nipponic approaches. *Social Science Information, 20,* 817–856.

Geertz, C. (1974). From the native's point of view: On the nature of anthropological understanding. In K. Basso & H. Selby (Eds.), *Meaning in anthropology* (pp. 221–237). Albuquerque: University of New Mexico Press.

Gergen, K. J. (1968). Personal consistency and the presentation of self. In C. Gordon & K. J. Gergen (Eds.), *The self in social interaction: Classic and contemporary perspectives* (Vol. 1, pp. 299–308). New York: Wiley.

Gergen, K. J., & Gergen, M. M. (1988). Narrative and the self as relationship. In L. Berkowitz (Ed.), *Advances in experimental social psychology* (Vol. 21, pp. 17–56). New York: Academic Press.

Gilligan, C. (1982). *In a different voice: Psychological theory and women's development.* Cambridge, MA: Harvard University Press.

Hallowell, A. I. (1955). *Culture and experience.* Philadelphia: University of Pennsylvania Press.

Hamaguchi, E. (1985). A contextual model of the Japanese: Toward a methodological innovation in Japan studies. *Journal of Japanese Studies, 11,* 289–321.

Head, H. (1920). *Studies in neurology.* London: Oxford University Press.

Heelas, P. L. F., & Lock, A. J. (Eds.). (1981). *Indigenous psychologies: The anthropology of
the self.* London: Academic Press.

Hofstede, G. (1980). *Culture's consequences: International differences in work-related values.* Beverly Hills, CA: Sage.

Holland, D., & Quionn, N. (1987). *Cultural models in language and thought.* Cambridge,
England: Cambridge University Press.

Hsu, F. L. K. (1975). *Iemoto: The heart of Japan.* New York: Wiley.

Hsu, F. L. K. (1981). *American and Chinese: Passage to differences.* Honolulu: University of
Hawaii Press.

Hsu, F. L. K. (1985).The self in cross-cultural perspective. In A. J. Marsella, G. De Vos, &
F.L.K. Hsu (Eds.), *Culture and self* (pp. 24–55). London: Tavistock.

Johnson, F. (1985). The Western concept of self. In A. Marsella, G. De Vos, & F. L. K. Hsu
(Eds.), *Culture and self.* London: Tavistock.

Kakar, S. (1978) *The inner world: A psychoanalytic study of childhood and society in India.*
Delhi, India: Oxford University Press.

Kennedy, S., Scheier, J., & Rogers, A. (1984). The price of success: Our monocultural science. *American Psychologist, 39,* 996–997.

Kondo, D. (1982). *Work, family and the self: A cultural analysis of Japanese family enterprise.* Unpublished doctoral dissertation, Harvard University.

Lebra, T. S. (1976). *Japanese patterns of behavior.* Honolulu: University of Hawaii Press.

Lykes, M. B. (1985). Gender and individualistic vs. collectivist bases for notions about the
self. In A. J. Stewart & M. B. Lykes (Eds.), *Gender and personality: Current perspectives on theory and research* (pp. 268–295). Durham, NC: Duke University Press.

Maehr, M., & Nicholls, J. (1980). Culture and achievement motivation: A second look. In
N. Warren (Ed.), *Studies in cross-cultural psychology* (Vol. 2, pp. 221–267). New York:
Academic Press.

Markus, H. (1977). Self-schemas and processing information about the self. *Journal of Personality and Social Psychology, 35,* 63–78.

Marriott, M. (1976). Hindu transactions: Diversity without dualism. In B. Kapferer (Ed.),
Transaction and meaning (pp. 109–142). Philadelphia: Institute for Study of Human Issues.

Marsella, A., De Vos, G., & Hsu, F. L. K. (1985). *Culture and self.* London: Tavistock.

McClelland, D. C. (1961). *The achieving society.* New York: Free Press.

Mead, G. H. (1934). *Mind, self and society.* Chicago: University of Chicago Press.

Miller, J. B. (1986). *Toward a new psychology of women* (2nd ed.). Boston: Beacon Press.

Miller, J. G. (1988). Bridging the content–structure dichotomy: Culture and the self. In M. H.
Bond (Ed.), *The cross-cultural challenge to social psychology* (pp. 266–281). Beverly
Hills, CA: Sage.

Miller, J. G., Bersoff, D. M., & Harwood, R. L. (1990). Perceptions of social responsibilities
in India and in the United States: Moral imperatives or personal decisions? *Journal of
Personality and Social Psychology, 58,* 33–47.

Moore, C. A. (Ed.). (1967). Introduction: The humanistic Chinese mind. In *The Chinese
mind: Essentials of Chinese philosophy and culture* (pp. 1–10). Honolulu: University of
Hawaii Press.

Northrop, F. S. C. (1946). *The meeting of East and West.* New York: Macmillan.

Phillips, D. C. (1976). *Holistic thought in social science.* Stanford, CA: Stanford University Press.

Roland, A. (1988). *In search of self in India and Japan: Toward a cross-cultural psychology.* Princeton, NJ: Princeton University Press.

Sampson, E. E. (1985). The decentralization of identity: Toward a revised concept of personal and social order. *American Psychologist, 40,* 1203–1211.

Sampson, E. E. (1988). The debate on individualism: Indigenous psychologies of the individual and their role in personal and societal functioning. *American Psychologist, 43,* 15–22.

Sampson, E. E. (1989). The challenge of social change for psychology: Globalization and psychology's theory of the person. *American Psychologist, 44,* 914–921.

Sass, L. A. (1988). The self and its vicissitudes: An "archaeological" study of the psychoanalytic avant-garde. *Social Research, 55,* 551–607.

Schwartz, S. H., & Bilsky, W. (1990). Toward a theory of the universal content and structure of values: Extensions and cross-cultural replications. *Journal of Personality and Social Psychology, 58,* 878-891.

Shweder, R. A. (1984). Preview: A colloquy of culture theorists. In R. A. Shweder & R. A. LeVine (Eds.), *Culture theory: Essays on mind, self, and emotion* (pp. 1–24). Cambridge, England: Cambridge University Press.

Shweder, R. A. (1990). Cultural psychology: What is it? In J. W. Stigler, R. A. Shweder, & G. Herdt (Eds.), *Cultural psychology: Essays on comparative human development* (pp. 1–46). Cambridge, England: Cambridge University Press.

Shweder, R. A., & Bourne, E. J. (1984). Does the concept of the person vary cross-culturally? In R. A. Shweder & R. A. LeVine (Eds.), *Culture theory: Essays on mind, self, and emotion* (pp. 158–199). Cambridge, England: Cambridge University Press.

Shweder, R. A., & LeVine, R. A. (Eds.). (1984). *Culture theory: Essays on mind, self, and emotion.* Cambridge, England: Cambridge University Press.

Smith, R. J. (1985). A pattern of Japanese society: In society or knowledgement of interdependence? *Journal of Japanese Studies, 11,* 29–45.

Stevenson, H., Azuma, H., & Hakuta, K. (1986). *Child development and education in Japan.* New York: Freeman.

Stigler, J. W., Shweder, R. A., & Herdt, G. (Eds.). (1990). *Cultural psychology: Essays on comparative human development.* Cambridge, England: Cambridge University Press.

Stryker, S. (1986). Identity theory: Developments and extensions. In K. Yardley & T. Honess (Eds.), *Self and identity* (pp. 89–104). New York: Wiley.

Tajfel, H. (1984). *The social dimension: European developments in social psychology.* Cambridge, England: Cambridge University Press.

Triandis, H. C. (1989). The self and social behavior in differing cultural contexts. *Psychological Review, 96.* 506–520.

Triandis, H. C., Bontempo, R., Villareal, M. J., Asai, M., & Lucca, N. (1988). Individualism and collectivism: Cross-cultural perspectives on self-ingroup relationships. *Journal of Personality and Social Psychology, 54,* 323–338.

Triandis, H. C., & Brislin, R. W. (Eds.). (1980). *Handbook of cross-cultural social psychology* (Vol. 5). Boston: Allyn & Bacon.

Triandis, H. C., Marin, G., Lisansky, J., & Betancourt, H. (1984). *Simpatía* as a cultural script of Hispanics. *Journal of Personality and Social Psychology, 47,* 1363–1375.

Veroff, J. (1983). Contextual determinants of personality. *Personality and Social Psychology Bulletin, 9,* 331–344.

Waterman, A. S. (1981). Individualism and interdependence. *American Psychologist, 36,* 762–773.

Weisz, J. R., Rothbaum, F. M., & Blackburn, T. C. (1984). Standing out and standing in: The psychology of control in America and Japan. *American Psychologist, 39,* 955–969.

White, G. M., & Kirkpatrick, J. (Eds.). (1985). *Personal, self, and experience: Exploring Pacific ethnopsychologies.* Los Angeles: University of California Press.

Yamagishi, T. (1989). Exit from the group as an individualistic solution to the free-rider problem in the United States and Japan. *Journal of Experimental Social Psychology, 24,* 530–542.

Yang, K. S. (1981b). Social orientation and individual modernity among Chinese students in Taiwan. *Journal of Social Psychology, 113,* 159–170.

3

Social Influence: Following and Resisting

Social influence is one of the most central processes in all of social psychology. It represents to some extent the bottom line, the key end result of people interacting redundant. Fundamental issues of influence, such as conformity and obedience, have been with us since the beginning of time, and matters such as advertising and cult conversions are often the topics of modern discussion.

Robert Cialdini, author of the highly regarded book *Influence,* is Professor of Psychology at Arizona State University. He is one of the most innovative and highly respected voices in the field of social psychology. In our conversation, Prof. Cialdini discusses the unusual way that he has gained insights into the strategies and practices of influence and the general principles that he has derived from his experiences. I am certain that, as you read this, you will recognize each of these, not just as they have been used by others, but as you have used them yourselves.

A CONVERSATION WITH ROBERT CIALDINI
Arizona State University

Krupat: *When we speak of social influence, the word conformity often comes up. Does the idea of conformity strike you as good, bad, or indifferent?*

Cialdini: Some people don't like that term because they view it only in its negative sense. I think conformity can often be quite an adaptive and even enlightened response to one's environment. It doesn't necessarily bespeak a weak-willed, wishy-washy individual who is at the mercy of the winds. In the role of an information processing efficiency expert, you may take a look at the evidence and decide that the most accurate information about how to behave comes from the behaviors of others. Conforming sometimes allows us a shortcut without having to think too hard about things in our information-overloaded day.

Krupat: *For years, social psychologists have been running experiments to gain a handle on the nature of influence. Based on what we know, would you say it is easy to change people?*

Cialdini: As social psychologists who study behavior in the laboratory, we frequently can't answer that question very well. In our laboratory procedures we eliminate all of the sources of influence in the situation except the one that we are studying. What we see very often, then, is change that we can't easily locate outside the antiseptic, artificial environment of the laboratory. I think we need to take a different approach and look at the prevalence and prominence of change tactics and strategies that exist in the influence professions.

Krupat: *When you say influence professions, I'm not quite sure whether to take you literally. Lawyers try to influence juries, teenagers try to get their friends to try alcohol, and college students try to get their roommates to lend them money. Aren't they all in the influence business?*

Cialdini: But they are not all in the influence *professions.* Only the attorney is, because there is an abiding commercial interest in getting other people to say yes to a request. That's what I mean by a profession. The economic livelihood of these people depends on the success of the influence strategies that they use. Those practitioners who use influence strategies and principles that work will flourish, and the principles themselves will remain as part of the pool of practices and procedures that are passed on to succeeding generations in the same way adaptive genes are passed on. The upshot is that, if we look across the widest range of influence professionals and we see that the same principles have risen to the surface and persisted, that's our best evidence of what the most powerful influences are in natural interaction.

Krupat: *Are you ever amazed that influence professionals do what they do so well even though they have never formally studied human behavior?*

Cialdini: It is interesting that they seem to be able to know how to do this without ever having studied social psychology. I think the reason for this is that they are beneficiaries of decades of trial and error. And to answer your earlier question as to whether it's easy to change people, my answer is yes. If one understands how the major principles of influence work and if one understands how to activate them, it's possible to change people and to change them reliably and regularly.

Krupat: *Even if influence professionals don't know why it works in any conceptual sense?*

Cialdini: It's not their job to know why it works. That's my job as a social scientist; that's what you and I do for a living. That's why we also need to go into the laboratory after we've looked to see what works powerfully and systematically in the natural environment.

Krupat: *But if the laboratory and the real world are both important, how can the research process best go about incorporating both?*

Cialdini: We need to begin with systematic observation of a phenomenon that is effective, that works on people. Then we take it to the laboratory to examine its psychological underpinnings, why it works the way it does. Then we take that new information into the natural environment to see if our new insights really represent the way the thing works in the real world. And that's the final arc in the cycle that I don't think is often enough closed by social psychologists. I once called this approach "full cycle social psychology." We seem to think that the laboratory is the standard against which we should base all our knowledge. I don't think so. The grand experiment that's going on outside is still the standard against which we should compare our results.

Krupat: *If I'm correct, you have observed that arena at close hand in a way that would be pretty unusual for the standard social psychologist. Can you tell me a little about that?*

Cialdini: I had always been a fan of the sociologists and anthropologists who used the method of participant observation, which involved a systematic immersing of the researcher into the setting to be understood. What I did was to infiltrate as many influence professions as I could possibly get access to. I would answer ads in the newspaper for sales trainees and would learn from the inside what an encyclopedia sales operator told trainees to do to get people to say yes. I did this with insurance sales, portrait photography sales, and automobile sales. I also drew on some contacts with friends of mine and managed to infiltrate some advertising agencies and a couple of charity organizations. I interviewed police bunco squad officers to see what the con artists try to do, and I even interviewed cult recruiters to see what they did that so powerfully got people to join. And across it all I looked for the commonalities, the things that occurred in parallel in each of these influence professions.

Krupat: *That's as fascinating as it is unusual. What did you find?*

Cialdini: I found six principles that had the character of universal mechanisms of influence, that seemed effective across professions, across people within those professions, across versions and varieties of techniques, and even across eras as far back as the turn of the century.

Krupat: *Let's take them one at a time. What's first?*

Cialdini: If we believe the sociologist Gouldner, there is not a single human society that does not subscribe to the principle of reciprocation, the rule that obligates people to give back to others some form of behavior that they have first received from them. That is a very powerful motivator of conduct in our culture. It applies to every single behavior, both on the positive and negative sides. We are socialized into it so thoroughly that we feel guilty taking without giving in return. So it becomes possible for people to influence us in their direction by giving us something first, by doing us a favor or a service or giving a gift. We can be made to say yes in that way, by the rules of reciprocity. The Disabled American Veterans Organization, for example, reports that when they send out a standard appeal for donations they get about an 18 percent return rate. But if they include in the envelope a little pack of individualized gummed address labels, the success rate jumps to 35 percent. It virtually doubles by adding 6 cents worth of material.

Krupat: *I see. You keep the labels and repay rather than stay forever in their debt.*

Cialdini: Right. And when a company wants you to fill out a survey, another tactic that's gaining popularity is to send you a dollar with the survey. Of course, people don't send the dollar back, but once they've kept it, they feel obligated to do something in return. So they fill out a survey that they would never had agreed to do for a dollar if they were being paid to do so after the fact.

Krupat: *Principle number one makes good sense. What is number two?*

Cialdini: Number two is scarcity. We all tend to want those things that are scarce, rare, and dwindling in their availability. You might remember the Mazda Miata craze, where people were spending more money on a used Miata than they would have spent for a new one if it were available. But it wasn't available, so that unavailability made the car more attractive by itself. Compliance professionals have limited-time-only and limited-availability sales. The scarcity is just manufactured to spur interest.

Krupat: *What is third on the list?*

Cialdini: Authority is next. I think here we've seen good evidence that people who are in positions of legitimate authority, experts for example, are able to get people to comply to their requests. People tend to defer to the directives of legitimate authority, and that makes all kinds of sense because legitimately constituted authorities typically have attained their positions by virtue of greater wisdom or experience or training. However, we often fall victim to authority directives even when they make no sense at all, it seems to me, because it's such an automatic response. Advertisers will sometimes try to misuse this principle by hiring spokespeople who have an aura of authority in a particular area when there is really no authority at all. I'm thinking for example of the television commercials starring the actor Robert Young. He talks about the health consequences of Sanka decaf coffee or the pain-relieving power of Arthritis Pain Relief formula. And the only reason he is so successful as a spokesman is that he used to play Marcus Welby, M.D., on television. But that's enough to produce persuasion in the minds of people who are not thinking, who are simply reacting to the influence.

Krupat: *I assume the reason that actors are no longer allowed to endorse products by saying they are doctors serves as testimony to the strength of this effect.*

Cialdini: I actually heard a commercial a couple of years ago where the actor began by saying, "I'm not a doctor, but I play one on TV." And then he proceeded to describe some product. That's the ultimate in mindlessness! Why should we expect that this guy who plays a doctor on TV should be more believable? But the Robert Young commercials were exceedingly effective in selling their products.

Krupat: *What is next on our list of strategies?*

Cialdini: Next is commitment. That really has to do with the principle of consistency and our tendency to want to be consistent with our attitudes, beliefs, words, and deeds. That means that, if I can get you to go on record, to take a stand in favor of some position at one point, I will be significantly more likely to get you to say yes to a request that is logically consistent with that stand at some subsequent time. The most famous consistency tactic is the foot-in-the-door technique in which a person asks a homeowner for a small favor, let's say to sign a petition favoring safe driving. Then two weeks later the homeowner is asked to put up a billboard on the lawn favoring safe driving. You may find people who will do that because they've gone on record at an earlier point as advocating safe driving and, in order to be consistent with that earlier commitment, they agree again.

Krupat: *I have fallen into that trap many a time. There's a problem in self-presentation, in terms of being able to say no once you've already said yes.*

Cialdini: You're right. Not only is there a desire on the part of people to be consistent within themselves, it is also important to be seen as consistent in the eyes of others, because consistency is a valued trait in our society. It speaks of rationality, logic, and honesty.

Krupat: *What's next?*

Cialdini: Liking is the fifth. It should come as no surprise that we prefer to say yes to the requests of the people we know and like. All you need to do is look at the wild success of the Tupperware party, which arranges for customers to buy not from a stranger across the counter, but from a friend, relative, or neighbor. When I investigated how a Tupperware party works, some of the people would say, "I really don't need any more plastic containers, but what can I do? My friend asked me."

Krupat: *That makes me think about a practice that cults are known to use. When potential recruits show up at a meeting, the group members huddle around them and say nice things. I recall reading that a young woman said it almost felt like sorority rush.*

Cialdini: It's called love bombing, in which you get unqualified positive regard from all the people around you. They tell you how much they like you and respect your decision to come and see what the group is all about.

Krupat: *Okay, what is principle number six?*

Cialdini: Social validation. We frequently decide what is appropriate behavior for ourselves by examining the behavior of the people around us. The evidence here indicates that we are most likely to follow the actions of others when those others are numerous, when there are many others. I remember the wonderful experiment that Milgram and his colleagues performed when they took a research assistant, had him stand on a crowded street corner in New York City, pick a spot in the sky, and stare at it for 60 seconds to see what would happen. Not a whole lot happened when that person was by himself, but the following day five research assistants stood on that street corner and stared at the same empty spot in the sky. Within 60 seconds 84 percent of the people who passed by had stopped to look up with them. It seems we assume that, if a lot of people are doing something, there must be value to it.

Krupat: *Now that we have gone through all six principles, does knowing about them make us any more likely to resist influence attempts?*

Cialdini: I think that's partially true. When we come upon one of these principles, we have to recognize that frequently they do steer us correctly; otherwise, we wouldn't use them as a guidepost for deciding when to comply. What we have to decide is whether it makes sense in that particular situation to use the influence of an authority or a lot of other people or someone we know and like. I would recommend that when we encounter one or another of these principles, we should take a step back from the situation before we decide how to behave. We should analyze what it is we are being requested to do in terms of its merits, not in terms of the way that it was requested of us. Especially in the important decisions that we have to face, it's worth taking that moment out before rushing in with a decision.

Peter B. Smith
Michael Harris Bond

Psychology Across Cultures: Conformity and Independence

This brief excerpt from an excellent book by Smith and Bond on cross-cultural studies in social psychology poses several interesting questions about the concepts of conformity and independence. As noted by the authors, versions of Solomon Asch's classic experiment on conformity and independence have been performed over several decades in places as far reaching as Great Britain and Zimbabwe, Brazil and Kuwait, Zaire and Fiji. In general, they note that countries with a collectivist orientation have higher conformity rates than those with more individualistic orientations, but the matter is not as simple as this. Consider one Japanese study in which people conformed greatly to others who were members of the same club, but relatively little when the others were strangers. This reading selection brings home the point of cultural relativity, that the motives that drive behavior and the forms of behavior found in one place may be different than the other. On the other hand, it invites the question of whether it is possible to generate some broad principles of social behavior that apply from culture to culture and time to time.

The most widely replicated social psychology experiment of all time is Asch's (1951) study of conformity, of which there are at least 24 published non-US replications, from 13 countries. In this study a naive subject is repeatedly asked to judge which of three lines matches another line, in the presence of several other people who frequently all give the same *wrong* answer. The replications show widely differing rates of conformity and independence in the different countries.

Aside from the differences found in the results from this experiment, there is another issue of interest here. The Asch experiment is almost invariably described as a study of conformity, even though the original study showed that two-thirds of the judgments made by subjects were independent of the pressure upon them to give the wrong judgment. Friend, Rafferty and Bramel (1990) examined reports of the Asch studies in 99 US social psychology texts. They found an increasing trend over time to concentrate upon the fact that one-third of the judgments were erroneous, and to use this as evidence of how widespread is the process of conformity in society. Friend et al. point out that this interpretation is precisely the opposite of what Asch was trying to show, and indeed succeeded in showing: namely, that his subjects were not entirely conformist and that most judgments were entirely correct. One can only speculate as to why this interpretation of Asch's finding occurs.

This type of reinterpretation of results is not an isolated instance. The findings of other classic studies, such as Milgram's work on obedience, are often also reported as though all subjects succumbed to social pressures. One possibility is that writers of texts—including the writers of this one—are seeking to persuade you, the reader, that social behaviour is understandable and predictable. To assert that people sometimes, even often, act independently of those around them might seem to undermine the case for a social psychology, and encourage instead the study of personality.

The value of Friend et al.'s critique for our purposes is that it alerts us to the fact that we cannot judge whether 37 percent of conforming responses and 63 percent of independent ones are *high* or *low* figures until we can compare them with figures from other cultures. In a society which values independence and initiative as highly as do many Americans, we might expect that any evidence of conformity would be interpreted negatively. In a cross-cultural context, we have to entertain the possibility that a 37 percent conformity rate is relatively low, as Asch believed, and not high, as many of the textbook writers assert.

If members of collectivist groups spend more time with one another and seek in-group harmony, then we should expect that social influence processes would lead them towards greater levels of conformity than those reported from groups in individualist cultures. These studies are not ideal for our present purpose, since we cannot be sure that judgments about physical stimuli of this kind respond to social pressure in the same way as do social stimuli such as attitudes or social representations. However, researchers have attempted precise replications of the Asch experiment in a much wider range of countries than is available for any other social psychological study, so they provide us with the firmest data available. Table 3.1 summarizes the results, subdividing between countries thought to be predominantly individualist and countries thought to be collectivist.

The comparison of errors recorded in the different studies should not be considered as very precise, because not all studies used exactly the same procedures. Some studies used the Asch (1951) procedure, whereby subjects have face-to-face contact with one another. Others used the Crutchfield (1955) technique, in which subjects communicate electronically. However, two trends are fairly clear from the table. First, the percentage of errors made is more consistently high in the studies done in collectivist societies. Second, more errors are recorded for subjects who were not students.

In interpreting what these results mean, we need to think more about who the subjects were in these studies. The original Asch studies were made with students who were mostly strangers to one another. While most of the studies reported following the same procedures in Asch, hardly any of them specify whether subjects

TABLE 3.1 Asch Conformity Studies By National Culture

Study	Subjects	% Errors
'Individualist' countries		
The original Asch studies (1951, 1956)	Students	37
Eight later US students (averaged)	Students	25
Four British studies (averaged)	Students	17
Vlaander and van Rooijen (1985)	Dutch students	24
Perrin and Spencer (1981)	British probation clients	22
Perrin and Spencer (1981)	British unemployed blacks	39
Hatcher (1982)	Belgian students	24
Doms (1983)	Belgian students	14
'Collectivist' countries		
Whittaker and Meade (1967)	Brazilian students	34
Whittaker and Meade (1967)	Hong Kong students	32
Whittaker and Meade (1967)	Lebanese students	31
Whittaker and Meade (1967)	Zimbabwean Bantu students	51
Claeys (1967)	Zairean students	36
Frager (1970)	Japanese students	25
Chandra (1973)	Fijian teachers	36
Chandra (1973)	Indian teachers in Fiji	58
Rodrigues (1982)	Brazilians	35
Amir (1984)	Kuwaiti students	29
Williams and Sogon (1984)	Japanese sports club members	51
Williams and Sogon (1984)	Japanese students not known to each other	27

Note: American students which were averaged: Deutsch and Gerard (1955); Whittaker et al. (1957); Levy (1960); Gerard et al. (1968); Larsen (1974); Larsen et al. (1979); Lamb and Alsifaki (1980); Nicholson et al. (1985). British studies: Seaborne (1962); Perrin and Spencer (1981); Nicholson et al. (1985); Abrams et al. (1990).

were or were not strangers to one another. This is crucial information, since we would expect a member of a cultural group with interdependent values to conform if the pressure came from in-group members, but not if it came from strangers. The studies from Japan are particularly interesting in this connection. Frager (1970) used students who were strangers to one another, and to his considerable surprise found a low level of conformity. Indeed, he also recorded high levels of anti-conformity, which is movement *away* from the majority opinion. This may have been related to the high level of student unrest and rebellion at the time in Keio University, where the study was undertaken. The more recent Japanese study by Williams and Sogon (1984) showed a much higher error rate for intact groups, and a lower rate for unacquainted students. The result supports the view that conformity rates for interdependent subjects are strongly influenced by their relationship to the other judges in the experiment.

Looking at the table more carefully, we can discover that some of the other high error rates are also recorded where the subjects may have had some strong reason to hold interdependent values linking them with other members of their group. For instance, conformity was particularly high among unemployed blacks in Britain and among members of the minority Indian population in Fiji. This way of looking at the findings encourages us to think not so much about levels of conformity in different national cultures, but about conformity as a consequence of interdependent values, whether those values characterize a whole culture or particular subcultures within a larger society. Indeed, interdependence need not necessarily stem from some long-lasting set of values, but may arise from the manner in which the experiment is set up. The recent British study by Abrams et al. (1990) found much greater conformity when subjects were led to believe that the other judges were fellow students of psychology than when they were told that they were students of ancient history.

We thus have a range of experimental results ranging from the ecological studies of conformity in agricultural and hunting societies by Berry (1967) and Berry and Annis (1974) to laboratory studies in individualistic and collectivist cultures, which all support a similar conclusion. The more one's fate is interdependent with that of others, the greater is the likelihood of conformity occurring.

Social Proof:
Monkey Me, Monkey Do

In this selection, Cialdini offers us insight into the concept of "social proof"—the idea that, if everyone else is doing it, it must be right. Citing the dramatic example of the mass suicide of the followers of the Reverend Jim Jones in Jonestown, Guyana, Cialdini suggests that no amount of charisma on the part of Jones can fully account for his behavior. Instead, Jones's isolation of the group from all outside influences generated a herd mentality in his followers. The members of the cult came to define reality for one another, and the perception that everyone else was willing to obey his demands led them to this mass act of self-destruction in a way that no physical force or personal appeal could have ever achieved.

The principle of social proof, like all other weapons of influence, works better under some conditions than under others. Without question, when people are uncertain they are more likely to use others' actions to decide how they themselves should act. In addition, there is another important working condition: similarity. The principle of social proof operates most powerfully when we are observing the behavior of people just like us (Festinger, 1954). It is the conduct of such people that gives us the greatest insight into what constitutes correct behavior for ourselves. Therefore, we are more inclined to follow the lead of a similar individual than a dissimilar one.

That is why I believe we are seeing an increasing number of average-person-on-the-street testimonials on TV these days. Advertisers now know that one successful way to sell a product to ordinary viewers (who compose the largest potential market) is to demonstrate that other "ordinary" people like and use it. Whether the product is a brand of soft drink or a pain reliever or a laundry detergent, we hear volleys of praise from John or Mary Everyperson.

More compelling evidence for the importance of similarity in determining whether we will imitate another's behavior comes from scientific research. An especially apt illustration can be found in a study done by psychologists at Columbia University (Hornstein, Fisch, & Holmes, 1968). The researchers placed wallets on the ground in various locations around midtown Manhattan to observe what would happen when they were found. Each wallet contained $2.00 in cash, a $26.30 check, and various information providing the name and address of the wallet's "owner." In addition to these items, the wallet also contained a letter making it evident that the wallet had been lost not once, but twice. The letter was written to the wallet's owner from a man who had found it earlier and whose intention was to return it. The finder indicated in his letter that he was happy to help and that the chance to be of service in this way had made him feel good.

It was evident to anyone who found one of these wallets that this well-intentioned individual had then lost the wallet himself on the way to the mail box—the wallet was wrapped in an envelope addressed to the owner. The researchers wanted to know how many people finding such a wallet would follow the lead of the first finder and mail it, intact, to the original owner. Before they dropped the wallets, however, the researchers varied one feature of the letter it contained. Some of the letters were written in standard English by someone who seemed to be an average American, while the other letters were written in broken English by the first finder, who identified himself as a recently arrived foreigner. In other words, the person who initially found the wallet and had tried to return it was depicted by the letter as being either similar or dissimilar to most Americans.

The interesting question was whether the people who found the wallet and letter would be more influenced to mail the wallet if the first person who had tried to do so were similar to them. The answer was plain: Only 33 percent of the wallets were returned when the first finder was seen to be dissimilar, but 70 percent were returned when he was thought to be a similar other. These results suggest an important qualification of the principle of social proof. We will use the actions of others to decide on proper behavior for ourselves, *especially when we view those others to be similar to ourselves.*

This tendency applies not only to adults but to children as well. Health researchers have found, for example, that a school-based antismoking program had lasting effects only when it used same-age peer leaders as teachers (Murray et al., 1984). Another study found that children who saw a film depicting a child's positive visit to the dentist lowered their own dental anxieties principally when they were the same age as the child in the film (Melamed et al., 1978). I wish I had known about this second study when, a few years before it was published, I was trying to reduce a different kind of anxiety in my son, Chris.

I live in Arizona where backyard swimming pools abound. Regrettably, each year, several young children drown after falling into an unattended pool. I was determined, therefore, to teach Chris how to swim at an early age. The problem was not that he was afraid of the water; he loved it, but he would not get into the pool without wearing his inflatable inner tube, no matter how I tried to coax, talk, or shame him out of it. After getting nowhere for two months, I hired a graduate student of mine to help. Despite his background as a lifeguard and swimming instructor, he failed as I had. He couldn't persuade Chris to attempt even a stroke outside of his plastic ring.

About this time, Chris was attending a day camp that provided a number of activities to its group, including the use of a large pool, which he scrupulously avoided. One day, shortly after the graduate student incident, I went to get Chris from camp and, with my mouth agape, watched him run down the diving board and jump into the deepest part of the pool. Panicked, I began pulling off my shoes to jump in to his rescue when I saw him bob to the surface and paddle safely to the side of the pool—where I dashed, shoes in hand, to meet him.

"Chris, you can swim!" I said excitedly. "You can swim!"

"Yes," he responded casually, "I learned how today."

"This is terrific! This is just terrific," I blurted, gesturing expansively to convey my enthusiasm. "But, how come you didn't need your plastic ring today?"

Looking somewhat embarrassed because his father seemed to be raving while inexplicably soaking his socks in a small puddle and waving his shoes around, Chris explained:

"Well, I'm 3 years old, and Tommy is 3 years old. And Tommy can swim without a ring, so that means I can, too."

I could have kicked myself. Of course it would be *to little Tommy,* not to a 6′2″ graduate student, that Chris would look for the most relevant information about what he could or should do. Had I been more thoughtful about solving Chris' swimming problem, I could have employed Tommy's good example earlier and, perhaps, saved myself a couple of frustrating months. I could have simply noted at the day camp that Tommy was a swimmer and then arranged with his parents for the boys to spend a weekend afternoon swimming in our pool. My guess is that Chris' plastic ring would have been abandoned by the end of the day.

MONKEY DIE

Any factor that can spur 70 percent of New Yorkers to return a wallet, with all its contents included, must be considered impressive. Yet the outcome of the lost-wallet study offers just a hint of the immense impact that the conduct of similar others has on human behavior. More powerful examples exist in addition to this one. To my mind, the most telling illustration of this impact starts with a seemingly nonsensical statistic: After a suicide has made front-page news, airplanes—private planes, corporate jet, airliners—begin falling out of the sky at an alarming rate.

For example, it has been shown (Phillips, 1979) that immediately following certain kinds of highly publicized suicide stories, the number of people who die in commercial-airline crashes increases by 1,000 percent! Even more alarming: The increase is not limited to airplane deaths. The number of automobile fatalities shoots up as well (Phillips, 1980). What would possibly be responsible?

One explanation suggests itself immediately: The same social conditions that cause some people to commit suicide cause others to die accidentally. For instance, certain individuals, the suicide-prone, may react to stressful societal events (economic downturns, rising crime rates, international tensions) by ending it all. Others will react differently to these same events; they might become angry, impatient, nervous, or distracted. To the degree that such people operate or maintain the cars and planes of our society, the vehicles will be less safe, and consequently, we will see a sharp increase in the number of automobile and air fatalities.

According to this "social conditions" interpretation, then, some of the same societal factors that cause intentional deaths also cause accidental ones, and that is why we find so strong a connection between suicide stories and fatal crashes. Another fascinating statistic indicates that this is not the correct explanation: Fatal crashes increase dramatically only in those regions where the suicide has been highly publicized. Other places, existing under similar social conditions, whose newspapers have *not* publicized the story, have shown no comparable jump in such fatalities. Furthermore, within those areas where newspaper space has been allotted, the wider the publicity given the suicide, the greater has been the rise in subsequent crashes. Thus, it is not some set of common societal events that stimulates suicides on the one hand and fatal accidents on the other. Instead, it is the publicized suicide story itself that produces the car and plane wrecks.

To explain the strong association between suicide-story publicity and subsequent crashes, a "bereavement" account has been suggested. Because, it has been argued, front-page suicides often involve well-known and respected public figures, perhaps their highly publicized deaths throw many people into states of shocked sadness. Stunned and preoccupied, these individuals become careless around cars and planes. The consequence is the sharp increase in in deadly accidents involving such vehicles that we see after front-page suicide stories. Although the bereavement theory can account for the connection between the degree of publicity given a story and subsequent crash fatalities—the more people who learn of the suicide, the larger will be the number of bereaved and careless individuals—it *cannot* explain another startling fact: Newspaper stories reporting suicide victims who died alone produce an increase in the frequency of single-fatality wrecks only, whereas stories reporting suicide-plus-murder incidents produce an increase in multiple-fatality wrecks only. Simple bereavement could not cause such a pattern.

The influence of suicide stories on car and plane crashes, then, is fantastically specific. Stories of pure suicides, in which only one person dies, generate wrecks in which only one person dies; stories of suicide-murder combination, in which there are multiple deaths, generate wrecks in which there are multiple deaths. If neither "social conditions" nor "bereavement" can make sense of this bewildering array of facts, what can? There is a sociologist at the University of California in San Diego who thinks he has found the answer. His name is David Phillips, and he points a convincing finger at something called the "Werther effect."

The story of the Werther effect is both chilling and intriguing. More than two centuries ago, the great man of German literature, Johann von Goethe, published a novel entitled *Die Leiden des jungen Werthers (The Sorrows of Young Werther)*. The book, in which the hero, named Werther, commits suicide, had a remarkable impact. Not only did it provide Goethe with immediate fame, but it also sparked a wave of emulative suicides across Europe. So powerful was this effect that authorities in several countries banned the novel.

Phillips' own work has traced the Werther effect to modern times (Phillips, 1974). His research has demonstrated that, immediately following a front-page suicide story, the suicide rate increases dramatically in those geographical areas where the story has been highly publicized. It is Phillips' argument that certain troubled people who read of another's self-inflicted death kill themselves in imitation. In a morbid illustration of the principle of social proof, these people decide how they should act on the basis of how some other troubled person has acted.

Phillips derived his evidence for the modern-day Werther effect from examining the suicide statistics in the United States between 1947 and 1968. He found that, within two months after every front-page suicide story, an average of 58 more people than usual killed themselves. In a sense, each suicide story killed 58 people who otherwise would have gone on living. Phillips also found that this tendency for suicides to beget suicides occurred principally in those parts of the country where the first suicide was highly publicized. He observed that the wider the publicity given the first suicide, the greater the number of later suicides (see Figure 3.1).

If the facts surrounding the Werther effect seem to you suspiciously like those surrounding the influence of suicide stories on air and traffic fatalities, the similarities have not been lost on Phillips, either. In fact, he contends that all the excess deaths following a front-page suicide incident can be explained as the same thing: copycat suicides. Upon learning of another's suicide, an uncomfortably large number of people decide that suicide is an appropriate action for themselves as well. Some of these individuals then proceed to commit the act in a straightforward, no-bones-about-it fashion, causing the suicide rate to jump.

Others, however, are less direct. For any of several reasons—to protect their reputations, to spare their families the shame and hurt, to allow their dependents to collect on insurance policies—they do not want to appear to have killed themselves. They would rather seem to have died accidentally. So, purposively but furtively, they cause the wreck of a car or a plane they are operating or are simply riding in. This can be accomplished in a variety of all-too-familiar-sounding ways. A commercial airline pilot can dip the nose of the aircraft at a crucial point of takeoff or can inexplicably land on an already occupied runway against the instructions from the control tower; the driver of a car can suddenly swerve into a tree or into oncoming traffic; a passenger in an automobile or corporate jet can incapacitate the operator, causing the deadly crash; the pilot of a private plane can, despite all radio warnings, plow into another aircraft. Thus the alarming climb in crash fatalities that we find following front-page suicides is, according to Phillips, most likely due to the Werther effect secretly applied.

I consider this insight brilliant. First, it explains all of the data beautifully. If these wrecks really are hidden instances of imitative suicide, it makes sense that we would see an increase in the wrecks should occur after the suicide stories that have been most widely publicized and have, consequently, reached the most people. It also makes sense that the number of crashes should jump appreciably only in those geographical areas where the suicide stories were publicized. It even makes sense that single-victim suicides should lead only to single-victim crashes. Imitation is the key.

In addition, there is a second valuable feature of Phillips' insight. Not only does it allow us to explain the existing facts, it also allows us to predict new facts that had never been uncovered before. For example, if the abnormally frequent crashes following publicized suicides are genuinely the result of imitative rather than accidental actions, they should be more deadly as a result. That is, people trying to kill

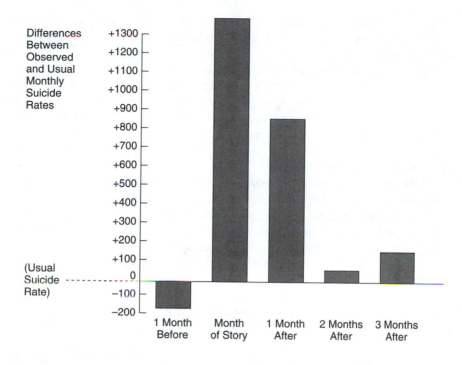

Differences Between Observed and Usual Monthly Suicide Rates

(Usual Suicide Rate)

1 Month Before | Month of Story | 1 Month After | 2 Months After | 3 Months After

(Based on 35 Suicide Stories 1947–68)

FIGURE 3.1

Fluctuation in Number of Suicides Before, During, and After Month of Suicide Story.

This evidence raises an important ethical issue. The suicides that follow these stories are *excess* deaths. After the initial spurt, the suicide rates do not drop below traditional levels but only return to those levels. Statistics like these might well give pause to newspaper editors inclined to sensationalize suicide accounts, as those accounts are likely to lead to the deaths of scores of people. More recent data indicate that in addition to newspaper editors, television broadcasters have cause for concern about the effects of the suicide stories they present. Whether they appear as news reports, information features, or fictional movies, these stories create an immediate cluster of self-inflicted deaths, with impressionable, imitation-prone teenagers being the most frequent victims (Bollen & Phillips, 1982; Gould & Shaffer, 1986; Phillips & Carsensen, 1986, 1988; Schmidtke & Hafner, 1988).

themselves will likely arrange (with a foot on the accelerator instead of the brake, with the nose of the plane down instead of up) for the impact to be as lethal as possible. The consequence should be quick and sure death. When Phillips examined the records to check on this prediction, he found that the average number of people killed in a fatal crash of a commercial airliner is more than three times greater if the crash happened one week after a front-page suicide story than if it happened one week before. A similar phenomenon can be found in traffic statistics where there is evidence for the deadly efficiency of post-suicide-story auto crashes. Victims of fatal car wrecks that follow front-page suicide stories die four times more quickly than normal (Phillips, 1980).

Still another fascinating prediction flows from Phillips' idea. If the increase in wrecks following suicide stories truly represents a set of copycat deaths, then the imitators should be most likely to copy the suicides of people who are similar to them. The principle of social proof states that we use information about the way others have behaved to help us determine proper conduct for ourselves. As the dropped-wallet experiment showed, we are most influenced in this fashion by the actions of people who are like us.

Therefore, Phillips reasoned, if the principle of social proof is behind the phenomenon, there should be some clear similarity between the victim of the highly publicized suicide and those who cause subsequent wrecks. Realizing that the clearest test of this possibility would come from the records of automobile crashes involving a single car and a lone driver, Phillips compared the age of the suicide-story victim with the ages of the lone drivers killed in single-car crashes immediately after the story appeared in print. Once again, the predictions were strikingly accurate: When the newspaper detailed the suicide of a young person, it was young drivers who then plowed their cars into trees, poles, and embankments with fatal results; but when the news story concerned an older person's suicide, older drivers died in such crashes (Phillips, 1980).

This last statistic is the clincher for me. I am left wholly convinced and, simultaneously, wholly amazed by it. Evidently, the principle of social proof is so wide-ranging and powerful that its domain extends to the fundamental decision for life or death. Phillips' findings illustrate a distressing tendency for suicide publicity to motivate certain people who are similar to the victim to kill themselves—because they now find the idea of suicide more legitimate. Truly frightening are the data indicating that many innocent people die in the bargain. A glance at the graphs documenting the undeniable increase of traffic and air fatalities following publicized suicides, especially those involving murder, is enough to cause concern for one's own safety. I have been sufficiently affected by these statistics to begin to take note of front-page suicide stories and to change my behavior in the period after their appearances. I try to be especially cautious behind the wheel of my car. I am reluctant to take extended trips requiring a lot of air travel. If I must fly during such a period, I purchase substantially more flight insurance than I normally would. Phillips has done us a service by demonstrating that the odds for survival when we travel change measurably for a time following the publication of certain kinds of front-page suicide stories. It would seem only prudent to play those odds (see Figure 3.2).

As if the frightening features of Phillips' suicide data weren't enough, his additional research (Phillips, 1983) brings more cause for alarm: Homicides in this country have a stimulated, copycat character after highly publicized acts of violence. Heavyweight championship prize fights that receive coverage on network evening news appear to produce measurable increases in the United States homicide rate. This analysis of heavyweight championship fights (between 1973 and 1978) is perhaps most compelling in its demonstration of the remarkably specific nature of

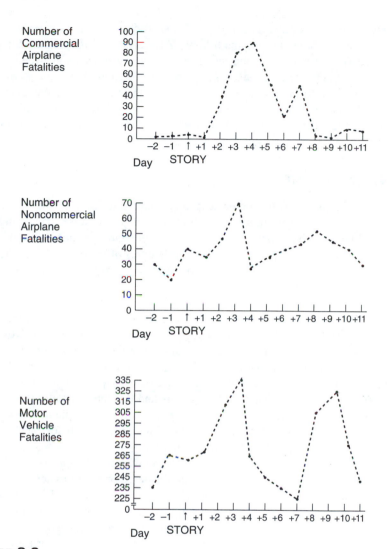

FIGURE 3.2

Daily Fluctuation in Number of Accident Fatalities Before, On, and After Suicide Story Date

As is apparent from these graphs, the greatest danger exists three to four days following the news story's publication. After a brief dropoff, there comes another peak approximately one week later. By the eleventh day, there is no hint of an effect. This pattern across various types of data indicates something noteworthy about secret suicides. Those who try to disguise their imitative self-destruction as accidents wait a few days before committing the act—perhaps to build their courage, to play the incident, or to put their affairs in order. Whatever the reason for the regularity of this pattern, we know that travelers' safety is most severely jeopardized three to four days after a suicide-murder story and then again, but to a lesser degree, a few days later. We would be well advised, then, to take special care in our travels at these times.

the imitative aggression that is generated. When such a match was lost by a black fighter, the homicide rate during the following 10 days rose significantly for young black male victims but not young white males. On the other hand, when a white fighter lost a match, it was young white men, but not young black men, who were killed more frequently in the next 10 days. When these results are combined with the parallel findings in Phillips' suicide data, it is clear that widely publicized aggression has the nasty tendency to spread to similar victims, no matter whether the aggression is inflicted on the self or on another.

MONKEY ISLAND

Work like Phillips' helps us appreciate the awesome influence of the behavior of similar others. Once the enormity of that force is recognized, it becomes possible to understand perhaps the most spectacular act of compliance of our time—the mass suicide at Jonestown, Guyana. Certain crucial features of the event deserve review.

The People's Temple was a cultlike organization that was based in San Francisco and drew its recruits from the poor of that city. In 1977, the Reverend Jim Jones—who was the group's undisputed political, social, and spiritual leader—moved the bulk of the membership with him to a jungle settlement in Guyana, South America. There, the People's Temple existed in relative obscurity until November 18, 1978, when Congressman Leo R. Ryan of California (who had gone to Guyana to investigate the cult), three members of Ryan's fact-finding party, and a cult defector were murdered as they tried to leave Jamestown by plane. Convinced that he would be arrested and implicated in the killings and that the demise of the People's Temple would result, Jones sought to control the end of the Temple in his own way. He gathered the entire community around him and issued a call for each person's death to be done in a unified act of self-destruction.

The first response was that of a young woman who calmly approached the now famous vat of strawberry-flavored poison, administered one dose to her baby, one to herself, and then sat down in a field, where she and her child died in convulsions within four minutes. Others followed steadily in turn. Although a handful of Jonestowners escaped and a few others are reported to have resisted, the survivors claim that the great majority of the 910 people who died did so in an orderly, willful fashion.

News of the event shocked us. The broadcast media and the papers provided a barrage of reports, updates, and analyses. For days, our conversations were full of the topic, "How many have they found dead now?" "A guy who escaped said they were drinking the poison like they were hypnotized or something." "What were they doing down in South America, anyway?" "It's so hard to believe. What caused it?"

Yes, "What caused it?"—the critical question. How are we to account for this most astounding of compliant acts? Various explanations have been offered. Some have focused on the charisma of Jim Jones, a man whose style allowed him to be loved like a savior, trusted like a father, and treated like an emperor. Other explanations have pointed to the kind of people who were attracted to the People's Temple. They were mostly poor and uneducated individuals who were willing to give up their freedoms of thought and action for the safety of a place where all decisions would be made for them. Still other explanations have emphasized the quasi-religious nature for the People's Temple, in which unquestioned faith in the cult's leader was assigned highest priority.

No doubt each of these features of Jonestown has merit in explaining what happened there, but I do not find them sufficient. After all, the world abounds with cults populated by dependent people who are led by a charismatic figure. What's more, there has never been a shortage of this combination of circumstances in the past. Yet virtually nowhere do we find evidence of an event even approximating the Jonestown incident among such groups. There must be something else that was critical.

One especially revealing question gives us a clue: "If the community had remained in San Francisco, would Reverend Jones' suicide command have been obeyed?" A highly speculative question to be sure, but the expert most familiar with the People's Temple has no doubt about the answer. Louis Jolyon West, chairman of psychiatry and biobehavioral sciences at UCLA and director of its neuropsychiatric unit, is an authority on cults, who had observed the People's Temple for eight years prior to the Jonestown deaths. When interviewed in the immediate aftermath, he made what strikes me as an inordinately instructive statement: "This wouldn't have happened in California. But they lived in total alienation from the rest of the world in a jungle situation in a hostile country."

Although lost in the welter of commentary following the tragedy, West's observation together with what we know about the principle of social proof, seems to me quite important to a satisfactory understanding of the compliant suicides. To my mind, the single act in the history of the People's Temple that most contributed to the members' mindless compliance that day occurred a year earlier with the relocation of the Temple to a jungle country of unfamiliar customs and people. If we are to believe the stories of Jim Jones' malevolent genius, he realized fully the massive psychological impact such a move would have on his followers. All at once, they found themselves in a place they knew nothing about. South America, and the rain forests of Guyana, especially, were unlike anything they had experienced in San Francisco. The country—both physical and social—into which they were dropped must have seemed dreadfully uncertain.

Ah, uncertainty—the right-hand man of the principle of social proof. We have already seen that when people are uncertain, they look to the actions of others to guide their own actions. In the alien, Guyanese environment, then, Temple members were very ready to follow the lead of others. As we have also seen, it is others of a special kind whose behavior will be most unquestioningly followed: similar others. Therein lies the awful beauty of Reverend Jones' relocation strategy. In a country like Guyana, there were no similar others for a Jonestown resident but the people of Jonestown itself.

What was right for a member of the community was determined to a disproportionate degree by what other community members—influenced heavily by Jones—did and believed. When viewed in this light, the terrible orderliness, the lack of panic, the sense of calm with which these people moved to the vat of poison and to their deaths seem more comprehensible. They hadn't been hypnotized by Jones;

they had been convinced—partly by him but, more importantly, by the principle of social proof—that suicide was the correct conduct. The uncertainty they surely felt upon first hearing the death command must have caused them to look around them for a definition of the appropriate response.

It is worth particular note that they found two impressive pieces of social evidence, each pointing in the same direction. The first was the initial set of their compatriots, who quickly and willingly took the poison drafts. There will always be a few such fanatically obedient individuals in any strong leader-dominated group. Whether, in this instance, they had been specially instructed beforehand to serve as examples, or whether they were just naturally the most compliant with Jones' wishes, is difficult to know. No matter, the psychological effect of the actions of those individuals must have been potent. If the suicides of similar others in news stories can influence total strangers to kill themselves, imagine how enormously more compelling such an act would be when performed without hesitation by one's neighbors in a place like Jonestown. The second source of social evidence came from the reactions of the crowd itself. Given the conditions, I suspect that what occurred was a large-scale instance of the pluralistic ignorance phenomenon. Each Jonestowner looked to the actions of surrounding individuals to assess the situation and—finding calmness because everyone else, too, was surreptitiously assessing rather than reacting—"learned" that patient turntaking was the correct behavior. Such misinterpreted, but nonetheless convincing, social evidence would be expected to result precisely in the ghastly composure of the assemblage that waited in the tropics of Guyana for businesslike death.

From my own perspective, most attempts to analyze the Jonestown incident have focused too much on the personal qualities of Jim Jones. Although he was without question a man of rare dynamism, the power he wielded strikes me as coming less from his remarkable personal style than from his understanding of fundamental psychological principles. His real genius as a leader was his realization of the limitations of individual leadership. No leader can hope to persuade, regularly and single-handedly, all the members of the group. A forceful leader can reasonably expect, however, to persuade some sizable proportion of group members. Then the raw information that a substantial number of group members has been convinced can, by itself, convince the rest. Thus the most influential leaders are those who know how to arrange group conditions to allow the principle of social proof to work in their favor.

It is in this that Jones appears to have been inspired. His masterstroke was the decision to move the People's Temple community from urban San Francisco to the remoteness of equatorial South America, where the conditions of uncertainty and exclusive similarity would make the principle of social proof operate for him as perhaps nowhere else. There a settlement of a thousand people, much too large to be held in persistent sway by the force of one man's personality, could be changed from a following into a *herd*. As slaughterhouse operators have long known, the mentality of a herd makes it easy to manage. Simply get some members moving in the desired direction and the others—responding not so much to the lead animal as to those immediately surrounding them—will peacefully and mechanically go along. The powers of the amazing Reverend Jones, then, are probably best understood not in terms of his dramatic personal style but in his profound knowledge of the art of social jujitsu.

References

Bollen, K. A., & Phillips, D. P. (1982). Imitative suicides: A national study of the effects of television news stories. *American Sociological Review, 47,* 802–809.

Festinger, L. (1954). A theory of social comparison processes. *Human Relations, 7,* 117–140.

Gould, M. S., & Shaffer, D. ((1986). The impact of suicide in television movies. *The New England Journal of Medicine, 315,* 690–694.

Hornstein, H. A., Fisch, E., & Holmes, M. (1968). Influence of a model's feeling about his behavior and his relevance as a comparison other on observers' helping behavior. *Journal of Personality and Social Psychology, 10,* 222–226.

Murray, D. A., Leupker, R. V., Johnson, C. A., & Mittlemark, M. B. (1984). The prevention of cigarette smoking in children: A comparison of four strategies. *Journal of Applied Social Psychology, 14,* 274–288.

Phillips, D. P. (1974). The influence of suggestion on suicide: Substantive and theoretical implications of the Werther effect. *American Sociological Review, 39,* 340–354.

Phillips, D. P. (1979). Suicide, motor vehicle fatalities, and the mass media: Evidence toward a theory of suggestion. *American Journal of Sociology, 84,* 1150–1174.

Phillips, D. P. (1980). Airplane accidents, murder, and the mass media: Towards a theory of imitation and suggestion. *Social Forces, 58,* 1001–1024.

Phillips, D. P. (1983). The impact of mass media violence on U.S. homicides. *American Sociological Review, 48,* 560–568.

Phillips, D. P., & Cartensen, L. L. (1986). Clustering of teenage suicides after television news stories about suicide. *The New England Journal of Medicine, 315,* 685–689.

Schmidtke, A., & Hafner, H. (1988). The Werther effect after television films: New evidence for an old hypothesis. *Psychological Medicine, 18,* 665–676.

Philip Meyer

If Hitler Asked You to Electrocute a Stranger, Would You?

In this article from *Esquire,* Meyer discusses one of the most dramatic and highly debated programs of research in social psychology—Stanley Milgram's studies on obedience. Meyer offers us some insights into Milgram's interests and motivation in performing this research in which people were asked to deliver clearly painful and possibly dangerous electric shocks to another person as part of an experiment. Noting that a majority of people obeyed, Meyer prompts us to answer the question of why people acted as they did—and in doing so to analyze the powerful situational factors present and to wonder how each of us would have reacted in that situation.

In the beginning, Stanley Milgram was worried about the Nazi problem. He doesn't worry much about the Nazis anymore. He worries about you and me, and, perhaps, himself a little bit too.

Stanley Milgram is a social psychologist, and when he began his career at Yale University in 1960 he had a plan to prove, scientifically, that Germans are different. The Germans-are-different hypothesis has been used by historians, such as William L. Shirer, to explain the systematic destruction of the Jews by the Third Reich. One madman could decide to destroy the Jews and even create a master plan for getting it done. But to implement it on the scale that Hitler did meant that thousands of other people had to go along with the scheme and help to do the work. The Shirer thesis, which Milgram set out to test, is that Germans have a basic character flaw which explains the whole thing, and this flaw is a readiness to obey authority without question, no matter what outrageous acts the authority commands.

The appealing thing about this theory is that it makes those of us who are not Germans feel better about the whole business. Obviously, you and I are not Hitler, and it seems equally obvious that we would never do Hitler's dirty work for him. But now, because of Stanley Milgram, we are compelled to wonder. Milgram developed a laboratory experiment which provided a systematic way to measure obedience. His plan was to try it out in New Haven on Americans and then go to Germany and try it out on Germans. He was strongly motivated by scientific curiosity, but there was also some moral content in his decision to pursue this line of research, which was, in turn, colored by his own Jewish background. If he could show that Germans are more obedient than Americans, he could then vary the conditions of the experiment and try to find out just what it is that makes some people more obedient than others. With this understanding, the world might, conceivably, be just a little bit better.

But he never took his experiment to Germany. He never took it any farther than Bridgeport. The first finding, also the most unexpected and disturbing finding, was that we Americans are an obedient people: not blindly obedient, and not blissfully obedient, just obedient. "I found so much obedience," says Milgram softly, a little sadly, "I hardly saw the need for taking the experiment to Germany."

There is something of the theatre director in Milgram, and his technique, which he learned from one of the old masters in experimental psychology, Solomon Asch, is to stage a play with every line rehearsed, every prop carefully selected, and everybody an actor except one person. That one person is the subject of the experiment. The subject, of course, does not know he is in a play. He thinks he is in real life. The value of this technique is that the experimenter, as though he were God, can change a prop here, vary a line there, and see how the subject responds. Milgram eventually had to change a lot of the script just to get people to stop obeying. They were obeying so much, the experiment wasn't working—it was like trying to measure oven temperature with a freezer thermometer.

The experiment worked like this: If you were an innocent subject in Milgram's melodrama, you read an ad in the newspaper or received one in the mail asking for volunteers for an educational experiment. The job would take about an hour and pay $4.50. So you make an appointment and go to an old Romanesque stone structure on High Street with the imposing name of The Yale Interaction Laboratory. It looks something like a broadcasting studio. Inside, you meet a young, crew-cut man in a laboratory coat who says he is Jack Williams, the experimenter. There is another citizen, fiftyish, Irish face, an accountant, a little overweight, and very mild and harmless-looking. This other citizen seems nervous and plays with his hat while the two of you sit in chairs side by side and are told that the $4.50 checks are yours no matter what happens. Then you listen to Jack Williams explain the experiment.

It is about learning, says Jack Williams in a quiet, knowledgeable way. Science does not know much about the conditions under which people learn and this experiment is to find out about negative reinforcement. Negative reinforcement is getting punished when you do something wrong, as opposed to positive reinforcement which is getting rewarded when you do something right. The negative reinforcement in this case is electric shock. You notice a book on the table, titled, *The Teaching– Learning Process,* and you assume that this has something to do with the experiment.

Then Jack Williams takes two pieces of paper, puts them in a hat, and shakes them up. One piece of paper is supposed to say, "Teacher" and the other, "Learner." Draw one and you will see which you will be. The mild-looking accountant draws one, holds it close to his vest like a poker player, looks at it, and says, "Learner." You look at yours. It says, "Teacher." You do not know that the drawing is rigged, and both slips say "Teacher." The experimenter beckons the mild-mannered "learner."

"Want to step right in here and have a seat, please?" he says. "You can leave your coat on the back of that chair . . . roll up your right sleeve, please. Now what I want to do is strap down your arms to avoid excessive movement on your part during the experiment. This electrode is connected to the shock generator in the next room.

"And this electrode paste," he says, squeezing some stuff out of a plastic bottle and putting it on the man's arm, "is to provide a good contact and to avoid a blister or burn. Are there any questions now before we go into the next room?"

You don't have any, but the strapped-in "learner" does.

"I do think I should say this," says the learner. "About two years ago, I was a at the veterans' hospital . . . they detected a heart condition. Nothing serious, but as long as I'm having these shocks, how strong are they—how dangerous are they?"

Williams, the experimenter, shakes his head casually. "Oh, no," he says. "Although they may be painful, they're not dangerous. Anything else?"

Nothing else. And so you play the game. The game is for you to read a series of word pairs: for example, blue-girl, nice-day, fat-neck. When you finish the list, you read just the first word in each pair and then a multiple-choice list of four other words, including the second word of the pair. The learner, from his remote, strapped-in position, pushes one of four switches to indicate which of the four answers he thinks is the right one. If he gets it right, nothing happens and you go on to the next one. If he gets it wrong, you push a switch that buzzes and gives him an electric shock. And then you go to the next word. You start with 15 volts and increase the number of volts by 15 for each wrong answer. The control board goes from 15 volts on one end to 450 volts on the other. So that you know what you are doing, you get a test shock yourself, at 45 volts. It hurts. To further keep you aware of what you are doing to that man in there, the board has verbal descriptions of the shock levels, ranging from "Slight Shock" at the left-hand side, through "Intense Shock" in the middle, to "Danger: Severe Shock" toward the far right. Finally, at the very end, under 435- and 450-volt switches, there are three ambiguous X's. If, at any point, you hesitate, Mr. Williams calmly tells you to go on. If you still hesitate, he tells you again.

Except for some terrifying details, which will be explained in a moment, this is the experiment. The object is to find the shock level at which you disobey the experimenter and refuse to pull the switch.

When Stanley Milgram first wrote this script, he took it to fourteen Yale psychology majors and asked them what they thought would happen. He put it this way: Out of one hundred persons in the teacher's predicament, how would their break-off points be distributed along the 15-to-450-volt scale? They thought a few would break off very early, most would quit someplace in the middle and a few would go all the way to the end. The highest estimate of the number out of one hundred who would go all the way to the end was three. Milgram then informally polled some of his fellow scholars in the psychology department. They agreed that very few would go to the end. Milgram thought so too.

"I'll tell you quite frankly," he says, "before I began this experiment, before any shock generator was built, I thought that most people would break off at 'Strong Shock' or 'Very Strong Shock.' You would only get a very, very small proportion of people going out to the end of the shock generator, and they would constitute a pathological fringe."

In his pilot experiments, Milgram used Yale students as subjects. Each of them pushed the shock switches, one by one, all the way to the end of the board.

So he rewrote the script to include some protests from the learner. At first, they were mild, gentlemanly, Yalie protests, but, "it didn't seem to have as much effect as I thought it would or should," Milgram recalls. "So we had more violent protestation on the part of the person getting the shock. All of the time, of course, what we were trying to do was not to create a macabre situation, but simply to generate disobedience. And that was one of the first findings. This was not only a technical deficiency of the experiment, that we didn't get disobedience. It really was the first finding, that obedience would be much greater than we had assumed it would be and disobedience would be much more difficult than we had assumed."

As it turned out, the situation did become rather macabre. The only meaningful way to generate disobedience was to have the victim protest with great anguish, noise, and vehemence. The protests were tape-recorded so that all the teachers ordinarily would hear the same sounds and nuances, and they started with a grunt at 75 volts, proceeded through a "Hey, that really hurts," at 125 volts, got desperate with, "I can't stand the pain, don't do that," at 180 volts, reached complaints of heart trouble at 195, an agonized scream at 285, a refusal to answer at 315, and only heartrending, ominous silence after that.

Still, sixty-five percent of the subjects, twenty- to fifty-year-old American males, everyday, ordinary people, like you and me, obediently kept pushing those levers in the belief that they were shocking the mild-mannered learner, whose name was Mr. Wallace, and who was chosen for the role because of his innocent appearance, all the way up to 450 volts.

Milgram was now getting enough disobedience so that he had something he could measure. The next step was to vary the circumstances to see what would encourage or discourage obedience. There seemed very little left in the way of discouragement. The victim was already screaming at the top of his lungs and feigning a heart attack. So whatever new impediment to obedience reached the brain of the subject had to gravel by some route other than the ear. Milgram thought of one.

He put the learner in the same room with the teacher. He stopped strapping the learner's hand down. He rewrote the script so that at 150 volts the learner took his hand off the shock plate and declared that he wanted out of the experiment. He rewrote the script some more so that the experimenter then told the teacher to grasp the learner's hand and physically force it down on the plate to give Mr. Wallace his unwanted electric shock.

"I had the feeling that very few people would go on at that point, if any," Milgram says. "I thought that would be the limit of obedience that you would find in the laboratory."

It wasn't.

Although seven years have now gone by, Milgram still remembers the first person to walk into the laboratory in the newly rewritten script. He was a construction worker, a very short man. "He was so small," says Milgram, "that when he sat on the chair in front of the shock generator, his feet didn't reach the floor. When the experimenter told him to push the victim's hand down and give the shock, he turned to the experimenter, and he turned to the victim, his elbow went up, he fell down on the hand of the victim, his feet kind of tugged to one side, and he said, 'Like this, boss?' ZZUMPH!''

The experiment was played out to its bitter end. Milgram tried with forty different subjects. And thirty percent of them obeyed the experimenter and kept on obeying.

"The protests of the victim were strong and vehement, he was screaming his guts out, he refused to participate, and you had to physically struggle with him in order to get his hand down on the shock generator," Milgram remembers. But twelve out of forty did it.

Milgram took his experiment out of New Haven. Not to Germany, just twenty miles down the road to Bridgeport. Maybe, he reasoned, the people obeyed because of the prestigious setting of Yale University. If they couldn't trust a center of learning that had been there for two centuries, whom could they trust? So he moved the experiment to an untrustworthy setting.

The new setting was a suite of three rooms in a run-down office building in Bridgeport. The only identification was a sign with a fictitious name: "Research Associates of Bridgeport." Questions about professional connections got only vague answers about "research for industry."

Obedience was less in Bridgeport. Forty-eight percent of the subjects stayed for the maximum shock, compared to sixty-five percent at Yale. But this was enough to prove that far more than Yale's prestige was behind the obedient behavior.

For more than seven years now, Stanley Milgram has been trying to figure out what makes ordinary Americans citizens so obedient. The most obvious answer—that people are mean, nasty, brutish and sadistic—won't do. The subjects who gave the shocks to Mr. Wallace to the end of the board did not enjoy it. They groaned, protested, fidgeted, argued, and in some cases, were seized by fits of nervous, agitated giggling.

"They even try to get out of it," says Milgram, "but they are somehow engaged in something from which they cannot liberate themselves. They are locked into a structure, and they do not have the skills or inner resources to disengage themselves."

Milgram, because he mistakenly had assumed that he would have trouble getting people to obey the orders to shock Mr. Wallace, went to a lot of trouble to create a realistic situation.

There was crew-cut Jack Williams and his grey laboratory coat. Not white, which might denote a medical technician, but ambiguously authoritative grey. Then there was the book on the table, and the other appurtenances of the laboratory which emitted the silent message that things were being performed here in the name of science, and were therefore great and good.

But the nicest touch of all was the shock generator. When Milgram started out, he had only a $300 grant from the Higgins Fund of Yale University. Later he got more ample support from the National Science Foundation, but in the beginning he had to create his authentic-looking machine with very scarce resources except for his own imagination. So he went to New York and roamed around the electronic shops until he found some little black switches at Lafayette Radio for a dollar apiece. He bought thirty of them. The generator was a metal box, about the size of a small foot-locker, and he drilled the thirty holes for the thirty switches himself in a Yale machine shop.

But the fine detail was left to professional industrial engravers. So he ended up with a splendid-looking control panel dominated by the row of switches, each labeled with its voltage, and each having its own red light that flashed on when the switch was pulled. Other things happened when a switch was pushed. Besides the ZZUMPHing noise, a blue light labeled "voltage energizer" went on, and a needle on a dial labeled "voltage" flicked from left to right. Relays inside the box clicked. Finally, in the upper left-hand corner of the control panel was this inscription, engraved in precise block letters:

SHOCK GENERATOR TYPE ZLB
DYSON INSTRUMENT COMPANY
WALTHAM, MASS.
OUTPUT: 15 VOLTS—450 VOLTS

One day a man from the Lehigh Valley Electronics Company of Pennsylvania was passing through the laboratory, and he stopped to admire the shock generator. "This is a very fine shock generator," he said. "But who is this Dyson Instrument Company?" Milgram felt proud at that, since Dyson Instrument Company existed only in the recesses of his imagination.

When you consider the seeming authenticity of the situation, you can appreciate the agony some of the subjects went through. It was pure conflict. As Milgram explains to his students, "When a parent says, 'Don't strike old ladies,' you are learning two things: the content, and, also, to obey authority. This experiment creates conflicts between the two elements."

Here is a partial transcription from one of the experiments. The naive "teacher" is a heavyset, worried-looking man with prematurely grey hair. He is wearing a polo shirt. He is very polite. He has just pushed the 180-volt lever. A hidden camera is recording the performance.

Learner (who, from the teacher's point of view is heard but not seen, an off-stage voice): Ow, I can't stand the pain. Don't do that. . . .

Teacher (pivoting around in his chair and shaking his head): I can't stand it. I'm not going to kill that man in there. You hear him hollering?

Experimenter: As I told you before, the shocks may be painful, but—

Teacher: But he's hollering. He can't stand it. What's going to happen to him?

Experimenter (his voice patient, matter-of-fact): The experiment requires that you continue, Teacher.

Teacher: Aah, but, unh, I'm not going to get that man sick in there . . . know what I mean?

Experimenter: Whether the learner likes it or not, we must go on, through all the word pairs.

Teacher: I refuse to take the responsibility. He's in there hollering!

Experimenter: It's absolutely essential that you continue, Teacher.

Teacher (indicating the unused questions): There's too many left here, I mean, Geez, if he gets them wrong, there's too many of them left. I mean who's going to take the responsibility if anything happens to that gentleman?

Experimenter: I'm responsible for anything that happens to him. Continue please.

Teacher: All right (Consults list of words.) The next one's "Slow—walk, truck, dance, music." Answer please. (A buzzing sound indicates the learner has signaled his answer.) Wrong. A hundred and ninety-five volts. "Dance." (Zzumph!)

Learner: Let me out of here. My heart's bothering me! (Teacher looks at experimenter.)

Experimenter: Continue, please.

Learner (screaming): Let me out of here, you have no right to keep me here. Let me out of here, let me out, my heart's bothering me, let me out! (Teacher shakes head, pats the table nervously.)

Teacher: You see, he's hollering. Hear that? Gee, I don't know.

Experimenter: The experiment requires. . . .

Teacher (interrupting): I know it does, sir, but I mean—hunh! He don't know what he's getting in for. He's up to 195 volts! (Experiment continues, through 210 volts, 225 volts, 240 volts, 225 volts, 270 volts, delivered to the man in the electric chair, at which point the teacher, with evident relief, runs out of word–pair questions.)

Experimenter: You'll have to go back to the beginning of that page and go through them again until he's learned them all correctly.

Teacher: Aw, no. I'm not going to kill that man. You mean I've got to keep going up with the scale. No sir. He's hollering in there. I'm not going to give him 450 volts.

Experimenter: The experiment requires that you go on.

Teacher: I know it does, but that man is hollering in there, sir.

Experimenter (same matter-of-fact tone): As I said before, although the shocks may be painful. . . .

Teacher (interrupting): Awwww. He—he—he's yelling in there.

Experimenter: Start with "Blue," please, at the top of the page. Continue, please, Teacher. Just go ahead.

Teacher (concentrating intently on list of words in front of him, as if to shut everything else out): "Blue—boy, girl, grass, hat." (Buzz indicates answer.) Correct. "Night—day, sky, job, chair. (Buzz) Wrong. The answer is "day." Two hundred and eighty-five volts. (Zzumph!)

Learner: Ohhuhhoohhh!

Experimenter: Continue, please.

Teacher: "Fat—man, lady, tub, neck." Answer, please. (Buzz) Wrong. The answer is "neck." Three hundred volts. (Zzumph!)

Learner: Ohhh. I absolutely refuse to answer any more. (Shouting urgently, now). Let me out of here. You can't hold me here. Get me out. Get—me—out—of—here.

Experimenter: Continue. The next word is "Green," please.

Teacher: "Green—grass, hat, ink, apple." (Nothing happens. No answering buzz. Just gloomy silence.)

Teacher: I don't think he is going to answer.

Experimenter: If the learner doesn't answer in a reasonable time, about four or five seconds, consider the answer wrong. And follow the same procedures you have been doing for wrong answers. Say "Wrong," tell him the number of volts, give him the punishment, read him the correct answer. Continue, please.

Teacher: "Green—grass, hat, ink, apple." Answer, please. (More silence. Teacher just sits there.)

Experimenter: Go on with the procedure, please, Teacher.

Teacher: Three hundred and fifteen volts. The answer is "ink." (Zzumph!)

Learner: Ohh. Ooohh.

Teacher (relieved to hear response): Next one.

Learner: I absolutely refuse to answer.

Teacher: You got to. You get a shock if you don't answer. (Experiment continues with learner refusing to answer, and, finally, failing even to grunt or groan. At 375 volts, the teacher stands up. Has he had enough? Will he break off the experiment? Will he disobey?)

Teacher: I think something's happened to that fellow in there. I don't get no answer. He was hollering at less voltage. Can't you check in and see if he's all right, please?

Experimenter (same detached calm): Not once we've started. Please continue, Teacher.

Teacher (sits down, sighs deeply): "Cool—day, shade, water, paint." Answer please. Are you all right in there? Are you all right?

Experimenter: Please continue, Teacher. Continue, please. (Teacher pushes lever. ZZUMPH!)

Teacher (swiveling around in his chair): Something's happened to that man in there. (Swiveling back) Next one. "Low—dollar, necklace, moon, paint." (Turning around again) Something's happened to that man in there. You better check in on him, sir. He won't answer or nothing.

Experimenter: Continue. Go on, please.

Teacher: You accept all responsibility.

Experimenter: The responsibility is mine. Correct. Please go on. (Teacher returns to his list, starts running through words as rapidly as he can read them, works through to 450 volts.)

Teacher: That's that.

Experimenter: Continue using the last switch on the board, please. The forty-five switch for each wrong answer. Continue please.

Teacher: But I don't get anything!

Experimenter: Please continue. The next word is "White."

Teacher: Don't you think you should look in on him, please.

Experimenter: Not once we've started the experiment.

Teacher: But what if something has happened to the man?

Experimenter: The experiment requires that you continue. Go on, please.

Teacher: Don't the man's health mean anything?

Experimenter: Whether the learner likes it or not. . . .

Teacher: What if he's dead in there? (Gestures toward the room with the electric chair.) I mean, he told me he can't stand the shock, sir. I don't mean to be rude, but I think you should look in on him. All you have to do is look in the door.

I don't get no answer, no noise. Something might have happened to the gentleman in there, sir.

Experimenter: We must continue. Go on, please.

Teacher: You mean keep giving him what? Four hundred fifty volts, what he's got now?

Experimenter: That's correct. Continue. The next word is "White."

Teacher (now at a furious pace): "White—cloud, horse, rock, house." Answer, please. The answer is "horse." Four hundred and fifty volts. (Zzumph!) Next word, "Bag—paint, music, clown, girl." The answer is "paint." Four hundred and fifty volts. (ZZUMPH!) Next word is "short—sentence, movie."

Experimenter: Excuse me, Teacher. We'll have to discontinue the experiment.

(Enter Milgram from camera's left. He has been watching from behind one-way glass.)

Milgram: I'd like to ask you a few questions. (Slowly, patiently, he dehoaxes the teacher, telling him that the shocks and screams were not real.)

Teacher: You mean he wasn't getting nothing? Well, I'm glad to hear that. I was getting upset there. I was getting ready to walk out.

(Finally, to make sure there are no hard feelings, friendly, harmless Mr. Wallace comes out in coat and tie. Gives jovial greeting. Friendly reconciliation takes place. Experiment ends.)*

Subjects in the experiment were not asked to give the 450-volt shock more than three times. By that time, it seemed evident that they would go on indefinitely. "No one," says Milgram "who got within five shocks of the end ever broke off. By that point, he had resolved the conflict."

Why do so many people resolve the conflict in favor of obedience?

Milgram's theory assumes that people behave in two different operating modes as different as ice and water. He does not rely on Freud or sex or toilet-training hang-ups for this theory. All he says is that ordinarily we operate in a state of autonomy, which means we pretty much have and assert control over what we do. But in certain circumstances, we operate under what Milgram calls a state of agency (after agent, *n* . . . one who acts for or in the place of another by authority from him; a substitute; a deputy.—*Webster's Collegiate Dictionary*). A state of agency, to Milgram, is nothing more than a frame of mind.

"There's nothing bad about it, there's nothing good about it," he says. It's a natural circumstance of living with other people. . . . I think of a state of agency as a real transformation of a person; if a person has different properties when he's in that state, just as water can turn to ice under certain conditions of temperature, a person can move to the state of mind that I call agency . . . the critical thing is that you see yourself as the instrument of the execution of another person's wishes. You do not

———

*Copyright 1965 by Stanley Milgram. From the film OBEDIENCE, distributed by the New York University Film Library.

see yourself as acting on your own. And there's a real transformation, a real change of properties of the person."

To achieve this change, you have to be in a situation where there seems to be a ruling authority whose commands are relevant to some legitimate purpose; the authority's power is not unlimited.

But situations can be and have been structured to make people do unusual things, and not just in Milgram's laboratory. The reason, says Milgram, is that no action, in and of itself, contains meaning.

"The meaning always depends on your definition of the situation. Take an action like killing another person. It sounds bad.

"But then we say the other person was about to destroy a hundred children, and the only way to stop him was to kill him. Well, that sounds good.

"Or, you take destroying your own life. It sounds very bad. Yet, in the Second World War, thousands of persons thought it was a good thing to destroy your own life. It was set in the proper context. You sipped some saki from a whistling cup, recited a few haiku. You said, 'May my death be as clean and as quick as the shattering of crystal.' And it almost seemed like a good, noble thing to do, to crash your kamikaze plane into an aircraft carrier. But the main thing was, the definition of what a kamikaze pilot was doing had been determined by the relevant authority. Now, once you are in a state of agency, you allow the authority to determine, to define what the situation is. The meaning of your action is altered."

So, for most subjects in Milgram's laboratory experiments, the act of giving Mr. Wallace his painful shock was necessary, even though unpleasant, and besides they were doing it on behalf of somebody else and it was for science. There was still strain and conflict, of course. Most people resolved it by grimly sticking to their task and obeying. But some broke out. Milgram tried varying the conditions of the experiment to see what would help break people out of their state of agency.

"The results, as seen and felt in the laboratory," he has written, "are disturbing. They raise the possibility that human nature, or more specifically the kind of character produced in American democratic society, cannot be counted on to insulate its citizens from brutality and inhumane treatment at the direction of malevolent authority. A substantial proportion of people do what they are told to do, irrespective of the content of the act and without limitations of conscience, so long as they perceive that the command comes from a legitimate authority. If, in this study, an anonymous experimenter can successfully command adults to subdue a fifty-year-old man and force on him painful electric shocks against his protest, one can only wonder what government, with its vastly greater authority and prestige, can command of its subjects."

This is a nice statement, but it falls short of summing up the full meaning of Milgram's work. It leaves some questions still unanswered.

The first question is this: Should we really be surprised and alarmed that people obey? Wouldn't it be even more alarming if they all refused to obey? Without obedience to a relevant ruling authority there could not be a civil society. And without a civil society, as Thomas Hobbes pointed out in the seventeenth century, we would live in a condition of war, "of every man against every other man," and life would be "solitary, poor, nasty, brutish and short."

In the middle of one of Stanley Milgram's lectures at C.U.N.Y. recently, some mini-skirted undergraduates started whispering and giggling in the back of the room. He told them to cut it out. Since he was the relevant authority in that time and that place, they obeyed, and most people in the room were glad that they obeyed.

This was not, of course, a conflict situation. Nothing in the coeds' social upbringing made it a matter of conscience for them to whisper and giggle. But a case can be made that in a conflict situation it is all the more important to obey. Take the case of war, for example. Would we really want a situation in which every participant in a war, direct or indirect—from front-line soldiers to the people who sell coffee and cigarettes to employees at the Concertina barbed-wire factory in Kansas—stops and consults his conscience before each action? It is asking for an awful lot of mental strain and anguish from an awful lot of people. The value of having civil order is that one can do his duty, or whatever interests him, or whatever seems to benefit him at the moment, and leave the agonizing to others. When Francis Gary Powers was being tried by a Soviet military tribunal after his U-2 spy plane was shot down, the presiding judge asked if he had thought about the possibility that his flight might have provoked a war. Powers replied with Hobbesian clarity: "The people who sent me should think of these things. My job was to carry out orders. I do not think it was my responsibility to make such decisions."

It was not his responsibility. And it is quite possible that if everyone felt responsible for each of the ultimate consequences of his own tiny contributions to complex chains of events, then society simply would not work. Milgram, fully conscious of the moral and social implications of his research, believes that people should feel responsible for their actions. If someone else had invented the experiment, and if he had been the naive subject, he feels certain that he would have been among the disobedient minority.

"There is no very good solution to this," he admits, thoughtfully. "To simply and categorically say that you won't obey authority may resolve your personal conflict, but it creates more problems for society which may be more serious in the long run. But I have no doubt that to obey is the proper thing to do in this [the laboratory] situation. It is the only reasonable value judgment to make."

The conflict between the need to obey the relevant ruling authority and the need to follow your conscience becomes sharpest if you insist on living by an ethical system based on a rigid code—a code that seeks to answer all questions in advance of their being raised. Code ethics cannot solve the obedience problem. Stanley Milgram seems to be a situation ethicist, and situation ethics does offer a way out: When you feel conflict, you examine the situation and then make a choice among the competing evils. You may act with a presumption in favor of obedience, but reserve the possibility that you will disobey whenever obedience demands a flagrant and outrageous affront to conscience. This, by the way, is the philosophical position of many who resist the draft. In World War II, they would have fought. Vietnam is a different, an outrageously different situation.

Life can be difficult for the situation ethicist, because he does not see the world in straight lines, while the social system too often assumes such a God-given, squared-off structure. If your moral code includes an injunction against all war, you may be deferred as a conscientious objector. If you merely oppose this particular war, you may not be deferred.

Stanley Milgram has his problems, too. He believes that in the laboratory situation, he would not have shocked Mr. Wallace. His professional critics reply that in his real-life situation he has done the equivalent. He has placed innocent and naive subjects under great emotional strain and pressure in selfish obedience to his quest for knowledge. When you raise this issue with Milgram, he has an answer ready. There is, he explains patiently, a critical difference between his naive subjects and the man in the electric chair. The man in the electric chair (in the mind of the naive subject) is helpless, strapped in. But the naive subject is free to go at any time.

Immediately after he offers this distinction, Milgram anticipates the objection.

"It's quite true," he says, "that this is almost a philosophic position, because we have learned that some people are psychologically incapable of disengaging themselves. But that doesn't relieve them of the moral responsibility."

The parallel is exquisite. "The tension problem was unexpected," says Milgram in his defense. But he went on anyway. The naive subjects didn't expect the screaming protests from the strapped-in learner. But they went on.

"I had to make a judgment," says Milgram. "I had to ask myself, was this harming the person or not? My judgment is that it was not. Even in the extreme cases, I wouldn't say that permanent damage results."

Sound familiar? "The shocks may be painful," the experimenter kept saying, "but they're not dangerous."

After the series of experiments was completed, Milgram sent a report of the results to his subjects and a questionnaire, asking whether they were glad or sorry to have been in the experiment. Eighty-three and seven-tenths percent said they were glad and only 1.3 percent were sorry; 15 percent were neither sorry nor glad. However, Milgram could not be sure at the time of the experiment that only 1.3 percent would be sorry.

Kurt Vonnegut, Jr., put one paragraph in the preface to *Mother Night,* in 1966, which pretty much says it for the people with their fingers on the shock-generator switches, for you and me, and maybe even for Milgram. "If I'd been born in Germany," Vonnegut said, "I suppose I would have *been* a Nazi, bopping Jews and gypsies and Poles around, leaving boots sticking out of snowbanks, warming myself with my sweetly virtuous insides. So it goes."

Just so. One thing that happened to Milgram back in New Haven during the days of the experiment was that he kept running into people he'd watched from behind the one-way glass. It gave him a funny feeling, seeing those people going about their everyday business in New Haven and knowing what they would do to Mr. Wallace if ordered to. Now that his research results are in and you've thought about it, you can get this funny feeling too. You don't need one-way glass. A glance in your own mirror may serve just as well.

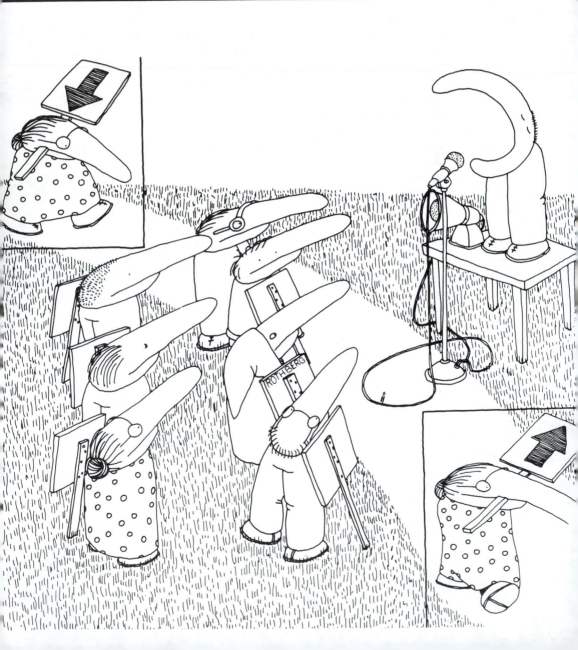

4

Attitudes: Feeling, Believing, and Behaving

To the extent that people have popular images of social psychologists, we are sometimes thought to be attitude pollsters or experts in persuasion. While social psychology involves a great deal more than this, the measurement and change of attitudes has been one of the central interests in the field from its early development to the current day.

Richard Petty, who is Professor of Psychology at Ohio State University, carries a well-deserved reputation as one of the leading names in the field of attitudes and attitude change. He is the former editor of the *Personality and Social Psychology Bulletin* and, along with his colleague John Cacioppo, has developed the Elaboration Likelihood Model, one of the most influential theories in social psychology today. In our conversation, we discussed the many ways in which the study of attitude change has advanced and changed in recent years. Having now clarified many conceptual and theoretical issues, Prof. Petty believes that attitude researchers are now on the verge of making major contributions to important issues, such as drug abuse and AIDS.

A CONVERSATION WITH RICHARD PETTY
Ohio State University

Krupat: *Let's begin at the beginning. Can you tell me what an attitude is and why it is that social psychologists seem to find this concept so important and interesting?*

Petty: The most common perspective today would be that attitudes refer to people's general evaluations of objects, issues, and people. There are a variety of sources that these general evaluations come from. They can be based on your emotions or specific information or beliefs or past behavioral experiences. The reason I think attitudes are important is that a good amount of evidence shows that these general evaluations are one of the most critical determinants of our behavior. So when people talk about social problems of the day, whether it's heart disease and cholesterol, AIDS, or drug abuse, one of the critical things we must do is to influence and modify people's attitudes. Most of our major social problems turn out to be problems of attitudes. For example, people think that they don't like low-fat food. They say it's not good tasting, or they are afraid to try it. So the first step in any kind of public education campaign is to look at what people's attitudes are and attempt to modify them so that behavior will follow.

Krupat: *But couldn't someone say, "Why bother with attitudes? Why not get right to the matter of interest and just get people to comply, to change their behavior without worrying about attitudes?"*

Petty: According to most attitude theorists, change through compliance is only temporary. Compliance occurs because of people's responses to particular aspects of some situation. The factors that produce compliance in one situation might not be present in another situation. On the other hand, people carry their attitudes with them from one situation to the next. So producing an internalized change in attitudes is the best way of influencing behavior across situations.

Krupat: *It's very interesting that you've been giving examples from a lot of very important social areas, such as AIDS and various kinds of health issues. Aren't attitude researchers often thought of as laboratory-type theoreticians rather than applied problem solvers?*

Petty: This has varied over the course of history to some extent. If you go back to Kurt Lewin, one of the founders of social psychology, he was trying to modify people's attitudes about eating generally disliked, but surplus, foods during World War II, and Carl Hovland's group was studying the morale of the troops during that war. Understanding attitudes and persuasion turned out to be more complex than it initially seemed, however, and lots of conflicting findings were produced. For example, expert sources were sometimes good for persuasion and sometimes they weren't. Sometimes variables influenced attitudes initially, but the effects were very short lived. These problems almost killed the field. It's only recently by back to the lab and trying to get more control over things that we are getting a handle on what's happening. Now we may finally be ready to reemerge and apply what we know. I think we have learned enough about when things work and why that it's time again to start looking at important problems in the real world.

Krupat: *You said that we are now just beginning to master the complexity of attitude change and to learn just when things work and why. When do things work, and why?*

Petty: That's a big question, isn't it?

Krupat: *Agreed. Too big and too general, but let's start out at that level if you don't mind, and then we can get more specific as we go along.*

Petty: Let me offer a sort of abstract answer in terms of what we've learned over the past 20 years that we didn't know before. In some ways, the whole approach to the field of attitudes and persuasion has changed. If you went back 15 to 20 years ago, we had all these competing theories, each trying to explain all phenomena all the time. And, of course, what happened was that it turned out that one theory worked here, but maybe it didn't work there. One of the biggest advances of the past 10 years or so is the recognition that different processes work in different situations. For example, in our own work on the Elaboration Likelihood Model, we find that classical conditioning is a very important mechanism, but it is especially effective in situations where people are relatively unmotivated or unable to think about the stimuli presented to them.

Krupat: *Let me interrupt you midstream, if I may. The model that you and John Cacioppo have developed—the Elaboration Likelihood Model (ELM)—is one of the most important in the field. Yet I am certain that some people aren't familiar with it. Maybe you could describe it for us.*

Petty: Sure. The basic idea is that sometimes people like to and are able to think before they make decisions and sometimes decisions are made without much thought. So we have this continuum of thinking from very high levels of thought where careful deliberation occurs before forming a judgment or decision, which we refer to as the central route, to very little thought, consideration, and elaboration, which we refer to as the peripheral route. The basic postulate of the model is that different attitude change processes work at different points along this continuum. Simple processes like classical conditioning or mere exposure work best when people are unmotivated or unable to think. But they don't work so well when people are motivated to think. Other variables, like a person's mood, work by different processes at different points along this continuum. If you're in a good mood and you're not really motivated to think about something, you'll generally like anything that's associated with that good mood. But if you are highly motivated to think, mood doesn't work that way. Instead, mood influences the nature of the thoughts that come to mind. So mood can work in a thoughtful way or a less thoughtful way.

Krupat: *I follow you. But why does it matter whether we change someone's attitude as the result of high or low levels of thoughtfulness or, as you say, by the central or peripheral route?*

Petty: The reason we care whether you are at one end of the continuum or the other is that, although you can be effective at changing a person's attitude at any point along the continuum using the appropriate process, the attitude changes resulting from careful and deliberative thinking tend to last longer and to be more resistant to counterpressures. That, for example, is important in the drug abuse field. For example, you could bring in celebrities or high-status figures to say "Don't use drugs" and you would get the kids to say "We don't like drugs." But the first time their attitudes were challenged, they would have no defense. Their attitudes wouldn't be very resistant to countervailing forces, even though it looked as though the researchers were successful. One of the lessons of a model like the ELM is that the amount of attitude change isn't necessarily the critical thing, it's the strength of the change. Some procedures produce strong attitudes—

ones that will persist over time, resist counterforces, and be predictive and directive of behavior. But other attitude changes which look exactly the same on an attitude change scale don't have those qualities.

Krupat: *Before I interrupted you to explain the ELM, we were on the verge of getting from the larger, more abstract issues into specific questions about what works and why. Let's get back to that.*

Petty: When you think about a theory like the ELM, there are a couple of kinds of variables that are highlighted. One very powerful consideration is that there are individual differences in the extent to which people like to think about issues. John Cacioppo and I have investigated this in our work on the "need for recognition." High-need-for-recognition people generally like to think, and they tend to form strong attitudes that persist over time and are predictive of behavior.

Krupat: *But if I were just facing an audience and I couldn't measure their need for recognition, how would I use that information?*

Petty: In a case like that you could take one step back. We know that there ar some correlates of the need for recognition, like education level. Or, if you are picking jurors for a trial, you could ask them a few questions related to the need for recognition scale to get a sense of whether you would need to use a central or a peripheral strategy. But if you knew absolutely nothing about your audience and wanted to induce central route change, what you'd want to do is to build some things into your message itself. I think the most powerful is self-relevance. If you can make people think that a message is relevant to themselves, they will naturally process it. We've demonstrated this in the lab by varying whether the consequences of the message are likely to affect the message recipients or not, like whether a tuition increase is for their university or some other university. One of my favorite studies on self-relevance simply varied the use of a pronoun. All the arguments were exactly the same, but, instead of having a detached third-person message that read, "*Students* will benefit by having an improved library," the message simply said, "*You* will benefit." And it showed the same kinds of effects that we got with more dramatic manipulations just by changing the pronouns and invoking the self-concept.

Krupat: *That sounds like a wonderful strategy. Are there others that work as well?*

Petty: Another thing that we found you can do quite easily is to use rhetorical questions. For one reason or another, people have learned that when they are asked questions they have to pay attention because they might have to give an answer. So simply by framing an argument in a way that says, "Wouldn't this be great if we did such-and-such?"

people think about it more than if you just say, "It would be great if we did such-and-such."

Krupat: *As I listen to you, I am trying to integrate some of the newer thinking on attitudes with some classic approaches. For instance, the old communications model tried to understand attitude change by asking "who says what to whom?" Would I be correct to say that you are taking things like this and trying to go one step beyond?*

Petty: That's the idea. We still need to deal with source variables, the question of who, and message variables, the question of what, and so forth. But we think about these variables in different ways now. Before, people would just take a long list of variables like expertise or attractiveness and say that these qualities are good for persuasion. You would think an expert source would be good for persuasion, right? But we now have research that shows that sometimes expert sources actually have the opposite effect. Now we recognize that some source variables can work by a simple peripheral process or they can motivate you to think. If an expert motivates you to think but presents weak arguments, your thinking will lead to greater rejection of the message.

Krupat: *But what happens when we try to export our knowledge to decision makers and policy developers? How do they feel about conditional statements that offer complex advice such as "If X then Y?"*

Petty: In the abstract it sounds complicated, but practically, if you are allowed to have control over the situation, you can move groups into the high-elaboration set by invoking self-relevance. As I mentioned, simple things can work, such as just changing the pronouns or including rhetorical questions. You might be able to assess what the level of interest is and use different persuasion strategies, depending on the nature of your audience. It means that you don't go in and mindlessly say, "Here's my message. I'm going to give it this way regardless." Once you get some sense of your audience, you can change your message to fit them.

Krupat: *Are you finding these days that people in "the real world" are still skeptical about the findings and advice of academic researchers?*

Petty: Just with the number of phone calls that come from advertising agencies, law firms, and government panels, I think it's certainly not the case anymore. They are becoming more aware of what's going on. For example, more and more I see commercials and messages that you think were taken right out of the professional journals.

Krupat: *It seems to me that social psychologists are using their knowledge not so much to sell commercial products as to promote ideas and* *behaviors that most people value. Is that a direction you think we should be going?*

Petty: Yes. When people talk about the drug problem, there is a growing recognition that it isn't just the supply of drugs that we need to affect, but also the demand for drugs. When you start talking about demand, you're talking about changing individuals and their attitudes. AIDS is also in large part a problem of attitudes. More and more social psychologists are getting involved in working with AIDS task forces. There's always resistance of some people who think, "This is common sense. We know what we are doing." But as people see the success rates you get from using laboratory-based persuasion techniques appropriately (as with Project DARE), their attitudes are definitely changing.

Leon Festinger
James M. Carlsmith

Cognitive Consequences of Forced Compliance

This article describes one of the classic experiments in social psychology, which tests Leon Festinger's cognitive dissonance theory. Festinger and Carlsmith begin with the assumption that if you do something as part of an experiment that is downright boring, and then find yourself telling someone else that it was interesting, an unpleasant feeling of dissonance will be produced. They then ask what difference it would make—in terms of changing people's attitudes toward the boring experiment—if you were induced to act this way for a small reward ($1) or a large one ($20). Although some people might think that paying a large sum would be a more successful approach to take, the results support the prediction of dissonance theory that the one dollar group changed their attitudes more to justify acting in a way that was inconsistent with their beliefs.

What happens to a person's private opinion if he is forced to do or say something contrary to that opinion? Only recently has there been any experimental work related to this question.

Recently, Festinger (1957) proposed a theory concerning cognitive dissonance from which come a number of derivations about opinion change following forced compliance. Since these derivations are stated in detail by Festinger (1957, Ch. 4), we will here give only a brief outline of the reasoning.

Let us consider a person who privately holds opinion "X" but has, as a result of pressure brought to bear on him, publicly stated that he believes "not X."

1. This person has two cognitions which, psychologically, do not fit together: one of these is the knowledge that he believes "X," the other the knowledge that he has publicly stated that he believes "not X." If no factors other than his private opinion are considered, it would follow, at least in our culture, that if he believes "X" he would publicly state "X." Hence, his cognition of his private belief is dissonant with his cognition concerning his actual public statement.

2. Similarly, the knowledge that he has said "not X" is consonant with (does fit

together with) those cognitive elements corresponding to the reasons, pressures, promises of rewards and/or threats of punishment which induced him to say "not X."

3. In evaluating the total magnitude of dissonance, one must take account of both dissonances and consonances. Let us think of the sum of all the dissonances involving some particular cognition as "D" and the sum of all the consonances as "C." Then we might think of the total magnitude of dissonance as being a function of "D" divided by "D" plus "C."

Let us then see what can be said about the total magnitude of dissonance in a person created by the knowledge that he said "not X" and really believes "X." With everything else held constant, this total magnitude of dissonance would decrease as the number and importance of the pressures which induced him to say "not X" increased.

Thus, if the overt behavior was brought about by, say, offers of reward or threats of punishment, the magnitude of dissonance is maximal if these promised rewards or threatened punishments were just barely sufficient to induce the person to say "not X." From this point on, as the promised rewards or threatened punishment become larger, the magnitude of dissonance becomes smaller.

4. One way in which the dissonance can be reduced is for the person to change his private opinion so as to bring it into correspondence with what he has said. One would consequently expect to observe such opinion change after a person has been forced or induced to say something contrary to his private opinion. Furthermore, since the pressure to reduce dissonance will be a function of the magnitude of the dissonance, the observed opinion change should be greatest when the pressure used to elicit the overt behavior is just sufficient to do it.

The present experiment was designed to test this derivation under controlled, laboratory conditions. In the experiment, we varied the amount of reward used to force persons to make a statement contrary to their private views. The prediction [from 3 and 4 above] is that the larger the reward given to the subject, the smaller will be the subsequent opinion change.

PROCEDURE

Seventy-one male students in the introductory psychology course at Stanford University were used in the experiment. In this course, students are required to spend a certain number of hours as subjects (Ss) in experiments. They choose among the available experiments by signing their names on a sheet posted on the bulletin board which states the nature of the experiment. The present experiment was listed as a two-hour experiment dealing with "Measures of Performance."

During the first week of the course, when the requirement of serving in experiments was announced and explained to the students, the instructor also told them about a study that the psychology department was conducting. He explained that, since they were required to serve in experiments, the department was conducting a study to evaluate these experiments in order to be able to improve them in the future. They were told that a sample of students would be interviewed after having served as *S*s. They were urged to cooperate in these interviews by being completely frank and honest. The importance of this announcement will become clear shortly. It enabled us to measure the opinions of our *S*s in a context not directly connected with our experiment and in which we could reasonably expect frank and honest expressions of opinion.

When the *S* arrived for the experiment on "Measures of Performance" he had to wait for a few minutes in the secretary's office. The experimenter (*E*) then came in, introduced himself to the *S* and, together, they walked into the laboratory room where the *E* said:

> This experiment usually takes a little over an hour but, of course, we had to schedule it for two hours. Since we have that extra time, the introductory psychology people asked if they could interview some of our subjects. [Offhand and conversationally.] Did they announce that in class? I gather that they're interviewing some people who have been in experiments. I don't know much about it. Anyhow, they may want to interview you when you're through here.

With no further introduction or explanation the *S* was shown the first task, which involved putting 12 spools onto a tray, emptying the tray, refilling it with spools, and so on. He was told to use one hand and to work at his own speed. He did this for one-half hour. The *E* then removed the tray and spools and placed in front of the *S* a board containing 48 square pegs. His task was to turn each peg a quarter turn clockwise, then another quarter turn, and so on. He was told again to use one hand and to work at his own speed. The *S* worked at this task for another half hour.

While the *S* was working on these tasks, the *E* sat, with a stop watch in his hand, busily making notations on a sheet of paper. He did so in order to make it convincing that this was what the *E* was interested in and that these tasks, and how the *S* worked on them, was the total experiment. From our point of view the experiment had hardly started. The hour which the *S* spent working on the repetitive, monotonous tasks was intended to provide, for each *S* uniformly, an experience about which he would have a somewhat negative opinion.

After the half hour on the second task was over, the *E* conspicuously set the stop watch back to zero, put it away, and said:

> O.K. Well, that's all we have in the experiment itself. I'd like to explain what this has been all about so you'll have some idea of why you were doing this. [*E* pauses.] Well, the way the experiment is set up is this. There are actually two groups in the experiment. In one, the group you were in, we bring the subject in and give him essentially no introduction to the experiment. That is, all we tell him is what he needs to know in order to do the tasks, and he has no idea of what the experiment is all about, or what it's going to be like, or anything like that. But in the other group, we have a student that we've hired that works for us regularly, and what I do is take him into the next room where the subject is waiting—the same room you were waiting in before—and I introduce him as if he had just finished being a subject in the experiment. That is, I say: "This is so-and-so, who's just finished the experiment, and I've asked him to tell you a little of what it's about before you start." The fellow who works for us then, in conversation with the next subject, makes these points: [The *E* then produced a sheet headed "For Group B" which had written on

it: It was very enjoyable, I had a lot of fun, I enjoyed myself, it was very interesting, it was intriguing, it was exciting. The *E* showed this to the *S* and then proceeded with his false explanation of the purpose of the experiment.] Now, of course, we have this student do this, because if the experimenter does it, it doesn't look as realistic, and what we're interested in doing is comparing how these two groups do on the experiment—the one with this previous expectation about the experiment, and the other, like yourself, with essentially none.

Up to this point the procedure was identical for *S*s in all conditions. From this point on they diverged somewhat. Three conditions were run, Control, One Dollar, and Twenty Dollars, as follows:

Control Condition

The *E* continued:

Is that fairly clear? [Pause.] Look, that fellow [looks at watch] I was telling you about from the introductory psychology class said he would get here a couple of minutes from now. Would you mind waiting to see if he wants to talk to you? Fine. Why don't we go into the other room to wait? [The *E* left the *S* in the secretary's office for four minutes. He then returned and said:] O.K. Let's check and see if he does want to talk to you.

One and Twenty Dollar Conditions

The *E* continued:

Is that fairly clear how it is set up and what we're trying to do? [Pause.] Now, I also have a sort of strange thing to ask you. The thing is this. [Long pause, some confusion and uncertainty in the following, with a degree of embarrassment on the part of the *E*. The manner of the *E* contrasted strongly with the preceding unhesitant and assured false explanation of the experiment. The point was to make it seem to the *S* that this was the first time the *E* had done this and that he felt unsure of himself.] The fellow who normally does this for us couldn't do it today—he just phoned in, and something or other came up for him—so we've been looking around for someone that we could hire to do it for us. You see, we've got another subject waiting [looks at watch] who is supposed to be in that other condition. Now Professor _____, who is in charge of this experiment, suggested that perhaps we could take a chance on your doing it for us. I'll tell you what we had in mind: the thing is, if you could do it for us now, then of course you would know how to do it, and if something like this should ever come up again, that is, the regular fellow couldn't make it, and we had a subject scheduled, it would be very reassuring to us to know that we had somebody else we could call on who knew how to do it. So, if you would be willing to do this for us, we'd like to hire you to do it now and then be on call in the future, if something like this should ever happen again. We can pay you a dollar (twenty dollars) for doing this for us, that is, for doing it now and then being on call. Do you think you could do that for us?

If the *S* hesitated, the *E* said things like, "It will only take a few minutes," "The regular person is pretty reliable; this is the first time he has missed," or "If we needed you we could phone you a day or two in advance; if you couldn't make it, of course, we wouldn't expect you to come." After the *S* agreed to do it, the *E* gave him the previously mentioned sheet of paper headed "For Group B" and asked him to read it through again. The *E* then paid the *S* one dollar (twenty dollars), made out a hand-written receipt form, and asked the *S* to sign it. He then said:

> O.K., the way we'll do it is this. As I said, the next subject should be here by now. I think the next one is a girl. I'll take you into the next room and introduce you to her, saying that you've just finished the experiment and that we've asked you to tell her a little about it. And what we want you to do is just sit down and get into a conversation with her and try to get across the points on that sheet of paper. I'll leave you alone and come back after a couple of minutes. O.K.?

The *E* then took the *S* into the secretary's office where he had previously waited and where the next *S* was waiting. (The secretary had left the office.) He introduced the girl and the *S* to one another saying that the *S* had just finished the experiment and would tell her something about it. He then left saying he would return in a couple of minutes. The girl, an undergraduate hired for this role, said little until the *S* made some positive remarks about the experiment and then said that she was surprised because a friend of hers had taken the experiment the week before and had told her that it was boring and that she ought to try to get out of it. Most *S*s responded by saying something like "Oh, no, it's really very interesting. I'm sure you'll enjoy it." The girl after this listened quietly, accepting and agreeing to everything the *S* told her. The discussion between the *S* and the girl was recorded on a hidden tape recorded.

After two minutes the *E* returned, asked the girl to go into the experimental room, thanked the *S* for talking to the girl, wrote down his phone number to continue the fiction that we might call on him again in the future and then said: "Look, could we check and see if that fellow from introductory psychology wants to talk to you?"

From this point on, the procedure for all three conditions was once more identical. As the *E* and the *S* started to walk to the office where the interviewer was, the *E* said: "Thanks very much for working on those tasks for us. I hope you did enjoy it. Most of our subjects tell us afterward that they found it quite interesting. You get a chance to see how you react to the tasks and so forth." This short persuasive communication was made in all conditions in exactly the same way. The reason for doing it, theoretically, was to make it easier for anyone who wanted to persuade himself that the tasks had been, indeed, enjoyable.

When they arrived at the interviewer's office, the *E* asked the interviewer whether or not he wanted to talk to the *S*. The interviewer said yes, the *E* shook hands with the *S*, said good-bye, and left. The interviewer, of course, was always kept in complete ignorance of which condition the *S* was in. The interview consisted of four questions, one each of which the *S* was first encouraged to talk about the matter and was then asked to rate his opinion on reaction on an 11-point scale. The questions are as follows:

> 1. Were the tasks interesting and enjoyable? In what way? In what way were they not? Would you rate how you feel about them on a scale from −5 to +5 where −5 means they were extremely dull and boring, +5 means they were extremely interest-

ing and enjoyable, and zero means they were neutral, neither interesting nor uninteresting.

2. Did the experiment give you an opportunity to learn about your own ability to perform these tasks? In what way? In what way not? Would you rate how you feel about this on a scale from 0 to 10 where 0 means you learned nothing and 10 means you learned a great deal.

3. From what you know about the experiment and the tasks involved in it, would you say the experiment was measuring anything important? That is, do you think the results may have scientific value? In what way? In what way not? Would you rate your opinion on this matter on a scale from 0 to 10 where 0 means the results have no scientific value or importance and 10 means they have a great deal of value and importance.

4. Would you have any desire to participate in another similar experiment? Why? Why not? Would you rate your desire to participate in a similar experiment again on a scale from −5 to +5, where −5 means you would definitely dislike to participate, +5 means you would definitely like to participate, and 0 means you have no particular feeling about it one way or the other.

As may be seen, the questions varied in how directly relevant they were to what the S had told the girl. This point will be discussed further in connection with the results.

At the close of the interview the S was asked what he thought the experiment was about and, following this, was asked directly whether or not he was suspicious of anything and, if so, what he was suspicious of. When the interview was over, the interviewer brought the S back to the experimental room where the E was waiting together with the girl who had posed as the waiting S. (In the control condition, of course, the girl was not there.) The true purpose of the experiment was then explained to the S in detail, and the reasons for each of the various steps in the experiment were explained carefully in relation to the true purpose. All experimental Ss in both One Dollar and Twenty Dollar conditions were asked, after this explanation, to return the money they had been given. All Ss, without exception, were quite willing to return the money.

The data from 11 of the 71 Ss in the experiment had to be discarded for the following reasons:

1. Five Ss (three in the One Dollar and two in the Twenty Dollar condition) indicated in the interview that they were suspicious about having been paid to tell the girl the experiment was fun and suspected that that was the real purpose of the experiment.

2. Two Ss (both in the One Dollar condition) told the girl that they had been hired, that the experiment was really boring but they were supposed to say it was fun.

3. Three Ss (one in the One Dollar and two in the Twenty Dollar condition) refused to take the money and refused to be hired.

4. One S (in the One Dollar condition), immediately after having talked to the girl, demanded her phone number saying he would call her and explain things, and also told the D he wanted to wait until she was finished so he could tell her about it.

These 11 Ss were, of course, run through the total experiment anyhow and the experiment was explained to them afterwards. Their data, however, are not included in the analysis.

Summary of Design

There remain, for analysis, 20 Ss in each of the three conditions. Let us review these briefly: 1. *Control condition.* These Ss were treated identically in all respects to the Ss in the experimental conditions, except that they were never asked to, and never did, tell the waiting girl that the experimental tasks were enjoyable and lots of fun. 2. *One Dollar condition.* These Ss were hired for one dollar to tell a waiting S their tasks, which were really rather dull and boring, were interesting, enjoyable, and lots of fun. 3. *Twenty Dollar condition.* These Ss were hired for twenty dollars to do the same thing.

RESULTS

The major results of the experiment are summarized in Table 4.1 which lists, separately for each of the three experimental conditions, the average rating which the Ss gave at the end of each question on the interview. We will discuss each of the questions on the interview separately, because they were intended to measure different things. One other point before we proceed to examine the data. In all the comparisons, the Control condition should be regarded as a baseline from which to evaluate the results in the other two conditions. The Control condition gives us, essentially, the reactions of Ss to the tasks and their opinions about the experiment as falsely explained to them, without the experimental introduction of dissonance. The data from the other conditions may be viewed, in a sense, as changes from this baseline.

How Enjoyable the Tasks Were

The average ratings on this question, presented in the first row of figures in Table 4.2, are the results most important to the experiment. These results are the ones most directly relevant to the specific dissonance which was experimentally created. It will be recalled that the tasks were purposely arranged to be rather boring and monotonous. And, indeed, in the Control condition the average rating was −.45, somewhat on the negative side of the neutral point.

In the other two conditions, however, the S told someone that these tasks were

TABLE 4.1 Average Ratings on Interview Questions for Each Condition

	Experimental Condition		
Question on Interview	Control (N = 20)	One Dollar (N = 20)	Twenty Dollars (N = 20)
How enjoyable tasks were (rated from −5 to +5)	−.45	+1.35	−.05
How much they learned (rated from 0 to 10)	3.08	2.80	3.15
Participate in similar exp. (rated from −5 to +5)	−.62	+1.20	−.25

interesting and enjoyable. The resulting dissonance could, of course, most directly be reduced by persuading themselves that the tasks were, indeed, interesting and enjoyable. In the One Dollar condition, since the magnitude of dissonance was high, the pressure to reduce this dissonance would also be high. In this condition, the average rating was +1.35, considerably on the positive side and significantly different from the Control condition.

In the Twenty Dollar condition, where less dissonance was created experimentally because of the greater importance of the consonant relations, there is correspondingly less evidence of dissonance reduction. The average rating in this condition is only −.05, slightly and not significantly higher than the Control condition. In short, when an S was induced, by offer of reward, to say something contrary to his private opinion, this private opinion tended to change so as to correspond more closely with what he had said. The greater the reward offered (beyond what was necessary to elicit the behavior) the smaller was the effect.

Desire to Participate in a Similar Experiment

The results from this question are shown in the last row of Table 4.2. This question is less directly related to the dissonance that was experimentally created for the Ss. Certainly, the more interesting and enjoyable they felt the tasks were, the greater would be their desire to participate in a similar experiment. But other factors would enter also. Hence, one would expect the results on this question to be very similar to the results on "how enjoyable the tasks were" but weaker. Actually, the result, as may be seen in the table, are in exactly the same direction, and the magnitude of the mean differences is fully as large as on the first question. The variability is greater, however, and the differences do not yield high levels of statistical significance.

How Much They Learned From the Experiment

The results on this question are shown in the second row of figures in Table 4.2. The question was included because it, as far as we could see, had nothing to do with the dissonance, was experimentally created, and could not be used for dissonance reduction. One would expect no differences at all among the conditions. We felt it was important to see that the effect was not a completely general one but was specific to the content of the dissonance which was created. As can be readily seen in Table 4.2, there are only negligible differences among conditions. The highest t value of any of these differences is only 0.48.

SUMMARY

Recently, Festinger (1957) has proposed a theory concerning cognitive dissonance. Two derivations from this theory are tested here. They are:

1. If a person is induced to do or say something which is contrary to his private opinion, there will be a tendency for him to change his opinion so as to bring it into correspondence with what he has done or said.

2. The stronger the pressure used to elicit the overt behavior (beyond the minimum needed to elicit it) the weaker will be the above-mentioned tendency.

A laboratory experiment was designed to test these derivations. Subjects were subjected to a boring experience and then paid to tell someone that the experience had been interesting and enjoyable. The amount of money paid the subject was varied. The private opinions of the subjects concerning the experiences were then determined.

The results strongly corroborate the theory that was tested.

References

Festinger, L. *A theory of cognitive dissonance.* Evanston, IL: Row Peterson, 1957.

Janis, I. L., & King, B. T. The influence of role-playing on opinion change. *J. Abnorm. Soc. Psychol.,* 1954, 49, 211–218.

Kelman, H. Attitude change as a function of response restriction. *Hum. Relat.,* 1953, 6, 185–214.

King, B. T., & Janis, I. L. Comparison of the effectiveness of improvised versus non-improvised role-playing in producing opinion changes. *Hum. Relat.,* 1956, 9, 177–186.

Richard E. Petty
John T. Cacioppo
David Schumann

Central and Peripheral Routes to Advertising Effectiveness: The Moderating Role of Involvement

This article is one of many discussing and testing the Elaborate Likelihood Model that was discussed in the conversation with Richard Petty. In this research, those students who heard that the product they were reading about would be test marketed in their city (high involvement) were most affected by the quality of the arguments offered. However, those who were low in involvement were more affected by the prominence of the endorser (a sports celebrity vs. an average citizen). These findings lend support for the existence of two routes of persuasion—central and peripheral.

Over the past three decades, a large number of studies have examined how consumers' evaluations of issues, candidates, and products are affected by media advertisements. Research on the methods by which consumers' attitudes are formed and changed has accelerated at a pace such that Kassarjian and Kassarjian were led to the conclusion that "attitudes clearly have become the central focus of consumer behavior research" (1979, p. 3). Not only are there a large number of empirical studies on consumer attitude formation and change, but there are also a large number of different theories of persuasion vying for the attention of the discipline (see Engle and Blackwell 1982; Kassarjian 1982).

In our recent reviews of the many approaches to attitude change employed in social and consumer psychology, we have suggested that—even though the different theories of persuasion possess different terminologies, postulates, underlying motives, and particular "effects" that they specialize in explaining—these theories emphasize one of two distinct routes to attitude change (Petty and Cacioppo 1981, 1983). One, called the *central route,* views attitude change as resulting from a person's diligent consideration of information that s/he feels is central to the true merits of a particular attitudinal position. Attitude changes induced via the central route are postulated to be relatively enduring and predictive of behavior (Cialdini, Petty, and Cacioppo 1981; Petty and Cacioppo 1980).

A second group of theoretical approaches to persuasion emphasizes a more *peripheral route* to attitude change. Attitude changes that occur via the peripheral route do not occur because an individual has personally considered the pros and cons of the issue, but because the attitude issue or object is associated with positive or negative cues—or because the person makes a simple inference about the merits of the advocated position based on various simple cues in the persuasion context. For example, rather than diligently considering the issue-relevant arguments, a person may accept an advocacy simply because it was presented during a pleasant lunch or because the source is an expert. Similarly, a person may reject an advocacy simply because the position presented appears to be too extreme. These cues (e.g., good food, expert sources, extreme positions) and inferences (e.g., "If an expert says it, it must be true") may shape attitudes or allow a person to decide what attitudinal position to adopt without the need for engaging in any extensive thought about issue- or product-relevant arguments.

The accumulated research on persuasion clearly indicates that neither the central nor the peripheral approach alone can account for the diversity of attitude-change results observed. Thus, a general framework for understanding attitude change must consider that in some situations people are avid seekers and manipulators of information, and in others they are best described as "cognitive misers" who eschew any difficult intellectual activity (Burnkrant 1976; McGuire 1969). An important question for consumer researchers then is: when will consumers actively seek and process product-relevant information, and when will they be more cursory in their analysis of ads? Recent research in consumer behavior and social psychology has focused on the concept of "involvement" as an important moderator of the amount and type of information processing elicited by a persuasive communication (see Burnkrant and Sawyer 1983; Petty and Cacioppo 1981, 1983). One major goal of the experiment reported in this paper was to test the hypothesis that under "high involvement," attitudes in response to an advertisement would be affected via the central route, but that under "low involvement," attitudes would be affected via the peripheral route.

INVOLVEMENT AND ATTITUDE CHANGE

Methods of Studying Involvement

Although there are many specific definitions of involvement within both social and consumer psychology, there is considerable agreement that high involvement messages have greater personal relevance and consequences or elicit more personal connections than low involvement messages (Engel and Blackwell 1982; Krugman 1965; Petty and Cacioppo 1979; Sherif and Hovland 1961). Various strategies have been employed in studying involvement.

A preferred procedure for studying involvement would be to hold recipient, message, and medium characteristics constant and randomly assign participants to high and low involvement groups. Apsler and Sears (1968) employed an ingenious method to manipulate involvement: some participants were led to believe that a persuasive proposal had personal implications for them (an advocated change in university regulations would take effect while the student participants were still in school), while others were led to believe that it did not (i.e., the change would not take effect until the students had graduated). A variation of this procedure was developed by Wright (1973, 1974) to manipulate involvement in an advertising study. Participants in the high involvement group were told that they would subsequently be asked to evaluate the product in an advertisement they were about to see, and were given some additional background information. Participants in the low involvement group did not expect to evaluate the product and were given no background information. The background information provided to the high involvement subjects explained the relevance of their product decisions to "their families, their own time and effort, and their personal finances" (Wright 1973, p. 56). However, it is somewhat unclear to what extent this background information made certain product-relevant arguments salient or suggested appropriate dimensions of product evaluation for high but not low involvement subjects.

In the present experiment, participants in both the high and low involvement groups were told that they would be evaluating advertisements for products, but subjects in the high involvement group were led to believe that the experimental advertised product would soon be available in their local area, and that after viewing a variety of advertisements they would be allowed to choose one brand from the experimental product category to take home as a gift. Low involvement participants were led to believe that the experimental advertised product would not be available in their local area in the near future, and that after viewing the ads they would be allowed to take home one brand from a category of products other than the experimental category.

Theories of Involvement

In addition to the methodological differences that have plagued the involvement concept, another area of disagreement concerns the effects on persuasion that involvement is expected to have. Perhaps the dominant notion in social psychology stems from the Sherifs' social judgment theory (Sherif et al. 1965). Their notion is that on any given issue, highly involved persons exhibit more negative evaluations of a communication because high involvement is associated with an extended "latitude of rejection." Thus, incoming messages on involving topics are thought to have an enhanced probability of being rejected because they are more likely to fall within the unacceptable range of a person's implicit attitude continuum. Krugman (1965) has proposed an alternative view that has achieved considerable recognition among consumer researchers. According to this view, increasing involvement does not increase resistance to persuasion, but instead shifts the sequence of communication impact. Krugman argues that under high involvement, a communication is likely to affect cognitions, then attitudes, and then behaviors, whereas under low involvement, a communication is more likely to affect cognitions, then behaviors, then attitudes (see also Ray et al. 1973).

As noted earlier, a focal goal of this study is to assess the viability of a third view of the effects of involvement on consumer response to advertisements. This view stems from our Elaboration Likelihood Model (ELM) of attitude change (Petty and Cacioppo 1981). The basic tenet of the ELM is that different methods of inducing persuasion may work best depending on whether the elaboration likelihood of the communication situation (i.e., the probability of message- or issue-relevant thought occurring) is high or low. When the elaboration likelihood is high, the central route to persuasion should be particularly effective, but when the elaboration likelihood is low, the peripheral route should be better. The ELM contends that as an issue or product increases in personal relevance or consequences, it becomes more important and adaptive to forming a reasoned and veridical opinion. Thus, people are more motivated to devote the cognitive effort required to evaluate the true merits of an issue or product when involvement is high rather than low. If increased involvement increases one's propensity to think about the true merits of an issue or product, then manipulations that require extensive issue- or product-relevant thought in order to be effective should have a greater impact under high rather than low involvement conditions. On the other hand, manipulations that allow a person to evaluate an issue or product without engaging in extensive issue- or product-relevant thinking should have a greater impact under low rather than high involvement.

Research in social psychology has supported the view that different variables affect persuasion under high and low involvement conditions. For example, the quality of the arguments contained in a message has had a greater impact on persuasion under conditions of high rather than low involvement (Petty and Cacioppo 1979; Petty, Cacioppo, and Heesacker 1981). On the other hand, peripheral cues such as the expertise or attractiveness of a message source (Chaiken 1980; Petty, Cacioppo, and Goldman 1981; Rhine and Severance 1970) have had a greater impact on persuasion under conditions of low rather than high involvement. In sum, under high involvement conditions people appear to exert the cognitive effort required to evaluate the issue-relevant arguments presented, and their attitudes are a function of this information-processing activity (central route). Under low involvement conditions, attitudes appear to be affected by simple acceptance and rejection cues in the persuasion context and are less affected by argument quality (peripheral route). Although the accumulated research in social psychology is quite consistent with the ELM, it is not yet clear whether or not the ELM predictions would hold when involvement concerns a product (such as toothpaste) rather than an issue (such as capital punishment), and when the persuasive message is an advertisement rather than a speech or editorial.

CENTRAL AND PERIPHERAL ROUTES TO ADVERTISING EFFECTIVENESS

One important implication of the ELM for advertising messages is that different kinds of appeals may be most effective for different audiences. For example, a person who is about to purchase a new refrigerator (high involvement) may scrutinize the product-relevant information presented in an advertisement. If this information is perceived to be cogent and persuasive, favorable attitudes will result, but if this information is weak and specious, unfavorable attitudes will result (central route). On the other hand, a person who is not considering purchasing a new refrigerator at the moment (low involvement) will not expend the effort required to think about the product-relevant arguments in the ad, but may instead focus on the attractiveness, credibility, or prestige of the product's endorser (peripheral route). Some evidence in consumer psychology is consistent with this reasoning. For example, Wright (1973, 1974) exposed people to an advertisement for a soybean product under high and low involvement conditions (see earlier description) and measured the number of source comments (derogations) and message comments (counterarguments) generated after exposure. Although Wright (1974) predicted that involvement would increase both kinds of comments, he found that more message comments were made under high rather than low involvement, but that more source comments were made under low involvement conditions. This finding, of course, is consistent with the ELM.

In an initial attempt to provide a specific test of the utility of the ELM for understanding the effectiveness of advertising messages (Petty and Cacioppo 1980), we conducted a study in which three variables were manipulated: (1) the personal relevance of a shampoo ad (high involvement subjects were led to believe that the product would be available in their local area, whereas low involvement subjects were not); (2) the quality of the arguments contained in the ad; and (3) the physical attractiveness of the endorsers of the shampoo. Consistent with the ELM predictions, the quality of the arguments contained in the advertisement had a greater impact on attitudes when the product was of high rather than low relevance. Contrary to expectations, however, the attractiveness of the endorsers was equally important under both the high and low involvement conditions. In retrospect, in addition to serving as a peripheral cue under low involvement, the physical appearance of the product endorsers (especially their hair) may have served as persuasive visual testimony for the product's effectiveness. Thus, under high involvement conditions, the physical attractiveness of the endorsers may have served as a cogent product-relevant argument.

The present study was a conceptual replication of previous work (Petty and Cacioppo 1980), except that we employed a peripheral cue that could not be construed as a product-relevant argument. In the current study, participants were randomly assigned to high and low involvement conditions and viewed one of four different ads for a fictitious new product, "Edge disposable razors." The ad was presented in magazine format and was embedded in an advertising booklet along with 11 other ads. Two features of the Edge ad were manipulated: the quality of the arguments in support of Edge (strong or weak), and the celebrity status of the featured endorsers of Edge (celebrity or average citizen). It is important to note that preliminary testing revealed that for most people, the celebrity status of the endorsers was irrelevant to an evaluation of the true merits of a disposable razor, but that because the celebrity endorsers were liked more than the average citizens, they could still serve as a positive peripheral cue.

We had two major hypotheses. First, we expected the quality of the arguments presented in the ad to have a greater impact on product attitudes under high rather than low involvement conditions. Second, we expect the celebrity status of the product endorsers to have a greater impact on product attitudes under low rather than high involvement conditions. If these hypotheses were supported, it would provide the first evidence to understanding the effects of involvement on attitudinal responses to advertisements.

METHOD

Subjects and Design

A total of 160 male and female undergraduates at the University of Missouri–Columbia participated in the experiment to earn credit in an introductory psychology course; 20 subjects were randomly assigned to each of the cells in a 2 (involvement: high or low) × 2 (argument quality: strong or weak) × 2 (cue: celebrity or noncelebrity status) factorial design. Subjects participated in groups of three to 15 in a very large classroom. The subjects were isolated from each other so that they could complete the experiment independently, and subjects in a single session participated in different experimental conditions.

Procedure

Two booklets were prepared for the study. The first contained the advertising stimuli and the second contained the dependent measures. The first page of the advertising booklet explained that the study concerned the evaluation of magazine and newspaper ads and that the psychology department was cooperating with the journalism school in this endeavor. The first page also contained part of the involvement manipulation (see below). It was explained that each ad in the booklet was preceded by an introductory statement that told a little about the advertisement that followed (e.g., "The _____ company of Paris, France has just opened an American office in New York City. This élite men's clothing company originally sold clothing only in Europe, but is now in the process of attempting to enter the American market. The ad on the next page is one that they will be testing soon in Tampa, Florida before running the ads in other major cities that will eventually carry their products"). The instructions told subjects to continue through the booklet at their own pace and to raise their hands when finished. The ad booklet contained 10 real magazine ads for both relatively familiar (e.g., Aquafresh toothpaste) and unfamiliar (e.g., Riopan antacid) products, and two bogus ads. The sixth ad in each booklet was the crucial fictitious ad for Edge razors (the nature of the other bogus ad was varied but is irrelevant to the present study). When subjects had completed perusing their ad booklets, they were given a questionnaire booklet to complete. Upon completion of the questionnaire, the subjects were thoroughly debriefed, thanked for their participation, and dismissed.

Independent Variables

Involvement. Involvement was embedded in two places in the ad booklet. First, the cover page offered subjects a free gift for participation in the experiment. Subjects were either informed that they would be allowed to choose a particular brand of disposable razor (high involvement with the fictitious Edge ad) or that they would be allowed to choose a brand of toothpaste (low involvement with Edge). A toothpaste ad did appear in the ad booklet, but it was the same ad for all subjects. To bolster the involvement manipulation, the page that introduced the Edge ad also differed in the high and low involvement conditions. High involvement subjects were told that the advertisement and product would soon be test-marketed in medium-sized cities throughout the Midwest, including their own city (Columbia, Missouri); low involvement subjects were told that the advertisement and product were being test-marketed only on the East Coast. Thus high involvement subjects were not only led to believe that they would soon have to make a decision about the product class, they were also led to believe that the product would be available in their area in the near future. Low involvement subjects, on the other hand, did not expect to make a decision about razors (but did expect to make one about toothpaste), and were led to believe that Edge razors would not be available for purchase in their area in the foreseeable future.

Argument quality. A variety of arguments for disposable razors were pretested for potency on a sample of undergraduates. In the *strong arguments* ad, the razor was characterized as "scientifically designed," and the following five statements were made about the product:

- New advanced honing method creates unsurpassed sharpness
- Special chemically formulated coating eliminates nicks and cuts and prevents rusting
- Handle is tapered and ribbed to prevent slipping
- In direct comparison tests, the Edge blade gave twice as many close shaves as its nearest competitor
- Unique angle placement of the blade provides the smoothest shave possible

In the *weak arguments* version of the ad, the razor was characterized as "designed for beauty," and the following five statements were made about the product:

- Floats in water with a minimum of rust
- Comes in various sizes, shapes, and colors
- Designed with the bathroom in mind
- In direct comparison tests, the Edge blade gave no more nicks or cuts than its competition
- Can only be used once but will be memorable

Peripheral cue. In the "famous endorser" conditions, the headline accompanying the advertisement read "Professional Athletes Agree: Until you try new Edge disposable razors you'll never know what a really close shave is." In addition, the ad featured the pictures of two well-known, well-liked golf (male) and tennis (female) celebrities. In the "nonfamous endorser" conditions, the headline read "Bakersfield, California Agrees: _____," and the ad featured pictures of average looking people who were unfamiliar to the subjects. The average citizens in the ad were middle-aged and characterized as coming from California to minimize perceptions of similarity to the subjects (Missouri college students). Figure 4.1 depicts two of the four Edge ads used in the present study.

Dependent Measures

On the first page of the dependent variable booklet, subjects were asked to try to list all of the product categories for which they had seen advertisements, and to try to re-call the brand name of the product in that category. On the next page, subjects were given descriptions of the 12 product categories and were asked to select the correct brand name from among seven choices provided. Although we had no specific hy-potheses about brand recall and recognition, these measures were included because of their practical importance and for purposes of comparison with the attitude data.

Next, subjects responded to some questions about one of the legitimate ads in the booklet; this was followed by the crucial questions about Edge razors. The questions about Edge were placed relatively early in the booklet to avoid subject fatigue and boredom and to maximize the effectiveness of the manipulations. Subjects were first asked to rate, on a four-point scale, how likely it would be that they would purchase Edge disposable razors "the next time you needed a product of this nature." The de-scription for each scale value were: 1 = "I definitely would not buy it," 2 = "I might or might not buy it," 3 = "I would probably buy it," and 4 = "I would definitely buy it." Following this measure of purchase intentions, subjects were asked to rate their overall impression of the product on three nine-point semantic differential scales an-chored at −4 and +4 (bad–good, satisfactory–unsatisfactory, and unfavorable–favor-able). Since the intercorrelations among these measures were very high, responses were averaged to assess a general positive or negative attitude toward the product.

Several questions were asked in order to check on the experimental manipula-tions, and subjects were asked to try to list as many of the attributes mentioned in the ad about Edge razors as they could recall. Following the questions about Edge were several questions about some of the other products and ads in the booklet. As a check on the involvement manipulation, the very last questions in the booklet asked subjects to recall the free gift they had been told to expect.

RESULTS

Manipulation Checks

In response to the last question in the dependent variable booklet asking subjects what gift they had been told to expect, 92.5 percent of the subjects in the high involvement conditions correctly recalled that they were to select a brand of disposable razor. In the low involvement conditions, none of the subjects indicated

PROFESSIONAL ATHLETES AGREE

Until you try new EDGE disposable razors you'll never know what a "really close shave" is.

- **Scientifically Designed**
- New advanced honing method creates unsurpassed sharpness
- Special chemically formulated coating eliminates nicks and cuts and prevents rusting
- Handle is tapered and ribbed to prevent slipping
- In direct comparison tests the EDGE blade gave twice as many close shaves as its nearest competitor
- Unique angle placement of the blade provides the smoothest shave possible

GET THE EDGE DIFFERENCE!

Note: Panel above shows celebrity endorser ad for Edge razors employing the strong arguments. Panel below shows average citizen endorser ad for Edge razors employing the weak arguments. Pictures of celebrities and citizens have been blacked out to preserve propriety and anonymity.

BAKERSFIELD, CALIFORNIA AGREES

Until you try new EDGE disposable razors you'll never know what a "really close shave" is.

- **Designed for Beauty**
- Floats in water with a minimum of rust
- Comes in various sizes, shapes, and colors
- Designed with the bathroom in mind
- In direct comparison tests the EDGE blade gave no more nicks or cuts than its competition
- Can only be used once but will be memorable

FIGURE 4.1

Example
Mock Ads

GET THE EDGE DIFFERENCE!

a razor and 78 percent correctly recalled that they were to select a brand of toothpaste. Thus, subjects presumably realized what product they were soon to make a decision about as they examined the ad booklet.

To assess the effectiveness of the endorser manipulation, two questions were asked. First, subjects were asked if they recognized the people in the ad for the disposable razor. When the famous athletes were employed, 94 percent indicated "yes," whereas when the average citizens were employed, 96 percent indicated "no." In addition, subjects were asked to rate the extent to which they liked the people depicted in the ad on an 11-point scale, where 1 indicated "liked very little" and 11 indicated "liked very much." An analysis of this measure revealed that the famous endorsers were liked more ($M = 6.06$) than the average citizens ($M = 3.64$); on average, women reported liking the endorsers more ($M = 5.32$) than did men ($M = 4.44$).

As a check on the argument-persuasiveness manipulation, two questions were asked. The first required respondents to "rate the reasons as described in the advertisement for using EDGE" on an 11-point scale anchored by "unpersuasive" and "persuasive"; the second question asked them to rate the reasons on an 11-point scale anchored by "weak reasons" and "strong reasons." In short, all of the variables were manipulated successfully. The tendency for females to be more positive in their ratings of both endorsers and the arguments in the ads is generally consistent with previous psychological research portraying women as more concerned with social harmony than men (Eagly 1978). Importantly, these sex differences did not lead to any significant gender effects on the crucial measures of attitude and purchase intention.

Attitudes and Purchase Intentions

Table 4.2 presents the means and standard deviations for each cell on the attitude index. A number of interesting main effects emerged. First, involved subjects were somewhat more skeptical of the product ($M = 0.31$) than were less involved subjects ($M = 0.99$). Second, subjects liked the product significantly more when the ad contained cogent arguments ($M = 1.65$) than when the arguments were specious ($M = -0.35$). Third, subjects tended to like the product more when it was endorsed by the famous athletes ($M = 0.86$) than by the average citizens of Bakersfield, California ($M = 0.41$).

Each of these main effects must be qualified and interpreted. First, the nature of the product endorser had a significant impact on product attitudes only under low involvement but not under high involvement (see top panel of Figure 4.2). On the other hand, although argument quality had an impact on product attitudes under both low involvement and high involvement, the impact of argument quality on attitudes was significantly greater under high rather than low involvement (see bottom panel of Figure 4.2).

Two significant effects emerged from the question asking subjects to rate their likelihood of purchasing Edge disposable razors the next time they needed a product of this nature. Subjects said that they would be more likely to buy the product when the arguments presented were strong ($M = 2.23$) rather than weak ($M = 1.68$). Additionally, argument quality was a more important determinant of purchase intentions under high rather than low involvement.

TABLE 4.3 Means and Standard Deviations for Each Experimental Cell on the Attitude Index

| | Low involvement | | High involvement | |
	Weak arguments	Strong arguments	Weak arguments	Strong arguments
Citizen endorser	−.12	.98	−1.10	1.98
	(1.81)	(1.52)	(1.66)	(1.25)
Celebrity endorser	1.21	1.85	−1.36	1.80
	(2.28)	(1.59)	(1.65)	(1.07)

Note: Attitude scores represent the average rating of the product on three nine-point semantic differential scales anchored at −4 and +4 (bad–good, unsatisfactory–satisfactory, and unfavorable–favorable). Standard deviations are in parentheses.

The correlation between attitudes and purchase intentions for low involvement subjects was 0.36; and for high involvement subjects it was 0.59. Although both correlations were significantly different from zero, it is interesting to note that the low involvement correlation was considerably smaller than the high involvement correlation. The fact that the argument quality manipulation affected behavioral intentions while the endorser manipulation did not (although it did affect attitudes), and the fact that attitudes were better predictors of behavioral intentions under high rather than low involvement, provide some support for the ELM view that attitudes formed via the central route will be more predictive of behavior than attitudes formed via the peripheral route.

Recall and Recognition Measures

Subjects were asked to list all of the products for which they had seen ads and all of the brand names they had encountered. Following this, all subjects were told that they had seen an advertisement for a disposable razor and were asked to select the correct brand name from a list of seven (Gillette, Wilkinson, Schick, Edge, Bic, Schaffer, and Remington).

The involvement manipulation had a significant impact on free recall of the product category, with more high involvement subjects (81 percent) recalling the product category than low involvement subjects (64 percent). Additionally, exposure to the famous endorser increased recall of the product category under low involvement conditions (from 52 percent to 75 percent), but had no significant effect on product category recall under high involvement (80 versus 82 percent).

Involvement affected free recall of the brand name of the product, increasing it from 42 percent in the low involvement conditions to 60 percent in the high involvement conditions. There was also an effect for gender on this measure, with males showing greater brand name recall (61 percent) than females (39 percent). The endorser manipulation had a marginally significant effect on brand name recall (43 versus 58 percent).

On the measure of brand name recognition, an interaction pattern emerged.

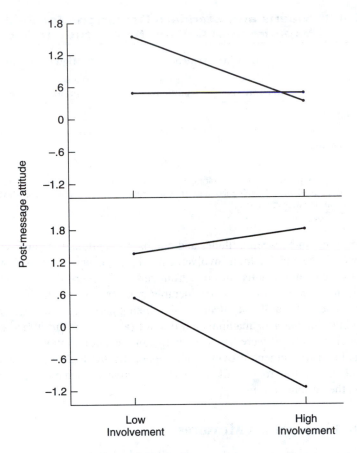

Note: Top panel shows interactive effect of involvement and endorser status on attitudes toward Edge razors. Bottom panel shows interactive effect of involvement and argument quality on attitudes toward Edge razors.

FIGURE 4.2

Product Attitudes

Under low involvement, the use of famous endorsers reduced brand name recognition from 85 to 70 percent, but under high involvement, the use of famous endorsers improved brand name recognition from 77 to 87 percent.

To summarize the recall and recognition data thus far, it appears that increasing involvement with the product enhanced recall not only of the product category, but also of the brand name of the specific product advertised. The effects of the endorser manipulation were more complex and depended on the level of involvement. In general, under low involvement a positive endorser led to increased recall of the product category but reduced brand name recognition. Thus, people may be more likely to notice the products in low involvement ads when they feature prominent personalities, but because of the enhanced attention accorded the people in the ads and the general lack of interest in assessing the merits of the product (due to low involvement), reductions in brand recognition may occur. This finding is similar to the results of studies on the use of sexually oriented material in ads for low involvement products—the sexual material enhances recognition of the ad, but not the brand name of the product (e.g., Chestnut, LaChance, and Lubitz 1977; Steadman 1969). Under high involvement, however, the use of prominent personalities enhanced brand name recognition. When people are more interested in the product category, they may be more motivated to assess what brand the liked personalities are endorsing. The manipulation of argument quality had no effect on recall of the product category, brand name recall, or brand name recognition.

A final recall measure assessed how many of the specific arguments for Edge razors the subjects could spontaneously recall after they had examined the entire ad booklet. Overall, subjects were able to correctly reproduce only 1.75 of the five arguments presented. This was not affected by any of the experimental manipulations.

Clearly, the manipulations produced a very different pattern of effects on the recall and recognition measures than on the attitude and purchase intention measures. In addition, the recall and recognition measures were uncorrelated with attitudes or intentions toward Edge razors. This finding is consistent with a growing body of research indicating that simple recall or recognition of information presented about an attitude object is not predictive of attitude formation and change (e.g., Cacioppo and Petty 1979; Greenwald 1968; Insko, Lind, and LaTour 1976).

The present data also argue against measures of brand name recall or recognition as the sole indicants of advertising effectiveness. For example, in the present study, enhancing involvement led to a significant improvement in brand name recall, but increasing involvement led to a decrement in attitude toward the brand when the arguments presented were weak.

DISCUSSION

As we noted earlier, previous research on attitude formation and change has tended to characterize the persuasion process as resulting either from a thoughtful (though not necessarily rational) consideration of issue-relevant arguments and product-relevant attributes (central route), or from associating the attitude object with various positive and negative cues and operating with simple decision rules (peripheral route). Over the past decade, investigators in both social psychology and consumer behavior have tended to emphasize the former process over the latter. Consider the comments of Fishbein and Ajzen (1981, p. 359):

> The general neglect of the information contained in a message . . . is probably the most serious problem in communication and persuasion research. We are convinced that the persuasiveness of a communication can be increased much more easily and dramatically by paying careful attention to its content . . . than by manipulation of credibility, attractiveness . . . or any of the other myriad factors that have caught the fancy of investigators in the area of communication and persuasion.

The present study suggests that, although the informational content of an advertisement may be the most important determinant of product attitudes under some circumstances, in other circumstances such noncontent manipulations as the celebrity status (likability) or credibility of the product endorsers may be even more important. Specifically, we have shown that when an advertisement concerned a product of low involvement, the celebrity status of the product endorsers was a very potent determinant of attitudes about the product. When the advertisement concerned a product of high involvement, however, the celebrity status of the product endorsers had no effect on attitudes, but the cogency of the information about the product contained in the ad was a powerful determinant of product evaluations. These data clearly suggest that it would be inappropriate for social and consumer researchers to overemphasize the influence of issue-relevant arguments or product-relevant attributes and ignore the role of peripheral cues. Each type of attitudinal influence occurs in some instances, and the level of personal involvement with an issue or product appears to be one determinant of which type of persuasion occurs.

According to the Elaboration Likelihood Model, personal relevance is thought to be only one determinant of the route to persuasion. Personal relevance is thought to increase a person's motivation for engaging in a diligent consideration of the issue- or product-relevant information presented in order to form a veridical opinion. Just as different situations may induce different motivations to think, different people may typically employ different styles of information processing, and some people will enjoy thinking more than others (Capioppo and Petty 1982, forthcoming). However, a diligent consideration of issue- or product-relevant information requires not only the motivation to think, but also the ability to process the information. Thus, situational variables (e.g., prior knowledge; Cacioppo and Petty 1980) may also be important moderators of the route to persuasion. In the present study, subjects' ability to think about the product was held at a high level across experimental conditions—that is, the messages were easy to understand, the presentation was self-paced, and so on. Thus, the primary determinant of the route to persuasion was motivational in nature.

It is important to note that although our "peripheral" manipulation was a source variable presented visually and our "central" manipulation was a message variable presented verbally, neither the source/message nor the visual/verbal dichotomy is isomorphic with the central/peripheral one. Thus, a source variable may induce persuasion via the central route, and a message variable may serve as a peripheral cue. For example, in one study described previously (Petty and Cacioppo 1980), we observed that a physically attractive message endorser might serve as a cogent product-relevant argument for a beauty product. In another study (Petty and Cacioppo, forthcoming), we found that the mere number of message arguments presented may activate a simple decision rule (the more the better) under low involvement, but not under high involvement, where argument quality is more important than number. Similarly, a "central" manipulation may be presented visually—e.g., depicting a kitten in an advertisement for facial tissue to convey the product-relevant attribute "softness" (Mitchell and Olson 1981)—and a "peripheral manipulation may be presented verbally—e.g., providing a verbal description of a message source as an expert or as likeable (Chaiken 1980; Petty, Cacioppo, and Goldman

1981). The critical feature of the central route to persuasion is that an attitude change is based on a diligent consideration of information that a person feels is central to the true merits of an issue or product. This information may be conveyed visually, verbally, or in source or message characteristics. In the peripheral route, attitudes change because of the presence of simple positive or negative cues, or because of the invocation of simple decision rules which obviate the need for thinking about issue-relevant arguments. Stimuli that serve as peripheral cues or that invoke simple decision rules may be presented visually or verbally, or may be part of source or message characteristics.

In sum, the present study has provided support for the view that different features of an advertisement may be more or less effective, depending upon a person's involvement with it. Under conditions of low involvement, peripheral cues are more important than issue-relevant argumentation, but under high involvement, the opposite is true. The realization that independent variables may have different effects, depending on the level of personal relevance of a message, may provide some insight into the conflicting pattern of results that is said to characterize much attitude research. It may well be that attitude effects can be arranged on a continuum, depending on the elaboration likelihood of the particular persuasion situation. This continuum would be anchored at one end by the peripheral route and at the other end by the central route to persuasion. Furthermore, these two routes may be characterized by quite different antecedents and consequences. If so, future work could be aimed at uncovering the various moderators of the route to persuasion and at tracking the various consequents of the two different routes.

References

Ajzen, Icek and Martin Fishbein (1980). *Understanding Attitudes and Predicting Social Behavior.* Englewood Cliffs, NJ: Prentice-Hall.

Apsler, Robert and David O. Sears (1968). Warning, Personal Involvement, and Attitude Change. *Journal of Personality and Social Psychology, 9* (June), 162–166.

Burnkrant, Robert E. (1976). A Motivational Model of Information Processing Intensity. *Journal of Consumer Research, 3* (June), 21–30.

Burnkrant, Robert E. and Alan G. Sawyer (1983). Effects of Involvement and Message Content on Information Processing Intensity, in *Information Processing Research in Advertising.* Richard Harris, ed. Hillsdale, NJ: Lawrence Erlbaum.

Cacioppo, John T. and Richard E. Petty (1979). Effects of Message Repetition and Position on Cognitive Responses, Recall, and Persuasion. *Journal of Personality and Social Psychology, 37* (January), 97–109.

Burnkrant, Robert E. and Richard E. Petty (1980). Sex Differences in Influenceability: Toward Specifying the Underlying Processes. *Personality and Social Psychology Bulletin, 6* (December), 651–656.

Burnkrant, Robert E. and Richard E. Petty (1982). The Need for Cognition. *Journal of personality and Social Psychology, 42* (January 116–131.

Burnkrant, Robert E. and Richard E. Petty (forthcoming). The Need for Cognition: Relationships to Social Influence and Self Influence, *Social Perception in Clinical Counseling Psychology.* Richard P. McGlynn, James E. Maddux, Cal D. Stoltenberg, and John H. Harvey, eds. Lubbock, TX: Texas Tech Press.

Chaiken, Shelly (1980). Heuristic Versus Systematic Information Processing and the Use of Source Versus Message Cues in Persuasion. *Journal of Personality and Social Psychology,* 39 (November), 752–766.

Chestnut, Robert W., Charles C. LaChance, and Amy Lubitz (1977). The Decorative Female Model: Sexual Stimuli and the Recognition of Advertisements. *Journal of Advertising Research,* 6, 11–14.

Cialdini, Robert B., Richard E. Petty, and John T. Caccioppo (1981). Attitude and Attitude Change. *Annual Review of Psychology,* 32, 357–404.

Eagly, Alice H. (1978). Sex Differences in Influenceability. *Psychological Bulletin,* 85 (January), 86–116.

Engel, James F. and Roger D. Blackwell (1982). *Consumer Behavior.* Hinsdale, IL: Dryden Press.

Fishbein, Martin and Icek Ajzen (1981). Acceptance, Yielding, and Impact: Cognitive Processes in Persuasion. *Cognitive Responses in Persuasion,* Richard E. Petty, Thomas Ostrom, and Timothy C. Brock, eds. Hillsdale, NJ: Lawrence Erlbaum, 339–359.

Greenwald, Anthony G. (1968). Cognitive Learning, Cognitive Response to Persuasion, and Attitude Change. *Psychological Foundations of Attitudes,* eds. Anthony G. Greenwald, Timothy C. Brock, and Thomas Ostrom, New York: Academic Press, 147–170.

Greenwald, Anthony G., Irving Janis, and Harold Kelley (1953). *Communication and Persuasion,* New Haven, CT: Yale University Press.

Insko, Chester A., E. Allen Lind, and Stephen LaTour (1976). Persuasion, Recall, and Thoughts. *Representative Research in Social Psychology,* 7, 66–78.

Kassarjian, Harold H. (1982). Consumer Psychology. *Annual Review of Psychology,* 33, 619–649.

Kassarjian, Harold H. and Waltraud M. Kassarjian (1979). Attitudes under Low Commitment Conditions. *Attitude Research Plays for High Stakes,* eds. John C. Maloney and Bernard Silverman, Chicago: American Marketing Association, 3–15.

Krugman, Herbert E. (1965). The Impact of Television Advertising: Learning without Involvement. *Public Opinion Quarterly,* 29 (Fall), 349–356.

Krugman, Herbert E. (1967). The Measurement of Advertising Involvement. *Public Opinion Quarterly,* 30 (Winter), 853–596.

McGuire, William J. (1969). The Nature of Attitudes and Attitude Change. *The Handbook of Social Psychology,* Vol. 3, Gardner Lindzey and Elliot Aronson, eds. Reading, MA: Addison-Wesley, 136–314.

Mitchell, Andrew A. and Jerry C. Olson (1981). Are Product Attribute Beliefs the Only Mediator of Advertising Effects on Brand Attitude? *Journal of Marketing Research,* 18 (August), 318–332.

Petty, Richard E. and John T. Caccioppo (1979). Issue Involvement Can Increase or Decrease Persuasion by Enhancing Message-Relevant Cognitive Responses. *Journal of Personality and Social Psychology,* 37 (October), 1915–1926.

Petty, Richard E. and John T. Caccioppo (1980). Effects of Issue Involvement on Attitudes in an Advertising Context. *Proceedings of the Division 23 Program,* Gerald G. Gorn and Marvin E. Goldberg, eds. Montreal, Canada: American Psychological Association, 75–79.

Petty, Richard E. and John T. Caccioppo (1981). *Attitudes and Persuasion: Classic and Contemporary Approaches,* Dubuque, IA: William C. Brown.

Petty, Richard E. and John T. Caccioppo (1983). Central and Peripheral Routes to Persuasion: Application to Advertising. *Advertising and Consumer Psychology,* Larry Percy and Arch Woodside, eds. Lexington, MA: Lexington Books, 3–23.

Petty, Richard E. and John T. Cacioppo (forthcoming). The effects of Involvement on Responses to Argument Quantity and Quality: Central and Peripheral Routes to Persuasion. *Journal of Personality and Social Psychology.*

Petty, Richard E., John T. Cacioppo, and Rachel Goldman (1981). Personal Involvement as a Determinant of Argument-Based persuasion. *Journal of Personality and Social Psychology,* 41 (November), 847–855.

Petty, Richard E., John T. Cacioppo, and Martin Heesacker (1981). The Use of Rhetorical Questions in Persuasion: A Cognitive Response Analysis. *Journal of Personality and Social Psychology,* 40 (March), 432–440.

Petty, Richard E., Gary L. Wells, and Timothy C. Brock (1976). Distraction Can Enhance or Reduce Yielding to Propaganda: Thought Disruption Versus Effort Justification. *Journal of Personality and Social Psychology,* 34 (November), 874–884.

Ray, Michael L., Alan G. Sawyer, Michael L. Rothschild, Roger M. Heeler, Edward C. Strong and Jerome B. Reed (1973). Marketing Communication and the Hierarchy of Effects. *New Models for Mass Communication Research,* Vol. 2, Peter Clarke, ed. Beverly Hills, CA: Sage Publications, 147–176.

Rhine, Ramon, and Laurence J. Severance (1970). Ego-Involvement, Discrepancy, Source Credibility, and Attitude Change. *Journal of Personality and Social Psychology,* 16 (October), 175–190.

Sherif, Muzifer and Carl I. Hovland (1961). *Social Judgment,* New Haven: Yale University Press.

Sherif, Carolyn W., Muzifer Sherif, and Roger E. Nebersall (1965). *Attitude and Attitude Change,* Philadelphia: Saunders.

Steadman, Major (1969). How Sexy Illustrations Affect Brand Recall. *Journal of Advertising Research,* 9 (1), 15–19.

Wright, Peter L. (1973). The Cognitive Processes Mediating Acceptance of Advertising. *Journal of Marketing Research,* 10 (February), 53–62.

Wright, Peter L. (1974). Analyzing Media Effects on Advertising Responses. *Public Opinion Quarterly,* 38 (Summer), 192–205.

Anthony Pratkanis
Elliot Aronson

The Fear Appeal

This selection asks an important and basic question about attitude change: Do fear tactics work? Reviewing the literature in this area, the authors tell us that the answer is "it depends"—on the nature of the audience and what the message contains. In particular, they point out that in order to bring positive results, a fear campaign must offer specific recommendations that are perceived as both effective and doable. You might consider, as the authors do, what these findings say about the likely effectiveness of an antidrug campaign whose main message is "Just say no."

In 1741, in the small New England town of Enfield, Jonathan Edwards delivered a sermon entitled "Sinners in the Hands of an Angry God." In this sermon, he preached:

> Thus it is that natural men are held in the hand of God, over the pit of hell; they have deserved the fiery pit, and are already sentenced to it . . . the devil is waiting for them, hell is gaping for them, and swallow them up. . . . In short, they have no refuge, nothing to take hold of; all that preserves them every moment is the mere arbitrary will and uncovenanted, unobliged forebearance of an incensed God.

Eyewitness accounts indicate that the sermon left the congregation "breathing of distress and weeping." The records show that thousands gave over their lives to Christ as part of the Great Awakening of eighteenth-century America.

Two centuries later, in 1932, Adolf Hitler inspired his fellow countrymen and women with the words:

> The streets of our country are in turmoil. The universities are filled with students rebelling and rioting. Communists are seeking to destroy our country. Russia is threatening us with her might, and the Republic is in danger. Yes—danger from within and without. We need law and order! Without it our nation cannot survive.

Millions of Germans gladly embraced Hitler's Nationalist Socialist party.

Although the goals of Edwards and Hitler were quite different, their method was the same—instilling fear. Both Edwards and Hitler threatened their audiences with dire consequences if, of course, a certain course of action was not followed.

Ministers and politicians are not the only ones who arouse fear in order to motivate and persuade. Life insurance agents use fear to induce purchase of their policies; parents use fear to persuade their children to come home early from a date; and physicians use fear to insure that patients adopt and maintain a prescribed medical regimen. Sometimes these fear appeals are based on legitimate concerns—smoking does cause cancer; "unsafe sex" increases one's chance of contracting AIDS; failure to brush and floss can lead to painful tooth decay. But often fear appeals are based on dark, irrational fears—fears stemming from racial prejudice or the notion that there is a communist under every bed. At times, a regime instills fear by terrorizing its own citizens, as in Hitler's Germany, Stalin's Soviet Union, Argentina of the junta, Hussein's Iraq, and at countless other times and places. Fear appeals are powerful because they channel our thoughts away from careful consideration of the issue at hand and toward plans for ridding ourselves of the fear. When illegitimate fears are used, the message promotes deception—not to mention the cruelty of the fear itself. It behooves us to look closely at just when and how fear appeals are effective.

Not all fear appeals are successful in obtaining their objectives. For the past few years, public service announcements have alerted viewers to the dangers of drug abuse and cigarette use, and have frightened Americans about the possibility of contracting AIDS. Opponents of the nuclear arms race have often painted a graphic picture of nuclear winter. Yet drug abuse and cigarette smoking remain *high,* the practice of safe sex *low,* and the possibility of world annihilation through the use of nuclear weapons ever present. Just what are the factors that make a fear-arousing appeal more or less effective?

Let's begin with a seemingly simple question. Suppose you wish to arouse fear in the hearts of your audience as a way of inducing opinion change. Would it be more effective to arouse just a little fear, or should you try to scare the hell out of them?

For example, if your goal is to convince people to drive more carefully, would it be more effective to show them gory technicolor films of the broken and bloody bodies of highway accident victims, or would it be more effective if you soft-pedaled your communication—showing crumpled fenders, discussing increased insurance rates due to careless driving, and pointing out the possibility that people who drive carelessly may have their driver's licenses suspended?

Common sense argues on both sides of this street. On the one hand, it suggests that a good scare will motivate people to action; on the other hand, it argues that too much fear can be debilitating—that is, it might interfere with a person's ability to pay attention to the message, to comprehend it, and to act upon it. We have all believed, at one time or another, that it only happens to the other guy, it can't happen to me. Thus people continue to drive at very high speeds and to insist on driving after they've had a few drinks, even though they should know better. Perhaps this is because the possible negative consequences of these actions are so great that we try not to think about them. Thus, if a communication arouses extreme fear, we tend *not* to pay close attention to it.

What does the evidence tell us? Experimental data overwhelmingly suggest that all other things being equal, the more frightened a person is by a communication, the more likely he or she is to take positive preventive action.

The most prolific researchers in this area have been Howard Leventhal and his associates. In one experiment, they tried to induce people to stop smoking and obtain chest X-rays. Some subjects were exposed to a low-fear treatment: They were simply presented with a recommendation to stop smoking and get their chests X-rayed. Others were subjected to moderate fear. They were shown a film depicting a young man whose chest X-rays revealed he had lung cancer. The people subjected to the high-fear condition saw the same film the "moderate-fear" people saw, and, in addition, they were treated to a vivid, gory, color film of a lung cancer operation. The results showed that those people who were most frightened were also most eager to stop smoking and most likely to sign up for chest X-rays.

Is this true for all people? It is not. There is good reason why common sense can lead us to believe that a great deal of fear leads to inaction: It does—for certain people, under certain conditions.

What Leventhal and his colleagues discovered is that the people who had a reasonably good opinion of themselves (high self-esteem) were the ones most likely to be moved by high degrees of fear arousal. People with low opinions of themselves were the least likely to take immediate action when confronted with a communication arousing a great deal of fear—but (and here is the interesting part) after a delay, they behaved very much like the subjects with high self-esteem. People who have a low opinion of themselves may have difficulty coping with threats to themselves. A high-fear communication overwhelms them and makes them feel like crawling into bed and pulling the covers up over their heads. Low or moderate fear is something they can more easily deal with at the moment they experience it. But, given time—that is, if it is not essential they act immediately—they will be more likely to act if the message truly scared the hell out of them.

Subsequent research by Leventhal and his colleagues lends support to this analysis. In one study, subjects were shown films of serious automobile accidents. Some subjects watched the films on a large screen from up close; others watched from from far away on a much smaller screen. Among those subjects with high or moderate self-esteem, those who saw the films on the large screen were much more likely to take subsequent protective action than were those who saw the films on the small screen. Subjects with low self-esteem were more likely to take action when they saw the films on a small screen; those who saw the films on a large screen reported a great deal of fatigue and stated they had great difficulty even thinking of themselves as victims of automobile accidents.

It should be relatively easy to make people with high self-esteem behave like people with low self-esteem. We can overwhelm them by making them feel there is nothing they can do to prevent or ameliorate a threatening situation. Much research has shown that if recipients of a fear appeal perceive that there is no way to cope effectively with the threat, they are not likely to respond to the appeal but will just bury their heads in the sand—even those who have high self-esteem. Franklin D. Roosevelt knew the debilitating effect of extreme fear and sought to counteract it when he announced in his first inaugural address, "The only thing we have to fear is fear itself."

Conversely, suppose you wanted to reduce the automobile accident rate or to help people give up smoking, and you were faced with low self-esteem people. How might you proceed? If you were to construct a message containing clear, specific, and optimistic instructions, it might increase the feeling among the members of your audience that they could confront their fears and cope with the danger.

These speculations have been confirmed; experiments by Howard Leventhal and his colleagues show that fear-arousing messages containing specific instructions about how, when, and where to take action are much more effective than recommendations that omit such instructions. For example, a campaign conducted on a college campus urging students to get tetanus shots included specific instructions about where and when they were available. The campaign materials included a map showing the location of the student health service and a suggestion that each student set aside a convenient time to stop by.

The results showed high-fear appeals to be more effective than low-fear appeals in producing favorable *attitudes* toward tetanus shots among the students, and they also increased the students' stated intentions to get the shots. The highly specific instructions about how to get the shots did not affect these opinions and intentions, but the instructions did have a big effect on the *actual behavior:* of those subjects who were instructed about how to proceed, 28% actually got the tetanus shots; but of those who received no specific instructions, only 3% got them. In a control group exposed only to the instructions, with no fear-arousing message, no one got the shots. Thus, specific instructions alone were not enough to produce action—fear was a necessary component for action in such situations.

Very similar results were obtained in Leventhal's cigarette experiment. Leventhal found that a high-fear communication produced a much greater *intention* to stop smoking. Unless it was accompanied by recommendations for specific behavior, however, it produced little result. Similarly, specific instructions (buy a magazine instead of a pack of cigarettes, drink plenty of water when you have the urge to smoke, and so on) without a fear-arousing communication were relatively ineffective. The combination of fear arousal and specific instructions produced the best results; the students in this condition were smoking less four months after they were subjected to the experimental procedure.

In sum, a fear appeal is most effective when (1) it *scares* the hell out of people, (2) it offers a *specific recommendation* for overcoming the fear-arousing threat, (3) the recommended action is perceived as effective for reducing the threat, and (4) the message recipient believes that he or she *can* perform the recommended action.

This is exactly what Jonathan Edwards and Adolf Hitler offered their listeners. Both men described rising menaces (sin, communism) that, if allowed free rein, would devastate the soul or the national spirit. Each man offered a specific remedy for the crisis (commitment to Christ, joining the Nazi party). These courses of action were easy enough to perform; one needed only to answer the altar call or to vote for a Nazi candidate.

In contrast, fear appeals to increase nuclear disarmament or to decrease drug abuse rarely incorporate all four components of a successful fear appeal. We have all been alerted to the dread of nuclear winter and the personal and social destruction of drug abuse. However, there have been few specific recommendations for removing these threats that have been generally perceived as *effective* and *doable.*

Two counterexamples of effective anti-nuclear arms appeals will make our point. First, during the 1950s and early 1960s, many people purchased and installed "nuclear fallout shelters" in their homes. The reason: fear of nuclear war was high and the installation of a home fallout shelter, at the time, appeared to be an effective, doable response.

Second, during the 1964 presidential campaign, Lyndon Johnson, in a series of television ads, was able to sway voters by portraying his opponent, Barry Goldwater, as a supporter of the use of nuclear weapons. One controversial ad featured a young girl counting to ten as she pulled petals from a daisy. A moment later, the television screen filled with the mushroom cloud of a nuclear bomb. Johnson's appeal was successful because it linked the fear of nuclear war to Goldwater, and then proposed a vote for Johnson as a specific, doable way to avoid this threat.

Or consider the recent campaign to reduce the incidence of drug abuse by telling kids to "just say no." Although many children and teenagers are probably frightened by the drug scene, "just saying no" is not perceived as an effective and doable response. Imagine yourself as a teenager whose friends are pressuring you to try cocaine. Just saying no is likely to result in even more pressure—"Come on, just one try. What are you? A fraidy-cat?" Such pressure is not easy to resist.

The drug problem, given its scope and complexity, will require more than just a cleverly worded advertisement to solve. However, we can design our appeals so that they are more effective. For example, a teacher recently asked her elementary school class to come up with specific ways to say no when their friends pressure them to use drugs. The students produced a book of "ways to say no," for example, walking away, calling the dealer the fraidy-cat, or offering the friend an alternative to doing drugs. Such an approach has the advantage of "self-selling" the class not to use drugs, and also provides a list of specific ways that children will perceive as effective for dealing with peer pressure, and the list can then be illustrated on television or role-played in the schools. But in the final analysis, for our fear appeals to work, we need to offer our children a more effective and doable solution to life's problems than the advice to "just say no."

There is a broader question: should fear appeals be used at all? Given the power of fear to motivate and direct our thoughts, there is much potential for abuse. Illegitimate fears can always be invented for any given propaganda purpose. As persuaders, it is our responsibility, if we decide to use a fear appeal, to insure that the fear we instill is, at least, legitimate and that it serves to alert the target to potential dangers as opposed to obscuring the issue with emotion. As targets of such appeals, we owe it to ourselves to first ask, "How legitimate is this fear?" before taking the propagandist's bait.

5

Groups: Working with Others

Some people have said that social psychologists today are not as interested in group behavior as they once were. Still, since we are members of so many different kinds of groups and because groups make so many of our most important decisions, an understanding of group behavior remains of critical importance. Whether we are speaking of work committees, athletic teams, government agencies, juries, or just a casual group of friends, we cannot escape their influences.

Richard Moreland, Professor in the Department Psychology (with a secondary appointment in the Katz Business School) at the University of Pittsburgh, is one of the leaders in this field. He has published widely on a variety of group-related topics, and is co-author (with colleague John Levine) of the definitive chapter on groups in the fourth edition of the *Handbook of Social Psychology*. Professor Moreland has been particularly interested in the formation and composition of groups, and the manner in which new members are socialized into them. In our conversation he raised a number of points dealing with both group composition and group size, pointing out that groups bring with them both advantages and disadvantages. In reference to ways in which groups treat new members, he pointed out that even newcomers to the Supreme Court face some of the same treatment that newcomers to any group or team do.

A CONVERSATION WITH RICHARD MORELAND

Krupat: *When given the choice, people usually choose to work and play in groups, but what's so good about belonging to a group? Why do humans seem to be attracted to them?*

Moreland: Some social psychologists now think that belonging to groups is part of an evolutionary plan, that humans are social animals who are not happy when they're by themselves. Groups do meet different kinds of needs, both physical and psychological.

Krupat: *Such as?*

Moreland: In terms of physical needs, groups are helpful for survival terms. Gathering and producing food is easier in a group than when you're by yourself. Protection from dangers is more likely when you're in a group, and caretaking of the ill, the young, and the elderly are all easier when you're in a group than when you're by yourself. In terms of other kinds of needs, social psychologists have argued that groups provide information about the world. They help to settle questions that are hard to settle on your own, questions that are inherently subjective like, "Does God exist?" and "What's the purpose of life?"

Krupat: *And groups give us the answers to these questions?*

Moreland: Well, they help anyway. Often we check our opinions against those of group members to see if we're thinking about things the same way that they are. Groups also fill psychological needs, in terms of feeling wanted and loved, feeling that other people approve of you. So they have a kind of therapeutic effect as well. Research on social support networks shows that people who don't have many friends are more prone to mental health as well as physical health problems. There's even some speculation that social support can strengthen the immunological system and help people deal with disease better.

Krupat: *Okay, but when I think about groups I think of working in a group. If I am part of a group, a committee, or a task force, can this actually help me accomplish things better or more efficiently?*

Moreland: In this area, there's a lot of research comparing how well groups perform tasks compared to how well individuals perform them. Researchers find that groups typically outperform the performance of their average member. So if you had a set of people to give an assignment to and you just picked somebody at random, chances are you'd be better off giving that assignment to a group. On the other hand, groups seldom achieve as well as their best member could. So there seems to be something that holds the group back.

Krupat: *Then trying to accomplish tasks in a group can sometimes be inefficient?*

Moreland: Right. And that gets us into what are called "process gains" and "process losses." Process gains involve something about the interaction among group members that raises the group above the level of its average member. These include things like informal training, where people in the group teach one another how to work together better, and the division of labor. You can not only divide the task into smaller pieces that each member can perform, but each person in the group can be given the piece that they're best suited for.

Krupat: *And what about process losses, the negative things that can cause problems?*

Moreland: These are what fascinate social psychologists. Process losses include coordination problems where people have miscommunications or fail to coordinate their efforts. For example, if I can't do my piece of the work until you finish yours, and you're late, there's nothing I can do. If you've ever worked on a project with somebody else you know something about that.

Krupat: *But overall, I would think that most people believe in the power of groups. For example, people typically believe that if you put a group of people in a room and ask them to brainstorm, they will come up with more and better solutions to their problems.*

Moreland: Actually, brainstorming is particularly interesting because it's a very popular technique in the real world, but in social scientists' laboratory experiments it regularly fails. In most experiments, real groups produce many fewer ideas than "nominal groups," which are simply the same number of people working independently.

Krupat: *Then why has a technique like brainstorming remained so popular when the data say it doesn't work?*

Moreland: One problem is the communication gap between scientists and people out in the real world. People in business are not aware of the research findings, or maybe we haven't helped them to become aware of them. Also, there are other benefits of brainstorming besides just producing lots of ideas. Robert Sutton published a book recently on a company in California that heavily relies on brainstorming. The people in that company love to brainstorm, it's a way for them to show off their talents to one another, which is a route to promotion and advancement. So in these meetings people would struggle to show how clever they were, how they had a new angle on the work. Even though it might not have worked as well as people think it did, it served as a kind of fringe benefit.

Krupat: *How about the size of the group. Is bigger better? Or is it that smaller groups are best?*

Moreland: As groups get larger than five or six members, strains on the interaction among people begin to appear. It's hard to coordinate, and people may start to feel alienated or that they're not making a contribution. So if you try and go above five or six members, the group will break down into smaller cliques. If you want to create a group with a sense of intimacy and have people feel like they're really enjoying the experience and contributing, you want to keep groups small.

Krupat: *But if smaller is better, why would we have juries set at twelve people?*

Moreland: My understanding is that it's not mandated that juries have twelve members, and I believe some states have experimented with smaller size juries. Unfortunately it's not possible to do experiments on real juries because there are laws forbidding that. So social psychologists study mock juries using college students or people from the community on the jury rolls, presenting them with testimony as if they were actually witnessing a trial.

Krupat: *And what do they find?*

Moreland: The research shows that smaller juries reach about the same verdicts as larger juries, so based on that we could have smaller juries and save a lot of time and money. On the negative side, though, there is some evidence that smaller juries are not as careful in how they handle evidence. There's a kind of sloppiness to their decision making. They spend less time discussing the case and arrive at a decision sooner. If you ask them afterwards to recall pieces of evidence that were presented, they have poorer recall. On the one hand, it's great that they go faster and arrive at the same decisions. On the other hand, if you're a defendant, I suppose you would rather have a jury that took its time and considered everything carefully instead of rushing into judgment.

Krupat: *How about the composition of the group? How much of a difference does it make who is part of the group?*

Moreland: There's quite an interest nowadays in diversity, in comparing homogeneous groups with heterogeneous groups, especially in business. We know from research that diversity has a good side and a bad side. The good side is that it appears to enhance creativity—a group that contains different kinds of members will come up with fresh ideas, new angles on things. They may discuss things more thoroughly and come up with a better understanding. On the other hand, we also know that some people don't like diversity. In diverse groups there's more turnover of members, more miscommunication, misunderstanding, and conflict. The trick is to find some way to keep the bad side of diversity from happening while still benefitting from the good.

Krupat: *Let's switch from the characteristics of groups to the way they work. For instance, how do people get integrated into an existing group? Are there good or bad things for a newcomer to do?*

Moreland: I think everyone has had the experience of joining a group and being a newcomer. John Levine and I have written quite a lot about how that process unfolds. There seems to be a very strong newcomer role, with role obligations attached, and people who are willing to play the role generally do better than people who violate it. You need to make yourself unobtrusive and not stand out, go with the flow and demonstrate that you realize that you're not as good as the other group members, that you need some time to prove your worth. People who violate these role requirements and don't act like proper newcomers, draw angry responses. So if you come into a group and you're outspoken or you criticize the way the group does things and suggest better ways, particularly better ways from another group you used to belong to, people don't think you are acting properly.

Krupat: *The examples that pop into my mind involve fraternities and especially rookie hazing in sports.*

Moreland: Yes, the newcomer role is very powerful. I've seen articles in *Sports Illustrated* recently on football or basketball players. Since they start right off earning millions of dollars, you would think their teams would treat them with kid gloves, but there's still newcomer hazing. I also read an article a few years ago about the Supreme Court. The newest Justice on the Supreme Court is given special duties that the others don't have to fulfill.

Krupat: *Hazing the new kid on the block in the Supreme Court? What do the new justices have to do?*

Moreland: They have to hold the door when the other judges file in. They take their seat last, and have to coordinate the law clerks and the typing pool and all that kind of stuff.

Krupat: *Amazing. How does one become a regular? Does it require that oldtimers move on, or do you eventually just shake the role and become accepted?*

Moreland: We call it a role transition of acceptance, when you stop being new and suddenly you're one of the guys. Some groups mark that change with a public ceremony of some kind, but often it's more subtle. It might involve being invited to lunch when you didn't used to get invited, or being privy to information that wasn't available to you before. Others start to include you in the gossip network and share skeletons in the closet about the group that they didn't trust you to know before.

Krupat: *As I listen to you, I am impressed with how un-simple things are. Size is good, but also bad. Diversity can be good, but not always. The idea of the newcomer role makes sense at one level, but it seems crazy at another. Are you, or others you deal with, frustrated that the answers usually aren't straightforward?*

Moreland: It is frustrating, and I run into it when I talk with people from the media. They're getting ready to write a newspaper story or a TV spot or something, and they really don't want to hear anything very complicated. They want one or two punchlines, things that will grab the audience's attention.

Krupat: *But isn't it doubly frustrating that so many of the people in the real world who are advising about groups probably don't know one tenth of what you and your research have to offer?*

Moreland: You may be right. My wife works for a large corporation, and she occasionally comes home and tells me about the consultants that they have hired for a weekend workshop. When she describes the things they advise I get agitated because the consultants seem to have grossly oversimplified the problems and the solutions. Still, I think it is possible to educate people about groups. I guess that is part of the function of the courses we teach and the books we write.

Krupat: *If you don't mind my asking, how did you come to be interested in studying groups in the first place?*

Moreland: I think everybody is interested in groups at some level, maybe because of family experiences. When I was a teenager I went to a middle school with about 500 kids. I belonged to a strongly-defined clique. It was a good clique, an esteemed clique, and I liked it. When we graduated from there and went on to high school, the high school in our area drew from many different middle schools. And by some process I never quite figured out, and I still don't understand it exactly, I went from being a high status person in this desirable clique, to being sort of lost and not in any clique at all. That caused me some personal difficulties at that age, which made me wonder, how could that have happened so quickly? So I think that may account for part of my interest in groups, especially in studying newcomers to groups, and how groups change over time.

Krupat: *You seem to have survived that experience pretty well. As a groups researcher do you find that you are also a group-oriented person?*

Moreland: I do kind of yearn for groups, but I'm not that comfortable in them. I always thought of myself as a sociable person, but in recent years my wife has pointed out to me that I'm rather anti-social. We live in a house out in the woods far away from everybody, and I get uncomfortable going to social gatherings, parties, that kind of stuff. But I still have this kind of yearning for a warm fuzzy group to belong to. I'm always on the lookout for that.

Wolfgang Stroebe
Michael Diehl
Georgios Abakoumkin

The Illusion of Group Effectivity

As discussed by Richard Moreland in the conversation at the beginning of this section, most people presume that brainstorming
in a group is more effective than working alone. Stroebe and his
colleagues in Germany, in this and other studies, find that this is
not so. Although people who problem solve in a group of four
generally believe that they had been much more productive than
when they worked alone, they were not. The authors try to understand the reason for this "illusion of group productivity" by testing two assumptions: 1) that people have a self-serving motivation to think of their performance in a positive manner; and 2) that
when they work in groups people have a hard time remembering
which ideas were theirs and which came from other group members. They find that group members report that over half the ideas
mentioned by the group had also occurred to them, which likely
leads them to believe—incorrectly—that they had been more creative when in the group setting.

There is a striking discrepancy between everyday beliefs and scientific evidence
concerning the usefulness of group discussions as a method of idea generation. Academics, politicians, and the business community are unshakable in their conviction
that groups can stimulate creativity (e.g., Adriani, Cornelius, Lasko, & Wetz, 1989;
Grossman, 1984; Thaima & Woods, 1984). Thus, brainstorming, a method of idea
generation in groups, is still widely used in business organizations and advertising
agencies, in spite of consistent empirical evidence that people produce many more
ideas when they work individually rather than in groups (Diehl & Stroebe, 1987,
1991; Mullen, Johnson, & Salas, 1991). This has been called the *illusion of group
effectivity* (Diehl & Stroebe, 1991).

We are all members of a variety of groups and, as such, are frequently involved
in group idea generation. Therefore, the illusion of group effectivity could not have
persisted unless group members typically experienced that they had been more creative in groups than they would have been on their own. Because subjects in brainstorming research are usually asked to indicate their enjoyment and to evaluate their

productivity after brainstorming either individually or in groups, such studies could provide a great deal of evidence to test this assumption. The first part of this article will use unpublished data from our research program on brainstorming (Diehl & Stroebe, 1987, 1991) to illustrate their illusion of group effectivity. The second part will present an experiment that was conducted to address the processes that cause this illusion.

THE EXPERIENCE OF GROUP EFFECTIVITY

In a series of studies in which the productivity of brainstorming groups was assessed by comparing the quantity and quality of the ideas produced by real groups and those produced by nominal groups (i.e., subjects who work individually and whose individual products are statistically aggregated), subjects produced fewer ideas when working in real groups than when working individually (Diehl & Stroebe, 1987, 1991).

Paradoxically, however, this difference in performance was not reflected by their experience. Thus, when asked at the end of either a group or an individual brainstorming session who would produce more ideas, someone working alone or a person who works in a group 80% of the subjects indicated that a person working in a group would be more productive (Diehl & Stroebe, 1987, Experiment 1). It did not make any difference whether these respondents had themselves worked individually or in a group. Similar findings were reported by Paulus, Dzindolet, and Camacho (1990).

For further evidence of the operation of the illusion of group effectivity, we compared the responses of subjects who worked either under group or under individual conditions to questions asking whether they enjoyed the brainstorming session, whether they were satisfied with their own performance, and whether they felt facilitated or inhibited by the group. Compared with subjects who worked individually, subjects who brainstormed in groups were more likely to enjoy the brainstorming session, and to be satisfied with their own performance.

Group members also felt facilitated by the presence of other members. The feeling of facilitation was linked to the fact that group members were able to communicate with one another rather than to their interdependence per se. This can be seen from our studies on production blocking, which used a communication apparatus that allowed the independent manipulation of interdependence and communication among group members. Interdependence was created by allowing each of the four subjects who were seated in separate rooms but formed a "group" to present their ideas only when a voice-activated light signal indicated that none of the others were talking. Communication was manipulated by either allowing subjects to hear one another's ideas through an intercom system or preventing them from doing so. When communication was permitted, subjects were more likely to feel facilitated by other group members, whereas when communication was not permitted, the presence of other group members was more likely to be perceived as inhibitory.

All in all, the responses of subjects who participated in brainstorming experiments nicely illustrate the operation of the illusion of group effectivity. Thus, even though the actual productivity of group members in all our experiments was markedly lower than that of subjects who brainstormed individually, group members felt facilitated by the presence of other group members, enjoyed their work more, and were more satisfied with their own performance. Both groups and individual subjects also left the experimental session with the firm conviction that a person working in a group is more productive than a person who generates ideas individually.

CAUSES OF THE ILLUSION OF GROUP EFFECTIVITY

How can one explain the persistence of this illusion, despite the performance deterioration associated with idea generation in groups? One reason could be a *baseline fallacy*. In brainstorming sessions more ideas are produced by a four-person group than by an individual. Members of such groups could therefore rightly be under the impression that they achieved much more as group members than they could have achieved on their own. This baseline fallacy, which is rflected by such sayings as "Two heads are better than one," led early group researchers such as Shaw (1932) to infer group superiority from the observation that more groups than individuals solved their problems.

A somewhat different interpretation assumes that after a session group members are unable to differentiate between the ideas they have had themselves and those that were suggested by other group members. Because individuals are usually motivated to view their own performance in a positive light (i.e., self-enhancement), the inability to differentiate between own and others' ideas could result in a tendency among group members to attribute some of the ideas of other group members to themselves. This tendency could result in an overestimation of ideas that subjects claim to have reported and/or ideas that they recall having had at the session without actually verbalizing them. It would explain why people who brainstorm in groups rate their productivity higher than people who generate ideas in individual sessions.

There is some support for the hypothesis that group members overestimate their own contribution to the group product. Ross and Sicoly (1979; Experiment 2) had subjects who were assembled in dyads exposed to different portions of a case study. The groups had to discuss various solutions to the case, and the discussions were tape-recorded. Half the dyads were informed that their group had performed poorly, whereas the other half were told that their group had performed well. Three to four days later the participants were asked back to write down as much as they could remember of the group discussion. They were also asked to indicate the source of each of these ideas. Although subjects attributed to themselves the majority of statements they recalled under both conditions, they claimed somewhat fewer statements after failure feedback than success feedback.

The interpretation of these results is somewhat unclear. As subjects had originally read different aspects of the case study and had had to present their part of the material to the other subject, it is not surprising that they remembered more of their own contributions. Furthermore, the analysis of the accuracy of these claims indicated there were very few instances in which subjects took credit for statements made by their partners. Thus, the only evidence for a self-enhancement bias is the fact that subjects overestimated their own contribution to a greater extent under success than failure conditions.

Thus, these experiments suffer from methodological weaknesses that make it difficult to draw firm conclusions. But even if the findings had been unambiguously supportive of overestimation, the evidence would have been sufficient to account for the illusion of group effectivity. After all, it is quite likely that the overestimation of individual productivity is not restricted to group situations. It seems plausible from a self-enhancement perspective that some overestimation should also occur when people produce ideas on their own. To establish the overestimation of individual productivity in groups as one of the causes of the illusion of group effectivity, it has, therefore, to be demonstrated that individuals overestimate their own productivity more when working in groups than when working individually.

SESSION 1

Method

Subjects. Subjects were 92 female students (aged 16 to 17) from local high schools who were paid for their participation. All subjects were signed up in four-person groups to participate in two experimental sessions. Forty-eight subjects were run individually, 44 subjects in four-person groups.

Task. In the first session, subjects had to generate ideas individually or in groups according to the usual brainstorming rules (see Osborn, 1957) on the issue of how to improve traffic safety in Germany.

Independent Variable. The independent variable was type of session (individual vs. group). Subjects brainstormed either individually or in groups.

Procedure. After all four subjects had arrived, they were given their topic and informed of the brainstorming rules (i.e., the more ideas the better, and the wilder the ideas the better; improve or combine ideas already suggested; do not be critical). They were then either seated alone in small rooms (individual condition) or led into a somewhat larger room (group condition). Subjects were assigned to conditions on a predetermined random basis.

Subjects were instructed that the purpose of the experiment was to compare the productivity of persons working individually with that of individuals working in groups. Subjects working in individual rooms were also told that for the purpose of such a comparison, their ideas would be combined with those of the other three women to form a "nominal" group. Subjects were then informed that because experience had shown that people had many ideas only after the end of a brainstorming session, they would be asked to return for a second session where they would be shown the ideas produced by their group and would be asked to list the ideas they had had in the meantime.

For individual as well as group sessions, subjects were given a clip-on microphone. They were then reminded of the brainstorming rules and instructed that they had 15 minutes to make suggestions on the topic they had been given. After giving these instructions, the experimenter left the room to switch on the tape recorder and stayed in the control room until the end of the session. She then returned and handed out the first postexperimental questionnaire.

Dependent Variables. The major dependent variable in Session 1 was the number of nonredundant ideas. In the postexperimental questionnaire, subjects were asked to estimate the number of ideas produced by their (nominal or real) group and the percentage of those ideas they had had themselves. They also indicated what proportion of the ideas that had occurred to them they had actually verbalized. Finally, they rated how satisfied they were with their personal performance, how much at ease they had been in the brainstorming session, and whether they would have had more ideas if they had worked in a group (individual subjects) or if they had worked alone (groups).

Scoring. Ideas were transcribed from the tape recording by a research assistant, who was instructed to write each separate idea on a separate card and to record the subject number on the back.

The cards were then assembled in sets that reflected the performance of either a real or a nominal group. An assistant went through these cards and identified any idea that had been suggested more than once within a given set. To assess the reliability of this judgment, a second assistant repeated the procedure for a subsample of six sets. Relating the number of choices in which the two raters agreed to the total number of pairs, it was found that the raters agreed in 99.92% of the total number of possible pairs.

Results

The number of nonredundant ideas produced by real groups ($M = 84.55$) was markedly lower than the number produced by nominal groups ($M = 110.83$). Subjects in nominal groups estimated the number of ideas produced by their group at $M = 35.46$. Subjects in real groups estimated this number at $M = 22.67$. There was no significant difference between conditions in subjects' estimates of the percentage of the ideas they had contributed themselves (nominal groups, $M = 26.74$; real groups, $M = 24.48$) or in their reports of how many of the ideas that had occurred to them they had verbalized. Under both conditions subjects indicated that they had verbalized nearly all their ideas ($M = 1.58$ for nominal groups; $M = 1.67$ for real groups; scale range: $1 = almost\ all$ to $5 = only\ a\ few$).

Responses to the other items on the postexperimental questionnaire indicated that, compared with subjects working individually, group members were significantly more satisfied with their personal performance and found the brainstorming session more enjoyable. Whereas subjects working individually thought that they would have had many more ideas if they had worked in groups, group members did not think that they would have had more ideas if they had worked individually.

Discussion

The performance data replicated the findings of all previous published studies using groups of more than two subjects: Subjects who brainstormed in real groups were significantly less productive than subjects who brainstormed individually (see Diehl & Stroebe, 1987; Mullen et al., 1991). It is interesting that this performance difference was also reflected in the performance estimates. "Members" of nominal groups gave a higher mean estimate of the number of ideas produced by their "group" than members of real groups. The fact that subjects under all conditions markedly underestimated the number of ideas produced by their nominal or real group suggests that subjects "chunk" ideas differently than our raters. Finally, subjects assessed the percentage of the ideas they themselves contributed to the group product at approximately 25%. This is hardly surprising, as subjects were aware that they were part of a four-person group.

To summarize, there was a marked discrepancy between group versus individual difference in actual performance and estimates of performance, on one hand, and subjects' *evaluation* of their performance, on the other. Compared with subjects who worked individually, group members were more satisfied with their performance and felt more at ease in the brainstorming session. Furthermore, subjects who worked individually believed they would have had many more ideas if they had been in a group, whereas group members did not believe that they would have done better individually. These evaluation data offer persuasive evidence for the operation of the illusion of group effectiveness.

SESSION 2

Method

Subjects. Subjects in Session 2 were 86 of the 92 participants in Session 1 who returned for the second session 2 weeks later. The postexperimental questionnaires of 4 subjects could not be used owing to failure to write on a code number.

Task. Subjects were presented with the total set of nonredundant ideas produced by their nominal or real group, each idea written on a card. Their task was to assign each idea to one of three categories: (a) suggested by me; (b) suggested by another group member but had also occurred to me; (c) suggested by another group member and had not occurred to me.

Procedure. Subjects, who were run individually this time, were told that they would be presented with all the ideas produced by their group, each idea written on a different card. Their task would be to decide whether they had suggested this idea during the first session. If they had suggested it, they should drop the card into the box on their left, labeled *Suggested by me*. If they had not suggested it, they should decide between one of the two boxes on their right, labeled *Suggested by another group member but had also occurred to me* or *Suggested by another group member*

TABLE 5.1 Percentage of Ideas Assigned to Each of Three Categories by Members of Nominal and Real Groups

Category	Nominal Group	Real Group
Suggested by me	34	28
Suggested by another group member but had also occurred to me	13	33
Suggested by another group member and had not occurred to me	53	39

and had not occurred to me. It was emphasized that the "also occurred to me" box should be used only if the idea had occurred to the subject during the first session. Cards were drawn from a card dispenser so that subjects could not see how many cards would be presented.

Dependent Variables. The major dependent variable was the percentage of the total number of nonredundant ideas produced by a group that the subject assigned to each of the three categories. In a postexperimental questionnaire subjects were also asked how confident they were about the accuracy of their assignment of ideas.

Results

Table 5.1 presents the percentage of the total number of nonredundant ideas produced by a group that was assigned to each of the three categories. Compared with subjects in nominal groups, members of real groups assigned a significantly lower percentage of ideas to the categories "Suggested by me," and "Suggested by another group member and had not occurred to me," but a higher percentage to the category "Suggested by another group member but had also occurred to me." When asked their reasons for not giving an idea, members of real groups typically stated that a similar idea had been suggested earlier. Members of nomi-

TABLE 5.2 Percentages of Ideas Correctly and Incorrectly Identified by Members of Nominal and Real Groups as Suggested by Themselves or Not Suggested by Themselves

	Identified as "Suggested by Me"		Identified as "Not Suggested by Me"	
	Nominal	Real	Nominal	Real
Suggested by subject	76[a]	57[a]	24	43
Not suggested by subject	20	18	80[a]	82[a]

[a]Hits (correct identifications).

nal groups, however, indicated that they had thought the idea not original enough to be mentioned.

To test the assumption that members of real groups were less accurate than members of nominal groups in identifying the ideas they had suggested, a comparison was made on the "hits" and "misses" for ideas that subjects identified as having been suggested by themselves and not having been suggested by themselves. The first row of Table 5.2 presents the percentage of ideas that subjects had actually suggested and identified as suggested (hits) and the percentage they had actually suggested but not identified accordingly (misses). The second row presents the percentage of ideas that subjects erroneously identified as suggested by themselves (misses) and the percentage that they correctly identified as not suggested by themselves (hits). On the whole, subjects identified a larger proportion of ideas correctly than incorrectly. But whereas there was no significant difference between the hit rates of members of real and nominal groups for ideas they had not suggested, there was a significant difference between their hit rates for ideas they *had* suggested. Members of real groups identified a significantly lower percentage of the ideas that they had actually suggested than members of nominal groups.

Subjects' responses to the postexperimental questionnaire also suggested that members of real groups felt less confidence in their ability to make these category assignments. Compared with members of nominal groups, members of real groups had less confidence in the accuracy of their assignment ideas, and thought that they were more likely to have made mistakes.

Discussion

There are two ways to look at the findings of this study. First, one can compare members of nominal and real groups in terms of the proportion of ideas that subjects claimed to have suggested. This analysis leads to conclusions that are contrary to our hypothesis. Members of real groups declared somewhat fewer contributions to the group product than members of nominal groups. In fact, whereas the 28% of the total product claimed by members of real groups comes very close to the actual average contribution of members of four-person groups, members of nominal groups show a tendency to overestimate their personal contribution.

A very different pattern emerges, however, if one compares the two conditions in terms of the proportion of ideas that subjects claimed to have had during the brainstorming session, regardless of whether or not they suggested them. Here, subjects of real groups asserted that 61% of the total set of ideas that constituted their group product had also occurred to them, while subjects of nominal groups claimed only 47%.

How can we explain this discrepancy? The failure to support our hypothesis with regard to the proportion of ideas subjects claimed to have suggested is puzzling, because there is persuasive evidence that members of real groups were less able than members of nominal groups to remember whether a given idea was suggested by self or other. Furthermore, members of nominal groups correctly identified 76% of the ideas they had suggested, whereas members of real groups recognized only 57% of these ideas (see Table 5.2). Finally, members of real groups indicated less confidence in the accuracy of their decisions on the postexperimental questionnaire.

Why did the apparent inability of members of real groups to differentiate between ideas that had originally been suggested by self and by others translate into the predicted overestimation effect for the proportion of total ideas that subjects claimed to have had but not for the proportion they claimed to have suggested? Members of real groups who claim to have suggested an idea imply at the same time that other members did not suggest it. Like any distribution task, this type of distribution is likely to be affected by fairness considerations. This assumption is consistent with the findings of Ross and Sicoly (1979), who reported that members rarely took credit for ideas suggested by other group members. Although Stephenson and Wicklund (1983) reported a somewhat discrepant result, their overestimation effect could have been due to their requirement that group members list twice all the ideas produced in their group.

For members of nominal groups, the claim to have verbalized an idea is much less exclusive. These subjects brainstormed individually and can therefore assume that the same idea might have been reported by several members of their nominal group. In fact, the members of our nominal groups estimated that approximately 50% of the ideas suggested by them had also been suggested by other subjects.

The failure to find an overestimation effect for subjects' own contribution to the group product for members of real groups is therefore likely to be due to the differential operation of a fairness norm. Whereas members of real groups were restrained from making this claim, members of nominal groups were not.

Fairness considerations are less relevant to the claim by subjects that an idea suggested by another subject also occurred to them even though they did not verbalize it. After all, even brilliant ideas could have occurred to several persons, and by stating that an idea also occurred to oneself, one does not deny that the other person had mentioned that idea first. Thus, when both groups were unrestrained by fairness norms, members of real groups showed a much stronger overestimation effect than members of nominal groups.

One problem in interpreting subjects' claims that ideas occurred to them that they did not mention is that whereas we know which ideas subjects did or did not verbalize, we have no such evidence with regard to ideas subjects claim to have had at the first session but not to have mentioned at that time. It would therefore seem possible that members of real groups were in fact stimulated by the ideas suggested by other subjects. In other words, they might be speaking the truth in stating that 33% of the ideas suggested by other subjects had also occurred to them.

This interpretation appears implausible, however, in the light of subjects' responses to the question about whether they reported all the ideas that had occurred to them. If members of real groups really reported fewer than half the ideas that occurred to them, it is difficult to understand how these subjects could have stated at the end of the first session that they had verbalized almost all the ideas that had occurred to them. Furthermore, in view of the marked difference between real and nominal groups in the proportion of ideas assigned to the category "occurred but not suggested," it is difficult to understand why subjects working under the two conditions did not differ in their answers to this question and on the postexperimental questionnaire.

A second alternative to our interpretation is the assumption of a need for impression management rather than self-enhancement. The difference between the two interpretations is in attributing the overestimation effect to an intentional (i.e., impression management) or an erroneous (i.e., self-enhancement) misclassification. Because subjects might have thought that the experimenter would be unable to check on their claim that ideas had occurred to them that they did not verbalize, they might have knowingly made false claims with the intent of creating a positive impression.

One argument against this hypothesis is that subjects' claims were inconsistent with their own answers to the postexperimental questionnaire administered at the end of the first session. Furthermore, this interpretation cannot account for the difference observed in the claims of real and nominal groups. It would be difficult to argue that members of real groups felt a stronger need to impress the experimenter than members of nominal groups. Finally, this assumption is inconsistent with the fact that members of real groups misidentified 43% of the ideas they actually did verbalize whereas members of nominal groups made such a mistake in only 24% of cases. If subjects knowingly (rather than erroneously) overstated the number of ideas they had suggested, it is difficult to understand why members of real groups failed to identify so many of the ideas they had actually suggested during the brainstorming session.

A third alternative to our interpretation is the suggestion of Wicklund and colleagues (Wicklund, 1989; Wicklund, Reuter, & Schiffmann, 1988) that the process of acting on the ideas of other group members (e.g., reworking, developing, improving, or merely writing down the ideas) might lead to an appropriation of these ideas (i.e., exaggeration of one's own relative contribution). However, although this theory could account for the overestimation effect reported by Stephenson and Wicklund (1983), several aspects of our findings are inconsistent with their hypothesis: Wicklund's theory would lead one to expect that members of real but not of nominal groups would claim responsibility for ideas that had actually been suggested by other people. In contrast, our evidence indicates that it is the members of nominal groups who overestimate their contributions. There is no evidence for this type of idea appropriation in real groups. In fact, members of real groups failed to claim responsibility for many of the ideas they had actually suggested. Thus, members of real groups misattributed 43% of the ideas they had suggested themselves to other members, a percentage nearly twice as high as that of subjects who worked alone (Table 5.2).

GENERAL DISCUSSION

The evidence reported in this article illustrates the operation of the illusion of group effectivity and goes some way toward explaining it. Even though in all our experiments (Diehl & Stroebe, 1987, 1991) subjects who brainstormed individually produced markedly more ideas than subjects who brainstormed in groups, this had no impact on subjects' impression that group sessions were more productive than individual sessions. Thus, members of real groups indicated that they felt facilitated in their idea production by the presence of other subjects. They enjoyed the brainstorming sessions more and were more satisfied with their own productivity than subjects who had brainstormed individually.

One plausible reason for the persistence of the illusion of group effectivity is what we call the baseline fallacy (Diehl & Stroebe, 1991). Because, unlike the experimenter, subjects lack the comparison between real and nominal groups, members of real groups might rightly feel that more was achieved by the group than they could have achieved by themselves. After all, real groups of four subjects typically produced more ideas than one person who brainstormed individually. However, the theoretical reasoning underlying the experimental study reported in this article goes beyond the baseline fallacy and argues that group members also overestimate the number of ideas that occurred to them in a group session.

As authors of multiauthor papers, many of us may have had the experience that coauthors claimed to have made suggestions in the writing of the paper that we clearly remembered to have originated ourselves. Unlike subjects who brainstormed individually, members of real groups were exposed to all the ideas produced by other group members, and it therefore seems plausible that they had real difficulties in differentiating their own ideas from those of the other group members. We further argue that, because of pervasive tendencies for self-enhancement, this confusion should result in an overestimation of subjects' own contributions.

The results of our experiment are generally consistent with these hypotheses. There is clear evidence that members of real groups not only were much less accurate than subjects who brainstormed individually in differentiating their own ideas from those of their colleagues but also felt less confident of the validity of their decisions. This confusion resulted in a marked overestimation of the ideas group members claimed to have had during the first session, but not of the ideas they claimed to have suggested.

We would like to argue that the first claim is much more relevant to our hypothesis than the second: First, there is reason to believe that members of real groups might have been reluctant to make such claims because they were affected by fairness norms that did not apply to subjects who brainstormed individually. More important, however, the illusion of group effectivity is based on assumptions about creativity rather than on claims about actual contributions. Thus, the fact that group members were under the illusion that more than half the ideas suggested by the group had also occurred to them at the time is sufficient to account for the illusion of group effectivity.

References

Adriani, B., Cornelius, R., Lasko, W., & Wetz, R. (1989). *Hurra ein Problem! Kreative Lösungen im Team.* Wiesbaden: Gabler.

Diehl, M., & Stroebe, W. (1987). Productivity loss in brainstorming groups. Toward the solution of a riddle. *Journal of Personality and Social Psychology, 53,* 497–509.

Diehl, M., & Stroebe, W. (1991). Productivity loss in idea-generating groups: Tracking down the blocking effect. *Journal of Personality and Social Psychology, 61,* 392–403.

Grossman, S. R. (1984). Brainstorming updated. *Training and Development Journal, 38,* 84–87.

Madsen, D. B., & Finger, J. R. (1978). Comparison of a written feedback procedure, group brainstorming, and individual brainstorming. *Journal of Applied Psychology, 63,* 120–123.

Mullen, B., Johnson, C, & Salas, E. (1991). Productivity loss in brainstorming groups: A meta-analytic integration. *Basic and Applied Social Psychology, 12,* 3–23.

Osborn, A. F. (1957). *Applied imagination* (rev. ed.). New York: Scribner's.

Paulus, P. B., Dzindolet, M., & Camacho, L. M. (1990, June). *Perceived and actual productivity in brainstorming groups.* Paper presented at the general meeting of the European Association of Experimental Social Psychology, Budapest.

Ross, M., & Sicoly, F. (1979). Egocentric biases in availability and attribution. *Journal of Personality and Social Psychology, 37,* 322–336.

Rotter, G. S., & Portugal, S. M. (1969). Group and individual effects in problem solving. *Journal of Applied Psychology, 53,* 338–341.

Shaw, M. (1932). A comparison of individuals and small groups in the rational solution of complex problems. *American Journal of Psychology, 44,* 491–403.

Stephenson, B., & Wicklund, R. A. (1983). Self-directed attention and taking the other's perspective. *Journal of Experimental Social Psychology, 19,* 58–77.

Thaima, S., & Woods, M. F. (1984). A systematic small group approach to creativity and innovation: A case study. *R & D Management, 14,* 25–35.

Torrance, E. P. (1970). Influence of dyadic interaction on creative functioning. *Psychological Reports, 26,* 391–394.

Wicklund, R. A. (1989). The appropriation of ideas. In P. Paulus (Ed.), *The psychology of group influence.* Hillsdale, NJ: Lawrence Erlbaum.

Wicklund, R. A. Reuter, T., & Schiffmann, R. (1988). Acting on ideas: Appropriation to one's self. *Basic and Applied Social Psychology, 9,* 13–31.

Stephen G. Harkins
Jeffrey M. Jackson

The Role of Evaluation in Eliminating Social Loafing

Harkins and Jackson's research concerns social loafing—a finding that on many tasks people will put out less effort when working with others than they do when alone. It has been argued that this occurs in group efforts because people will loaf when their individual contributions cannot be identified and they cannot receive blame or praise for their efforts. Harkins and Jackson find that to overcome social loafing the individual's output must be identifiable, but in addition group members must also feel that their output can be evaluated against those of their fellow group members.

For a variety of tasks it has been found that participants when working alone put out greater effort than when working with others, an effect that has been termed "social loafing" (Latané, Williams, & Harkins, 1979). This effect has been demonstrated on tasks requiring physical effort (e.g., rope-pulling: Ingham, Levinger, Graves, & Peckham, 1974; shouting: Latané et al., 1979; pumping air: Kerr & Bruun, 1981) and cognitive effort (evaluating essays: Petty, Harkins, & Williams, 1980; brainstorming and vigilance: Harkins & Petty, 1982) by females as well as males (Harkins, Latané, & Williams, 1980). Using Steiner's (1972) typology, some of these tasks have been maximizing (requiring the participant to produce as much as possible: e.g., rope-pulling, pumping air), whereas others have been optimizing (requiring the participant to achieve some criterion performance: e.g., evaluating essays, vigilance); but on the "group" trials of all of these tasks, individual outputs have been pooled to arrive at a group product.

Williams, Harkins, and Latané (1981) have suggested that loafing arises at least in part from the fact that when the participants' outputs are pooled, individual outputs are lost in the crowd, submerged in the total, and are separately unrecoverable by the experimenter. Because participants can receive neither credit nor blame for their individual performances, they loaf. Williams et al. (1981) tested this notion in two experiments in which shouting was used as the effortful activity. In Experiment I, participants performed alone and together and, consistent with previous research (Latané et al., 1979), produced less noise when performing together than when performing alone. However, in phase two of the experiment, after having donned individual microphones, which they were told allowed monitoring of individual outputs even when they performed in groups, participants produced as much noise in groups as when alone. Experiment I was replicated in a second experiment in which a between-groups design was used. In a condition that replicated previous loafing experiments, participants performed alone and together, and were thus identifiable only when they performed alone (social-loafing replication). In a second condition, participants performed alone and together but wore individual microphones and were identifiable at all times, replicating phase two of Experiment I (always identifiable). Finally in a new condition, participants performed alone and together, but were told that interest centered on the group totals and so individual performances would be summed and compared to their group performances (never identifiable). As in phase one of Experiment I, in the social-loafing replication in which participants were identifiable only when alone, they put out greater effort when shouting alone than when shouting together. When always identifiable, participants put out as much effort when shouting together as when alone, replicating phase two of Experiment I. Finally when never identifiable, participants put out as little effort when shouting alone as when shouting together.

The results of these studies are consistent with the notion that identifiability of individual effort is a critical factor in social loafing. When individual outputs were always identifiable, people exerted consistently high levels of effort; and when outputs were never identifiable, they exerted consistently low levels. However, in this research, what has been termed identifiability has actually involved more than identifiability alone. Participants in these experiments have all worked on the same tasks; thus when their performances were identifiable, they could also be directly compared to the performances of the other participants. Identifiability alone may not be sufficient to eliminate loafing. Motivation may come from the participant's knowledge that his or her performance can be compared to the performances of other participants. The opportunity for comparison may lead the participants to believe that their performance can be evaluated, and this potential for evaluation may motivate performance. In the present research, we attempted to test this notion by manipulating identifiability and evaluation potential separately to allow an assessment of their independent effects.

We used a brainstorming task in which groups of four participants were asked to generate as many uses as they could for an object. These uses were written on slips of paper that were deposited in a box that was either divided into four compartments so that each participant's uses were collected separately (individually identifiable) or not divided so that each participant's uses were combined with those of the other group members (pooled). Crossed with this identifiability manipulation was a manipulation of evaluation potential. Participants were told that we were interested in the number of uses that could be generated for a range of objects. Some of these objects were difficult to generate uses for and some were easy, and as a result their outputs could be compared only to the outputs of participants who had the same object. By then telling participants that they had the same object as or different objects from the others we were able to manipulate evaluation potential. Of course, everyone was actually generating uses for the same object.

We hypothesized that social loafing would be eliminated only when individual outputs were identifiable and could be compared because only then could evaluation take place. When outputs were pooled or were identifiable but not comparable, evaluation was not possible, which was expected to lead to loafing.

METHOD

Participants

One hundred sixty male and female participants took part in this research as a means of fulfilling an introductory psychology course requirement. The participants were run in groups of four that were randomly assigned to one of four conditions comprising a 2 (Individually Identifiable outputs vs. Pooled outputs) × 2 (Comparability vs. No Comparability) factorial.

Procedure

When the participants arrived, they were seated at a table with partitions that prevented them from seeing one another and were informed that we were studying the performance of individuals and groups on a task called brainstorming. They would be given the name of an object and their task would be to generate as many uses as they could for this object.

Participants in the identifiable conditions read the following: "We are interested in the number of uses generated for this (these) object(s) by each of you. So, at the end of the experimental session, we will count the number of uses generated by each of you individually and determine how many you generated." If the group was in the pooled condition, members read these instructions: "We are interested in the total number of uses generated for this (these) object(s) by your group. So, at the end of the experimental session we will count the total number of uses generated by your group and determine how many the four of you generated." All then read that they should not be concerned about the quality of their uses, but should make sure that each use was a possible use for the object.

Comparability was manipulated by informing participants that the object for which they would be generating uses was the same as or different from the object the others were to be given. All participants were told that we were interested in the number of uses that could be generated for a range of objects and that because some of these objects were easy and some were difficult to generate uses for, the number of uses they generated was comparable only to the number generated by others working on the same object.

In the comparability condition, after having read the previous instructions, the participants read that each of the members of their group would be presented with this particular object and they were to generate as many uses for this object as they could. In the no comparability condition the participants read that each of the members of their group would be presented with a different object and they were to generate as many uses for this object as they could.

After having read their respective instructions, participants selected an envelope that contained the name of their particular object and were given a number of slips of paper on which they were to write their uses. The envelopes were presented in a manner consistent with the participants' previous instructions. Thus if the participants were in the comparability condition, each participant selected one of a number of envelopes after having been told that each envelope contained a different object. All participants actually generated uses for the same object, a knife.

After the participants selected their envelopes, they were asked to remove their object slips, memorize their object name, fold their object slips three times, and slide them down the tubes in front of them, which extended into a box. The top of the box was then removed, and the participants were shown either that the box was divided into four compartments, allowing us to determine exactly how many uses each of them individually generated (individually identifiable), or that there were no dividers, allowing us to determine only how many total uses the group generated (pooled).

The participants were told to write one use per slip, to fold it, and to slide it down the tube. They were then asked to don headsets, to begin writing when the music started, and to continue until they were stopped. The music (Beethoven's Fifth Symphony) served as a masking noise so that participants could not hear the others sliding their uses down the tubes. The participants were given 12 minutes to list uses, a length of time that previous research suggested would be more than ample (Harkins & Petty, 1982), and were then asked to respond to a set of questions on anchored 11-point scales. Among these measures were manipulation checks for identifiability. (To what extent do you believe the experimenter could tell exactly how many uses you individually generated on this task?) and comparability (To what extent do you feel that your performance can be directly compared to that of the other participants who are present now?) Also included were measures of how much effort the participants thought they expended on the task, how unusual they thought their uses were, how much pressure to perform there was, how competitive they felt, and to what extent they felt that their uses represented a unique contribution unlikely to be duplicated by other participants. After completing the questionnaire, participants were debriefed and dismissed.

Unknown to the subjects, each of the envelopes contained exactly 100 slips of paper. By counting the number of slips left by each person, we arrived at the number of uses generated by each person in the pooled conditions.

RESULTS

Manipulation Checks

Participants whose uses were pooled reported that the experimenter was less able to determine exactly how well they performed, M = 6.2, then participants whose uses were individually identifiable, M = 7.6. Participants in the comparability condition felt that their performances were more comparable to those of the others in their group, M = 6.7, than participants in the no comparability condition who had been told that each person in their group had been given a different object, M = 5.9.

Uses

Analysis of the uses data revealed that consistent with previous research on social loafing, participants whose uses were individually identifiable generated more uses, M = 22.3, than those whose uses were pooled, M = 19.6. In addition, there was a main effect for comparability such that participants for whom there was comparability generated more uses, M = 22.4, than those whose uses were not comparable, M = 19.5.

However, these main effects must be viewed in light of the significant Identifiability × Comparability interaction. When the participants' outputs were identifiable and comparable to those of the others in their group, they produced more uses, M = 24.9, than were produced in any of the other three conditions. In the pooled/comparability condition, participants generated no more uses, M = 19.8, than participants in the pooled/no comparability condition, M = 19.3. When individual outputs *were* identifiable, but *not* directly comparable to the outputs of the others in their group, the participants generated no more uses, M = 19.7, than participants in the pooled conditions.

DISCUSSION

Williams et al. (1981) suggested that social loafing arises from the fact that when participants "work together," individual outputs are not identifiable, and because participants can receive neither credit nor blame for their performances, they loaf. In the current research we argued that more than identifiability alone may be required to eliminate loafing. In the Williams et al. (1981) research when the participants' individual outputs could be monitored, not only were their outputs identifiable, but these outputs could be compared to those of the other performers. This potential for evaluation, which was absent when outputs were pooled, could motivate performance. To test this notion we orthogonally manipulated identifiability and comparability. Replicating previous research using this brainstorming task (Harkins & Petty, 1982), we found that when outputs were identifiable participants generated more uses than when their outputs were pooled. However, this difference emerged *only* when participants believed that their outputs could be compared to their co-workers' performances. When participants believed that their individual performances were not comparable and thus could not be evaluated, there was no difference in the number of uses generated by participants whose outputs were identifiable and those whose outputs were pooled.

Superficially, it may appear that these findings and results from other loafing research are at variance with what one might expect on the basis of social facilitation research. After all, "social psychological theory holds that at least for simple well-learned tasks involving dominant responses, the presence of others, whether as coactors or spectators, should facilitate performance (Latané et al., 1979, p. 823)." Pulling ropes, shouting, clapping, and generating uses for an ordinary object are all easily accomplished, but using these tasks loafing researchers have found that people working individually put out more, not less, effort than people working together. However, we would like to argue that the findings from loafing and facilitation are consistent.

Two explanations, mere presence (Zajonc, 1980) and learned drive (Cottrell, 1972), have been used most often to account for facilitation effects. Mere presence cannot account for loafing effects given that—in all published loafing studies save one (Kerr & Bruun, 1981)—the number of people present for both individual and group trials has actually been held *constant*. However, it appears that learned drive can. Cottrell (1972) has suggested that the presence of others is often associated with evaluation and/or competition and it is this association that leads to increased drive and enhanced performance on simple tasks. In facilitation research, when participants work together (coact), their outputs can be evaluated (compared) and they work harder than participants working alone. In social loafing research, when participants work together, their outputs are pooled and evaluation is not possible, leading to loafing. In both cases, evaluation potential is central. In social facilitation, working together enhances evaluation potential; in social loafing, working together reduces it.

This analysis suggests that evaluation potential plays a central role in both facilitation and loafing effects, but what is necessary for evaluation to take place? We would suggest that two pieces of information must be known: the participant's individual output and a standard against which this output can be compared. The necessity for a standard can be satisfied in a number of ways. For example, in the present research the standard of comparison was the number of uses generated by the other participants. When this standard was not available either because each person in the group had a different object or because outputs were pooled, performance dropped. Norms generated from the performances of previous participants could also provide a standard. If the task were optimizing (requiring some criterion performance, Steiner, 1972) rather than maximizing (requiring as much as effort as possible), the criterion could serve as the standard. Whatever the standard, we would argue that the standard—as well as the participant's output—must be known for evaluation to be possible, but known by whom?

In loafing research the role of the experimenter as evaluator has been emphasized. For example, Harkins et al. (1980) write: "The results (social loafing) are easily explained by a minimizing strategy where participants are motivated to work only as hard as necessary to gain credit for a good performance or to avoid blame for a bad one. Whenever the experimenter was unable to monitor individual outputs directly, performers sloughed off" (p. 464). However, the experimenter is only one of three potential sources of evaluation in loafing research. When outputs are pooled, participants may also feel that they cannot evaluate their own output, nor can their output be evaluated by their fellow participants. In our experiment, when individual outputs were identifiable and comparable within a group, each of these sources could evaluate an individual's performance. Social facilitation researchers have employed each of these sources in their explanations of coaction effects (e.g., experimenter evaluation: Seta, Paulus, & Schkade, 1976; coactor evaluation: Klinger, 1969; self-evaluation: Sanders, Baron, & Moore, 1978). However, although the potential for evaluation by each of these sources could motivate performance, clear evidence of their independent contributions is lacking.

The same is true of the evaluation conditions of loafing research. In some loafing research the fact that everyone would see scores after the performance was mentioned (e.g., Ingham et al., 1974; Latané et al., 1979), whereas in other research (e.g., Harkins, et al., 1980; Kerr & Bruun, 1981; Harkins & Petty, 1982), nothing was said about to whom performance scores would be made available. By manipulating to whom information about the individual outputs and standard is made available, it will be possible to determine how each of these sources of evaluation functions independently and in concert to motivate performance in group performance settings.

References

Cottrell, N. (1972). Social facilitation. In C. McClintock (Ed.), *Experimental social psychology*. New York: Holt, Rinehart & Winston.

Harkins, S., Latané, B., & Williams, K. (1980). Social loafing: Allocating effort or taking it easy? *Journal of Experimental Social Psychology, 16,* 457–465.

Harkins, S., & Petty, R. (1982). Effects of task difficulty and uniqueness on social loafing. *Journal of Personality and Social Psychology, 43,* 1214–1229.

Ingham, A., Levinger, G., Graves, J., & Peckham, V. (1974). The Ringelmann effect: Studies of group size and group performance. *Journal of Experimental Social Psychology, 10,* 371–384.

Kerr, N., & Bruun, S. (1981). Ringelmann revisited: Alternative explanations for the social loafing effect. *Personality and Social Psychology Bulletin, 7,* 224–231.

Kirk, R. (1982). *Experimental design*. Belmont, CA: Wadsworth.

Klinger, E. (1969). Feedback effects and social facilitation of vigilance performance: Mere coaction versus potential evaluation. *Psychonomic Science, 14,* 161–162.

Latané, B., Williams, K., & Harkins, S. (1979). Many hands make light the work: The causes and consequences of social loafing. *Journal of Personality and Social Psychology, 37,* 823–832.

Petty, R., Harkins, S., & Williams, K. (1980). The effects of group diffusion of cognitive effort on attitudes: An information-processing view. *Journal of Personality and Social Psychology, 38,* 81–92.

Sanders, G., Baron, R., & Moore, D. (1978). Distraction and social comparison as mediators of social facilitation effects. *Journal of Experimental Social Psychology, 14,* 291–303.

Seta, J., Paulus, P., & Schkade, J. (1976). Effects of group size and proximity under cooperative and competitive conditions. *Journal of Personality and Social Psychology, 34,* 47–53.

Steiner, I. (1972). *Group process and productivity*. New York: Academic Press.

Williams, K., Harkins, S., & Latané, B. (1981). Identifiability as a deterrent to social loafing: Two cheering experiments. *Journal of Personality and Social Psychology, 40,* 303–311.

Zajonc, R. (1980). Compresence. In P. Paulus (Ed.), *Psychology of group influence*. Hillsdale, NJ: Lawrence Erlbaum.

Gregory Moorhead
Richard Ference
Chris P. Neck

Group Decision Fiascoes Continue: Space Shuttle Challenger and a Revised Groupthink Framework

In this article, the authors review the events surrounding the tragic decision to launch the space shuttle Challenger. Moorhead and his colleagues assert that the decision-making process demonstrates *groupthink,* a phenomenon wherein cohesive groups become so concerned with their own process that they lose sight of the true requirements of their task. The authors review the events in light of this concept, suggesting that the groupthink concept needs to be expanded to consider time pressures, which were surely present in the Challenger situation, as well as the kind of leadership patterns that exist in a group.

In 1972, a new dimension was added to our understanding of group decision making with the proposal of the groupthink hypothesis by Janis (1972). Janis coined the term "groupthink" to refer to "a mode of thinking that people engage in when they are deeply involved in a cohesive in-group, when the members' striving for unanimity override their motivation to realistically appraise alternative courses of action" (Janis, 1972, p. 8). The hypothesis was supported by his hindsight analysis of several political-military fiascoes and successes that are differentiated by the occurrence or non-occurrence of antecedent conditions, groupthink symptoms, and decision making defects.

In a subsequent volume, Janis further explicates the theory and adds an analysis of the Watergate transcripts and various published memoirs and accounts of principals involved, concluding that the Watergate cover-up decision also was a result of groupthink (Janis, 1983). Both volumes propose prescriptions for preventing the occurrence of groupthink, many of which have appeared in popular press, in books on executive decision making, and in management textbooks. Multiple advocacy decision-making procedures have been adopted at the executive levels in many organizations, including the executive branch of the government. One would think that by

1986, 13 years after the publication of a popular book, that its prescriptions might be well ingrained in our management and decision-making styles. Unfortunately, it has not happened.

On January 28, 1986, the space shuttle Challenger was launched from Kennedy Space Center. The temperature that morning was in the mid-20's, well below the previous low temperatures at which the shuttle engines had been tested. Seventy-three seconds after launch, the Challenger exploded, killing all seven astronauts aboard, and becoming the worst disaster in space flight history. The catastrophe shocked the nation, crippled the American space program, and is destined to be re-membered as the most tragic national event since the assassination of John F. Kennedy in 1963.

The Presidential Commission that investigated the accident pointed to a flawed decision-making process as a primary contributory cause. The decision was made the night before the launch in the Level I Flight Readiness Review meeting. Due to the work of the Presidential Commission, information concerning the meeting is available for analysis as a group decision possibly susceptible to groupthink.

In this paper, we report the results of our analysis of the Level I Flight Readi-ness Review meeting as a decision-making situation that displays evidence of group-think. We review the antecedent conditions, the groupthink symptoms, and the pos-sible decision-making defects, as suggested by Janis (1983). In addition, we take the next and more important step by going beyond the development of another example of groupthink to make recommendations for renewed inquiry into group decision-making processes.

THEORY AND EVIDENCE

The meeting(s) took place throughout the day and evening from 12:36 P.M. (EST), January 27, 1986 following the decision to not launch the Challenger due to high crosswinds at the launch site. Discussions continued through about 12:00 midnight (EST) via teleconferencing and Telefax systems connecting the Kennedy Space Center in Florida, Morton Thiokol (MTI) in Utah, Johnson Space Center in Hous-ton, and the Marshall Space Flight Center. The Level I Flight Readiness Review is the highest level of review prior to launch. It comprises the highest level of manage-ment at the three space centers and at MTI, the private supplier of the solid rocket booster engines.

To briefly state the situation, the MTI engineers recommended not to launch if temperatures of the O-ring seals on the rocket were below 53 degrees Fahrenheit, which was the lowest temperature of any previous flight. Laurence B. Mulloy, man-ager of the Solid Rocket Booster Project at Marshall Space Flight Center, states:

> The bottom line of that, though, initially was that Thiokol engineering, Bob Lund, who is the Vice President and Director and Engineering, who is here today, recom-mended that 51-L [the Challenger] not be launched if the O-ring temperatures pre-dicted at launch time would be lower than any previous launch, and that was 53 de-grees. (*Report of the Presidential Commission on the space Shuttle Accident*, 1986, p. 91–92).

This recommendation was made at 8:45 P.M., January 27, 1986 (*Report of the Presidential Commission on the Space Shuttle Accident,* 1986). Through the ensuing discussions the decision to launch was made.

Antecedent Conditions

The three primary antecedent conditions for the development of groupthink are: a highly cohesive group, leader preference for a certain decision, and insulation of the group from qualified outside opinions. These conditions existed in this situation.

Cohesive Group. The people who made the decision to launch had worked together for many years. They were familiar with each other and had grown through the ranks of the space program. A high degree of *esprit de corps* existed between the members.

Leader Preference. Two top level managers actively promoted their pro-launch opinions in the face of opposition. The commission report states that several managers at space centers and MTI pushed for launch, regardless of the low temperatures.

Insulation from Experts. MTI engineers made their recommendations relatively early in the evening. The top level decision-making group knew of their objections but did not meet with them directly to review their data and concerns. As Roger Boisjoly, a Thiokol engineer, states in his remarks to the Presidential Commission:

> and the bottom line was that the engineering people would not recommend a launch below 53 degrees Fahrenheit. . . . From this point on, management formulated the points to base their decision on. There was never one comment in favor, as I have said, of launching by any engineer or other nonmanagement person. . . . I was not even asked to participate in giving any input to the final decision charts (*Report of the Presidential Commission on the Space Shuttle Accident,* 1986, p. 91–92).

This testimonial indicates that the top decision-making team was insulated from the engineers who possessed the expertise regarding the functioning of the equipment.

Groupthink Symptoms

Janis identified eight symptoms of groupthink. They are presented here along with evidence from the *Report of the Presidential Commission on the Space Shuttle Accident* (1986).

Invulnerability. When groupthink occurs, most or all of the members of the decision-making group have an illusion of invulnerability that reassures them in the face of obvious dangers. This illusion leads the group to become overly optimistic and willing to take extraordinary risks. It may also cause them to ignore clear warnings of danger.

The solid rocket joint problem that destroyed Challenger was discussed often at flight readiness review meetings prior to flight. However, Commission member Richard Feynman concluded from the testimony that a mentality of overconfidence existed due to the extraordinary record of success of space flights. Every time we send one up it is successful. Involved members may seem to think that on the next one we can lower our standards or take more risks because it always works (*Time*, 1986).

The invulnerability illusion may have built up over time as a result of NASA's own spectacular history. NASA had not lost an astronaut since 1967 when a flash fire in the capsule of Apollo 1 killed three. Since that time NASA had a string of 55 successful missions. They had put a man on the moon, built and launched Skylab and the shuttle, and retrieved defective satellites from orbit. In the minds of most Americans and apparently their own, they could do no wrong.

Rationalization. Victims of groupthink collectively construct rationalizations that discount warnings and other forms of negative feedback. If these signals were taken seriously when presented, the group members would be forced to reconsider their assumptions each time they re-commit themselves to their past decisions.

In the Level I flight readiness meeting when the Challenger was given final launch approval, MTI engineers presented evidence that the joint would fail. Their argument was based on the fact that in the coldest previous launch (air temperature 30 degrees) the joint in question experienced serious erosion and that no data existed as to how the joint would perform at colder temperatures. Flight center officials put forth numerous technical rationalizations faulting MTI's analysis. One of these rationalizations was that the engineer's data were inconclusive. As Mr. Boisjoly emphasized to the Commission:

> I was asked, yes, at that point in time I was asked to quantify my concerns, and I said I couldn't. I couldn't quantify it. I had no data to quantify it, but I did say I knew that it was away from goodness in the current data base. Someone on the net commented that we had soot blow-by on SRM-22 [Flight 61-A, October, 1985] which was launched at 75 degrees. I don't remember who made the comment, but that is where the first comment came in about the disparity between my conclusion and the observed data because SRM-22 [Flight 61-A, October 1985] had blow-by at essentially a room temperature launch. I then said that SRM-15 [Flight 51-C, January, 1985] had much more blow-by indication and that it was indeed telling us that lower temperature was a factor. I was asked again for data to support my claim, and I said I have none other than what is being presented (*Report of the Presidential Commission on the Space Shuttle Accident*, 1986, p. 89).

Discussions became twisted (compared to previous meetings) and no one detected it. Under normal conditions, MTI would have to prove the shuttle boosters readiness for launch, instead they found themselves forced to prove that the boosters were unsafe. Boisjoly's testimony supports this description of the discussion:

> This was a meeting where the determination was to launch, and it was up to us to prove beyond a shadow of a doubt that it was not safe to do so. This is in total re-

verse to what the position usually is in a preflight conversation or a flight readiness review. It is usually exactly the opposite of that. (*Report of the Presidential Commission on the Space Shuttle Accident,* 1986, p. 93).

Morality. Group members often believe, without question, in the inherent morality of their position. They tend to ignore the ethical or moral consequences of their decision.

In the Challenger case, this point was raised by a very high level MTI manager, Allan J. McDonald, who tried to stop the launch and said that he would not want to have to defend the decision to launch. He stated to the Commission:

> I made the statement that if we're wrong and something goes wrong on this flight, I wouldn't want to have to be the person to stand up in front of board in inquiry and say that I went ahead and told them to go ahead and fly this thing outside what the motor was qualified to. (*Report of the Presidential Commission on the Space Shuttle Accident,* 1986, p. 95).

Some members did not hear this statement because it occurred during a break. Three top officials who did hear it ignored it.

Stereotyped Views of Others. Victims of groupthink often have a stereotyped view of the opposition of anyone with a competing opinion. They feel that the opposition is too stupid or too weak to understand or deal effectively with the problem.

Two of the top three NASA officials responsible for the launch displayed this attitude. They felt that they completely understood the nature of the joint problem and never seriously considered the objections raised by the MTI engineers. In fact they denigrated and badgered the opposition and their information and opinions.

Pressure on Dissent. Group members often apply direct pressure to anyone who questions the validity of these arguments supporting a decision or position favored by the majority. These same two officials pressured MTI to change its position after MTI originally recommended that the launch not take place. These two officials pressured MTI personnel to prove that it was not safe to launch, rather than to prove the opposite. As mentioned earlier, this was a total reversal of normal preflight procedures. It was this pressure that top MTI management was responding to when they overruled their engineering staff and recommended launch. As the Commission report states:

> At approximately 11 P.M. Eastern Standard Time, the Thiokol/NASA teleconference resumed, the Thiokol management stating that they had reassessed the problem, that the temperature effects were a concern, but that the data was admittedly inconclusive (p. 96).

This seems to indicate the NASA's pressure on these Thiokol officials forced them to change their recommendation from delay to execution of the launch.

Self-Censorship. Group members tend to censor themselves when they have opinions or ideas that deviate from the apparent group consensus. Janis feels that this reflects each member's inclination to minimize to himself or herself the importance of his or her own doubts and counter-arguments.

The most obvious evidence of self-censorship occurred when a vice president of MTI, who had previously presented information against launch, bowed to pressure from NASA and accepted their rationalizations for launch. He then wrote these up and presented them to NASA as the reasons that MTI had changed its recommendation to launch.

Illusion of Unanimity. Group members falling victim to groupthink share an illusion of unanimity concerning judgments made by members speaking in favor of the majority view. This symptom is caused in part by the preceding one and is aided by the false assumption that any participant who remains silent is in agreement with the majority opinion. The group leader and other members support each other by playing up points of convergence in their thinking at the expense of fully exploring points of divergence that might reveal unsettling problems.

No participant from NASA ever openly agreed with or even took sides with MTI in the discussion. The silence from NASA was probably amplified by the fact that the meeting was a teleconference linking the participants at three different locations. Obviously, body language which might have been evidenced by dissenters was not visible to others who might also have held a dissenting opinion. Thus, silence meant agreement.

Mindguarding. Certain group members assume the role of guarding the minds of others in the group. They attempt to shield the group from adverse information that might destroy the majority view of the facts regarding the appropriateness of the decision.

The top management at Marshall knew that the rocket casings had been ordered redesigned to correct a flaw 5 months previous to this launch. This information and other technical details concerning the history of the joint problem was withheld at the meeting.

Decision-Making Defects

The result of the antecedent conditions and the symptoms of groupthink is a defective decision-making process. Janis discusses several defects in decision making that can result.

Few Alternatives. The group considers only a few alternatives, often only two. No initial survey of all possible alternatives occurs. The Flight Readiness Review team had a launch/no-launch decision to make. These were the only two alternatives considered. Other possible alternatives might have been to delay the launch for further testing, or to delay until the temperatures reached an appropriate level.

No Re-Examination of Alternatives. The group fails to re-examine alternatives that may have been initially discarded based on early unfavorable information. Top

NASA officials spent time and effort defending and strengthening their position, rather than examining the MTI position.

Rejecting Expert Opinions. Members make little or no attempt to seek outside experts opinions. NASA did not seek out other experts who might have some expertise in this area. They assumed that they had all the information.

Rejecting Negative Information. Members tend to focus on supportive information and ignore any data or information that might cast a negative light on their preferred alternative. MTI representatives repeatedly tried to point out errors in the rationale the NASA officials were using to justify the launch. Even after the decision was made, the argument continued until a NASA official told the MTI representative that it was no longer his concern.

No Contingency Plans. Members spend little time discussing the possible consequences of the decision and, therefore, fail to develop contingency plans. There is no documented evidence in the Rogers Commission Report of any discussion of the possible consequences of an incorrect decision.

Summary of the Evidence

The major categories and key elements of the groupthink hypothesis have been presented (albeit somewhat briefly) along with evidence from the discussions prior to the launching of the Challenger, as reported in the President's Commission to investigate the accident. The antecedent conditions were present in the decision-making group, even though the group was in several physical locations. The leaders had a preferred solution and engaged in behaviors designed to promote it rather than critically appraise alternatives. These behaviors were evidence of most of the symptoms leading to a defective decision-making process.

DISCUSSION

This situation provides another example of decision making in which the group fell victim to the groupthink syndrome, as have so many previous groups. It illustrates the situation characteristics, the symptoms of group think, and decision-making defects as described by Janis. This situation, however, also illustrates several other aspects of situations that are critical to the development of groupthink that need to be included in a revised formulation of the groupthink model. First, the element of time in influencing the development of groupthink has not received adequate attention. In the decision to launch the space shuttle Challenger, time was a crucial part of the decision-making process. The launch had been delayed once, and the window for another launch was fast closing. The leaders of the decision team were concerned about public and congressional perceptions of the entire space shuttle program and its continued funding and may have felt that further delays of the launch could seriously impact future funding. With the space window fast closing, the decision team was faced with a launch now or seriously damage the program decision. One top level manager's response to Thiokol's initial recommendation to postpone the launch indicates the presence of time pressure:

> With this LCC (Launch Commit Criteria), i.e., do not launch with a temperature greater [sic] than 53 degrees, we may not be able to launch until next April. We need to consider this carefully before we jump to any conclusions. (*Report of the Presidential Commission on the Space Shuttle Accident,* 1986, p. 96).

Time pressure could have played a role in the group choosing to agree and to self-censor their comments. We propose that in certain situations where there is pressure to make a decision quickly, the elements may combine to foster the development of groupthink.

The second revision needs to be in the role of the leadership of the decision-making group. In the space shuttle Challenger incident, the leadership of the group varied from a shared type of leadership to a very clear leader in the situation. This may indicate that the leadership role needs to be clearly defined and a style that demands open disclosure of information, points of opposition, complaints, and dissension. We propose the leadership style is a crucial variable that moderates the relationship between the group characteristics and the development of the symptoms. Janis (1983) is a primary form of evidence to support the inclusion of leadership style in the enhanced model. His account of why the *same* group succumbed to groupthink in one decision (Bay of Pigs) and not in another (Cuban Missile Crisis) supports the depiction of leadership style as a moderator variable. In these decisions, the only condition that changed was the leadership style of the President. In other words, the element that seemed to distinguish why groupthink occurred in the Bay of Pigs decision and not in the Cuban Missile Crisis situation is the president's change in his behavior.

These two variables, time and leadership style, are proposed as moderators of the impact of the group characteristics on groupthink symptoms. This relationship is portrayed graphically in Figure 5.1. In effect, we propose that the groupthink symptoms result from the group characteristics, as proposed by Janis, but only in the presence of the moderator variables of time and certain leadership styles.

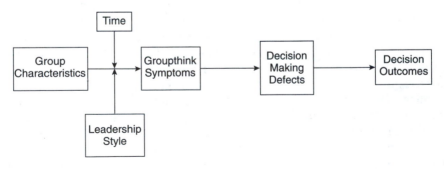

FIGURE 5.1
Revised Groupthink Framework

Time, as an important element in the model, is relatively straightforward. When a decision must be made within a very short time frame, pressure on members to agree, to avoid time-consuming arguments and reports from outside experts, and to self-censor themselves may increase. These pressures inevitably cause group members to seek agreement. In Janis's original model, time was included indirectly as a function of the antecedent condition, group cohesion. Janis (1983) argued that time pressures can adversely affect decision quality in two ways. First, it affects the decision makers' mental efficiency and judgment, interfering with their ability to concentrate on complicated discussions, to absorb new information, and to use imagination to anticipate the future consequences of alternative courses of action. Second, time pressure is a source of stress that will have the effect of inducing a policy-making group to become more cohesive and more likely to engage in groupthink.

Leadership style is shown to be a moderator because of the importance it plays in either promoting or avoiding the development of the symptoms of the groupthink. The leader, even though she or he may not promote a preferred solution, may allow or even assist the group seeking agreement by not forcing the group to critically appraise all alternative courses of action. The focus of this leadership variable is on the degree to which the leader allows or promotes discussion and evaluation of alternatives. It is not a matter of simply not making known a preferred solution; the issue is one of stimulation of critical thinking among the group.

Impact on Prescriptions for Prevention

The revised model suggests that more specific prescriptions for prevention of groupthink can be made. First, group members need to be aware of the impact that a short decision time frame has on decision processes. When a decision must be made quickly, there will be more pressure to agree, i.e., discouragement of dissent, self-censorship, avoidance of expert opinion, and assumptions about unanimity. The type of leadership suggested here is not one that sits back and simply does not make known her or his preferred solution. This type of leader must be one that requires all members to speak up with concerns, questions, and new information. The leader must know what some of these concerns are and which members are likely to have serious doubts so that the people with concerns can be called upon to voice them. This type of group leadership does not simply assign the role of devil's advocate and step out of the way. This leader actually plays the role or makes sure that others do. A leader with the required style to avoid groupthink is not a laissez faire leader or non-involved participative leader. This leader is active in directing the activities of the group but does not make known a preferred solution. The group still must develop and evaluate alternative courses of action, but under the direct influence of a strong, demanding leader who forces critical appraisal of all alternatives.

Finally, a combination of the two variables suggests that the leader needs to help members to avoid the problems created by the time element. For example, the leader may be able to alter an externally imposed time frame for the decision by negotiating an extension or even paying late fees, if necessary. If an extension is not possible, the leader may need to help the group eliminate the effects of time on the decision processes. This can be done by forcing attention to issues rather than time, encouraging dissension and confrontation, and scheduling special sessions to hear reports from outside experts that challenge prevailing views within the group.

Janis presents, in both editions of his book, several recommendations for preventing the occurrence of groupthink. These recommendations focus on the inclusion of outside experts in the decision-making process, all members taking the role of devil's advocate and critically appraising all alternative courses of action, and the leader not expressing a preferred solution. The revised groupthink framework suggests several new prescriptions that may be helpful in preventing further decision fiascoes similar to the decision to launch the space shuttle Challenger.

References

Time. Fixing NASA. June 9, 1986.

Janis, I. L. (1983) *Victims of groupthink.* Boston: Houghton Mifflin.

Janis, I. L. (1983) *Groupthink* (2nd ed., revised). Boston: Houghton Mifflin.

Report of the Presidential Commission on the Space Shuttle Accident. Washington, D.C.: July 1986.

6

Relationships: What Makes Them Work?

Everyone has an opinion as well as an interest in what makes relationships work. If you walk into a a paperback bookstore, you can find volume after volume containing pop philosophy and simple advice about what makes men and women satisfied in their relationships, and how to make them last. The problem is that so very little of this advice is based on solid theory or careful research.

Caryl Rusbult, Professor of Psychology at the University of North Carolina, has been studying relationships for the past 20 years. The models she has developed are widely respected and widely applied from the realm of romantic relationships to that of organizational behavior and job commitment. In our conversation she discussed the reasons why some relationships persist and other do not, considering determinants of commitment such as satisfaction, investment in the relationship, and the available level of alternatives. Discussing the ways in which people respond to conflict amid dissatisfaction in relationships, Prof. Rusbult pointed out that the negative or hurting things one person does may carry far greater weight in the course of the relationship than all the good acts that the person may bring.

A CONVERSATION WITH
CARYL RUSBULT

Krupat: *There are so many different issues that fascinate people about long term relationships. How did you become interested in relationships, and what about them interests you the most?*

Rusbult: My work addresses the question of how and why relationships persist over time. During a cross-country trip about twenty years ago a friend asked me "Why do people stick with their partners?" I answered my friend with a fairly standard textbook lecture, given the state of our knowledge at that time. I talked about research on proximity, attitudinal similarity, physical attractiveness, and other issues concerning interpersonal attraction. At the end of this my friend said, "So tell me, why do people stick with their partners?" My friend was right. We didn't have a very good answer to the question at that time because the literature was focused almost exclusively on positive affect in initial interactions between strangers—on attraction, satisfaction, liking, and so on.

Krupat: *So what did you focus on instead?*

Rusbult: My work examines long-term relationships, and emphasizes commitment, rather than positive affect, as the main cause of persistence. We suggest that commitment is influenced by three categories of variables. The first variable that influences commitment is satisfaction level—the degree to which the individual has positive feelings about a partner in relationship. The degree to which one has positive feelings is affected by the extent to which a partner gratifies one's most important needs—needs centering on issues such as companionship, intimacy, sexuality, and intellectual stimulation. To the degree that those needs are met in a relationship, you're going to feel satisfied with it.

Krupat: *But that's only one part of it. I assume we have to go beyond mere satisfaction.*

Rusbult: Right. A second category of variable has to do with quality of alternatives, or the degree to which those same needs could be met elsewhere, outside of the relationship. We've defined alternatives broadly—your best available alternative might not be a specific relationship. Quality of alternatives is also influenced by the general quality of the field of eligibles—by the number of suitable partners there are in your geographic region or in your age range.

Krupat: *So the second variable deals with "other options." What is the third?*

Rusbult: These two issues—satisfaction level and quality of alternatives—were identified by Thibaut and Kelly in their interdependence theory. We have added a third variable, investments. Investment size refers to the degree to which important resources have become attached to a relationship—resources that would be lost or would decline in value if the relationship were to end.

Krupat: *Such as?*

Rusbult: Some investments are things that you put directly in the relationship actually intending to improve it, like time and effort. Others are indirect investments—things that really are independent of the relationship but that can become linked to it, like a shared friendship network or owning a house together. Investments of both sorts increase the costs of ending a relationship, and therefore serve as powerful psychological inducements to persist. So a person's commitment level should be positively associated with satisfaction level and with investment size, and should be negatively associated with quality of alternatives. And in fact, the empirical evidence consistently provides support for this model.

Krupat: *Do you find in some situations that one factor will be more important than the other, or do they tend to have equal weighting?*

Rusbult: The formula is really a simple one. It's satisfaction level minus quality of alternatives plus investments. But you're right—across different types of relationships these variables may be weighted quite differently. Sometimes satisfaction is a powerful cause of commitment, and sometimes it's irrelevant. For example, we've found that in abusive relationships, satisfaction has nothing to do with whether a relationship will persist. The main issue is quality of alternatives. Women who remain in abusive relationships have terrible economic alternatives—for example, some women stick with their partners because they have fifty-seven cents in their pocket, an eighth grade education, no driver's license, and no place to live. They also tend to have a lot invested in the relationship—they're more likely to be married to their partners than not, and more likely to have children with their partners. So women often persist in abusive relationships because they've got terrible alternatives and because they have a great deal invested in the relationship. This model differs from many of the existing models of persistence in an abusive relationship, such as models that imply that it's somehow the victim's fault. Many existing models suggest there must be something wrong with a woman who persists in an abusive relationship—she must be masochistic, she must have acquired a pattern of learned helplessness, or she must have seriously depressed self-esteem. Our work suggests that the decision to persist in a bad relationship may be understandable once you take a look at quality of alternatives and investment size.

Krupat: *And taking your point of view would have very different implications for how to deal with this problem?*

Rusbult: Right—the policy implications are quite different when you adopt this point of view. If you think there's something wrong with the abused woman herself, you're likely to recommend psychotherapy and work on her self-esteem. But once you recognize that alternatives and investments may play a role, you become more likely to work on her alternatives, providing job training, a place to live, and economic support. Improving the quality of her alternatives is tantamount to giving her choice.

Krupat: *So if satisfaction, commitment, and investment increase commitment, what kinds of things have you found undermine relationships?*

Rusbult: Years ago I was interested in how individuals react to dissatisfaction in their relationships, and I happened to read a book by Albert Hirschman (an economist) called "Exit, Voice and Loyalty: Response to Decline in Firms, Organizations and States." Hirschman had developed a typology of reactions to dissatisfaction in formal organizations that seemed like a good model for understanding how people react to dissatisfaction in close relationships.

Krupat: *Let me interrupt you for a second. Wouldn't some people be skeptical of a business model for talking about close relationships? Do the same principles hold?*

Rusbult: I think that the abstract principles that govern commitment and reactions to dissatisfaction in one domain of life, for example in close relationships, are basically the same abstract principles that govern behavior in many other domains of life. We've used our model of commitment not only to understand commitment to close relationships but also to understand job commitment, and the model works very well in that domain as well.

Krupat: *I can buy that. So then let's get back to the model.*

Rusbult: Based on Hirschman's writings, we developed a typology of responses to dissatisfaction that has two dimensions. First of all, responses to dissatisfaction can be either constructive or destructive to the relationship. Second, responses can be relatively more active or passive with respect to the problem at hand.

Krupat: *So when we put these together we should have four possible kinds of reaction, right?*

Rusbult: Yes. The destructive and active reaction is "exit." Exit includes all kinds of actively destructive reactions—not just ending a relationship, but also any actively harmful behavior such as yelling at the partner, screaming "I don't know why I ever married you," or hitting the partner. Then there's a constructive and active category of response—"voice." For example, voice involves talking things over, seeing a couples counselor, asking friends for advice, or simply changing your behavior so as to solve the problem. Then we've got a constructive but passive reaction, "loyalty," which involves passively but optimistically hanging in there. Examples would be continuing to support the partner when others criticize him or her, continuing to wear symbols of the relationship (like a wedding ring), or simply praying for improvement. Finally, the destructive but passive way of reacting is "neglect," where the person passively allows conditions to deteriorate. The individual might refuse to discuss matters, spend long hours at work or away from the partner, or criticize the partner for matters that are really unrelated to the problem.

Krupat: *That seems like a very useful typology. Are any of these strategies particularly more useful or dangerous to use if you want to maintain a happy, long term relationship?*

Rusbult: Yes. We've done quite a bit of research using this typology and we've discovered two really interesting principles. The first might be called a good manners model. If you simply look at the level of exit, voice, loyalty and neglect that each partner exhibits, you find that levels of exit and neglect, the two destructive responses, powerfully predict couple functioning. High levels of exit and neglect are very harmful to a relationship. But there's an asymmetry. Corresponding levels of voice and loyalty are not equally constructive or helpful to a relationship. So good manners is the rule. Avoid dipping into the negatives, exit and neglect.

Krupat: *And the second principle?*

Rusbult: The second principle is accommodation, which describes an interdependent pattern of response. Individuals don't maintain uniformly good manners. Eventually, even the best-behaved partner will behave badly—the partner will be rude, inconsiderate, or just act like a jerk. We find that the way in which individuals react to a partner's destructive actions is very important. Accommodation is the willingness—when your partner engages in exit or neglect behaviors—to inhibit the impulse to react with exit or neglect and instead react with voice or loyalty. Even though your impulse may be to be equally rude and inconsiderate in turn (for example, to yell at your partner), it's important to control that impulse, count to ten, and instead react constructively. And that's hard to do.

Krupat: *What happens when you react in kind and yell or insult your partner right back?*

Rusbult: If partners do not accommodate, the initially rude act escalates into something more negative, until before you know it, the interaction has escalated to the point where partners are really at each other's throats. Then they have real problems.

Krupat: *But what if one partner accommodates and the other just escalates?*

Rusbult: Unless at least one partner accommodates, the couple really doesn't have a chance. But you're right in suggesting that one person's accommodative act does not fully solve the problem—it just provides the chance for the partners to cool things down. If Mary accommodates rather than retaliating, she creates a better set of options for John. Instead of being confronted with an angry partner, which may make him even angrier, he's confronted with a calm partner who is making it easier for him to calm down and begin to behave in a constructive manner.

Krupat: *But a relationship can't be successful in the long term if one person constantly accommodates and the other doesn't respond constructively in turn. Wouldn't you get to feel taken advantage of eventually?*

Rusbult: Definitely. Mutuality is a key issue—mutuality of accommodation, mutuality of commitment, mutuality of sacrifice is the ideal model. Mutuality represents an ideal environment for relationships to persist and remain healthy and vital.

Krupat: *I can see people besieging you to do couples counseling and* *things like that. How much do you see yourself or would you hope your field goes in the direction of practical application versus careful science?*

Rusbult: They have to go hand in hand.

Krupat: *How compatible or incompatible are they?*

Rusbult: They're completely compatible. The ideal model is one where you try to achieve both basic and applied goals. A good scientist will work to uncover the basic, abstract principles that govern a given behavior, and then take the second step of trying to communicate these findings to the public through a variety of means. This occurs through presenting papers at conferences, attending workshops that include practicing clinical psychologists (people who do couples counseling as well as scientists), and speaking to journalists who are writing articles for popular outlets like Bride Magazine or Ladies Home Journal. It's important to get a more accurate picture out there to the public, because a lot of the books that are written about relationships are really very bad—often, so-called "self-help" books give people really poor advice about how to develop a successful relationship.

Caryl E. Rusbult
Dennis J. Johnson
Gregory D. Murrow

Impact of Couple Patterns of Problem Solving on Distress and Nonstress in Dating Relationships

Having proposed a model of the ways in which couple solve problems, Rusbult and her colleagues tested the model, using a sample
of dating couples at the University of Kentucky. They found that
a major difference between those couples that function effectively
and those that do not has to do with the extent to which each re-
acts to problems in a destructive fashion. That is, the bad things
that partners do to one another rather than the good seem to have
a greater role in determining whether the relationship goes well or
not. Readers should check the details of these findings and ask
whether they hold true in their own personal relationships.

What determines whether a relationship will function successfully? Are certain couple patterns of problem solving more promotive of healthy functioning than others?
One of the most important goals in the study of close relationships is to understand
how couples react to inevitable, perhaps reparable, periodic decline and to identify
the patterns of response that produce the most favorable consequences. Unfortunately, despite the abundance of theory and research devoted to understanding the
development and deterioration of relationships (Altman & Taylor, 1973; Johnson,
1982; Lee, 1984; Levinger, 1979; Murstein, 1970; Rusbult, 1983), people still know
relatively little about the form and effectiveness of various patterns of couple problem solving.

The classic model for identifying what "works" in relationships is to compare
the behavior of partners in nondistressed relationships with comparable behavior in
distressed relationships (Billings, 1979; Birchler, Weis, & Vincent, 1975; Fiore &
Swensen, 1977; Frederickson, 1977; Gottman, 1979; Gottman et al., 1976; Margolin
& Wampold, 1981; Nettels & Loevinger, 1983; Schaap, 1984). This approach to the
study of relationships is predicated on the assumption that the problem-solving behavior of nondistressed couples in comparison with that of distressed couples, is reflective of healthy functioning. Unfortunately, very little of the prior work on dis-

tress/nondistress in close relationships is based on a larger, more comprehensive theory of problem solving.

According to Kelley (1979; Kelley et al., 1983), in formulating a comprehensive theory of relationships, one should take into consideration not only the behaviors of the individual partners but also, and more importantly, the interdependence of the partners, or the impact of their joint behaviors on their relationship (Kelley & Thibault, 1978). In addition, Kelley suggested that one take into consideration the types of attributions that the partners form about one another's dispositions. Accordingly, the theory of problem solving that we advance deals with three important components of close relationships: first, it addresses the simple effects of each individual's problem-solving responses on the quality of the relationship; second, it addresses the more complex effects of various interdependent patterns of problem-solving responses on relationship quality; and third, it enables one to explore the impact of partner perceptions of one another's problem-solving responses on relationship functioning. Our goal in developing such a theory is to understand the effects of each of these variables on the couple; that is, we use as the unit of analysis the relationship itself, rather than the individual partners. In our theory we use an extant typology of problem solving in close relationships with demonstrated utility: the exit–voice–loyalty–neglect typology (Rusbult & Zembrodt, 1983). This typology is a useful means of characterizing couple problem solving in that it is an abstract and comprehensive model that specifies the dimensions on which a variety of responses differ from one another.

THE EXIT–VOICE–LOYALTY–NEGLECT TYPOLOGY

The Rusbult and Zembrodt (1983) typology is based loosely on the writings of Hirschman (1970), who discussed three characteristic reactions to decline in economic domains; (a) *exit,* actively destroying the relationship; (b) *voice,* actively and constructively attempting to improve conditions; and (c) *loyalty,* passively but optimistically waiting for conditions to improve. To assess the comprehensiveness of this model, Rusbult and Zembrodt (1983) carried out a multidimensional scaling analysis of couple problem-solving responses. They found that Hirschman's three categories characterize behaviors in romantic involvements, and also identified a fourth important response: *neglect,* passively allowing one's relationship to deteriorate. The following are examples of behaviors representative of each category of response:

Exit—separating, moving out of a joint residence, actively [physically] abusing one's partner, getting a divorce;

Voice—discussing problems, compromising, seeking help from a friend or therapist, suggesting solutions, changing oneself or one's partner;

Loyalty—waiting and hoping that things will improve, supporting the partner in the face of criticism, praying for improvement;

Neglect—ignoring the partner or spending less time together, refusing to discuss problems, treating the partner badly [insulting], criticizing the partner for things unrelated to the real problem, just letting things fall apart.

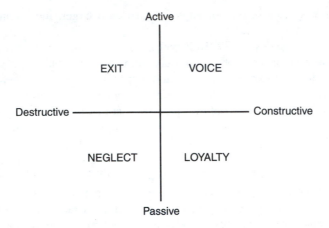

FIGURE 6.1

Exit, voice, loyalty, and neglect: a typology of problem-solving responses in close relationships.

As is shown in Figure 6.1, the four responses differ from one another along two dimensions: Voice and loyalty are *constructive* responses, wherein the individual attempts to revive or maintain the relationship, whereas exit and neglect are relatively more *destructive*.

Previous researchers have demonstrated that the four responses are influenced by a variety of relationship- and individual-level variables. Unfortunately, none of this research answers the question "What 'works' in relationships?" If the typology is to serve as a useful model of problem solving, the adaptive value of the four responses must be empirically established.

A MODEL OF PROBLEM SOLVING IN DISTRESSED RELATIONSHIPS

What implications does the prior work on distressed and nondistressed relationships have for understanding the functional value of exit, voice, loyalty, and neglect responses? First, previous researchers have demonstrated that partners in distressed relationships react more negatively and less positively to problems: Billings (1979) found that in comparison with nondistressed couples, distressed couples exhibit more negative and fewer positive problem-solving acts (e.g., more hostile–dominant, rejecting, and coercive–attacking behaviors, and fewer friendly–dominant behaviors). In the light of the consistency of these findings, we predict that couple distress will be greater to the degree that partners exhibit higher levels of the destructive problem-solving responses and lower levels of the constructive responses. We should find that distress is greater in relationships in which couples respond to problems in an abusive manner, threatening to end their relationships (i.e., exiting), or by refusing to discuss problems, ignoring the partner, spending less time together, and so on (i.e., engaging in neglect). In contrast, distress should be lower to the extent that partners compromise, suggest solutions to problems, and talk things over (i.e., voice), or quietly but optimistically wait for things to improve (i.e., remain loyal).

Previous researchers have also demonstrated that interdependent patterns of response may distinguish between well- and poorly-functioning couples. In the language of interdependence theory (Kelley & Thibault, 1978), distressed couples appear to engage in fewer relationship "transformations" of the problem situation, and thus react to destructive actions from partners with destructive responses in return. Thus we predict that couples will evince greater distress to the degree that partners reciprocate negative problem-solving responses, reacting to exit and neglect from partners with higher levels of exit and neglect in return.

Previous researchers have also demonstrated that partners in well- and poorly-functioning couples may perceive one another's behaviors quite differently. Some research has shown that distress is a function not so much of how partners intend their behaviors as it is a function of how they experience one another's behaviors (Gottman, 1979; Gottman et al., 1976; Markman, 1979, 1981). Thus the prediction advanced earlier about individual response tendencies may also apply to *perceptions* of partner behaviors; partners in distressed couples may *receive* one another's response more negatively, attributing to one another greater tendencies toward exit and neglect and lesser tendencies toward voice and loyalty.

Lastly, in light of prior work on the differences in problem-solving responses of men and women, we expected to uncover some gender differences in response style. On the basis of previous research, we can characterize the behavior of women, in relation to that of men as showing greater direct communication, a more contactful and less controlling style, greater emphasis on maintenance behavior, a desire to confront and discuss problems and feelings, lesser tendencies toward conflict–avoidance, a greater desire for affectional behaviors and a lesser emphasis on instrumental behaviors, and higher levels of intimate self-disclosure (Hawkins, Weisberg, & Ray, 1980; Kelley et al., 1978; Kitson & Sussman, 1982; Morgan, 1976; Rubin, Hill, Peplau, & Dunkel-Schetter, 1980). Given the woman's generally greater affiliative/communal orientation, we predicted that in comparison with men, women will evince greater tendencies to respond constructively and lesser tendencies to respond destructively to relationship problems.

As a preliminary test of the current model, we obtained information, from both members of dating couples, regarding (a) self-reports of response tendencies; (b) perceptions of partner's response tendencies; (c) reports of probable reactions to exit, voice, loyalty, and neglect from partner (i.e., interdependent patterns); and (d) reported satisfaction with and commitment to relationship, liking and loving for partner, and perceived effectiveness of own and partner's pattern of problem-solving. Furthermore, in light of the Gottman et al. (1976) argument that high-conflict situations may be a better means of evaluating the adaptive value of problem-solving responses, we examined interdependent patterns of response for both mild and serious relationship problems.

METHOD

Respondents

The respondents were 68 dating couples from the University of Kentucky. One member of each couple completed the questionnaire during an on-campus research session in partial fulfillment of the requirements for introductory psychology, and was asked to take a packet of materials to his or her partner. This packet included an identical questionnaire (coded with the same number as on that of the first partner's), a cover explaining the purpose of the study, and a stamped return envelope. In the cover letter we asked that individuals complete and return their questionnaires without showing them to their partners, and we assured them that their partners would not be privy to their responses.

The respondents were approximately 20 years old, 21 for male subjects (range = 17 to 36) and 19 for female subjects (range = 17 to 26), had been involved with one another for about 18 months (range = 2 to 66 months), spent about 3 or 4 evenings a week together (range = 1 to 7), and were in one another's company for about 37 hours per week (range = 2 to 110). Seventy-eight percent reported that they were dating regularly, 12% were engaged to be married, and 10% reported that they were dating casually. Eighty-two percent reported that neither partner dated others, 5% reported that one partner dated others and the other partner did not, and 13% reported that both partners dated other persons as well. Ninety-eight percent of the respondents were white.

Questionnaires

In addition to the demographic information mentioned earlier, each questionnaire also enabled us to assess the following:

Self-reported responses and perceptions of partner's responses. Each respondent completed a 28-item scale in order to measure his or her own self-reported tendencies to engage in exit, voice, loyalty, and neglect. Each of the seven items designed to measure each response category was a 9-point Likert-type scale (1 = never do this; 9 = always do this). Items from the four response categories were randomly ordered in the questionnaire. The verbatim items were as follows:

> *Exit*—"When I'm unhappy with my partner, I consider breaking up," "When I'm angry at my partner, I talk to him/her about breaking up," "When we have serious problems in our relationship, I take action to end the relationship," "When I'm irritated with my partner, I think about ending our relationship," "When we have problems, I discuss ending our relationship," "When things are going really poorly between us, I do things to drive my partner away," and "When I'm dissatisfied with our relationship, I consider dating other people."
>
> *Voice*—"When my partner says or does things I don't like, I talk to him/her about what's upsetting me," "When my partner and I have problems, I discuss things with him/her," "When I am unhappy with my partner, I tell him/her what's bothering

me," "When things aren't going well between us, I suggest changing things in the relationship in order to solve the problem," "When my partner and I are angry with one another, I suggest a compromise solution," "When we've had an argument, I work things out with my partner right away," and "When we have serious problems in our relationship, I consider getting advice from someone else (friends, parents, minister, or counselor)."

Loyalty—"When we have problems in our relationship, I patiently wait for things to improve," "When I'm upset about something in our relationship, I wait awhile before saying anything to see if things will improve on their own," "When my partner hurts me, I say nothing and simply forgive him/her," "When my partner and I are angry with each other, I give things some time to cool off on their own rather than take action," "When there are things about my partner that I don't like, I accept his/her faults and weaknesses and don't try to change him/her," "When my partner is inconsiderate, I give him/her the benefit of the doubt and forget about it," and "When we have troubles, no matter how bad things get I am loyal to my partner."

Neglect—"When I'm upset with my partner I sulk rather than confront the issue," "When I'm really bothered about something my partner has done, I criticize him/her for things that are unrelated to the real problem," "When I'm upset with my partner, I ignore him/her for awhile," "When I'm really angry, I treat my partner badly (for example, by ignoring him/her or saying cruel things)," "When we have a problem in our relationship, I ignore the whole thing and forget about it," "When I'm angry at my partner, I spend less time with him/her (for example, I spend more time with my friend, watch a lot of television, work longer hours, etc.)," and "When my partner and I have problems, I refuse to talk to him/her about it."

We assessed individuals' perceptions of their partners' problem-solving responses, using the same items, reworded to describe partner's rather than own response tendencies (e.g., "When I say or do things my partner doesn't like, he/she talks to me about what's upsetting him/her").

Interdependent patterns of response. Twenty open-ended items were designed to enable us to assess response tendencies in reaction to partner's exit, voice, loyalty, and neglect. Respondents wrote brief (one-sentence) responses to statements of the form "If we had a minor problem in our relationship and my partner wanted to ignore it, I would probably. . . ." These responses were coded for exit, voice, loyalty, and neglect content (e.g., 0 = no exit, 1 = some exit) by two judges naive to each couple's distress level.

Exit—"If my partner was irritated by something I had done and started dating someone else, I would probably. . . ."; "If we had a minor problem in our relationship and my partner thought about ending our relationship, I would probably. . . .";

Voice—"If my partner was irritated by something I had done and wanted to have a heart-to-heart talk about it, I would probably. . . ."; "If we had a minor problem in our relationship and my partner wanted to talk it over, I would probably. . . .";

Loyalty—"If my partner was annoyed by one of my personal habits and graciously tried to live with it rather than trying to change me, I would probably. . . ."; If my partner was irritated by something I had done and just waited patiently for it to pass away, I would probably. . . .";

Neglect—"If we had a minor problem in our relationship and my partner wanted to ignore, I would probably. . . ."; "If my partner was annoyed by one of my personal habits and started to treat me badly (ignoring me or saying cruel things), I would probably. . . .";

On the basis of these data, we calculated six dependent measures for each response: response to mild problems (e.g., total voice for the 12 mild-problem statements), response to severe problems (e.g., total loyalty for the eight severe problems), and response to exit, voice, loyalty, and neglect from partner (e.g., total neglect in response to the five partner–voice problems). The responses to mild and severe problem measures were used as additional measures of individual response tendencies.

Distress measures. The questionnaire also included Rubin's (1973) liking and loving instrument, a set of 18 items to which respondents indicated degree of disagreement/agreement on a 9-point Likert-type scale (1 = don't agree at all, 9 = agree completely). Using Rusbult's (1983) items, we measured satisfaction with and commitment to maintain relationships. Five 9-point Likert-type scales enabled us to measure each construct (e.g., for satisfaction, "To what extent are you satisfied with your current relationship?" and "How does your relationship compare to other people's?"; for commitment, "To what extent are you committed to maintaining your relationship?" and "For how much longer do you want your relationship with your partner to last?"). In addition, we assessed participants' perceptions of the effectiveness of their own and their partners' problem-solving styles, using eight 9-point Likert-type scales. The items with which we assessed perceived effectiveness of participants' own behaviors were "Do you think that *your* method of solving problems works?" "Do you think that *you* respond to problems in your relationship in a healthy manner?"; "Does *your* method of solving problems make you feel good afterwards?"; and "Does the way in which *you* react to periods of dissatisfaction make your relationship stronger?" We used the same items, reworded appropriately, to assess participants' perceptions of the effectiveness of their partners' problem-solving behaviors (e.g., "Do you think that *your partner's* method of solving problems works?)

Socially desirable responding. Respondents also completed the Marlow-Crowne (Crowne & Marlow, 1964) instrument, designed to enable us to assess tendencies to describe oneself in a socially desirable manner.

RESULTS

Validity of Exit, Voice, Loyalty, and Neglect Measures

To assess the validity of our measures of problem solving, we calculated the correlation between respondents' descriptions of their own tendencies to react to problems with exit, voice, loyalty, and neglect, and partners' descriptions of the individual's tendencies. These analyses provided fairly good evidence of convergence: the correlations were .53 for exit, .34 for voice, .30 for loyalty, and .42 for neglect. Also, the relation between self-reported tendencies toward exit, voice, loyalty, and neglect and the total coded measure of each response tendency (mild plus severe) from the open-ended items were significant for exit (.48), voice (.53), loyalty (.28), and neglect (.39).

Distress Measure

We calculated a total score for each respondent by summing his or her reported satisfaction, commitment, liking, loving, and perceived effectiveness of own and partner's problem-solving style (each measure first scaled from 1 to 9). Then we calculated a single distress score for each couple by summing male and female partners' reported distress. This composite score captures the feelings of both partners, and should be a valid means of assessing couple distress/nondistress.

Relation Between Problem-Solving Responses and Distress/Nondistress

Impact of individual responses. In the regression models in which we used measures of self-reported response tendencies and measures of responses to both mild and severe problems, both exit and neglect were consistently negatively predictive of couple distress/nondistress. Thus the prediction that destructive tendencies would be deleterious to couple functioning was strongly supported. However, although the tendency to voice in reaction to mild problems was associated with nondistress, voice did not contribute to the prediction of distress/nondistress for models in which we used the measures of self-reported tendencies or responses to severe problems. Furthermore, there was no evidence that loyalty responses contributed to the prediction of couple functioning.

To further examine the power of each mode of response in predicting couple functioning, we performed additional analyses in which we regressed the three measures of each response onto overall couple nondistress. These analyses revealed that the exit, voice, and neglect measures significantly improved the prediction of nondistress beyond that accounted by loyalty; for the weakest improvement (voice). Also, both the exit and voice measures improved the prediction of nondistress beyond that accounted for by voice; for the weakest improvement (neglect). Lastly, the exit measures improved the prediction of nondistress beyond that accounted for by neglect.

Impact of perceptions of partner responses. As predicted, the multiple regression analysis demonstrated that perceptions of partners' tendencies toward exit, voice, and neglect contributed significantly, and perceptions of loyalty contributed marginally, to the prediction of nondistress. Thus there is some evidence that perceptions of partner voice (and perhaps loyalty) do contribute to our understanding of couple functioning, though the analyses of individual response tendencies revealed only weak evidence of such effects.

Impact of interdependent patterns of response. According to our model, couple distress will be greater to the degree that persons react to destructive responses from partners with destructive responses in return. Using data from the open-ended measures of interdependent responses to test this prediction, we found that nondistress was negatively associated with tendencies to respond to partner's exit with exit and neglect (though the latter coefficient was only marginally significant), and with tendencies to respond to partner's neglect with exit and neglect. But tendencies to react with voice and loyalty to partner's exit were also significantly related to nondistress, as were voice reactions in response to partner's neglect. In general, then, we find that couple distress is associated not only with tendencies to reciprocate destructive responses, but also with failure to respond constructively to destructive partner responses.

Gender Differences

Gender differences in the relationships between problem-solving responses and couple distress/nondistress. To determine whether the aforementioned relations between problem-solving responses and couple distress/nondistress hold for both male and female subjects, we performed hierarchical regression analyses. First, we found that female subjects' tendencies to engage in exit exerted a more deleterious impact on couple functioning than did male subjects' exit tendencies. Second, female subjects' tendencies to engage in neglect were more destructive to the relationship in terms of their responses to severe problems. Thus the destructive behaviors of female partners (exit, and perhaps neglect) appear to be particularly deleterious to couple functioning.

Gender differences in mean level of problem-solving responses. To assess gender differences in response tendencies, we performed four two-factor multivariate analyses of variance. The results of these analyses are summarized in Table 6.1. As predicted, females engaged in higher levels of voice than did their male partners. Lastly, as predicted, female subjects evinced somewhat lower neglect scores than did male subjects.

Discussion

The results of this study provide good support for the predictions advanced in our model. First, we found that couples evince poorer functioning to the extent that partners report that they engage in higher levels of destructive responses (i.e., exit and neglect). However, there was no evidence of any link between couple functioning and tendencies to respond to problems with loyalty, and only weak evidence that voice affects couple functioning (voice contributed significantly to predicting nondistress only for mild problems). Thus it appears that the destructive problem-

TABLE 6.1   Gender Differences in Tendencies to Engage in Exit, Voice, Loyalty and Neglect

Subject Responses	Men	Women
Exit		
Self-reported responses	17.26	18.86
Responses to mild problems	1.84	1.56
Responses to severe problems	1.87	2.03
Voice		
Self-reported responses	41.74	45.22
Responses to mild problems	15.69	17.70
Responses to severe problems	11.23	11.92
Loyalty		
Self-reported responses	37.26	37.13
Responses to mild problems	5.07	6.11
Responses to severe problems	3.67	5.17
Neglect		
Self-reported responses	23.50	22.63
Responses to mild problems	5.35	4.08
Responses to severe problems	1.94	1.35

solving responses may be more powerful determinants of couple functioning than are the constructive responses. It is not so much the good, constructive things that partners do or do not do for one another that determines whether a relationship "works" as it is the destructive things that they do or not do in reaction to problems. Why might this be so? We entertain three possible explanations: First, the constructive responses may be more congruent with individuals' schemata for close relationships. If individuals expect their partners to behave well, the constructive responses may be taken for granted; constructive behavior, being the norm, gains one no benefits. Second, there may be an affective asymmetry in the impact of the various responses, destructive responses producing far more negative affect than constructive responses produce positive affect. Third, the response may be differentially salient; destructive responses may simply be more cognitively salient than their constructive counterparts. These speculations remain to be further explored.

Second, we found that couples evince greater health to the degree that partners attribute to one another greater constructive and lesser destructive problem-solving style. Thus in a result that is consistent with the work of Gottman and his colleagues (Gottman, 1979; Gottman et al., 1976; Markman, 1979, 1981), we find that the actual impact of partners' actions is critical in determining how well the relationship functions. Interestingly, the perception that one's partner engages in voice and is loyal (though the loyalty effect was only marginal) contributes to couple functioning, whereas other measures of loyalist tendencies bear no significant relation to couple health, and voice contributes to couple functioning only in response to mild problems.

Third, we found that certain interdependent patterns of couple response distinguish between well- and poorly-functioning couples. In accordance with predictions, tendencies to behave destructively (with exit or neglect) in reaction to destructive problem-solving behaviors from partners (exit or neglect) were especially powerful in enabling us to predict level of distress/nondistress (though the impact of neglect in response to partner's exit was only marginal). In addition, distress is greater to the degree that individuals react to partners' exit and neglect with voice, and react to partners' exit with loyalty. However, the models wherein we attempted to predict couple distress/nondistress on the basis of reactions to partners' voice and loyalty were only marginally predictive of overall couple functioning (though tendencies to voice in response to partners' loyalty were, individually, significantly predictive of nondistress). Together, these findings suggest that a critical issue in solving problems in relationships may be the manner in which individuals react to destructive responses from their partners: distress is greater to the extent that partners react destructively and fail to react constructively when their partners behave in ways that might be destructive to their relationship. Reactions when partners are behaving well (i.e., constructively) are not as effectively predictive of couple health.

Lastly, we found some support for hypotheses regarding gender differences in problem solving. In comparison with their male partners, female subjects were more likely to engage in voice and loyalty, and were somewhat less likely to engage in neglect (the latter effect was weak and inconsistently observed, however). The result of sex role socialization may be to teach women to attend more closely to the social–emotional domain, encouraging them to behave in ways that should promote healthy functioning in relationships. In contrast, men learn to attend to the instrumental domain, and are more likely to ignore or not wish to attend to interpersonal matters (i.e., engage in neglect). It is interesting to note that those behaviors at which women excelled—voice and loyalty—have much less impact on the functioning of the relationship; though women are very "good" at engaging in constructive responses, these response tendencies have very little impact on the quality of their relationships.

We found some evidence of gender differences in the aforementioned relations between problem-solving responses and couple functioning. Specifically, though we advanced no predictions in this regard, we found that the female subjects' tendencies to engage in exit are more damaging to the relationship than were their partners' exit tendencies. Also, there was a weak tendency for the female subjects' neglect tendencies to be more deleterious to the health of the relationship. Why are the women's destructive responses, particularly exit, more harmful to the relationship than are those of the male subjects? This may be due to absolute differences between men and women in mean level of each form of problem solving. Recall that in comparison with women, men are less likely to attempt to solve problems through the constructive reactions of voice and loyalty, and are somewhat more likely to engage in neglect. When his female partner engages in destructive behaviors—exit or neglect—the man is thus somewhat less likely than his partner would be under similar circumstances to help matters by engaging in voice or loyalty or by avoiding neglect. Under such circumstances, then, we may observe a pattern whereby the woman's destructive behaviors are not compensated for by adaptive partner reactions, and thus exert a strongly destructive effect on the couple's functioning. Also, it may be, because the woman generally shows greater tendencies toward constructive responding, that when she does behave destructively, it is a sign of serious trouble. However, this line of reasoning is clearly speculative, and remains to be further explored.

Before concluding, we note some of the strengths and weaknesses of this work. The most critical weakness concerns the validity of our measures. Specifically, our measure of couple distress is based entirely on self-reported feelings regarding partners and relationships. In the classic studies of distress/nondistress, distress and nondistressed couples differ in terms of both counseling status and in terms of standard measures of marital satisfaction (cf. Billings, 1979; Birchler et al., 1975; Gottman et al., 1976). The critical question is assessing the validity of our measure of distress is "What defines healthy functioning?" Is the critical issue how the partners feel about one another? If so, several of our distress component measures (i.e., liking, love, satisfaction) have been shown to be essential components of partners' affective reactions to one another (cf. Rubin, 1973; Rusbult, 1983). Is the critical issue whether the relationship persists? If so, the commitment component of our distress measure has been shown to be powerfully predictive of long-term stability in relationships (cf. Rusbult, 1983). Thus we feel that our distress measure is a valid one. Furthermore, if our couple distress measure was not as sensitive as it could have been, the strength and consistency of our findings suggest that these effects are especially powerful and robust. Nevertheless, it would be fruitful to replicate this work, using the traditional means of differentiating between distressed and nondistressed couples: counseling status.

A second drawback concerns the validity of our exit, voice, loyalty, and neglect measures. These measures were based entirely on verbal report: responses to Likert-type or responses to open-ended statements. It is possible that verbal reports bear little relation to actual problem-solving behaviors. However, two aspects of our findings are comforting in this regard: First, the various measures of individual response tendencies were significantly correlated with one another. Second, the fact that we obtained a relatively complicated, yet consistent, pattern of results—wherein constructive responses were not always positively related to couple functioning and destructive responses were not always negatively related to couple functioning—suggests that our findings do not result from artifacts of self-report such as positive response bias.

Our work has several strengths that render it particularly noteworthy. First, we used multiple modes of measurement in assessing tendencies toward exit, voice, loyalty, and neglect: self-reported tendencies, partner reports of tendencies, and relatively more behavioral measures obtained from responses to open-ended questions. The fact that we obtained similar patterns of findings across the several modes of measurement suggests that our findings should be regarded as relatively more dependable. Second, we have developed and obtained support for a model of problem solving in close relationships that is a relatively complex one, addressing the effects of individual response tendencies, partner perceptions of one another's' response tendencies, and interdependent patterns of couple responding.

One final issue concerns causal ordering: We must ask whether the couple patterns of problem solving observed herein cause level of couple distress, or whether level of distress causes the observed patterns of problem solving. Given that we are assessing the relation between an attribute variable—couple distress/nondistress—and various problem-solving behaviors, we cannot be certain of direction of causality. The only way to determine which of these causal orderings is the more valid account is to carry out a longitudinal investigation of dating or married couples: to follow newly formed couples, charting the development of their relationships as well as changes in patterns of individual and couple problem solving (cf. Markman, 1981). We are at present carrying on such an investigation.

Our work contributes to the understanding of couple problem solving by demonstrating first, that whether a couple functions effectively appears to have much to do with tendencies to (or not to) react to relationship problems in a destructive fashion. It is the bad things that individual partners do rather than the good things that they do not do that distinguishes between well- and poorly-functioning couples. Second, partners' perceptions of one another's problem-solving styles are also predictive of level of couple health; relationships benefit from individual perceptions that their partners engage in high levels of voice and loyalty and low levels of exit and neglect. Third, interdependent patterns of response are effectively predictive of nondistress. In more distressed relationships, when partners engage in exit or neglect, individuals tend to respond with high levels of destructive behaviors and low levels of constructive behaviors in return. Thus it is the way in which partners react during difficult times rather than the way they behave when things are going well that determines whether a relationship "works." Lastly, we observed some gender differences in problem-solving style: In comparison with men, women are more likely to evince voice and loyalty and may be somewhat less likely to engage in neglectful responses. These findings contribute to the understanding of behavior in close relationships by identifying several variables that appear to be critical in determining whether a relationship functions successfully. These results extend the domain to which one can apply the exit–voice–loyalty–neglect typology of responses to periodic decline in close relationships, and demonstrate that this typology is a useful means of portraying what "works" in close relationships.

References

Altman, I., & Taylor, D. A. (1973). *Social penetration: The development of interpersonal relationships.* New York: Holt, Rinehart & Winston.

Billings, A. (1979). Conflict resolution in distressed and nondistressed married couples. *Journal of Consulting and Clinical Psychology, 47,* 368–376.

Birchler, G. R., Weiss, R. L., & Vincent, J. P. (1975). Multimethod analysis of social reinforcement exchange between maritally distressed and nondistressed spouse and stranger dyads. *Journal of Personality and Social Psychology, 31,* 349–360.

Cohen, J., & Cohen, P. (1975). *Applied multiple regression/correlation analysis for the behavioral sciences.* Hillsdale, NJ: Erlbaum.

Crowne, D., & Marlowe, D. (1964). *The approval motive.* New York: Wiley.

Fiore, A., & Swensen, C. H. (1977). Analysis of love relationships in functional and dysfunctional marriages. *Psychological Reports, 40,* 707–714.

Frederickson, C. G. (1977). Life stress and marital conflict: A pilot study. *Journal of Marriage and Family Counseling, 3,* 41—47.

Gottman, J. (1979) *Experimental investigation of marital interaction.* New York: Academic Press.

Gottman, J. M., Notarius, C., Markman, H., Bank, S., Yoppi, B., & Rubin, M. E. (1976). Behavior exchange theory and marital decision making. *Journal of Personality and Social Psychology, 34,* 14—23.

Hagistad, G. O., & Smyer, M. A. (1982). Dissolving long-term relationships: Patterns of divorcing in middle age. In S. Duck (Ed), *Personal relationships 4: Dissolving personal relationships* (pp. 155—188). London: Academic Press.

Hawkins, J. L., Weisberg, C., & Ray, D. W. (1980). Spouse differences in communication and style: Preference, perception, behavior. *Journal of Marriage and the Family, 42,* 585—593.

Hill, C. T., Rubin, Z., & Peplau, L. A. (1976). Breakups before marriage: The end of 103 affairs. *Journal of Social Issues, 32*(1), 147—168.

Hirschman, A. O. (1970). *Exit, voice, and loyalty: Responses to decline in firms, organizations, and states.* Cambridge, MA: Harvard University Press.

Johnson, M. P. (1982). Social and cognitive features of the dissolution of commitment to relationships. In S. Duck (Ed.), *Personal relationships 4: Dissolving personal relationships* (pp. 51—73). London: Academic Press.

Kelley, H. H. (1979). *Personal relationships: Their structures and processes.* Hillsdale, NJ: Erlbaum.

Kelley, H. H., Berscheid, E., Christensen, A., Harvey, J. H., Huston, T. L., Levinger, G., McClintock, E. Peplau, L. A., & Peterson, D. R. (1983). Analyzing close relationships. In H. H. Kelley, E. Berscheid, A. Christensen, J. H. Harvey, T. L. Huston, G. Levinger, E. McClintock, L. A. Pellau, & D. R. Peterson (Eds.), *Close relationships* (pp. 20—67). San Francisco: W. H. Freeman.

Kelley, H. H., Cunningham, J. D., Grisham, J. A. Lefebvre, L. M., Sink, C. R., & Yablon, g. (1978). Sex differences in comments during conflict within close heterosexual pairs. *Sex Roles, 4,* 473—492.

Kitson, G. C., & Sussman, M. B. (1982). Marital complaints, demographic characteristics, and symptoms of mental distress in divorce. *Journal of Marriage and the Family, 44,* 87—101.

Lee, L. (1984). Sequences in separation: A framework for investigating endings of the personal (romantic) relationship. *Journal of Social and Personal Relationships, 1,* 49—73.

Levinger, G. (1979). A social exchange view on the dissolution of pair relationships. In R. L. Burgess & T. L. Huston (Eds.), *Social exchange in developing relationships* (pp. 169—193). New York: Academic Press.

Margolin, G., & Wampold, B. E. (1981). Sequential analysis of conflict and accord in distressed and nondistressed marital partners. *Journal of Counseling and Clinical Psychology, 49,* 554—567.

Markman, H. J. (1979). Application of behavioral model of marriage in predicting relationship satisfaction of couples planning marriage. *Journal of Consulting and Clinical Psychology, 47,* 743—749.

Markman, H. J. (1981). Prediction of marital distress: A 5-year follow-up. *Journal of Consulting and Clinical Psychology, 49,* 760-762.

Morgan, B. (1976). Intimacy of disclosure topic and sex differences in self-disclosure. *Sex Roles, 2,* 161—166.

Murstein, B. I. (1970). Stimulus–value–role: A theory of marital choice. *Journal of Marriage and the Family, 32,* 465—481.

Nettles, E. J., & Loevinger, J. (1983). Sex role expectations and ego level in relation to problem marriages. *Journal of Personality and Social Psychology, 45,* 676—687.

Rubin, Z. (1973). *Liking and loving.* New York: Holt, Rinehart & Winston.

Rubin, Z., Hill, C. T., Peplau, L. A., & Dunkel-Schetter, C. (1980). Self-disclosure in dating couples: Sex roles and the ethic of openness. *Journal of Marriage and the Family, 42,* 305—317.

Rusbult, C. E. (1983). A longitudinal test of the investment model: The development (and deterioration) of satisfaction and commitment in heterosexual involvements. *Journal of Personality and Social Psychology, 45,* 101—117.

Rusbult, C. E., & Zembrodt, I. M. (1983). Responses to dissatisfaction in romantic involvements: A multidimensional scaling analysis. *Journal of Experimental Social Psychology, 19,* 274—293.

Schaap, C. (1984). A comparison of the interaction of distressed and nondistressed married couples in a laboratory situation: Literature survey, methodological issues, and an empirical investigation. In K. Hahlweg & N. S. Jacobson (Eds.), *Marital interaction: Analysis and modification* (pp. 133—158). New York: Guilford.

Susan Sprecher
Quintin Sullivan
Elaine Hatfield

Mate Selection Preferences: Gender Differences Examined in a National Sample

What do men and women look for in a potential mate? Although lots of people talk about this question, and a few studies of college students have tried to answer it, Sprecher and her colleagues offer us some answers from a large nationwide sample of adults. As expected, they found that youth and physical attractiveness are more valued by men than women, and that earning potential was more important to women in their choice of a mate. The authors also report that while these broader preferences stood regardless of other characteristics of those in the survey, older versus younger people, and blacks versus whites had some additional unique preferences. At the end of the article the authors ask whether the different preferences of men and women are likely to change as our culture changes, especially as cultural values change and as women come to have greater career opportunities. What do you think?

Mate selection criteria have long been a topic of interest for family researchers and social psychologists. In one frequently used methodology dating back to an early study by Hill (1945), partner attributes or characteristics are listed and subjects (typically college students) are asked to rate each in importance. One issue that has been frequently examined with this "mate selection questionnaire paradigm" (Feingold, 1990) is how men and women differ in the attributes they desire in a partner (e.g., Buss & Barnes, 1986; Howard, Blumstein, & Schwartz, 1987). In this study, we extend previous research on this topic by examining gender differences in mate preferences with data from single adults in a national probability sample—the National Survey of Families and Households (NSFH).

THEORETICAL BACKGROUND TO GENDER
DIFFERENCES IN MATE PREFERENCES

One reason for psychologists' renewed interest in gender differences in mate selection criteria has been the development of evolutionary explanations for human social behavior (e.g., Buss & Schmitt, 1993; Cunningham, 1986; Kenrick & Trost, 1989). Evolutionary psychologists make clear predictions as to how men and women should differ in the traits they desire in a mate (e.g., Buss, 1989; Trivers, 1972). Buss (1989), for example, predicted that men should prefer mates with traits that signal their reproductive value (traits such as youth and good looks). Women should prefer mates with traits that signal their potential for resource acquisition (traits such as ambition and status). With these strategies, both men and women choose partners that enhance their reproductive success.

One could also explain such gender differences by referring to sociocultural factors (e.g., Buss & Barnes, 1986; Howard et al., 1987). That is, men's greater preference for a partner who is attractive and young and women's greater preference for a partner who can provide material wealth can be explained by traditional sex role socialization and the poorer economic opportunities for women.

Both theories help explain the gender differences in mate selection preferences predicted in this study. As explained by Feingold (1990), "Because evolutionary forces could shape sociocultural roles, the two types of explanations are not necessarily mutually exclusive" (p. 990).

PREVIOUS RESEARCH ON GENDER DIFFERENCES
IN MATE PREFERENCES

Evolutionary theory and the sociocultural perspective are in agreement in predicting gender differences in the desire for the following three partner attributes: physical attractiveness, youth (both predicted to be preferred by men), and earning potential and related socioeconomic characteristics (predicted to be preferred by women). Research, reviewed below, provides support for these gender differences. Although gender differences in traits desired in a partner have been examined primarily through the mate selection questionnaire, other methods have also been used, including content analysis of personal want ads.

In studies that use the mate selection questionnaire format, men have rated physical attractiveness or good looks as more important than have women (see recent studies by Allgeier & Wiederman, 1991; Buss, 1989; Buxx & Barnes, 1986; Goodwin, 1990; Howard et a., 1987; Townsend, 1989; Wiederman & Allgeier, 1991; for a meta-analysis of several studies, see Feingold, 1990). Content analysis of personal want ads, a recently developed method for studying mate selection preferences, has also demonstrated a similar gender difference: Men are more likely than women to request physical attractiveness in a partner, whereas women are more likely than men to offer it (Cameron, Oskamp, & Sparkes, 1977; Deauz & Hanna, 1984; Harrison & Saeed, 1977; Koestner & Wheeler, 1988; Rajecki, Bledsoe, & Rasmussen, 1991; see also Feingold, 1990). However, research conducted on people's reactions or behaviors toward real or hypothetical romantic others suggests that men and women value physical attractiveness to nearly the same degree (e.g., Feingold, 1990; Sprecher, 1989).

Whereas gender differences in physical attractiveness have been examined in many studies, gender differences in age preferences have not. However, in a cross-cultural study on mate preferences, Buss (1989) asked the ages respondents preferred in a marriage partner. In each of the 37 samples (from 33 countries), men generally preferred mates who were younger and women generally preferred mates who were older. Buss reported that these gender differences in age preferences were the largest gender differences found in his study on mate preferences. Research on personal want ads demonstrates a similar gender difference. Men are more likely than women to express a preference for a younger mate, whereas women are more likely than men to say they want an older mate (Bolig, Stein, & McKenry, 1984; Cameron et al., 1977; Harrison & Saeed, 1977; Rajecki et al., 1991). Furthermore, studies on decision making in video dating services indicate that men are more concerned than women with the age of a prospective match and are more likely to prefer a younger partner (Woll, 1986).

Previous research on gender differences in preferences for earning potential also provides support for the gender difference predicted about this characteristic from both evolutionary theory and the sociocultural perspective. When asked in a mate selection questionnaire what they prefer in a mate, women express a greater preference than men for earning potential or social status (e.g., Buss, 1989; Buss & Barnes, 1986; Howard et al., 1987; Townsend, 1989). Furthermore, in personal ads, financial security is more likely to be requested by women but more likely to be offered by men (Cameron et al., 1977; Harrison & Saeed, 1977; Koestner & Wheeler, 1988). In a study of the decisions made by clients in video dating organizations, Woll (1986) found that women were more likely than men to say that occupation was a factor they considered in deciding whether to request additional information about a prospective match.

In sum, there is substantial evidence for the gender differences in mate preferences predicted by evolutionary theory and the sociocultural perspective. Men value physical attractiveness and youth to a greater degree than women, and women value earning potential to a greater degree than men. There is also some evidence to indicate that actual matches in real life reflect these sex-specific exchanges of resources (Elder, 1969; Taylor & Glenn, 1976; Udry, 1977; Udry & Eckland, 1984).

PURPOSES OF THIS INVESTIGATION

Although gender differences in mate preferences for the above three characteristics have been examined in a number of recent studies, no previous study on this topic has been conducted with a national probability sample. Because questions on mate selection preferences were asked of the single respondents in the NSFH, we can, for the first time, examine gender differences in mate selection preferences with a nationally representative sample of single adults. The NSFH assesses mate preferences for 12 attributes, 8 of which are related to physical attractiveness, youth, and earning potential—the 3 characteristics discussed above. We hypothesized that men, compared with women, would be more concerned that their partner be physically attractive and younger than themselves and that women, compared with men, would be more eager to marry someone who has earning potential. We also explored gender differences in preferences for the other attributes included in the NSFH.

The second purpose of this study was to examine whether the magnitude of the gender differences in mate preferences varies across particular sociodemographic groups in the national sample. The NSFH data allow us to look at gender differences in mate preferences among single adults of different ages (from 19 to 35) and different races (Blacks and Whites). Although we expected that our predicted gender differences in mate preferences would be found in each of the sociodemographic groups, some gender differences may be more pronounced in one age group or race than in the others.

For example, we have reason to expect men's greater desire for someone younger increases with age. Kenrick and Keefe (1992) have noted that the evolutionary perspective would predict that as men age, they must become interested in younger and younger women if they are to mate with a woman still in her reproductive years (women's preferences should remain relatively constant over different ages). They found support for their hypothesis in content analyses of personal want ads collected from the United States and other countries and from an examination of actual age differences from marriage statistics.

Furthermore, Spaner and Glick (1980) and others have speculated that the shortage of men for Black women could lead to a tendency for Black women to marry men with less education who are younger or much older, and who have previously married. In other words, Black women, because of their limited field of eligibles, may be more willing to lower their criteria for a mate. On the other hand, Black men, who enjoy an abundance of Black women, can afford to be particularly choosy. Other ways that race and age may moderate the effect of gender on mate selection preferences are explored in this study.

METHOD

Sample

The hypotheses in this study were tested with a subsample from the NSFH, which was conducted in a 14-month period ending in May 1988. The NSFH is a multistage, area probability sample survey of 13,017 English or Spanish-speaking persons age 19 and older, living in households in the United States. Data were collected through both a face-to-face interview and a self-administered questionnaire.

Only the unmarried respondents in the NSFH study who were age 35 or younger who had never been married and were either White or Black were included in the analyses. Our subsample, then, consisted of 1,329 respondents, 648 (49%) men and 681 (51%) women and 854 (64%) White and 475 (36%) Black. The mean age of the subsample was 25 ($SD = 4.6$).

Measurement of Mate Preferences

In one section of the self-administered questionnaire presented to the single adults, a section was included that began "Listed below are considerations that are important to some people in thinking about WHETHER TO MARRY someone. Please circle how willing you would be to marry someone who. . . ." This introduction was followed by a list of 12 characteristics:

1. was older than you by 5 or more years,
2. was younger than you by 5 or more years,
3. had been married before,
4. already had children,
5. was not likely to hold a steady job,
6. was of a different religion,
7. was of a different race,
8. would earn much less than you,
9. would earn much more than you,
10. was not "good-looking,"
11. had more education than you, and
12. had less education than you.

Each of these items was followed by a 7-point (1 = not at all and 7 = very willing) Likert response scale. We used Items 1 and 2 to measure preference for youth, Item 10 to measure preference for physical attractiveness, and items 5, 8, 9, 11, and 12 to measure preference for earning potential (and social status).

RESULTS

Overview of Analyses

To examine the effect of gender on mate selection preferences, and the moderating influence of race and age, we conducted a $2 \times 2 \times 3$ analysis of variance (ANOVA). The independent variables were gender (male vs. female), race (White vs. Black), and age (19–22, 23–27, and 28–35). The dependent variables were the 12 mate selection preferences measured in the NSFH study. Because the theoretical focus of this study is on gender, the only results presented below for race and age are for the interaction effects that also included gender.

Gender Differences in Mate Preferences

First, the main effect of gender was examined to see if there was any support for the hypothesis that men and women differ in their preferences for physical attractiveness, youth, and earning potential. Table 6.2 shows that the main effect for gender was consistent with this hypothesis and statistically significant. Women were more willing than men to marry someone who was not good-looking, someone who was older by 5 years, someone who earned more, and someone who had more education.

TABLE 6.2 Gender Differences in Mate Preferences for a National Sample

Theoretical variables	M		F
	Men	Women	
Physical appearance			
Not "good-looking"	3.41	4.42	172.39**
Age			
Older by 5 years	4.15	5.29	182.48**
Younger by 5 years	4.54	2.80	394.17**
Earning potential			
Not likely to hold steady job	2.73	1.62	213.25**
Earn less than you	4.60	3.76	88.44**
Earn more than you	5.19	5.93	98.89**
More education	5.22	5.82	73.69**
Less education	4.67	4.08	39.00*
Other variables			
Married before	3.35	3.44	2.03
Already had children	2.84	3.11	9.56*
Different religion	4.24	4.31	0.76
Different race	3.08	2.84	12.97**

$*p < .01$
$**p < .001$

Men were more willing than women to marry someone who was younger by 5 years, someone not likely to have a steady job, someone who earned less, and someone who had less education.

Gender Differences in Different Sociodemographic Groups

The above results provide support for the gender differences predicted from evolutionary theory and from the sociocultural perspective concerning preferences for physical attractiveness, youth, and earning potential. The findings are also consistent with previous research. Next, we examined whether gender differences in mate preferences depend on race or age. To consider this, we look at the Gender × Race, the Gender × Age, and the Gender × Race × Age interactions from the ANOVA results.

Race. The Gender × Race interaction was significant for only two attributes. For both Blacks and Whites, women were less willing than men to marry someone who was unlikely to hold a steady job. This gender difference, however, was greater among Whites ($M = 2.76$ for White men and 1.48 for White women) than among Blacks ($M = 2.56$ for Black men and 2.01 for Black women). Of these four sociodemographic groups, White women were least willing to marry someone who was not likely to hold a steady job.

The second Significant Gender × Race interaction was found for the attribute not good-looking. For both races, men were less willing than women to marry someone who was not good-looking. This gender difference, however, was greater among Whites ($M = 3.42$ for White men and 4.55 for White women) than among Blacks ($M = 3.31$ for Black men and 4.05 for Black women; −3.81). Of the four sociodemographic groups, White women were most willing to marry someone who was not attractive.

Age. A Gender × Age interaction was significant for three attributes, two of which were among our theoretical variables. In all three age groups (19–22, 23–27, and 28–35), men were more willing than women to marry someone who earned less than they. This difference between men and women, however, was greater for the middle age group ($M = 4.72$ for men and 3.60 for women) than for the oldest age group ($M = 4.48$ for men and 3.43 for women) and the youngest age group ($M = 4.56$ for men and 3.96 for women). When we consider the six sociodemographic groups formed by combining gender and age, the group least willing to marry someone who earned less than they did was the female group aged 28–35.

Another significant Gender × Age interaction was found for "had more education." In all three age groups, women were more willing than men to marry someone with more education. The difference between the genders, however, was greater for the youngest age group ($M = 5.17$ for men and 5.96 for women) than for either the middle age group ($M = 5.35$ for men and 5.69 for women), or the oldest age group ($M = 5.13$ for men and 5.61 for women). Young women were particularly willing to marry someone who had more education.

Race and age. For both the youngest and the middle age groups, the degree of difference between men and women in willingness to marry someone younger by 5 years was very similar in both races. Men of both races were more willing than women of both races to marry someone younger ($M = 4.29$ for women and 2.41 for women among 19- to 22-year-old Blacks; $M = 4.27$ for men and 2.60 for women for women among 19- to 22-year-old Whites; $M = 4.24$ for men and 2.53 for women among 23- to 27-year-old Blacks; and $M = 4.75$ for men and 2.78 for women among 23- to 27-year-old Whites). In the 28–35 age group, however, the difference between men and women was exceptionally large among Blacks ($M = 5.00$ for men and 2.55 for women) but smaller among Whites ($M = 5.06$ for men and 4.07 for women). Thus, it seems that men's willingness to marry someone younger increased with age, and this is true regardless of race. For women, however, changes over age depend on race. Black women experienced no change with age in their willingness to marry someone younger, whereas White women, the older they got, became more willing to marry someone younger and, hence, became more similar to men in this preference.

DISCUSSION

We had two goals in this study. First, we wanted to know whether the gender differences in mate preferences found in earlier research would replicate in a national probability sample. The second goal was to examine whether the magnitude of the gender differences in mate selection preferences depends on age and race.

Do the Gender Differences Replicate?

We found clear support that the gender differences found in previous studies replicate in a national probability sample. More specifically, men were more willing than women to marry someone younger by 5 years (the largest gender difference found), someone who was not likely to hold a steady job, someone who earned less, and someone who had less education. Women were more willing than men to marry someone who was not good-looking, someone older by 5 years, someone who earned more than they, and someone who had more education. All of these gender differences were fairly large in magnitude.

These gender differences are consistent with previous research and with two theoretical perspectives on gender differences in human behavior. In evolutionary terms, men should prefer mates who possess traits signaling their reproductive value—traits such as youth and good looks—whereas women should prefer men who possess traits that signal their potential for resource acquisition—men who are able and willing to provide resources. These same gender differences, however, can also be explained by women's relative lack of access to societal resources and by traditional sex role socialization (the sociocultural perspective).

Although most of the items included in the list of assets and liabilities in the NSFH data refer to preferences for either youth, physical attractiveness, or earning potential (our theoretical variables), there were four other assets and liabilities included. No gender differences were found in either willingness to marry someone who had been married before or willingness to marry someone of a different religion. However, women were more willing than men to marry someone who already had children, and men were more willing than women to marry someone who was of a different race. These gender differences, however, were smaller in magnitude than the gender differences found for the theoretical variables.

Women may be more willing than men to marry someone who already has children because, compared with men, women have a limited number of years in which they are fertile and thus they may be more willing to consider alternative routes to parenthood. (According to this argument, we would expect to find that women's, but not men's, willingness to marry someone with children increases with age—indeed, we did secure a significant Gender × Age interaction on this item that reflects this pattern, which we discuss below.) Men may also express more reluctance than women to marry someone who already has children because they may be more likely than women to assume that they will have to be involved in the raising of the children (thus, taking away scarce resources from their own actual or future biological children). Custody of children is still more likely to go to mothers than to fathers. The finding that men expressed more willingness to marry someone of a different race may be explained, in part, by differential socialization of men and women. For example, daughters get more pressure than sons to marry according to endogamous norms (e.g., Prather, 1990), most likely because daughters are considered the link to the next generation and more generally are subject to greater parental influence. Although Black men's greater willingness, relative to Black women's, to marry a person of another race is consistent with actual marriage statistics, White men's greater willingness, relative to White women's, is not. Marriages between White women and Black men are more common than those between White men and Black women (see discussion by Murstein, 1986). This discrepancy between mate selection preferences and actual marriage statistics (at least for marriages between White men and Black women) is interesting and should be further investigated. In the formation of interracial relationships, opportunities may predominate over personal preferences.

Are Gender Differences in Mate Preferences Modified by Age or Race?

One second goal was to examine the extent to which gender differences found in mate preferences depend on age and race. We found that, in the main, the gender differences summarized above existed regardless of age (from 19 to 35) or race (Black vs. White). However, the various sociodemographic groups did differ slightly in the magnitude of gender differences for some of the preferences.

Let us first consider how gender differences in mate preferences depend on race. A significant interaction between gender and race was found for the item "was not likely to hold a steady job." We found that White men were more willing than Black men to marry a woman who did not possess a steady job. Women, White and Black, were less willing to marry a man who did not have a regular job. However, White women indicated more often than Black women that a man must have a steady job before they would consider marriage. White women do not face the same kind of shortage of "acceptable" men that Black women face, and hence this may be reflected in their tendency to be more demanding that their mate have a steady job. However, note that this interaction was not found for the other traits referring to earning potential (relative earning and relative education).

We also secured a weak but significant interaction between gender and race on the question about willingness to marry someone who was not good-looking. For both groups, men were more insistent than women that their mates be attractive. Again, however, race tempers these preferences. Black women were less willing than White women to marry someone who was not good-looking. In a small study conducted with professional Black women, Sparrow (1991) also found that physical attractiveness was rated as a relatively important quality for a mate to have (rated 7th out of 20 and rated as more important than money and occupation). It is not quite clear why White women rated looks as less important than other assets, whereas Black women did not. As we discuss later, the benefits of marriage may be less for Black women.

Age also shapes the pattern of gender differences found in mate preferences. First, an interaction between gender and age was found on the question "earns less than you." In the younger age group (19–22), both men and women were fairly willing to marry someone who earned less than they (and men were slightly more willing than women). As men and women aged, however, their concerns began to diverge. The older women got, the less willing they became to marry a man who earned less than they. There may be at least two reasons for this. First, as women got older, they may increasingly hear their "biological clocks" ticking. They may become more concerned about finding a man who can, if not support them, at least pull his own financial weight during their childbearing years. Second, as men and women get older, they begin to "hit their economic stride." When men and women are young, perhaps in college, it would not be surprising for both of them to work at low-paying jobs. They may not be too concerned about who makes more money. As men and women get older, the gap between what men and women "normally" make begins to diverge. Perhaps when an older woman thinks of marrying a man who earns less, she envisions a man far below her in socioeconomic status; in any case the consequences of a discrepancy may now be far more serious. At every age group, women were more willing than men to marry someone with more education. Younger women, however, were especially willing to marry someone with more education than themselves. This does not seem to make sense, either from a sociobiological or a practical perspective. As women get older, the marriage market begins to close in on them. We would expect them to get more tolerant, not less. However, this finding does make sense if we consider that many of the young women, who may not have yet finished their own educational pursuits, would likely be looking at a dating market of slightly older men. Longitudinal research is needed to further clarify how gender differences in mate preferences might depend on age. In cross-sectional analyses, as done in this study, the group of individuals who reach 28 years of age or older and are not yet married may be different from individuals who have married by this age. Furthermore, gender differences in the age range past the years of fertility are important to examine and are not addressed here.

For relatively young (19–27) men and women, the pattern of gender differences was similar in both races: men were more willing than women to marry someone who was younger. However, in the age group 28–35, Black women and White women diverged in their preferences. Black women experienced no change with age in their willingness to marry someone younger, whereas White women, the older they got, became more willing to marry someone younger. (Men's desire to marry someone younger increased with age, regardless of race.) It is not quite clear why Black women in this older age group did not, like their White counterparts, also become more willing to marry older men. South (1991) offered a number of possible reasons why Black women do not seem to respond to "marriage market" pressures:

> Thus, the economic benefits to marriage are less for black women. . . . This differential could lead black women to limit their field of acceptable mates, as well as to delay marriage or to remain unmarried. . . .
> In addition, among African Americans (and perhaps other groups) there may exist norms and social networks supportive of singlehood, which render marriage a less desired state. These norms and networks may reduce the financial and emotional costs of nonmarriage, allowing those who do marry greater discrimination in choosing a spouse. (p. 938)

Conclusion

The gender differences in mate preferences that we secured were consistent with those that are predicted by both evolutionary theory and the sociocultural perspective and consistent with those secured in previous research. This means that even though the previous studies used nonprobability samples, their results were essentially correct. That is, the gender patterns previously observed in mainly White college students appear to be found among both Whites and Blacks and among adults of different ages (19–35). With increased egalitarianism in heterosexual relationships, will men and women continue to have different mate selection preferences? The evolutionary explanation for gender differences in preferences suggests that we will continue to find differences between men and women in desire for physical attractiveness, youth, and earning potential—even with changing social conditions. On the other hand, gender differences in mate selection preferences could narrow in the next 2 decades as young males and females are socialized to value the same traits and are presented with equal opportunities in the larger social structure.

References

Allgeier, E. R., & Wiederman, M. W. (1991). Love and mate selection in the 1990s. *Free Inquiry, 11,* 25–27.

Bolig, R., Stein, P. J., & McKenry, P. C. (1984). The self-advertisement approach to dating: Male–female differences. *Family Relations, 33,* 587–592.

Bulcroft, R. A., & Bulcroft, K. A. (1993). Race differences in attitudinal and motivational factors in the decision to marry. *Journal of Marriage and the Family, 55,* 338–355.

Buss, D. M. (1989). Sex differences in human mate preferences: Evolutionary hypotheses tested in 37 cultures. *Behavioral and Brain Sciences, 12,* 1–49.

Buss, D. M., & Barnes, M. (1986). Preferences in human mate selection. *Journal of Personality and Social Psychology, 50,* 559–570.

Buss, D. M., & Schmitt, D. P. (1993). Sexual strategies theory: An evolutionary perspective on human mating. *Psychological Review, 100,* 204–232.

Cameron, C., Oskamp, S., & Sparkes, W. (1977). Courtship American style: Newspaper ads. *Family Coordinatory, 26,* 27–30.

Cunningham, M. R. (1986). Measuring the physical in physical attractiveness: Quasi-experiments on the sociobiology of female facial beauty. *Journal of Personality and Social Psychology, 50,* 925–935.

Deaux, K., & Hanna, R. (1984). Courtship in the personals column: The influence of gender and sexual orientation. *Sex Roles, 11,* 363–375.

Elder, G. H., Jr. (1969). Appearance and education in marriage mobility. *American Sociological Review, 34,* 519–533.

Feingold, A. (1990). Gender differences in effects of physical attractiveness on romantic attraction: A comparison across five research paradigms. *Journal of Personality and Social Psychology, 59,* 981–993.

Goodwin, R. (1990). Sex differences among partner preferences: Are the sexes really very similar? *Sex Roles, 23,* 501–513.

Harrison, a. A., & Saeed, L. (1977). Let's make a deal: An analysis of revelations and stipulations in lonely hearts advertisements. *Journal of Personality and Social Psychology, 35,* 257–264.

Hill, R. (1945). Campus values in mate selection. *Journal of Home Economics, 37,* 554–558.

Howard, J. A., Blumstein, P., & Schwartz, P. (1987). Social or evolutionary theories? Some observations on preferences in human mate selection. *Journal of Personality and Social Psychology, 53,* 194–200.

Hudson, J. W., & Henze, L. P. (1969). Campus values in mate selection: A replication. *Journal of Marriage and the Family, 31,* 772–778.

Kenrick, D. T., & Keefe, R. C. (1992). Age preferences in mates reflect sex differences in human reproductive strategies. *Behavioral and Brain Sciences, 15,* 75–133.

Kenrick, D. T., & Trost, M. R. (1989). A reproductive exchange model of heterosexual relations: Putting proximate economics in ultimate perspective. In C. Hendrick (Ed.), *Close relationships* (pp. 92–118). Newbury Park, CA: Sage.

Koestner, R., & Wheeler, L. (1988). Self-presentation in personal advertisements: The influence of implicit notions of attraction and role expectations. *Journal of Social and Personal Relationships, 5,* 149–160.

Murstein, E. I. (1986). *Paths to marriage.* Beverly Hills, CA: Sage.

Prather, J. E. (1990). "It's just as easy to marry a rich man as a poor one!": Students' accounts of parental messages about marital partners. *Mid-American Review of Sociology, 14,* 151–162.

Rajecki, D. W., Bledsoe, S. B., & Rasmussen, J. L. (1991). Successful personal ads: Gender differences and similarities in offers, stipulations, and outcomes. *Basic and Applied Social Psychology, 12,* 457–469.

South, S. J. (1991). Sociodemographic differentials in mate selection preferences. *Journal of Marriage and the Family, 53,* 928–940.

Spanier, G. B., & Glick, P. C. (1980). Mate selection differentials between Whites and Blacks in the United States. *Social Forces, 58,* 707–725.

Sparrow, K. H. (1991). Factors in mate selection for single Black professional women. *Free Inquiry in Creative Sociology, 19,* 103–109.

Sprecher, S. (1989). The importance to males and females of physical attractiveness, earning potential, and expressiveness in initial attraction. *Sex Roles, 21,* 591–607.

Sweet, J. A., Bumpass, L. L., & Call, V. R. A. (1988). *The design and content of the National Survey of Families and Households* (NSFH Working Paper No. 1). Madison: University of Wisconsin. Center for Demography and Ecology.

Taylor, P. A., & Glenn, N. D. (1976). The utility of education and attractiveness for females' status attainment through marriage. *American Sociological Review, 41,* 484–497.

Townsend, J. M. (1989). Mate selection criteria: A pilot study. *Ethology and Sociobiology, 10,* 241–253.

Townsend, J. M., & Levy, G. D. (1990). Effects of potential partners' physical attractiveness and socioeconomic status on sexuality and partner selection. *Archives of Sexual Behavior, 19,* 149–164.

Trivers, R. L. (1972). Parental investment and sexual selection. In B. Campbell (Ed.), *Sexual selection and the descent of man* (pp. 136–179). Chicago: Aldine.

Udry, J. R. (1977). The importance of being beautiful: A re-examination and racial comparisons. *American Journal of Sociology, 83,* 154–160.

Udry, J. R., & Eckland, B. K. (1984). The benefits of being attractive: Differential payoffs for men and women. *Psychological Reports, 54,* 47–56.

Wiederman, M. W., & Allgeier, E. R. (1992). Gender differences in mate selection criteria: Sociobiological or socioeconomic explanation. *Ethology and Sociobiology, 13,* 115–124.

Woll, S. (1986). So many to choose from: Decision strategies in video-dating. *Journal of Social and Personal Relationships, 3,* 43–53.

Robert J. Sternberg

The Ingredients of Love

In this clearly and simply written excerpt from his book, Robert Sternberg outlines the basic ingredients of his triangular theory of love. By recalling his past relationships, Sternberg points out that all "loves" have some degree of three elements: 1) intimacy, which consists of those feelings that promote a close and tight bond; 2) passion, an intense longing to be with the other person, which may be expressed sexually; and 3) decision/commitment, which involves a desire to maintain a relationship with the other, and to do what it takes to keep it going. By consideration of the strength or intensity of the three elements, Sternberg develops a taxonomy of differing kinds of love. You might contrast, for instance, the differing kinds of love found between two people who have been married for 40 years versus a couple that has been living together for a month. While both may have a tight, sharing bond (intimacy), it is likely that that the long marriage is great evidence of commitment, even though the passion has likely cooled over the years. The couple living together is likely to be strong on passion, but it is hard to be sure what their level of commitment is.

I first fell in love in the first grade. The girl, whom I will call Irene, was a classmate of mine and lived right up the block. She and I spent a lot of time together, playing (the usual childhood games, like hide and seek, tag, and house), walking to school, and helping each other out in any way we could. Irene and I had a modest plan: to become king and queen of the world, and to have everyone else in the world as our subjects. Irene eventually moved away, and that was the end of both our friendship and our kingdom: I never saw her again. But it seems clear in retrospect that she and I had at least one critical element of love: We were close friends and shared with each other intimacies we shared with no one else. We communicated well with each other and always felt comforted in each other's presence. Although we may not have had all the ingredients of love, we certainly had one of the most important: we cared about each other and supported each other. In short, we had an emotionally intimate relationship.

I next fell in love with Patti, who sat in front of me in tenth-grade biology class.

The very first day I laid eyes on her, I fell madly in love. I spent whole classes just staring at her—but I never told her how I felt about her. My lack of communication was not for lack of feelings. I thought about Patti almost constantly and, for a year of my life, about little else. I did my schoolwork on automatic pilot. When I would talk to other people, I would be, at most, half there, because I was secretly thinking about Patti. I would go home at the end of the day and pine away thinking about her. The months went by, but I couldn't move myself to express my feelings toward her; indeed, I acted coldly toward her, because I was afraid of giving myself away (which I probably did, anyway). I was crushed when, right after New Year's Day, I saw her clandestinely reading a handwritten letter, and her best friend told me that Patti had met a boy at a New Year's Eve party and falling in love with him. To make matters worse, the boy was captain of one of the school's athletic teams, and I wasn't even on a team. Eventually, I got over my obsession with Patti, and we even became somewhat friendly, though I discovered that I liked her decidedly less than I had loved her.

The feeling I had for Patti was a second ingredient of love: passion. And whereas the intimacy I felt with Irene was mutual, as intimacy almost has to be, the passion I felt for Patti was one-sided, as passion often is. In retrospect, of course, I would call my love for Patti infatuation, since it developed without my even knowing her and continued in the absence of any real mutual relationship between us. But infatuation is fueled more vigorously by doubts and uncertainties than by knowledge of what a person is like. Eventually, Patti went away to college, and I never saw her again.

The third time I fell in love was with Cindy, whom I met relatively soon after I met Patti. My relationship with Cindy was everything my relationship with Patti was not, and vice versa. In a word, my relationship with Cindy was "sensible." We had relatively similar backgrounds and upbringings; we both did well in school and were career oriented; and in a nutshell, we were what people would call a good match. Our relationship had neither the deep intimacy of my relationship with Irene nor the overwhelming passion of my one-sided relationship with Patti, but it did have something that the other two relationships had lacked. Cindy and I believed we loved each other, and relatively quickly committed ourselves to each other. We worked out a system whereby we would call each other every night and see each other regularly. We were viewed as an "item" by others, and viewed ourselves that way as well. Our relationship was pretty much exclusive; and as time went on and our commitment to each other increased, the time we spent with others decreased. Our commitment continued to grow; eventually, though, it declined, and we later split up. It is always hard to say why particular couples split up, but in our case I believe that, with the waning of passion over time, we had not developed sufficient intimacy to fuel our commitment to each other.

Paramount in each of these relationships of mine was one of the three ingredients, or components, of love: intimacy (with Irene), passion (for Patti), and commitment (to Cindy). I believe that love can be understood as a triangle (which should not be confused with a "love triangle" of three people) of which each point is one of these three components: intimacy (the top point of the triangle), passion (the left-hand point), and decision/commitment (the right-hand point) (see Figure 6.2).

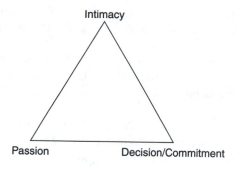

FIGURE 6.2

The Triangle of Love

The assignment of components to vertices is one of convenience; it is essentially arbitrary.

A substantial body of evidence suggests that the components of intimacy, passion, and commitment play a key role in love over and above other attributes. Even before I collected the first bit of data to test my theory, I had several reasons for choosing these three components as the building blocks for it.

First, many of the other aspects of love prove, on close examination, to be either parts or manifestations of these three components. Communication, for example, is a building block of intimacy, as is caring or compassion. Were one to subdivide intimacy and passion and commitment into their own subparts, the theory would eventually contain so many elements as to become unwieldy. There is no one, solely correct fineness of division. But a division into three components works well in several ways, as I hope to show.

Second, my review of the literature on couples in the United States, as well as in other lands, suggested that, whereas some elements of love are fairly time-bound or culture-specific, the three I propose are general across time and place. The three components are not equally weighted in all cultures, but each component receives at least some weight in virtually any time or place.

Third, the three components do appear to be distinct, although, of course, they are related. You can have any one without either or both of the others. In contrast, other potential building blocks for a theory of love—for example, nurturance and caring—tend to be difficult to separate, logically as well as psychologically.

Fourth, many other accounts of love seem to boil down to something similar to my own account, or a subset of it. If we take away differences in language and tone, the spirit of many other theories converges with mine. Finally, and perhaps most important, the theory works.

INTIMACY

In the context of the triangular theory, intimacy refers to those feelings in a relation-

ship that promote closeness, bondedness, and connectedness. My research with Susan Grajek indicates that intimacy includes at least ten elements:

1. *Desiring to promote the welfare of the loved one.* The lover looks out for the
partner and seeks to promote his or her welfare. One may promote the other's welfare at the expense of one's own—but in the expectation that the other will reciprocate when the time comes.

2. *Experiencing happiness with the loved one.* The lover enjoys being with his
or her partner. When they do things together, they have a good time and build a store
of memories upon which they can draw in hard times. Furthermore, good times
shared will spill over into the relationship and make it better.

3. *Holding the loved one in high regard.* The lover thinks highly of and respects
his or her partner. Although the lover may recognize flaws in the partner, this recognition does not detract from the overall esteem in which the partner is held.

4. *Being able to count on the loved one in times of need.* The lover feels that the
partner is there when needed. When the chips are down, the lover can call on the
partner and expect that he or she will come through.

5. *Having mutual understanding with the loved one.* The lovers understand each
other. They know each other's strengths and weaknesses and how to respond to each
other in a way that shows genuine empathy for the loved one's emotional states.
Each knows where the other is "coming from."

6. *Sharing oneself and one's possessions with the loved one.* One is willing to
give of oneself and one's time, as well as one's things, to the loved one. Although
all things need not be joint property, the lovers share their property as the need
arises. And, most important, they share themselves.

7. *Receiving emotional support from the loved one.* The lover feels bolstered
and even renewed by the loved one, especially in times of need.

8. *Giving emotional support to the loved one.* The lover supports the loved one
by empathizing with, and emotionally supporting, him or her in times of need.

9. *Communicating intimacy with the loved one.* The lover can communicate
deeply and honestly with the loved one, sharing innermost feelings.

10. *Valuing the loved one.* The lover feels the great importance of the partner in
the scheme of life.

These are only some of the possible feelings one can experience through the intimacy of love; moreover, it is not necessary to experience all of these feelings in order to experience intimacy. To the contrary, our research indicates that you experience intimacy when you sample a sufficient number of these feelings, with that
number probably differing from one person and one situation to another. You do not
usually experience the feelings independently, but often as one overall feeling.

What makes for intimacy? Different psychologists say similar things, albeit in
different ways. For Harold Kelley and his colleagues, intimacy results from strong,
frequent, and diverse interconnections between people. Intimate couples, then, have
strong ties and interact frequently in a variety of ways. Lillian Rubin lists as the
qualities of friendship what I view here as some of the keys to intimacy: trust, hon-

esty, respect, commitment, safety, support, generosity, loyalty, mutuality, constancy, understanding, and acceptance.

Intimacy probably starts in self-disclosure. To be intimate with someone, you need to break down the walls that separate one person from another. It is well known that self-disclosure begets self-disclosure: if you want to get to know what someone else is like, let him or her learn about you. But self-disclosure is often easier in same-sex friendships than in loving relationships, probably because people see themselves as having more to lose by self-disclosure in a loving relationship. And odd as it may sound, there is actually evidence that spouses may be less symmetrical in self-disclosure than are strangers, again probably because the costs of self-disclosure can be so high in love.

Many of us have had the experience of confiding a deep, dark secret to someone, only to get burned for having done so. I once had a friend to whom I confided what I considered to be an intimate secret. In talking to a friend of my friend, I became painfully aware of the fact that this person, who was no friend of mine, knew every detail. Needless to say, I was for a while hesitant to confide in anyone.

Intimacy, then, is a foundation of love, but a foundation that develops slowly, through fits and starts, and is difficult to achieve. Moreover, once it starts to be attained, it may, paradoxically, start to go away because of the threat it poses. It poses a threat in terms not only of the dangers of self-disclosure but of the danger one starts to feel to one's existence as a separate, autonomous being. Few people want to be "consumed" by a relationship, yet many people start to feel as if they are being consumed when they get too close to another human being. The result is a balancing act between intimacy and autonomy which goes on throughout the lives of most couples, a balancing act in which a completely stable equilibrium is often never achieved. But this in itself is not necessarily bad: the swinging back and forth of the intimacy pendulum provides some of the excitement that keeps many relationships alive.

PASSION

The passion component of love includes what Elaine Hatfield and William Walster refer to as a "state of intense longing *for union* with the other." Passion is largely the expression of desires and needs—such as for self-esteem, nurturance, affiliation, dominance, submission, and sexual fulfillment. The strengths of these various needs vary across persons, situations, and kinds of loving relationship. For example, sexual fulfillment is likely to be a strong need in romantic relationships but not in filial ones. These needs manifest themselves through psychological and physiological arousal, which are often inseparable from each other.

Passion in love tends to interact strongly with intimacy, and often they fuel each other. For example, intimacy in a relationship may be largely a function of the extent to which the relationship meets a person's need for passion. Conversely, passion may be aroused by intimacy. In some close relationships with members of the opposite sex, for example, the passion component develops almost immediately; and intimacy, only after a while. Passion may have drawn the individuals into the relationship in the first place, but intimacy helps sustain the closeness in the relationship. In other close relationships, however, passion, especially as it applies to physical attraction, develops only after intimacy. Two close friends of the opposite sex may find themselves eventually developing a physical attraction for each other once they have achieved a certain emotional intimacy.

Sometimes intimacy and passion work against each other. For example, in a relationship with a prostitute, a man may seek to maximize fulfillment of the need for passion while purposefully minimizing intimacy. An inverse relation between intimacy and passion can be a function of the person as well as of the situation: some people find that the attainment of emotional closeness and intimacy actually interferes with sexual fulfillment, or that passionate involvement is detrimental to emotional intimacy. The point, quite simply, is that although the interaction between intimacy and passion will vary across people and across situations, these two components of love will almost certainly interact in close relationships in one way or another.

Most people, when they think of passion, view it as sexual. But any form of psychophysiological arousal can generate the experience of passion. For example, an individual with a high need for affiliation may experience passion toward an individual who provides him or her with a unique opportunity to affiliate. For example, Debbie grew up in a broken home, with no extended family to speak of, and two parents who were constantly at war with each other and eventually divorced when she was an adolescent. Debbie felt as though she never had a family, and when she met Arthur, her passion was kindled. What he had to offer was not great sex but a large, warm, closely knit family that welcomed Debbie with open arms. Arthur was Debbie's ticket to the sense of belongingness she had never experienced but had always craved, and his ability to bring belongingness into her life aroused her passion for him. As time went on, though, she found that an extended family did not a marriage make, and eventually divorced Arthur. She is still close to his family, however.

For other people, the need for submission can be the ticket to passion. Connie's father was happy with nothing less than the complete subjugation of her mother, physical as well as psychological. For Connie, as well as for other women who grew up in Connie's working-class milieu, being loved may be tantamount to being submissive or even subjugated. To some extent, the stimuli that ignite passion constitute a learned response. Thus, Connie learned to be dominated in body as well as mind. Social workers are often frustrated when, after months spent getting a battered woman to leave her husband, the woman ultimately goes back to the batterer. To some observers, her return may seem incomprehensible; to others, it may seem like a financial decision. But often it is neither. Such a woman has had the misfortune to identify abuse with being loved and, in going back to the abuse, is returning to what is, for her, love as she has learned it.

DECISION AND COMMITMENT

The decision/commitment component of love consists of two aspects—one short-term and one long-term. The short-term aspect is the decision to love a certain other, whereas the long-term one is the commitment to maintain that love. These two aspects of the decision/commitment component of love do not necessarily occur together. The decision to love does not necessarily imply a commitment to that love. Oddly enough, the reverse is also possible, where there is a commitment to a relationship in which you did not make the decision, as in arranged marriages. Some people are committed to loving another without ever having admitted their love. Most often, however, a decision precedes the commitment both temporally and logically. Indeed, the institution of marriage represents a legalization of the commitment to a decision to love another throughout life.

While the decision/commitment component of love may lack the "heat" or "charge" of intimacy and passion, loving relationships almost inevitably have their ups and downs, and in the latter, the decision/commitment component is what keeps a relationship together. This component can be essential for getting through hard times and for returning to better ones. In ignoring it or separating it from love, you may be missing exactly that component of a loving relationship that enables you to get through the hard times as well as the easy ones. Sometimes, you may have to trust your commitment to carry you through to the better times you hope are ahead.

The decision/commitment component of love interacts with both intimacy and passion. For most people, it results from the combination of intimate involvement and passionate arousal; however, intimate involvement or passionate arousal can follow from commitment, as in certain arranged marriages or in close relationships in which you do not have a choice of partners. For example, you do not get to choose your mother, father, siblings, aunts, uncles, or cousins. In these close relationships, you may find that whatever intimacy or passion you experience results from your cognitive commitment to the relationship, rather than the other way around. Thus, love can start off as a decision.

The expert in the study of commitment is the UCLA psychologist Harold Kelley, who believes that love and commitment overlap, but that you can have one without the other. He gives as an example the Michelle Triola–Lee Marvin lawsuit, in which Triola sued the actor Marvin for "palimony." Although they had lived together for some time, they had never been married. And, however they may have loved each other, permanent commitment was clearly not in Marvin's mind.

For Kelley, commitment is the extent to which a person is likely to stick with something or someone and see it (or him or her) through to the finish. A person who is committed to something is expected to persist until the goal underlying the commitment is achieved. A problem for contemporary relationships is that two members of a couple may have different ideas about what it means to stick with someone to the end or to the realization of a goal. These differences, moreover, may never be articulated. One person, for example, may see the "end" as that point where the relationship is no longer working, whereas the other may see the end as the ending of one of the couple's lives. In a time of changing values and notions of commitment, it is becoming increasingly common for couples to find themselves in disagreement about the exact nature and duration of their commitment to each other. When marital commitments were always and automatically assumed to be for life, divorce was clearly frowned upon. Today, divorce is clearly more acceptable than it was even fifteen years ago, in part because many people have different ideas about how durable and lasting the marital commitment need be.

Difficulties in mismatches between notions of commitment cannot always be worked out by discussing mutual definitions of it, because these may change over time and differently for the two members of a couple. Both may intend a life-long commitment at the time of marriage, for example; but one of them may have a change of mind—or heart—over time. Moreover, as Kelley points out, it is important to distinguish between commitment to a person and commitment to a relationship. While two people may both be committed to each other, one may see the commitment as extending to the person and to a relationship with that person, but not necessarily to the type of relationship the couple have had up to a certain point. This person may wish to alter the kind of relationship they have. For example, one may be committed to one's husband and to having a relationship with that husband, but not to the kind of submissive role one has taken in the past with respect to him.

PROPERTIES OF THE COMPONENTS OF LOVE

The three components of love have different properties. For example, intimacy and commitment seem to be relatively stable in close relationships, whereas passion tends to be relatively unstable and can fluctuate unpredictably. You have some degree of conscious control over your feelings of intimacy (if you are aware of them), a high degree of control over the commitment of the decision/commitment component that you invest in the relationship (again, assuming awareness), but little control over the amount of passionate arousal you experience as a result of being with or even looking at another person. You are usually aware and conscious of passion, but awareness of the intimacy and decision/commitment components can be highly variable. Sometimes you experience warm feelings of intimacy without being aware of them or able to label them. Similarly, you are often not certain of how committed you are to a relationship until people or events intervene to challenge that commitment.

The importance of each of the three components of love varies, on the average, according to whether a loving relationship is short-term or long-term. In short-term involvements, and especially romantic ones, passion tends to play a large part, whereas intimacy may play only a moderate part, and decision/commitment may play hardly any part at all. In contrast, in a long-term close relationship, intimacy and decision/commitment typically must play relatively large parts. In such a relationship, passion typically plays only a moderate part, and its role may decline somewhat over time.

The three components of love also differ in their presence in various loving relationships. Intimacy appears to be at the core of many loving relationships, whether that relationship is with parent, sibling, lover, or close friend. Passion tends to be limited to certain kinds of loving relationship, especially romantic ones; whereas decision/commitment can be highly variable across different loving relationships. For example, commitment tends to be high in love for one's children, but relatively low in love for friends who come and go throughout the span of a life.

The three components also differ in the amount of psychophysiological involvement they offer. Passion is highly dependent on psychophysiological involvement, whereas decision/commitment appears to involve little psychophysiological response. Intimacy involves an intermediate amount of psychophysiological involvement.

In sum, the three components of love have somewhat different properties, which tend to highlight some of the ways they function in the experiences of love as they occur in various close relationships.

KINDS OF LOVING

How do people love, and what are some examples of ways in which they love? A summary of the various kinds of love captured by the triangular theory is shown in Table 6.3.

Intimacy Alone: Liking

Joe was intensely jealous. He had thought he and Stephanie were "a couple." But Stephanie seemed to be spending almost as much time with Alex as she was spending with Joe. Joe was afraid she was two-timing him. Finally, he confronted her.

"I just can't stand this any more."

"Huh? What can't you stand?"

"Your relationship with Alex. If you prefer him to me, that's fine. Just say the word, and I'll be on my way. But you seem to want us both, and I just won't stand for it any longer."

"I don't know what you're talking about. Alex is no competition for you—none at all. What in the world makes you think he is?"

"But you're spending as much time with him as you are with me, not to mention what you may be doing with that time."

"Joe, you're off, you're way off. Alex is a good friend. I do like his company. I like doing things with him. I like talking to him. But I don't love him, and I never

TABLE 6.3 Taxonomy of Kinds of Love

Kind of Love	Intimacy	Passion	Decision/ Commitment
Non-love	–	–	–
Liking	+	–	–
Infatuated love	–	+	–
Empy love	–	–	+
Romantic love	+	+	–
Companionate love	+	–	+
Fatuous love	–	+	+
Consummate love	+	+	+

Note: + = component present; – = component absent. These kinds of love represent idealized cases based on the triangular theory. Most loving relationships will fit between categories, because the components of love occur in varying degrees, rather than being simply present or absent.

will. I don't plan to spend my life with him. He's a friend, and nothing more, but nothing less either."

"Oh, I see." But Joe didn't really see that Stephanie's relationship with Alex was a friendship, and nothing more.

Liking results when you experience only the intimacy component of love without passion or decision/commitment. The term *liking* is used here in a nontrivial sense, to describe not merely the feelings you have toward casual acquaintances and passersby, but rather the set of feelings you experience in relationships that can truly be characterized as friendships. You feel closeness, bondedness, and warmth toward the other, without feelings of intense passion or long-term commitment. Stated another way, you feel emotionally close to the friend, but the friend does not arouse your passion or make you feel that you want to spend the rest of your life with him or her.

It is possible for friendships to have elements of passionate arousal or long-term commitment, but such friendships go beyond mere liking. You can use the absence test to distinguish mere liking from love that goes beyond liking. If a typical friend whom you like goes away, even for an extended period of time, you may miss him or her but do not tend to dwell on the loss. You can pick up the friendship some years later, often in a different form, without even having thought much about the friendship during the intervening years. When a close friendship goes beyond liking, however, you actively miss the other person and tend to dwell on or be preoccupied with his or her absence. The absence has a substantial and fairly long-term effect on your life. When the absence of the other arouses strong feelings of intimacy, passion, or commitment, the relationship has gone beyond liking.

Passion Alone: Infatuated Love

Tom met Lisa at work. One look at her was enough to change his life: he fell madly in love with her. Instead of concentrating on his work, which he hated, he would think about Lisa. She was aware of this, but did not much care for Tom. When he tried to start a conversation with her, she moved on as quickly as possible. Tom's staring and his awkwardness in talking to her made her feel uncomfortable. He, on the other hand, could think of little else besides Lisa, and his work began to suffer as the time he should have been devoting to it went instead to thinking about Lisa. He was a man obsessed. The obsession might have gone on indefinitely but Lisa moved away. Tom never saw Lisa again, and after several unanswered love letters, he finally gave up on her.

Tom's "love at first sight" is infatuated love or, simply, infatuation. It results from the experiencing of passionate arousal without the intimacy and decision/commitment components of love. Infatuation is usually obvious, although it tends to be somewhat easier for others to spot than for the person who is experiencing it. An infatuation can arise almost instantaneously and dissipate as quickly. Infatuations generally manifest a high degree of psychophysiological arousal and bodily symptoms such as increased heartbeat or even palpitations of the heart, increased hormonal secretions, and erection of genitals (penis or clitoris). Infatuation is essentially what the love researcher Dorothy Tennov calls "limerence" and, like it, can be quite lasting.

Decision/Commitment Alone: Empty Love

John and Mary had been married for twenty years, for fifteen of which Mary had been thinking about getting a divorce, but could never get herself to go through with it. Because she did not work outside the home, she was afraid she would be unable to make a living; besides, life alone might be worse than with John. And life with John was not bad. Basically, he left her alone. He was almost never home; and when he was, he pretty much stuck to doing his work. Whatever passion they might once have had was long since gone—Mary had long felt that John had found other women, and even the little intimacy they had once had had vanished. At this point, they hardly ever even talked. Mary often wondered whether John would leave, and sometimes wished he would. But he seemed content to have her wash his clothes, prepare his meals, keep house, and do all the things that she had long ago been taught a wife should do. Mary often felt that her life would be completely empty were it not for her children.

Mary's kind of love emanates from the decision that you love another and are committed to that love even without having the intimacy or the passion associated with some loves. It is the love sometimes found in stagnant relationships that have been going on for years but that have lost both their original mutual emotional involvement and physical attraction. Unless the commitment to the love is very strong, such love can be close to none at all. Although in our society we see empty love generally as the final or near-final stage of a long-term relationship, in other societies empty love may be the first stage of a long-term relationship. As I have said, in societies where marriages are arranged, the marital partners start with the commitment to love each other, or to try to do so, and not much more. Here, *empty* denotes a relationship that may come to be filled with passion and intimacy, and thus marks a beginning rather than an end.

Intimacy + Passion: Romantic Love

Susan and Ralph met in their junior year of college. Their relationship started off as a good friendship, but rapidly turned into a deeply involved romantic love affair. They spent as much time together as possible, and enjoyed practically every minute of it. But Susan and Ralph were not ready to commit themselves permanently to the relationship: both felt they were too young to make any long-term decisions, and that until they at least knew where they would go after college, it was impossible to tell even how much they could be together. Ralph was admitted to graduate study at UCLA and decided to go there. Susan, an engineer, had applied to the California Institute of Technology and was accepted, but without financial aid. She was also accepted by the Massachusetts Institute of Technology with a large fellowship. The difference in financial packages left her with little choice but to go to Massachusetts. When she went out east, neither she nor Ralph had much confidence that their relationship would survive the distance; and in fact, after a year of occasional commutes and not so occasional strains, it ended.

Ralph and Susan's relationship combines the intimacy and passion components of love. In essence, it is liking with an added element: namely, the arousal brought about by physical attraction. Therefore, in this type of love, the man and woman are not only drawn physically to each other but are also bonded emotionally. This is the view of romantic love found in the classic works of literature, such as *Romeo and Juliet*.

Intimacy + Commitment: Companionate Love

In their twenty years of marriage, Sam and Sara had been through some rough times. They had seen many of their friends through divorces, Sam through several jobs, and Sara through an illness that at one point had seemed as though it might be fatal. Both had friends, but there was no doubt in either of their minds that they were each other's best friend. When the going got rough, each of them knew he or she could count on the other. Neither Sam nor Sara felt any great passion in their relationship, but they had never sought out others, because they both believed they had what mattered most to them: the ability to say or do anything they might want without fear of attack or reprisal. Although they each knew there were probably limits to their regard for each other, they had never sought to test these limits, because they were happy to live within them.

Sam and Sara's kind of love evolves from a combination of the intimacy and decision/commitment components of love. It is essentially a long-term, committed friendship, the kind that frequently occurs in marriages in which physical attraction (a major source of passion) has waned.

Passion + Commitment: Fatuous Love

When Tim and Diana met at a resort in the Bahamas, they were each on the rebound. Tim's fiancée had abruptly broken off their engagement and essentially eloped with the man who had been Tim's close colleague. Moreover, Tim had just lost his job. Diana was recently divorced, the victim of the "other woman." Each felt desperate for love, and when they met each other, they immediately saw themselves as a match made in heaven. Indeed, it was as though someone had watched over them, seen their plight, and brought them together in their time of need. The manager of the resort, always on the lookout for vacation romances as good publicity, offered to marry them at the resort and to throw a lavish reception at no charge, other than cooperation in promotional materials. After thinking it over, Tim and Diana agreed. They knew they were right for each other, and because neither was particularly well off at the moment, the possibility of a free wedding was appealing. Regrettably, the marriage proved to be a disaster once Tim and Diana returned from their vacation. Although he was great fun to be with, Tim had never been one for taking employment seriously, whereas Diana expected him to get a job and support her. Tim, in turn, was shocked to learn that Diana did not expect to work, thus disappointing his expectations of receiving at least some financial support from her in order to further his aspiration to become a poet.

Fatuous love, as in the case of Tim and Diana, results from the combination of passion and decision/commitment without intimacy, which takes time to develop. It is the kind of love we sometimes associate with Hollywood, or with a whirlwind courtship, in which a couple meet one day, get engaged two weeks later, and marry the next month. This love is fatuous in the sense that the couple commit themselves to one another on the basis of passion without the stabilizing element of intimate involvement. Since passion can develop almost instantaneously, and intimacy cannot, relationships based on fatuous love are not likely to last.

Intimacy + Passion + Commitment: Consummate Love

> Harry and Edith seemed to all their friends to be the perfect couple. And what made them distinctive from many such "perfect couples" is that they pretty much fulfilled the notion. They felt close to each other, they continued to have great sex after fifteen years, and they could not imagine themselves happy over the long term with anyone else. Harry had had a few flings, none of them serious, and eventually told Edith about them, unaware of the fact that she already knew about them because he was so transparent. Edith, on the other hand, had had no extramarital affairs. But they had weathered their few storms, and each was delighted with the relationship and with each other.

Consummate, or complete, love like Edith and Harry's results from the combination of the three components in equal measure. It is a love toward which many of us strive, especially in romantic relationships. Attaining consummate love is analogous, in at least one respect, to meeting your goal in a weight-reduction program: reaching your ideal weight is often easier than maintaining it. Attaining consummate love is no guarantee that it will last; indeed, one may become aware of the loss only after it is far gone. Consummate love, like other things of value, must be guarded carefully.

I do not believe that all aspects of consummate love are necessarily difficult either to develop or to maintain. For example, love for one's children often carries with it the deep emotional involvement of the intimacy component, the satisfaction of motivational needs (such as nurturance, self-esteem, self-actualization) of the passion component, and the firm commitment of the decision/commitment component. For many but not all parents, formation and maintenance of this love is no problem. Perhaps the bonding between parents and children at birth renders this love relatively easier to maintain, or perhaps evolutionary forces are at work to ensure that parent-child bonding survives at least the formative years in which the child must depend heavily on the parent's love and support. Whichever of these possibilities holds (and it may be more than one), whether consummate love is easy or hard to form and maintain depends on the relationship and the situation.

The Absence of the Components: Non-love

> Jack saw his colleague Myra at work almost every day. They interacted well in their professional relationship, but neither was particularly fond of the other. Neither felt particularly comfortable talking to the other about personal matters; and after a few tries, they decided to limit their conversations to business.

Non-love, as in the relationship of Jack and Myra, refers simply to the absence of all three components of love. Non-love characterizes many personal relationships, which are simply casual interactions that do not partake of love or even liking.

7

Helping: Whether and When to Give Aid

Questions about when and why people help have always set off great debate and speculation. We can cite dramatic examples of people who risked their lives for the sake of strangers, at the same time recounting acts of apparent callousness where witnesses to a crime failed to offer any assistance to the victim. In ways that are rarely scientific or systematic, we all seek answers to what motivates helping and what sets it off.

Daniel Batson, Professor of Psychology at the University of Kansas, is a social psychologist who has studied helping behavior for over two decades, trying to identify and disentangle the complex motives that lead people to act on another person's behalf. In his recent book, *The Altruism Question,* he reviews his own careful research and that of others, making a strong case for the relationship between empathy, altruism, and helping. In our conversation he deals with some of these same basic issues, noting his discoveries in this field and tracing the evolution of his own interest in it.

A CONVERSATION WITH
DANIEL BATSON
University of Kansas

Krupat: *Let me begin by asking you a question that sounds simple, but probably has no simple answer: Why do people help one another?*

Batson: That's been a question that has intrigued philosophers for centuries because it raises the possibility that maybe people are capable of caring for something beyond just their own interests. Obviously, there are lots of reasons, but the thing that's particularly intriguing about the fact that people do help others is the possibility that maybe we're more social than we thought.

Krupat: *In what sense?*

Batson: Clearly, helping is a social behavior—it's doing something for someone else. But it goes beyond that because it suggests or at least raises the possibility that there is a social or prosocial motive, where one person actually has the other person's welfare as the goal. To try to sort out motives for helping is a delicate operation because there are a lot of subtle benefits that one can get from helping someone else. So the philosophical debates swing back and forth: Is it because helpers really are trying to benefit themselves, or is there somewhere within us a capacity to care about the other as an ultimate goal—not as a means for something else, but as an end in itself?

Krupat: *For example?*

Batson: Anytime you see a dramatic, wonderful example like the rescuing of Jews in Nazi Europe or the fellow who dove into the icy

Potomac to rescue a plane crash victim, you look at it and you say, "Gee, that's remarkable." But still, from Mother Teresa on down, it's possible to say, "Yes, but they do get benefits." That's part of the logical confusion. Simply to say that a person does get benefits from helping another doesn't rule out the possibility that getting those benefits was not the person's ultimate goal. It's a tricky issue, but I actually think that it's one of those problems where the experimental methods of social psychology are ideally suited—so far as I know, *uniquely* suited—to providing an answer.

Krupat: *Now, if I'm correct, you have some very strong feelings about what the answer is to this.*

Batson: When I started out doing research on helping behavior, I shared with most social psychologists the belief that people were always egoistic—self-interested. I took that as a given, relatively uncritically. But, working with a graduate student here at Kansas, Jay Coke, doing some research on empathy and helping, I was surprised by what we found. People seemed to be much more caring about the welfare of the other person than I, at least, would have expected. So that got us thinking that maybe there is more to this than we had imagined, and also thinking about how we could tease the possible motives apart.

Krupat: *Now one word that I don't think either one of us has used— and certainly we ought to introduce into the rest of the equation—is the term altruism. When you talk about helping behavior, where does altruism fit? Is it a special kind of helping?*

Batson: I think of helping as a *behavior*. Conceptually, it's important to distinguish that from the motive that promotes the behavior. I think of altruism as a *motive*. Altruism is a motivational state with the ultimate goal of increasing another's welfare. By ultimate goal here, I don't mean something cosmic, but just what the person is after in the situation. I juxtapose altruism with egoism, which is a motivational state with the ultimate goal of increasing one's own welfare. There are a whole range of possible helping motives, egoistic and altruistic. Both types of motives can operate at the same time. It's not an either/or. The fact that they can be mixed together simply makes it a more complicated problem.

Krupat: *Then where is the problem? Why do people have such a hard time accepting that altruistic motives could be driving social behaviors?*

Batson: Historically, and this goes back to the philosophical tradition, we have taken a very strong stand. The strong stand is that altruistic motivation as I've defined it does not exist. It's like a unicorn, something that you can imagine, but just doesn't happen to be part of the real world. The dominant position in Western thought is one of universal egoism, that anytime you see somebody doing something nice for somebody, ultimately they're doing it for themselves. That's a view within philosophy that we've gotten from Thomas Hobbes and his descendants. Within psychology, it comes to us in part from the Darwinian tradition, especially as interpreted by Freud. Reinforcement theory and behaviorism have also contributed. In part, psychologists' belief in universal egoism comes from a very fundamental insight that Freud had about our enormous capacity for ulterior or unconscious motives. We may think that we're doing something because we care about somebody else, but in fact we may be doing it for self-benefits of which we may not even be aware. What has happened historically, both within psychology and society at large, is that this has turned into a basic assumption that whatever we do, that there has to be some self-benefit.

Krupat: *So what I'm hearing you say is that, at a minimum, your goal has been to establish firmly that people are at least capable of altruistic motivation. Is that right?*

Batson: Not establish—find out. If we're not capable of altruism, then we don't need to worry about ways to promote it. We don't spend a lot of time worrying about trying to help people fly without airplanes because doing so is not within our physical repertoire. If altruism is without our psychological repertoire, if at least some people some of the time get interested in the welfare of others in much the same way they get invested in their own, then this changes our conception of human nature; then we humans are more social than we have thought.

Krupat: *Would I be correct in saying that you believe that helping and altruism are not only real, but that they are useful or necessary in helping us survive as a species?*

Batson: When you ask in what ways altruistic impulses could actually promote genetic survival, I think about mammalian species. At least within many mammalian species, the young live in a very vulnerable state for some period of time. Obviously, if the parents didn't give a rip about the needs or the welfare of their offspring, these species would quickly die out.

Krupat: *Okay, then to what extent is it built in and to what extent is it learned?*

Batson: I don't know the answer to that one. It may be hardwired, it may be learned, or it may be a mixture of the two. In my research the factor that I have tended to focus on in looking for altruistic motives is an empathic emotional response, a sort of feeling of compassion, sympathy, or tenderness. And in my more metaphorical moments, I tend to think of this empathy as an emotional umbilical cord, perhaps like the parental reaction to the child, which involves a very strong sense of attachment and an emotional feeling of concern for the child. It may be that the empathic emotions that we're looking at in the behavior of one undergraduate responding to the need of another or to the need of someone in society whom they have never met may be extensions of that parental impulse. It's just speculation, of course, but I think it is worth considering.

Krupat: *And I assume that, as you've pursued this empathic response further in your research, it doesn't disappear with closer scrutiny.*

Batson: No, it has not seemed to. There's always the danger of jumping too quickly to a flattering interpretation of human behavior based on altruistic motives. So it becomes a job of trying to be very, very careful and thinking as hard as we can about plausible self-benefits or egoistic motives that could hide behind and motivate helping evoked by empathic feelings. We have to take every plausible egoistic alternative seriously.

Krupat: *Now, you were saying that empathy and altruism do not disappear even when you study them critically and carefully. Yet in one of your more poetic moments, you describe the concern for others as "a fragile flower easily crushed by self-concern," suggesting that it needs to be carefully nurtured in order to survive. Can you recommend ways in which we can encourage and promote altruistic motives?*

Batson: To the degree that we have assumed that all human motivation is exclusively egoistic, when you ask, "How do I raise my son or daughter so that he or she is a kind, caring person?" what's likely to come to mind is that we need to reinforce these behaviors, praise our children when they do nice things, punish them when they do not, try to teach them the basic norms of reciprocity, sharing and fairness, and principles such as these. Pursuing this strategy, we haven't even entertained the possibility that there may be other sources of prosocial motivation, of motivation for helping, such as empathic feelings. If there are other sources, then maybe we need to think about trying to inculcate those as well, maybe we need to ask what we might do to increase our capacity to feel these empathic emotions for a wider range of individuals.

Krupat: *Such as?*

Batson: Such as giving children experiences of feeling these emotions. In fact, they get a fair number. A lot of children's fairy tales, the Disney sorts of movies, and things like that are designed, at least in part, to generate these kinds of feelings. But we may need to have children read these stories and watch these films in a context where they can recognize these feelings; we may need to help them label their feelings to understand what's going on. We don't tend to see teaching emotional sensitivity as integral to developing a caring individual.

Krupat: *I can see how we need to do this one-on-one, parent to child. But are there other things we can do on a large scale?*

Batson: In terms of social organization, it may be that there are certain community configurations—mainly stability in the community and contact with neighbors—that increase the likelihood of these kinds of emotional reactions. So the research on empathy and altruism carries implications for how one organizes society. If we assume that, in fact, everybody's only out for themselves and the only way that you're going to have them help other people is to make it worth their while, that leads to a strategy like introducing good samaritan laws—people get paid if they help a stranger or punished if they don't. But that strategy is dramatically different from one that says, "No, we've got some other resources that we can employ. If the structure of the community is of a particular type, people can actually care for one another." Now another alternative is to say, "OK, then let's encourage that as well; let's beat every drum. Let's try to reinforce the child and punish and so forth, and at the same time let's encourage the emotional reactions and caring." But that may backfire.

Krupat: *Is there something wrong with* not *putting all your eggs in one basket?*

Batson: It may be that the two things—shaping prosocial behavior with rewards and punishments and encouraging empathy and altruism—at least under certain circumstances—work against each other. To the degree that you make salient the self-benefits and the sort of self-gratification reasons for caring for somebody else, you may undermine the ability to care for them as an end in itself, just as extrinsic rewards have been found to undermine intrinsic actions in other areas of human behavior. So, what we may be doing with our current strategy is inadvertently undermining that altruistic motivation that does exist. Back to the fragile flower.

Krupat: *Up till now, we have been talking about other people's motives. At this point, I'd like to change from the motives of others to your own motivation. Some people take a topic, study it for a few years, and get tired of it. You've been at the business of studying altruism and helping for many years now. Can you tell me a little about how you came to be interested and how it is that you remain interested?*

Batson: When I left college, I went to theological seminary, planning to be a minister. After a few years, it was clear to me that I wasn't cut out for that; I really enjoyed research. I applied to graduate school at Princeton to work with Harry Schroeder, whom I had worked with before. Well, between the spring when I applied and the fall when I matriculated, Harry left Princeton. That placed me in an awkward situation;

I think the rest of the faculty at Princeton was a bit appalled at having this seminarian. That's not the normal route into psychology. So I was casting about for somebody to work with and I met John Darley who had recently come to Princeton. Through him I came to find out that you could take behavioral measures on something as complex as helping behavior. To think that one could study ethical issues in a scientific way was a real eye-opener for me and an exciting possibility. So, in the initial work that we did, we actually used seminary students as subjects in a study looking at some situational variables, but also looking at different dimensions of personal religion and the way that these related to a person's helpfulness.

Krupat: *That sounds like a good start. What has kept you going?*

Batson: When I was being considered for a position here at Kansas and came for an interview, I gave a talk about my dissertation work, which was an attributional analysis of how people help, focused on the cognitive factors in helping. In the audience was Fritz Heider, the originator of many attribution notions and emeritus professor at Kansas at that time. After my talk, I had a chance to sit down with Fritz and ask him what he thought. He was extremely nice. He said that the talk was very interesting, but then he added, "It seems to me that you're talking a matter of the heart and trying to turn it into a matter of the head." I really didn't know what to do with his comment. Basically I let it drop because within social psychology at that time people were studying helping behavior by looking at situational factors in a cognitive framework. But later, when Jay Coke and I collected our data and it looked like helping was much more a matter of the heart than I had imagined, I remembered the comment. I think now I have at least some understanding of what Fritz Heider was talking about: feeling and desire. When I began to think about prosocial emotion and motivation, it was like coming out of the woods into a clearing, and there was this huge landscape ahead—much bigger than I had imagined. People looking at my research over the years have said, "My God, how can you possibly stay at one thing this long?" implying that I ought to move on. But I've been pleased that so far it has stayed interesting, and so far, at least, I feel like I'm still learning. The question of the existence of altruism is wonderfully complex and, I believe, fundamentally important.

Bibb Latané
John M. Darley

Social Determinants of Bystander Intervention in Emergencies

In 1964 Bibb Latané and John Darley sat down over dinner, and discussed the story that everyone was talking about: the murder of a young woman, witnessed by 38 neighbors, in which not one person offered help. That night the authors sketched out on a dinner napkin one of the most important theories of helping behavior. That model, described here, says that before acting a potential helper must 1) notice an event, 2) determine that it is an emergency, something that requires intervention, and 3) decide that he or she must take personal responsibility. Although many people might expect that there would be "strength in numbers," the authors suggest that the presence of others is likely to inhibit rather than encourage helping in emergency situations. After presenting three studies to test their model, they conclude that it is not so much the relationship between the victim and the helper that may hold the key to understanding when and why people help, but the relationship among the bystanders themselves.

Almost 100 years ago, Charles Darwin wrote: "as man is a social animal, it is almost certain that he would . . . from an inherited tendency be willing to defend, in concert with others, his fellowmen; and be ready to aid them in any way, which did not too greatly interfere with his own welfare or his own strong desires" (*The Descent of Man*). Today, although many psychologists would quarrel with Darwin's assertion that altruism is inherited, most would agree that men will go to the aid of others even when there is no visible gain for themselves. At least, most would have agreed until a March night in 1964. That night, Kitty Genovese was set upon by a maniac as she returned home from work at 3:00 A.M. Thirty-eight of her neighbors in Kew Gardens came to their windows when she cried out in terror; but none came to her assistance, even though her stalker took over half an hour to murder her. No one even so much as called the police.

Since we started our research on by-stander response to emergencies, we have heard about dozens of such incidents. We have also heard many explanations: "I would assign this to the effect of the megalopolis in which we live, which makes closeness very difficult and leads to the alienation of the individual from the group," contributed a psychoanalyst. "A disaster syndrome," explained a sociologist, "that shook the sense of safety and sureness of the individuals involved and caused psychological withdrawal from the event by ignoring it." "Apathy," others claim. "Indifference." "The gratification of unconscious sadistic impulses." "Lack of concern for our fellow men." "The Cold Society." These explanations and many more have been applied to the surprising failure of bystanders to intervene in emergencies—failures which suggest that we no longer care about the fate of our neighbors.

But can this be so? We think not. Although it is unquestionably true that the witness in the incidents above did nothing to save the victim, "apathy," "indifference," and "unconcern" are not entirely accurate descriptions of their reactions. The 38 witnesses of Kitty Genovese's murder did not merely look at the scene once and then ignore it. Instead they continued to stare out of their windows at what was going on. Caught, fascinated, distressed, unwilling to act but unable to turn away, their behavior was neither helpful nor heroic; but it was not indifferent or apathetic either.

Actually, it was like crowd behavior in many other emergency situations; car accidents, drownings, fires, and attempted suicides all attract substantial numbers of people who watch the drama in helpless fascination without getting directly involved in the action. Are these people alienated and indifferent? Are the rest of us? Obviously not. It seems only yesterday we were being called overconforming. But why, then, do we not act?

Paradoxically, the key to understanding these failures of intervention may be found exactly in the fact that so surprises us about them: so many bystanders fail to intervene. If we think of 38, or 11, or 100 individuals, each looking at an emergency and callously deciding to pass by, we are horrified. But if we realize that each bystander is picking up cues about what is happening and how to react to it from the other bystanders, understanding begins to emerge. There are several ways in which a crowd of onlookers can make each individual member of that crowd less likely to act.

DEFINING THE SITUATION

Most emergencies are, or at least begin as, ambiguous events. A quarrel in the street may erupt into violence or it may be simply a family argument. A man staggering about may be suffering a coronary, or an onset of diabetes, or he simply may be drunk. Smoke pouring from a building may signal a fire, but on the other hand, it may be simply steam or air-conditioner vapor. Before a bystander is likely to take action in such ambiguous situations, he must first define the event as an emergency and decide that intervention is the proper course of action.

In the course of making these decisions, it is likely that an individual bystander will be considerably influenced by the decisions he perceives other bystanders to be taking. If everyone else in a group of onlookers seems to regard an event as nonserious and the proper course of action as nonintervention, this consensus may strongly affect the perceptions of any single individual and inhibit his potential intervention.

The definitions that other people hold may be discovered by discussing the situation with them, but they may also be inferred from their facial expressions or behavior. A whistling man with his hands in his pockets obviously does not believe he is in the midst of a crisis. A bystander who does not respond to smoke obviously does not attribute it to fire. An individual, seeing the inaction of others, will judge the situation as less serious that he would if alone.

But why should the others be inactive? Probably because they are aware that other people are also watching them. The others are an audience to their own reactions. Among American males, it is considered desirable to appear poised and collected in times of stress. Being exposed to the public view may constrain the actions and expressions of emotion of any individual as he tries to avoid possible ridicule and embarrassment. Even though he may be truly concerned and upset about the plight of a victim, until he decides what to do, he may maintain a calm demeanor.

If each member of a group is, at the same time, trying to appear calm and also looking around at the other members to gauge their reactions, all members may be led (or misled) by each other to define the situation as less critical than they would if alone. Until someone acts, each person sees only other nonresponding bystanders and is likely to be influenced not to act himself. A state of "pluralistic ignorance" may develop.

It has often been recognized that a crowd can cause contagion of panic, leading each person in the crowd to overreact to an emergency to the detriment of everyone's welfare. What we suggest here is that a crowd can also force inaction on its members. It can suggest by its passive behavior that an event is not to be reacted to as an emergency, and it can make any individual uncomfortably aware of what a fool he will look for behaving as if it is.

Where There's Smoke, There's (sometimes) Fire[1]

In this experiment we presented an emergency to individuals either alone or in groups of three. It was our expectation that the constraints on behavior in public combined with social influence processes would lessen the likelihood that members of three-person groups would act to cope with the emergency,

College students were invited to an interview to discuss "some of the problems involved in life at an urban university." As they sat in a small room waiting to be called for the interview and filling out a preliminary questionnaire, they faced an ambiguous but potentially dangerous situation. A stream of smoke began to puff into the room through a wall vent.

Some subjects were exposed to the potentially critical situation while alone. In a second condition, three naive subjects were tested together. Since subjects arrived at slightly different times, and since they each had individual questionnaires to work on, they did not introduce themselves to each other or attempt anything but the most rudimentary conversation.

As soon as the subjects had completed two pages of their questionnaires, the experimenter began to introduce the smoke through a small vent in the wall. The "smoke," copied from the famous Camel cigarette sign in Times Square, formed a moderately fine-textured but clearly visible stream of whitish smoke. It continued to jet into the room in irregular puffs, and by the end of the experimental period, it obscured vision.

All behavior and conversation were observed and coded from behind a one-way window (largely disguised on the subject's side by a large sign giving preliminary instructions). When and if the subject left the experimental room and reported the smoke, he was told that the situation "would be taken care of." If the subject had not reported the smoke within 6 minutes from the time he first noticed it, the experiment was terminated.

The typical subject, when tested alone, behaved very reasonably. Usually, shortly after the smoke appeared, he would glance up from his questionnaire, notice the smoke, show a slight but distinct startle reaction, and then undergo a brief period of indecision, perhaps returning briefly to his questionnaire before again staring at the smoke. Soon, most subjects would get up from their chairs, walk over to the vent and investigate it closely, sniffing the smoke, waving their hands in it, feeling its temperature, etc. The usual Alone subject would hesitate again, but finally would walk out of the room, look around outside, and, finding somebody there, calmly report the presence of the smoke. No subject showed any sign of panic; most simply said: "There's something strange going on in there, there seems to be some sort of smoke coming through the wall . . ." The median subject in the Alone condition had reported the smoke within 2 minutes of first noticing it. Three-quarters of the 24 people run in this condition reported the smoke before the experimental period was terminated.

Because there are three subjects present and available to report the smoke in the Three Naive Bystanders condition, as compared to only one subject at a time in the Alone condition, a simple comparison between the two conditions is not appropriate. We cannot compare speed in the Alone condition with the average speed of the three subjects in a group because, once one subject in a group had reported the smoke, the pressures on the other two disappeared. They could feel legitimately that the emergency had been handled and that any action on their part would be redundant and potentially confusing. Therefore, we used the speed of the first subject in a group to report the smoke as our dependent variable. However, since there were three times as many people available to respond in this condition as in the Alone condition, we would expect an increased likelihood that at least one person would report the smoke by chance alone. Therefore, we mathematically created "groups of three scores from the Alone condition to serve as a baseline.

In contrast to the complexity of this procedure, the results were quite simple.

Subjects in the three-person-group condition were markedly inhibited from reporting the some. Since 75% of the Alone subjects reported the smoke, we would expect over 98% of the three-person groups to include at least one reporter. In fact, in only 38% of the eight groups in this condition did even one person report. Of the 24 people run in these eight groups, only one person reported the smoke within the first 4 minutes before the room got noticeably unpleasant. Only three people reported the smoke within the entire experimental period. Social inhibition of reporting was so strong that the smoke was reported faster when only one person saw it than when groups of three were present.

Subjects who had reported the smoke were relatively consistent in later describing their reactions to it. They thought the smoke looked somewhat "strange." They were not sure exactly what it was or whether it was dangerous, but they felt it was unusual enough to justify some examination. "I wasn't sure whether is was a fire, but it looked like something was wrong." "I thought it might be steam, but it seemed like a good idea to check it out."

Subjects who had not reported the smoke were also unsure about exactly what it was, but they uniformly said that they had rejected the idea that it was a fire. Instead, they hit upon an astonishing variety of alternative explanations, all sharing the common characteristic of interpreting the smoke as a non-dangerous event. Many thought the smoke was either steam or air-conditioning vapor, several thought it was smog, purposely introduced to simulate an urban environment, and two actually suggested that the smoke was a "truth gas" filtered into the room to induce them to answer the questionnaire accurately! Predictably, some decided that "it must be some sort of experiment" and stoically endured the discomfort of the room rather than overreact.

The results of this study clearly support the prediction. Groups of three naive subjects were less likely to report the smoke than solitary bystanders. Our predictions were confirmed—but this does jot necessarily mean that our expiation of these results is the correct one. As a matter of fact, several alternative explanations center around the fact that the smoke represented a possible danger to the subject himself as well as to others in the building. For instance, it is possible that the subjects in groups saw themselves as engaged in a game of "chicken" in which the first person to report would admit his cowardliness. Or it may have been that the presence of others made subjects feel safer, and thus reduced their need to report.

To rule out such explanations, a second experiment was designed to see whether similar group inhibition effects could be observed in situations where there is no danger to the individual himself for not acting. In this study, male Columbia University undergraduates waited either alone or with a stranger to participate in a market research study. As they waited they heard a woman fall and apparently injure herself in the room next door. Whether they tried to help and how long they took to do so were the main dependent variables of the study.

The Fallen Woman[2]

Subjects were telephoned and offered $2 to participate in a survey of game and puzzle preferences conducted at Columbia by the Consumer Testing Bureau (CTB), a market research organization. When they arrived, they were met at the door by an attractive young woman and taken to the testing room. On the way, they passed the CTB office, and through its open door they were able to see a desk and bookcase piled high with papers and filing cabinets. They entered the adjacent testing room, which contained a table and chairs and a variety of games, and they were given questionnaires to fill out. The representatives told subjects that she would be working next door in her office for about 10 minutes while they were completing the questionnaire, and left by opening the collapsible curtain which divided the two rooms. She made sure that subjects were aware that the curtain was unlocked and easily opened and that it provided a means of entry to her office. The representative stayed in her office, shuffling papers, opening drawers, and making enough noise to remind the subjects of her presence. Four minutes after leaving the testing area, she turned on a high-fidelity stereophonic tape recorder.

The Emergency. If the subject listened carefully, he heard the representative climb up on a chair to reach for a stack of papers on the bookcase. Even if he were not listening carefully, he heard a loud crash and a scream as the chair collapsed and she fell to the floor. "Oh, my God, my foot . . . I . . . I . . . can't move . . . it. Oh . . . my ankle," the representative moaned. "I . . . can't get this . . . thing . . . off me." She cried and moaned for about a minute longer, but the cries gradually got more subdued and controlled. Finally she muttered something about getting outside, knocked over the chair as she pulled herself up and thumped to the door, closing it behind her as she left. The entire incident took 130 seconds.

The main dependent variable of the study, of course, was whether the subjects took action to help the victim and how long it took them to do so. There were actually several modes of intervention possible: A subject could open the screen dividing the two rooms, leave the testing room and enter the CTB office by the door, find someone else, or most simply, call out to see if the representative needed help. In one condition, each subject was in the testing room alone while he filled out the questionnaire and heard the fall. In the second condition, strangers were placed in the testing room in pairs. Each subject in the pair was unacquainted with the other before entering the room and they were not introduced.

Across all experimental groups, the majority of subjects who intervened did so by pulling back the room divider and coming in to the CTB office (61%). Few subjects came the round-about way through the door to offer their assistance (14%), and a surprisingly small number (24%) chose the easy solution of calling out to offer help. No one tried to find someone else to whom to report the accident.

Since 70% of Alone subjects intervened, we should expect that at least one person in 91% of all two-person groups would offer help if members of a pair had no influence upon each other. In fact, members did influence each other. In only 40% of the groups did even one person offer help to the injured woman. Only eight subjects of the 40 who were run in this condition intervened. This response rate is significantly below the hypothetical baseline. Social inhibition of helping was so strong that the victim was actually helped more quickly when only one person heard her distress than when two did.

When we talked to subjects after the experiment, those who intervened usually claimed that they did so either because the fall sounded very serious or because they were uncertain what had occurred and felt they should investigate. Many talked about intervention as the "right thing to do" and asserted they would help again in any situation.

Many of the noninterveners also claimed that they were unsure what had happened (59%), but had decided that it was not too serious (46%). A number of subjects reported that they thought other people would or could help (25%), and three said they refrained out of concern for the victim—they did not want to embarrass her. Whether to accept these explanations as reasons or rationalizations is moot—they certainly do not explain the differences among conditions. The important thing to note is that noninterveners did not seem to feel that they had behaved callously or immorally. Their behavior was generally consistent with heir interpretation of the situation. Subjects almost uniformly claimed that in a "real" emergency they would be among the first to help the victim.

These results strongly replicate the findings of the Smoke study. In both experiments, subjects were less likely to take action if they were in the presence of others than if they were alone. This congruence of findings from different experimental settings supports the validity and generality of the phenomenon; it also helps rule out a variety of alternative explanations suitable to either situation alone. For example, the possibility that smoke may have represented a threat to the subject's personal safety and that subjects in groups may have had a greater concern to appear "brave" than single subjects does not apply to the present experiment. In the present experiment, nonintervention cannot signify bravery. Comparison of the two experiments also suggests that the absolute number of nonresponsive bystanders may not be a critical factor in producing social inhibition of intervention; pairs of strangers in the present study inhibited each other as much as did trios in the former study.

Other studies we have done show that group inhibition effects hold in real life as well as in the laboratory, and for members of the general population as well as college students. The results of these experiments clearly support the line of theoretical argument advanced earlier. When bystanders to an emergency can see the reactions of other people, and when other people can see their own reactions, each individual may, through a process of social influence, be led to interpret the situation as less serious than he would if he were alone, and consequently be less likely to take action.

These studies, however, tell us little about the case that stimulated our interest in bystander intervention: the Kitty Genovese murder. Although the 38 witnesses to that event were aware, through seeing lights and silhouettes in other windows, that others watched, they could not see what others were doing and thus be influenced by their reactions. In the privacy of their own apartments, they could not be clearly seen by others, and thus inhibited by their presence. The social influence process we have described above could not operate. Nevertheless, we think that the presence of other bystanders may still have affected each individual's response.

DIFFUSION OF RESPONSIBILITY

In addition to affecting the interpretations that he places on a situation, the presence of other people can also alter the rewards and costs facing an individual bystander. Perhaps most importantly, the presence of other people can reduce the cost of not acting. If only one bystander is present at an emergency, he carries all of the responsibility for dealing with it; he will feel all of the guilt for not acting; he will bear all of any blame others may lever for nonintervention. If others are present, the onus of responsibility is diffused, and the individual may be more likely to resolve his conflict between intervening and not intervening in favor of the latter alternative.

When only one bystander is present at an emergency, if help is to come it must be from him. Although he may choose to ignore them out of concern for his personal safety, or desire "not to get involved," any pressures to intervene focus uniquely on him. When there are several observers present, however, the pressures to intervene do not focus on any of the observers; instead, the responsibility for intervention is shared among all the onlookers and is not unique to any one. As a result, each may be less likely to help.

Potential blame may also be diffused. However much we wish to think that an individual's moral behavior is divorced from considerations of personal punishment or reward, there is both theory and evidence to the contrary. It is perfectly reasonable to assume that under circumstances of group responsibility for a punishable act, the punishment or blame that accrues to any one individual is often slight or nonexistent.

Finally, if others are known to be present, but their behavior cannot be closely observed, any one bystander may assume that one of the other observers is already taking action to end the emergency. If so, his own intervention would only be redundant—perhaps harmfully or confusingly so. Thus, given the presence of other onlookers whose behavior cannot be observed, any given bystander can rationalize his own inaction by convincing himself that "somebody else must be doing something."

These considerations suggest that even when bystanders to an emergency cannot see or be influenced by each other, the more bystanders who are present, the less likely any one bystander would be to intervene and provide aid. To test this suggestion, it would be necessary to create an emergency situation in which each subject is blocked from communicating with others to prevent his getting information about their behavior during the emergency.

A Fit to be Tried[3]

A college student arrived in the laboratory, and was ushered into an individual room from which a communication system would enable him to talk to other participants (who were actually figments of the tape recorder). Over the intercom, the subject was told that the experimenter was concerned with the kinds of personal problems faced by normal college students in a high-pressure, urban environment, and that he would be asked to participate in a discussion about these problems. To avoid embarrassment about discussing personal problems with strangers, the experimenter said, several precautions would be taken. First, subjects would remain anonymous, which was why they had been placed in individual rooms rather than face-to-face. Second, the experimenter would not listen to the initial discussion himself, but would only get the subject's reactions later by questionnaire.

The plan for the discussion was that each person would talk in turn for 2 minutes, presenting his problems to the group. Next, each person in turn would comment on what others had said, and finally there would be a free discussion. A mechanical switching device regulated the discussion, switching on only one microphone at a time.

The Emergency. The discussion started with the future victim speaking first. He said he found it difficult to get adjusted to New York and to his studies. Very hesitantly and with obvious embarrassment, he mentioned that he was prone to seizures, particularly when studying hard or taking exams. The other people, including the one real subject, took their turns and discussed similar problems (minus the proneness to seizures). The naive subject talked last in the series, after the last prerecorded voice.

When it was again the victim's turn to talk, he made a few relatively calm comments, and then, growing increasingly loud and incoherent, he continued:

> I er I think I I need er if if could er er somebody er er er er er er er give me a little er give me a little help because I er I'm er er h-h-having a a a a real problem er right now and I er if somebody could help me out it would er er s-s-sure be good . . . because er there er er a cause I er I uh I've got a a one of the er sie . . . er er things coming on and and and I could really er use some help so if somebody would er give me a little h-help uh er-er-er-er-er-er c-could somebody er er help er uh uh uh (choking sounds). . . . I'm gonna die er er I'm . . . gonna die er help er er seizure (chokes, then quiet).

The major independent variable of the study was the number of people the subject believed also heard the fit. The subject was led to believe that the discussion group was one of three sizes: a two-person group consisting of himself, the victim, and four other persons.

The major dependent variable of the experiment was the time elapsed from the start of the victim's seizure until the subject left his experimental cubicle. When the subject left his room, he saw the experimental assistant seated at the end of the hall, and invariably went to the assistant to report the seizure. If 5 minutes elapsed without the subject's having emerged from his room, the experiment was terminated.

Ninety-five percent of all the subjects who ever responded did so within the first half of the time available to them. No subject who had not reported within 3 minutes after the fit ever did so. This suggests that even had the experiment been allowed to run for a considerable longer period of time, few additional subjects would have responded.

Eight-five percent of the subjects who thought they alone knew of the victim's plight reported the seizure before the victim was cut off; only 31% of those who thought four other bystanders were present did so. Every one of the subjects in the two-person condition, but only 62% of the subjects in the six-person condition ever reported the emergency.

Subjects, whether or not they intervened, believed the fit to be genuine and serious. "My God, he's having a fit," many subjects said to themselves (and we overheard via their microphones). Others gasped or simply said, "Oh." Several of the male subjects swore. One subject said to herself, "it's just my kind of luck, something has to happen to me!" Several subjects spoke aloud of their confusion about what course of action to take: "Oh, God, what should I do?"

When those subjects who intervened stepped out of their rooms, they found the experimental assistant down the hall. With some uncertainty but without panic, they reported the situation. "Hey, I think Number 1 is very sick. He's having a fit or something." After ostensibly checking on the situation, the experimenter returned to report that "everything is under control." They subjects accepted these assurances with obvious relief.

Subjects who failed to report the emergency showed few signs of the apathy and indifference thought to characterize "unresponsive bystanders." When the experimenter entered the room to terminate the situation, the subject often asked if the victim was all right. "Is he being taken care of?" "He's all right, isn't he?" Many of these subjects showed physical signs of nervousness; they often had trembling hands and sweating palms. If anything, they seemed more emotionally aroused than did the subjects who reported the emergency.

Why, then, didn't they respond? It is not our impression that they had decided not to respond. Rather, they were still in a state of indecision and conflict concerning whether to respond or not. The emotional behavior of these nonresponding subjects was a sign of their continuing conflict, a conflict that other subjects resolved by responding.

The fit created a conflict situation of the avoidance–avoidance type. On the one hand, subjects worried about the guilt and shame they would feel if they did not help the person in distress. On the other hand, they were concerned not to make fools of themselves by overreacting, not to ruin the ongoing experiment by leaving their intercoms, and not to destroy the anonymous nature of the situation, which the experimenter had earlier stressed as important. For subjects in the two-person condition, the obvious distress of the victim and his need for help were so important that their conflict was easily resolved. For the subjects who knew that there were other bystanders present, the cost of not helping was reduced and the conflict they were in was more acute. Caught between the two negative alternatives of letting the victim continue to suffer or rushing, perhaps foolishly, to help, the nonresponding bystanders vacillated between them rather than choosing not to respond. This distinction may be academic for the victim, since he got no help in either case, but it is an extremely important one for understanding the causes of bystanders' failures to help.

Although subjects experienced stress and conflict during the emergency, their general reactions to it were highly positive. On a questionnaire administered after the experimenter had discussed the nature and purpose of the experiment, every single subject found the experiment either "interesting" or "very interesting" and was willing to participate in similar experiments in the future. All subjects felt that they understood what the experiment was all about and indicated that they thought the deceptions were necessary and justified. All but one felt they were better informed about the nature of psychological research in general.

CONCLUSION

We have suggested two distinct processes which might lead people to be less likely to intervene in an emergency if there are other people present than if they are alone. On the one hand, we suggested that the presence of other people may affect the interpretations each bystander puts on an ambiguous emergency situation. If other people are present at an emergency, each bystander will be guided by their apparent reactions in formulating his own impressions. Unfortunately, their apparent reactions may not be a good indication of their true feelings. It is possible for a state of "pluralistic ignorance" to develop, in which each bystander is led by the apparent lack of concern of the others to interpret the situation as being less serious than he would if alone. To the extent that he does not feel the situation is an emergency, he will be unlikely to take any helpful action.

Even if an individual does decide that an emergency is actually in process and that something ought to be done, he still is faced with the choice of whether he himself will intervene. Here again, the presence of other people may influence him—by reducing the costs associated with nonintervention. If a number of people witness the same event, the responsibility for action is diffused, and each may feel less necessity to help.

"There's safety in numbers," according to an old adage and modern city dwellers seem to believe it. They shun deserted streets, empty subway cars, and lonely dark walks in dark parks, preferring instead to go where others are or to stay at home. When faced with stress, most individuals seem less afraid when they are in the presence of others than when they are alone.

A feeling so widely shared should have some basis in reality. Is there safety in numbers? If so, why? Two reasons are often suggested: Individuals are less likely to find themselves in trouble if there are others about, and even if they do find themselves in trouble, others are likely to help them deal with it. While it is certainly true that a victim is unlikely to receive help if nobody knows of his plight, the experiments above cast doubt on the suggestion that he will be more likely to receive help if more people are present. In fact, the opposite seems to be true. A victim may be more likely to get help, or an emergency be reported, the fewer the people who are available to take action.

Although the results of these studies may shake our faith in "safety in numbers," they also may help us begin to understand a number of frightening incidents where crowds have heard but not answered a call for help. Newspapers have tagged these incidents with the label, "apathy." We have become indifferent, they say, callous to the fate of suffering of others. Our society has become "dehumanized" as it has become urbanized. These glib phrases may contain some truth, since startling cases such as the Genovese murder often seem to occur in our large cities, but such terms may also be misleading. Our studies suggest a different conclusion. They suggest that situational factors, specifically factors involving the immediate social environment, may be of greater importance in determining an individual's reaction to an emergency than such vague cultural or personality concepts as "apathy" or "alienation due to urbanization." They suggest that the failure to intervene may be better understood by knowing the relationship among bystanders rather than that between a bystander and the victim.

Reference Notes

1. A more complete account of this experiment is provided in Latané and Darley (1968). Keith Gerritz and Lee Ross provided thoughtful assistance in running the study.
2. This experiment is more fully described in Latané and Rodin (1969).
3. Further details of this experiment can be found in Darley and Latané (1968).

References

Darley, J.M., and Latané, B. Bystander intervention in emergencies: Diffusion of responsibility. Journal of Personality and Social Psychology, 1968, 8, 377–383.

Latané, B., & Darley, J.M. Group inhibition of bystander intervention. Journal of Personality and Social Psychology, 1968, 10, 215–221.

Latané, B., & Rodin, J. A Lady in distress: Inhibiting effects of friends and strangers on bystander intervention. Journal of Experimental Social Psychology, 1969, 5, 189–202.

Samuel P. Oliner
Pearl M. Oliner

The Altruistic Personality: Concern into Action

This selection by Oliner and Oliner is based on extensive research done in Nazi occupied Europe investigating those factors that led some Germans to help save the lives of Jews during World War II. Although many people *felt* they should help, the authors found that those who actually helped did so for several different reasons. They note three different kinds of motivation: an empathic orientation by which the people were able to identify with the plight of the victims; a feeling that helping was expected of them by others whose opinions they valued; or a belief that the persecution of the Jews was a moral violation and a need to act out of principle in order to save them.

My parents were loving and kind. I learned from them to be helpful and considerate. There was a Jewish family living in our apartment building, but I hardly noticed when they left. Later, when I was working in the hospital as a doctor, a Jewish man was brought to the emergency room by his wife. I knew that he would die unless he was treated immediately. But we were not allowed to treat Jews; they could only be treated at the Jewish hospital. I could do nothing.

These are the words of a German nonrescuer, a kind and compassionate woman predisposed by sentiment and the ethics of her profession to help a dangerously ill man but who nonetheless did not do so. Thus, it is clearly not enough—in explaining rescuers' activities—to cite sentiments of caring and compassion. Several nonrescuers shared similar tendencies.

Rescuers' attachments to others and their inclusive view of humanity influenced their interpretations of events and situations and may have inclined them toward benevolent behavior. But the step from inclination to action is a large one. To understand what actually aroused rescuers to act on behalf of Jews, submerging or overriding fundamental considerations regarding their own and their families' survival, we must examine yet another motivational source.

It took a catalyst to translate predisposition into action—an external event that challenged rescuers' highest values. However, such actions were not the consequence of objective external events but rather of the subjective meanings rescuers conferred on them. Rescuers and nonrescuers interpreted the demands on themselves differently. Faced with the same knowledge, observation of needs, or requests, only rescuers felt compelled to help.

Based on theoretical proposals developed by Janusz Reykowski, we were able to discern three kinds of catalysts that generally aroused a response. They were able to serve as catalysts because they were congruent with the ways rescuers characteristically made important life decisions. Rescuers who were characteristically *empathically* oriented responded to an external event that aroused or heightened their empathy. Rescuers who were characteristically *normocentrically* oriented responded to an external even which they interpreted as a normative demand of a highly valued social group. Rescuers who characteristically behaved according to their own overarching *principles,* in the main autonomously derived, were moved to respond by an external event which they interpreted as violating these principles.

As the illustrative profiles of individual rescuers and their situations reveal, the altruistic act of rescue was not a radical departure from previous ways of responding but an extension of characteristic forms of relating to others.

An empathic orientation is centered on the needs of another, on that individual's possible fate. It emerges out of a direct connection with the distressed other. Compassion, sympathy, and pity are its characteristic expressions. The reactions may be emotional or cognitive; frequently they contain elements of both. An empathic reaction aroused more than a third (37 percent) of rescuers to their first helping act.

The impact of a direct encounter with a distressed Jew was sometimes overpowering. Consider, for example, the following episode related by a Polish woman, then approximately thirty-five years of age:

> In 1942, I was on my way home from town and was almost near home when M. came out of the bushes. I looked at him, in striped camp clothing, his head bare, shod in clogs. He might have been about thirty or thirty-two years old. And he begged me, his hands joined like for a prayer—that he had escaped from Majdanek and could I help him? He joined his hands in this way, knelt down in front of me, and said: "You are like the Virgin Mary." It still makes me cry. "If I get through and reach Warsaw, I will never forget you."
>
> Well, how could one not have helped such a man? So I took him home, and I fed him because he was hungry. I heated the water so that he could have a bath. Maybe I should not mention this, but I brushed him, rinsed him, gave him a towel to dry himself. Then I dressed him in my husband's underwear, a shirt, and a tie. I had to do it for him because I wasn't sure if he could do it himself. He was shivering, poor soul, and I was shivering too, with emotion. I am very sensitive and emotional.

Despite the striped clothes and the shaven head, the stranger emerged as a human being, the vital connection perhaps being made by his prayerlike gesture. Overcoming what may have been some feelings of aversion and modesty, the respondent took him home to take care of his most basic needs. The interaction terminated quickly. The rescuer gave the man about ten zloty (less than a dollar), and he went on his way.

In the case of "Stanislaus" empathic motivations were central and consistent.

Stanislaus was born in 1920 to a poor Polish Roman Catholic family. His mother had come to Warsaw from the countryside, where she worked as a domestic and part-time midwife. His father, who had some high school education, was disabled by an accident when Stanislaus was eight years old and lived on a pension thereafter. He had one brother, four years older than himself. He graduated from high school in 1939 but was unable to resume his studies until after the war, when he completed a degree in the diplomatic-consular department of the Academy of Political Science. During the war, he and his family lived near the Warsaw Ghetto. His helping activities continued over several years:

> The gallery of people changed all the time—it comprised several tens of people. Some obtained help in the form of a bowl of soup, others came for temporary shelter during the roundups. Still others, whom I had never met before, came and stayed with us until some other hideout was found.

One of the most noteworthy clues to Stanislaus' motivation is his recollection of details regarding almost all the individuals he helped—details not only of their physical appearance but also their psychological condition. He makes few references to himself; sentences that begin with "I" quickly change to focus on others. "I had my friends" in the ghetto, he says, and then begins to describe what life in the ghetto was like from the point of view of those who were there. Stanislaus thus appears particularly capable of centering on others' needs.

Understanding others, taking their perspective, and anticipating their futures may have left Stanislaus little psychological room to consider his own needs. He speaks little of his own wartime deprivations or even his mother's. His understanding of how others felt left him with the feeling of "no choice" regarding his response:

> Human compassion: When someone comes and says "I escaped from the camp," what is the alternative? One alternative is to push him out and close the door—the other is to pull him into the house and say, "Sit down, relax, wash up. You will be as hungry as we are because we have only this bread."

Caring for others and respect in its universal sense were both taught by his mother explicitly and by example. "I learned to respect the world from my mother," he said. His mother modeled caring behaviors in many ways. His childhood and adolescence were spent in a household filled with his mother's relatives, who sought her support as they looked for work or studied in the big city. His mother herself worked as a maid and midwife occasionally to earn the money necessary to provide for the boys' education. Stanislaus credits her with initiating his wartime helping activities.

Unlike an empathic reaction, a normocentric reaction is not rooted in a direct connection with the victim, but rather in a feeling of obligation to a social reference group with who the actor identifies and whose explicit and implicit rules he feels obliged to obey. The social group, rather than the victim him- or herself, motivates the behavior. The actor perceives the social group as imposing norms for behavior, and for these rescuers, inaction was considered a violation of the group's code of proper conduct. Feelings of obligation or duty are frequently coupled with anticipation of guilt or shame if one fails to act. For their first helping act, the majority of rescuers (52 percent) responded to a normocentric expectation.

In some cases, a normocentric response was activated when a person or authority representing the salient social group simply asked the rescuer to help. In the following episode, a very religious German woman, the wife of a parish minister, himself a member of the Bekennende Kirche, responded to a joint request by her husband and a prestigious intermediary:

> I was called to the parish office by my husband. I was then expecting my eighth child. The wife of Professor T. was there and said she had come on account of two Jews who appeared to her as poor animals escaping from the hunt. Could they come that very afternoon to stay with me? I said yes, but with a heavy heart because of the expected child. K. came at midday—she was a bundle of nerves. They stayed for three weeks. I was afraid.

Asked for the main reasons why she became involved, she said: "One cannot refuse someone who is concerned about the fate of others." The "someone" she was concerned about was not the Jews but her husband and the professor's wife.

Requests came from various authoritative sources whom rescuers felt obliged to obey: political groups, family members or friends. Frequently, they came from resistance groups. For example, a Polish member of PLAN (Polska Ludowa Akcja Niepodleglosciowa, Polish National Independence Action) found himself cooperating with Jewish resistance organizations. Asked why he did it, he responded:

> It was not a personal, individual activity—I had orders from the organization. In helping these people, I was helping myself since it weakened the Germans. It was an act of cooperation, military cooperation.

In general, normocentric motivations were more conducive to group actions than to strictly individual undertakings. Although such motivations could lead to extraordinary sacrifices, they were usually less likely to result in close personal relationships with the victims. For rescuers like "Dirk," an internalized normocentrically motivated Dutch rescuer, help was more often perceived as a matter of "duty" rather than sympathy or affection.

> It's not because I have an altruistic personality. It's because I am an obedient Christian. I know that is the reason why I did it. I know it. The Lord wants you to do good work. What good is it to say you love your neighbor if you don't help them. There was never any question about it. The Lord wanted us to rescue those people and we did it. We could not let those people go to their doom.

A principled motivation, like a normative one, is rooted in an indirect connection with the victim. The indirect connection, however, does not come about through a social group with whom the actor identifies but is rather mediated by a set of overarching axioms, largely autonomously derived. People with this orientation interpreted the persecution of Jews as a violation of moral precepts, and the main goal of their rescue behavior was to reaffirm and act on their principles. Even when their actions might prove futile, individuals tended to believe that the principles were kept alive as long as there were people who reaffirmed them by their deeds. Somewhat more than a tenth (11 percent) of rescuers were aroused to action by principles.

Rescuers, like most people, had multiple values, any one of which might assume supremacy at a given moment. For some rescuers, however, certain values became central principles around which they characteristically interpreted events and organized their lives. For these people, their principles were fundamental canons of belief whose violation was accompanied by strong moral indignation. They felt compelled to act more out of a sense of these principles than empathy for the victims.

These rescuers most frequently highlighted two kinds of moral principles—the principle of justice (the right of innocent people to be free from persecution) and the principle of care (the obligation to help the needy). Those motivated by the principle of justice tended to exhibit different emotional characteristics than did those who were motivated by the principle of care. They usually had more impersonal relationships with those they assisted and reserved strong emotions (anger and hate) for those who violated the principle of justice they held dear. Rescuers motivated primarily by care, on the other hand, usually focused on the subjective states and reactions of the victims. Kindness toward the victim was the dominant theme, while hate and indignation toward the violators were more transitory. In some cases the rescuer was even ready to extend help to the enemy if he was in pain or danger.

High independence from external opinions and evaluations is the major characteristic of people who share this orientation. Hence, they are more likely to act alone and on their own initiative. If other people are involved, it is mostly for instrumental reasons rather than for psychological support or guidance.

The capacity for such independent action has also been noted in individuals characterized by internalized norms. But principles differ in their origins from internalized norms. While internalized norms can be traced directly back to particular authoritative social groups, those who have a principled motivation appear to a great extent to develop their principles on the basis of their own intellectual and moral efforts. Normocentrically motivated persons refer repeatedly to certain groups or categories of people who espouse the same norms: religious groups, professional groups, friends, or family. Such references are rarely made by people with a principled motivation. To the extent that relationships are mentioned, they are presented as deliberately chosen on the basis of support for the principles to which the subject was previously committed. Adherence to the principles reappears to play the primary role in determining the association. Among normocentrically oriented persons, it is the other way around—the reference group with which one is associated appears to be the source of values. As one representative of rescuers who had a principled motivation, we offer "Suzanne," who emphasizes the principles of justice.

Suzanne's reason for helping was simple: "All men are equal and are born free and equal by right." Pressed by the interviewer to add other reasons, she replied, "There is no other." This is a fundamental conception of the principle of justice—universal in character, it extends to all persons. For Suzanne this principle was rooted in an intellectual world view that made infractions immediately obvious. Fascism, Nazism, and totalitarianism by their very nature violated the principle.

"Consequently," she explained, "I am against all dictatorial systems." The Pétan regime was a dictatorship; she recognized its implications immediately and reacted immediately.

Personal relationships played no part in Suzanne's helping activities. Over three years, in various ways, she helped several hundred people, including over a hundred children, all of whom [were] previously unknown to her. In all these cases she initiated helping and actively sought out people to help. She worked independently and was not connected with any resistance group. She did not seem to seek nor need any external reinforcement for her activity; the opinions of others apparently did not interest her. When asked what her neighbors who had found out about her activities felt, she replied, "Don't know." She was remarkably consistent in her action from the moment she made the decision until the end of the war. Stable and sustained task orientation, the impersonal context of helping, independence from external opinions or reinforcement, and engagement in action as long as injustice persisted—all testify to a principled motivation, as did her scores on the personality scales.

How did Suzanne develop into such a person? She describes her family as "very close and very united." Unity came from a convergence of values shared by both parents as well as her brother, twelve years her senior. Both mother and father emphasized above all being a responsible person. It was a value she learned well; "I always finish a task I commit myself to," she said. Her father particularly emphasized the need "to take care of one's neighbor and the duty to be an example to others." She credits her brother with having "taught me to practice and to live a good life." Her brother was a much-decorated hero of the resistance.

The variation in motivations leading to rescue behavior highlights the important point that the paths to virtue are neither uniform nor standardized. Rather, they represent alternative pathways through which individuals are equipped and disposed to interpret events of moral significance. Different rescuers found different meanings in what was happening to Jews, but once their plight was understood through the prism of the individual's orientation, the necessity to act became compelling.

Most commonly, rescuers were normocentrically oriented. Thus, they were aroused to act by external authorities whose values and standards they had internalized to varying degrees. The majority of rescuers (52 percent) perceived helping Jews as a means of expressing and strengthening their affiliations with their social groups. Those whose group norms were only weakly internalized depended on overt pressure from some authoritative group member to initiate and sustain their activity. (This suggests the potential power authoritative social groups might have galvanized in the service of rescue had more of them chosen to do so.) Those who had internalized their group norms deeply did not require such external pressure.

The empathic orientation was the next most common. An empathic reaction was characteristic of more than a third (37 percent) of rescuers. They had a particular capacity to focus on others' needs and to be moved by their distress. While visible cues were necessary for some, for others merely knowing that others were suffering was sufficient to arouse them. Principled motivations largely autonomously derived were the least common type of motivation. Only 11 percent of rescuers were aroused to action by principles alone.

While in many cases, the motivation appeared to be similar over a number of different helping acts, in several others the motivation for the first helping act was not necessarily the same for the second or third. Nor did the motivation that first aroused the rescuer to action necessarily remain the same during the course of the behavior, even in relation to the same person or people being helped. A normocentric initial motivation sometimes became more empathic as bonds formed between the rescuer and rescued. The same was true for principled rescuers. As one rescuer motivated by the principle of justice explained it, "I began to like the people I was helping and became very distressed at what was happening to them."

What is of final importance is that receptivity to such diverse catalysts did not suddenly emerge in the context of the traumas of the Holocaust. Rather, preparation began long before in the emotions and cognitions through which rescuers normally and routinely related to others and made their decisions. Thus, their responses were less explicit conscious choices than characteristic ways of attending to routine events. Already attuned to conferring meaning on events through their particular moral sensibilities, they depended on familiar patterns to discern the significance of the unprecedented events at hand. To a large extent, then, helping Jews was less a decision made at a critical juncture than a choice prefigured by an established character and way of life. As Iris Murdoch observes, the moral life is not something that is switched on at a particular crisis but is rather something that goes on continually in the small piecemeal habits of living. Hence, "at crucial moments of choice most of the business of choosing is already over." Many rescuers themselves reflected this view, saying that they "had no choice" and that their behavior deserved no special attention, for it was simply an "ordinary" thing to do.

Mark Snyder
Allen M. Omoto

Who Volunteers and Why? The Psychology of AIDS Volunteerism

This article asks many of the same questions of the previous article by Oliner & Oliner, but within a different context. The question here is what are the motives of people who volunteer to help people with AIDS. Snyder and Omoto consider the extent to which people who volunteer do it out of a sense of altruism, a concern for the community, and even a desire to feel good about themselves. The authors note that they could not find a simple profile that distinguished volunteers from others, and also that the complex pattern of motives for beginning to help and continuing to help over the long term were even different. In reading this article, it might be interesting to consider the range of motives uncovered here and compare these to the findings of Oliner & Oliner, comparing the various reasons guiding AIDS volunteers and those who helped save Jews from the Nazis.

Countless generations of Sunday school students (and others familiar with the curriculum) will recognize the following parable:

> A man was going down from Jerusalem to Jericho, and he fell among robbers, who stripped him and beat him, and departed, leaving him half dead. Now by chance a priest was going down the road; and when he saw him he passed by on the other side. So likewise a Levite, when he came to the place and saw him, passed by on the other side. But Samaritan, as he journeyed, came to where he was; and when he saw him, he had compassion, and went to him and bound his wounds, pouring on oil and wine; then he set him on his own beast and brought him to an inn, and took care of him. And the next day he took out two dennarii and gave them to the innkeeper, saying, "Take care of him; and whatever you spend, I will repay you when I come back." (Luke 10:29–37, RSV)

This, of course, is the story of the Good Samaritan. We begin our chapter with this parable because it raises a central question of who helps others in the real world.

The general question is: Who chooses to help people—like the assault victim in the parable—who are alone, in dire straits, and shunned by others? In particular, why do some people do as the Samaritan did, and engage in sustained helpfulness and make a continuing commitment to the ongoing care and well-being of those in need? Our specific research question is: Who volunteers to help people with AIDS (referred to as PWAs) and, relatedly, why do these helpers engage in their Samaritan acts?

To set the stage for answering this question, this chapter first provides a brief overview of our program of research on AIDS volunteerism, with special emphasis on people's perceptions of and motivations for AIDS volunteer work. Next, it presents data that speak to questions of who helps PWAs and why.

AIDS IN CONTEMPORARY SOCIETY

There is no doubt that AIDS extracts huge economic, medical, and psychological tolls from those struck by the disease, from their loved ones and associates, and from society at large. In 1981, the Centers for Disease Control reported the first case of what would come to be known as AIDS. Now, less than a decade later, an estimated 1.5 million Americans are infected with the HIV virus that is thought to cause AIDS (Morin, 1988). Up to 99% of these infected individuals are expected to develop AIDS (Lui, Darrow, & Rutherford, 1988). AIDS is also no longer a disease restricted to certain "high risk" groups (Morgan & Curran, 1986). Thus, with neither a vaccine nor a cure for AIDS on the horizon, the full impact of AIDS—as devastating and profound as it already has been—has yet to be felt, and it will touch all segments of the population.

AIDS, it should be recognized, is more than a medical crisis, and has had profound social, legal, and political ramifications. Society has responded to the AIDS epidemic on a number of fronts and in a variety of ways, both medical and nonmedical. Not only have new medical treatments and drugs been developed in response to AIDS, but also AIDS-related issues have been the focus of legislative activities, religious and ethical debates, community education and public health campaigns, and media and popular culture presentations. Understanding AIDS therefore involves understanding not just its medical aspects but also its psychological, social, and societal effects.

An increasingly critical component of society's response to AIDS has been the development of community-based grass-roots organizations that recruit, train, assign, and supervise volunteers who assist with the care of PWAs and with AIDS public-education efforts. For example, some volunteers help PWAs with their household chores; some provide emotional and social support as "buddies" to PWAs; others staff AIDS hotlines providing information, counseling, and referral services; still others volunteer for speaking, educational, and public-information assignments. Indeed, it has been observed that "one of the most remarkable and heartening byproducts of the HIV epidemic has been the development of grass-roots organizations (of volunteers) dedicated to serving the needs of people with AIDS" (Fineberg, 1989, P. 117). AIDS volunteerism clearly is a testimonial to human kindness and to the power of communities of "ordinary people" to unite and organize in response to extraordinary events.

AIDS volunteerism not only benefits the recipients of services, but also may provide rewards for those who donate their time and energy. Volunteerism promotes a sense of community spirit and civic solidarity. Volunteering offers tangible evidence to people that they live in a kind and gentle culture in which people choose to "give something back" to society. AIDS volunteers themselves have a great deal to say about their experiences and the benefits of volunteerism. Almost without exception, their narrative accounts reveal that volunteers find their work to be psychologically moving and powerful; many claim that it has substantially and irrevocably changed their lives (Omoto & Snyder, 1989a). Volunteers report, for example, that their work "makes me feel good all over," "gives me purpose in life," and that they feel they are "making a difference as an AIDS buddy." Through their work, moreover, many volunteers believe that they are gaining an awareness of other people's overwhelming problems and unfulfilled needs.

APPLIED AND THEORETICAL ASPECTS OF AIDS VOLUNTEERISM

In our research, we are working to understand the social and psychological aspects of volunteerism. We seek not only to find out who volunteers and why, but also to explore the consequences of volunteering for volunteers themselves, for the recipients of their efforts, and for society at large. The research is guided both by applied concerns regarding the role of volunteers in society's response to AIDS and by theoretical concerns with the nature of helping relationships and the social phenomenon of volunteerism.

At an *applied level,* by all accounts the number of AIDS cases will only increase in the years ahead as many of the millions of people already infected with the HIV virus actually develop AIDS and related illnesses. In addition, as medical advances extend the life expectancy of PWAs, more and more people will be living with AIDS (and living longer with AIDS). In fact, life expectancy after an AIDS diagnosis is over 50% longer now than it was at the beginning of the epidemic (Lemp, Payne, Neal Temelso, & Rutherford, 1990), and it is estimated that 11% of those diagnosed with AIDS are now living longer than three years ("HIV; Longer Life," 1990). As society and an already greatly burdened health care system struggle to care for an increasing number of PWAs who are living longer, then, one can expect an escalating demand for the benefits and services provided by AIDS volunteers. These volunteers will also be taxed by this increasing reliance on them, however, as many will experience weariness and distress from repeatedly confronting the sorrow of AIDS. Eventually, volunteers may experience battle fatigue and burnout from watching people with AIDS suffer and eventually die (e.g., "Noble Experiment," 1990). In fact, there are already troubling indications that in some communities, the supply of volunteers is falling short of the demand for their services (e.g., "Volunteering Drops," 1990).

At a *theoretical* level, studying AIDS volunteerism may be highly informative about the nature of helping behavior and about human relationships more generally. The study of helping behavior has long been a central area of research in personality and social psychology, with researchers attracted to it both because of its obvious social relevance and because it speaks to the issue of whether or not there is an intrinsically altruistic side to human nature (Batson, 1990).

Generally speaking, volunteer efforts and volunteer organizations constitute intriguing social phenomena of helping in the real world. For not only do people help in AIDS organizations, but citizens volunteer themselves in providing companionship to the elderly, health care to the sick, tutoring to the illiterate, and counseling to the troubled. Volunteer activity is quite prevalent in American society. According to the most recent Gallup Poll on the subject, 80 million American adults engaged in some form of volunteerism in 1987, with 21 million giving five or more hours per week to volunteer work (Independent Sector, 1988). By at least one estimate, there were almost 10,000 people actively involved as AIDS volunteers in the United States in 1989 (National AIDS Network, personal communication, March 7, 1990). What is common to all of these volunteer acts is that they are prosocial in nature and involve people devoting substantial amounts of their time and energy to aiding and benefiting others, often giving of themselves for extended periods of time.

Studying AIDS volunteerism provides an arena for examining *sustained, planned,* and *potentially costly* helping behavior. As such, it stands in contrast to much of the social psychological literature on helping, which has focused on situations in which potential helpers encounter unexpected opportunities to help that may also require quick decisions about whether or not to offer assistance (the classic example being the "bystander intervention: situation; Latané & Darley, 1970). The helping that occurs in such situations typically is confined to relatively brief and limited periods of time and to acts that are not particularly costly or risky, and that usually entail no future contact between the helper and the recipient.

In volunteerism, however, people have sought out opportunities to help others, rather than simply reacting to situations that have confronted them. Instead of being pressed to make quick decisions about whether or not to offer assistance, people may have deliberated for considerable amounts of time about whether or not to become a volunteer, the extent of their involvement, and the degree to which particular volunteer opportunities fit with their own personal patterns of needs, goals, and motivations. And, instead of limited and relatively low-cost assistance, many types of volunteer work involve commitment to an ongoing helping relationship that is of relatively long duration and involves considerable personal sacrifice in time, energy, emotional and psychological resources, and even financial expense (for a review of psychological research on volunteerism, see Clary & Snyder, 1991).

AIDS volunteerism embodies each of these features: AIDS volunteers have made deliberate decisions to engage in sustained helpfulness that is characterized by continuing commitment to the recipient's care and well-being. Like the Good Samaritan of the parable, they have gone beyond offering immediate help and instead made long-term investments in the well-being of another person. Thus they provide an excellent opportunity to investigate the dynamics of sustained ongoing

TABLE 7.1   Stages of the Volunteer Process

Level of analyses	Antecedents	Experiences	Consequences
Individual volunteer	Personality Demographics Personal history Motivations Psychological functions	Relationship development	Satisfaction Commitment Increased knowledge Attitude change
Broader social influences	Recruitment of volunteers	Effects of PWAs Treatment process	Social diffusion Public education

helping relationships. Perhaps because of the relatively recent emergence of AIDS volunteerism, there is very little in the way of a published literature, and what little of it there is tends to focus on reports of the development of volunteer programs (Arno, 1988: Dumont, 1989; Lopez & Getzel, 1987; for an exception, see Williams, 1988). Nevertheless, we believe that, in studying AIDS volunteerism, we have isolated a socially significant laboratory in which to extend, evaluate, refine, and apply psychological theories of individual and social behavior. The benefits of this research should be an increased understanding of AIDS volunteerism, to be sure, but also a greater understanding of prosocial action and of helping relationships.

In recognition of volunteerism as sustained, ongoing, and potentially costly helping behavior, we have developed a conceptual model that identifies three stages of the *volunteer process*. As shown in Table 7.1, this model (which guides our program of research) specifies the psychological and behavioral features associated with each stage and the social, organizational, and societal contexts in which they occur. In the specific case of AIDS volunteerism, the first stage involves *antecedents* of volunteerism, and addresses the questions of who volunteers and why. The second stage concerns *experiences* of volunteers and the PWAs they work with, and the effects of AIDS volunteerism on the general treatment and coping processes. The third stage focuses on *consequences* of volunteerism and looks at changes in attitudes, knowledge and behavior that occur in volunteers themselves, in the members of their immediate social networks, and in society at large. At each stage, psychological theories and the evidence of basic research are helping us frame research questions, the answers to which in turn should have implications for applied issues. To illustrate, let us focus on the antecedents stage of the AIDS volunteer process and consider the motivations behind volunteering, and the implications of these motivations for what transpires in voluntary helping relationships.

A FUNCTIONAL APPROACH TO AIDS VOLUNTEERISM

For all prospective volunteers, there are many costs associated with volunteerism and formidable barriers that may help keep them from getting involved in it. In the specific case of AIDS, not only are there limits of time and energy, but also fear of AIDS and death, and concerns about stigmatization. What, then, motivates some people to volunteer to help PWAs, to staff AIDS hotlines, or be "buddies" for PWAs? Who are the Good Samaritans when it comes to PWAs?

As Kurt Lewin, father of the "action research" tradition in the social sciences, suggested many years ago, "there is nothing so practical as a good theory" (Lewin, 1951, p. 169). In our research on AIDS volunteerism, we have taken this dictum to heart, as well as associated prescriptions that "we must infuse the field of applied social psychology with theory—and good theory at that" (Mark & Bryant, 1984, p. 247). To answer the questions of who volunteers and why they volunteer, we have adopted a *functional approach* to understanding the antecedents of AIDS volunteerism. We are extending psychological theories that suggest that people may engage in what appear to be the same behaviors for very different motivational reasons and to serve quite different psychological functions. This type of approach may hold great promise for unraveling the complex web of personal and social motivations that serve as the foundation of volunteer activity.

Functional Approaches

In personality and social psychology, functional approaches are most strongly identified with theories of attitudes and persuasion. To answer the question, "Of what use to people are their attitudes?" functional theorists argue that attitudes help people meet needs, execute plans, and achieve goals. Functional theorists further propose that the same attitudes may serve very different psychological functions for different people (Herek, 1987; Katz, 1960; Smith, Bruner, & White, 1956; Snyder & DeBono, 1987, 1989). For example, in the case of prejudice, one person's negative attitudes toward minorities may reflect the fact that others in the community hold such attitudes; this person's prejudices are serving the function of allowing him or her to fit into important social groups and to interact smoothly with others. But another person's equally negative and hostile prejudices may derive from anxieties and uncertainties about his or her self-worth, concerns that are alleviated by downward social comparison (Wills, 1981) and the derogation of others; this person's prejudices are serving the function of protecting him or her from accepting unpleasant truths about the self.

The logic of a functional approach is readily applicable to understanding the antecedents of volunteerism. Acts of volunteerism that appear to be quite similar on the surface may reflect markedly different underlying motivational processes; that is, they may be serving different psychological functions. Thus a functional approach brings into sharp focus the second question in the title of this chapter: Why do people help?

The specific case of AIDS volunteerism can illustrate the set of functions that has been identified with some regularity in diverse theoretical treatments of attitudes (e.g., Katz, 1960; Smith et al., 1956). The act of volunteering may for one person serve a *social* function, reflecting the normative influences of friends and significant others who are AIDS volunteers, or the desire to make friends and solidify certain social ties through volunteering. For another person, the same act of volunteering may flow from underlying values that prescribe altruistic contributions to society, thereby serving what may be termed a *value-expressive* function. For yet another person, volunteering may serve a *knowledge* function, providing a sense of understanding and information about AIDS and what it does to people. And, in still other cases, volunteering may service a *defensive* or protective function, helping people to cope with personal fears of AIDS, illness, and death.

These distinctions have several implications. If, in fact, volunteering serves different functions for different people, then it follows that volunteer organizations may do well to consider targeting their recruitment efforts at the particular motivations of selected sets of potential volunteers. For example, people struggling with their own fears, anxieties, and uncertainties about AIDS may be indifferent to recruitment appeals that stress societal obligations to help the needy. Rather, they may be stirred to action if the recruitment appeal makes clear how AIDS volunteer work provides opportunities for working through precisely the fears and anxieties that grip them.

In addition, a functional analysis has implications for understanding why some volunteers continue to donate their time and services, whereas others do not. A persistent frustration in volunteer programs is the high rate of attrition (i.e., dropout of their volunteers). As difficult as it may be to recruit volunteers, it is sometimes even more difficult to ensure their continued participation and service. One source of attrition may be a failure of volunteer programs to attend to the psychological functions served by volunteerism. That is, AIDS volunteers whose personal needs and motivations are being adequately fulfilled by their experiences should be more likely than those whose purposes for volunteering are not being addressed to be effective volunteers, to be satisfied with their work and to plan to continue their services.

INVESTIGATING THE VOLUNTEER PROCESS

In our program of research on AIDS volunteerism, we are conducting coordinated cross-sectional and longitudinal field studies coupled with experiments carried out in the laboratory. In these investigations, moreover, we are sampling from diverse subject populations, including people actually working as AIDS volunteers, individuals in training to become AIDS volunteers, volunteers for non-AIDS causes, and nonvolunteers as well.

What have we found? Specifically, what do we know at this point about who volunteers and why? Specifically, what do we know at this point about who volunteers and why? Because much of our research is still in progress, what follows is a preliminary and selective illustration of some of the motivational foundations of volunteerism.

Perceptions of AIDS Volunteer Work

We began our research with two studies of people's perceptions of AIDS volunteerism and of AIDS volunteers (Omoto & Snyder, 1989b). We chose this point of departure because the decision to become involved in AIDS volunteer work, as much as it may intrinsically invoke humanitarian values and altruistic concerns, may also be very much influenced by factors such as stereotyped beliefs and prejudicial attitudes toward AIDS, people with AIDS, and people potentially at risk for AIDS. For this reason, the prospect of providing emotional support and companionship to a terminally ill person may take on a very different meaning when that person is afflicted with AIDS than when that person suffers from, say, terminal cancer. It seems reasonable to expect that these different meanings will influence not only *who* volunteers, but the *reasons* why individuals would choose to donate their time and energy.

In this investigation of people's perceptions of volunteer work, 135 undergraduates anonymously reported on the extent to which they thought different factors would make them more or less likely to volunteer to provide emotional support and practical assistance to a terminally ill patient. Participants were then randomly assigned to read about volunteer work with a cancer patient or a PWA, work that included providing "emotional support and companionship through regular home and hospital visits, as well as telephone contact." Even though the volunteer activities and responsibilities were described in absolutely identical terms in the two conditions, students felt that they had many more good reasons (i.e., reasons that made them *more* likely to serve as a volunteer, such as general personal gains, humanitarian values, and community responsibility) to volunteer to help a patient with cancer than one who had AIDS—and they foresaw more potential barriers to doing AIDS volunteer work (i.e., reasons that made them *less* likely to volunteer, such as prejudice and fear). Clearly, the results of this experiment suggest that AIDS volunteer work is perceived by some to be very "different" kind of volunteer activity.

Consistent with a functional approach to volunteerism, then, quite different reasons and motivations are required for the very same acts depending on who will be the recipient. This finding was reinforced by a companion study in which 39 volunteers from non-AIDS organizations (that is, people with histories of donating their time and energy to helping others) were questioned about their reasons for engaging in their current work and the reasons they saw as being important for doing AIDS-related volunteer work (Omoto & Snyder, 1989b). The results of this study revealed that active volunteers claimed rather pragmatic and *selfish* reasons (such as resumé building, feeling good about oneself, and gaining experience) for their current work. But when it came to doing AIDS volunteer work, they cited different and distinctly altruistic and *selfless* reasons (such as an obligation to help others in need) as critical in decisions to help. In other words, these "Samaritans" said they would require *different* reasons for engaging in AIDS volunteer work than for their current volunteer work, and these were reasons that entailed concern for rather remote rewards that may be unlikely to motivate many people.

Motivations for Becoming an AIDS Volunteer

Thus, even those who volunteer for non-AIDS work perceive AIDS volunteerism to be a "special" form of volunteer activity, one requiring unique motivations for its engagement and one that might serve psychological functions quite different than other forms of volunteer work. But what about the motivations of AIDS volunteers themselves?

In systematic attempt to address the motivational foundations of AIDS volunteerism, we conducted an extensive questionnaire survey of 116 currently active AIDS volunteers at a community-based volunteer organization in Minneapolis, Minnesota. AIDS volunteers in this study filled out a confidential questionnaire about themselves, their backgrounds, and their experiences as volunteers. This survey included sections assessing their demographic characteristics, their involvement in past and current volunteer activity, and standard psychological measures of potentially relevant personality attributes (e.g., self-esteem, empathic tendencies, nurturance, death anxiety, need for social recognition, and concerns about social responsibility). The survey also contained items relevant to developing a structured self-report inventory for assessing motivations for AIDS volunteer work.

The simple question of who volunteers to do AIDS-related work actually has a very complex answer. The volunteers were a diverse groups, with considerable variability in their backgrounds and experiences as volunteers, and running the gamut on the measures of personality (see Omoto & Snyder, 1990). In terms of demographics, these volunteers ranged in age from 20 to 66 years, with a median age of 35. Sixty-four percent (64%) of them were males, 36% females; 60% defined themselves as exclusively or predominantly homosexual, 34% as exclusively or predominantly heterosexual, and the remaining 6% claimed to be bisexual. Rural (35%) and urban (32%) backgrounds were fairly equally represented in this group, as were income levels (ranging from less than $10,000 to over $100,000 annually). Collectively, and interestingly, these respondents were highly educated, with 91% having attended at least some college and 67% having earned a college degree. Finally, these volunteers had serviced anywhere from 2 to 42 months, and devoted approximately 4 hours per week on their volunteer tasks.

In spite of the diversity of their backgrounds, of course, all of these individuals shared something in common—they were all donating their time as AIDS volunteers. But did they share a common motivation for volunteering, and did volunteer work serve a common function for them? To assess their motivations, these volunteers rated how important each one of a set of different reasons was for their AIDS volunteer work. Included in this set were items designed to tap each of the motivations suggested by previous theorizing on psychological functions (i.e., the value expressive, knowledge, social, and defensive functions), as well as motivations thought to be particularly relevant to AIDS volunteer work (e.g., concern for the communities particularly affected by AIDS, knowing someone who has AIDS). In constructing a motivation inventory, factor analytic techniques were employed, and they revealed five distinguishable sets of motivations for AIDS volunteer work.

Of the five motivational functions obtained, some partially overlap with those specified by prior theory on psychological functions and some do not. The first set of motivations for doing AIDS volunteer work involved *community concern*, reflecting people's sense of obligation to or concern about a community or social grouping (e.g., "because of my concern and worry about the gay community," "to help

members of the gay community"). The second set of motivations invoked considerations related to personal *values* (e.g., "because of my humanitarian obligation to
help others," "because people should do something about issues that are important
to them"). The third set of motivations was characterized as relevant to concerns
about *understanding* (e.g., "to learn about how people cope with AIDS," "to deal
with my personal fears and anxiety about AIDS"). The fourth set of motivations was
labeled *personal development* and centered on issues of personal growth (e.g., "to
challenge myself and test my skills," "to gain experience dealing with emotionally
difficult topics"). Finally, the fifth category of motivations concerned *esteem enhancement* and included considerations about current voids or deficits in one's life
(e.g., "to feel better about myself," "to feel less lonely").

This inventory, as rough as it yet may be, has made possible a more thorough
analysis of the psychological functions of AIDS volunteerism, including directly addressing the question of why people volunteer. In spite of what appears to be a com-
monality of purpose in being a volunteer, the data show striking individual-to-
individual variability in which motivations are most and least important to volunteers. Some indication of the diversity of motivations behind AIDS volunteerism is
provided by the information presented in Figure 7.1, which displays the percentage

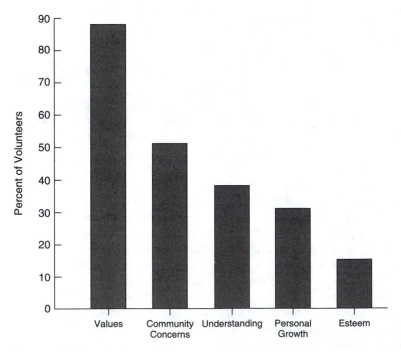

FIGURE 7.1

Percentage of Volunteers Choosing Each Type of Reason

of volunteers choosing each of the five categories of reasons for volunteering. This state of affairs is, of course anticipated by a functional approach, which emphasizes that different motivations for engaging in the same acts of volunteerism.

In attempting to understand these motivations, it is informative to view them against the backdrop of global personality dispositions. For instance, AIDS volunteer work, by its very nature, should provide excellent opportunities for expressing values central to nurturing, empathetic, and socially responsible personalities. In fact, AIDS volunteers who were motivated in their work by *value* concerns (as frequently represented as these motivations are among volunteers; see Figure 7.1) also scored relatively high on measures of nurturance, empathy, and social responsibility. To the extent that volunteers have nurturing dispositions, easily feel empathy for others, and think that people should take action on social issues, their work as volunteers may allow them to express these aspects of themselves.

As another example, AIDS volunteer work may provide opportunities for people to work on unresolved internal conflicts about their self-worth, their social regard, and their mortality. And, in point of fact, *esteem enhancement* motivations were associated with volunteer perceptions of having little social support and were also related to relatively low self-esteem, high need for social recognition, and high death anxiety. It appears that these people may be doing AIDS volunteer work to feel less lonely, to feel better about themselves, or to cope with their personal fears and anxieties about AIDS and death. Overall, these esteem enhancement motivations tended to be relatively less frequent among AIDS volunteers (as indicated, for example, in Figure 7.1), but it nevertheless seems possible to identify subsets of people for whom, by virtue of features of their personalities, such motivations seem to be particularly central in their volunteer activities.

Motivations for Continuing as an AIDS Volunteer

Just as motivations for volunteering may be traced backward to differences in personality, the preceding analysis also implies that they may foreshadow certain volunteer outcomes. Consider, for example, the specific types of work that volunteers choose to do and some of the differences between people who choose to work directly with PWAs (e.g., as a buddy or providing in-home care and assistance) and those who make decisions to work in other capacities (e.g., staffing the phone lines, doing general office work, or joining a speakers' bureau). We found that people who chose to work as buddies scored higher on motivations revolving around a concern for others, and incorporating feelings of compassion and empathy for PWAs and a desire to learn how to help PWAs, than did people who took on other volunteer assignments. Motivations for volunteering that are more selfish and that involve primarily esteem enhancement (wanting to feel better about oneself) and perhaps cravings for recognition and social reward, by contrast, were more characteristic of volunteers who did not have direct or extensive contact with PWAs than they were of those who worked as buddies.

Returning to our conceptual framework, it appears that the influence of psychological and motivational functions may extend well beyond the antecedents of volunteerism, and into the experiences and consequences stages of the volunteer process. In fact, the particular motivations that lead people to become volunteers may subsequently interact with their experiences so as to influence their ultimate effectiveness as volunteers, their satisfaction with their work, or even the length of time that they remain active. For that matter, people may develop very different reasons for staying involved in AIDS volunteer work than they had for getting started with it in the first place. The volunteer who enlisted for esteem enhancement or community concern reasons, for example, may derive little satisfaction from being assigned the solitary task of stuffing and licking envelopes, and may decide to quit the organization as soon as social conventions will allow. Similarly, volunteer work that is performed primarily for knowledge or understanding reasons may wear thin fairly quickly, for volunteers may become well-informed about AIDS relatively early—perhaps even as a result of training. Rather than continuing in the organization, then, these volunteers may turn their attention and energy to other challenges, causes and questions, or they may decide that remaining active in the organization is a good way to fulfill value motivations that have become salient.

To examine some of these possibilities, we recontacted the volunteers who had completed the extensive questionnaire approximately 1 year after the first survey, successfully reaching 78% o them. As part of this follow-up, volunteers were asked whether or not they were still active in the AIDS volunteer organization and about their satisfaction and complaints with their experiences. A year after the first contact, approximately one half of this group of AIDS volunteers was still active. There were no differential rates of attrition between men and women, nor between volunteers who had chosen to work as buddies and those who had donated their time and energy in other capacities. Hence, we moved on to examine the psychological and motivational characteristics of these people.

In focusing on the quitters, it was somewhat surprising that they reported their volunteer experiences to have been satisfying overall and that they were still personally committed to the purposes and philosophy of their AIDS organization. In fact, their levels of satisfaction and commitment were comparable to people who were persevering in their work. Quitters were apparently particularly affected, however, by the *costs* of volunteer work. That is, even though they had found their AIDS work satisfying and rewarding, they claimed that volunteering was taking up too much of their time and, importantly, that it caused them to feel embarrassed, stigmatized, or uncomfortable. Quitters claimed these costs to be much greater and more severe than continuing volunteers. The negative repercussions and *not* the benefits or rewards of their work, then, distinguished quitters from the volunteers who continued to serve.

Beyond these post hoc characterizations, however, a key question was whether we could have predicted who would continue and who would drop out from our first contact a year earlier. For example, were there certain people or personalities who were more likely to stay with the organization and others who were more likely to drop out?

In addressing these issues, the results showed that the initial measures were successful at predicting which volunteers would persevere and which ones would quit.

However, it was *not* the measures of global personality dispositions that proved to be strongly related to these decisions about continued involvement. Quitters, in general, scored no higher or lower than those who remained active in the organization on measures of empathy, nurturance, social responsibility, self-esteem, death anxiety, and need for social recognition.

Rather, people's initial reasons for volunteering, or the measures of psychological *functions,* successfully predicted volunteer attrition and longevity of service. To the extent that people espoused esteem enhancement or personal development reasons for their work (rather than community concern, values, or understanding motivations), they were more likely still to be active volunteers at the 1-year follow-up. Relatedly, in comparable analyses for predicting the total length of time that volunteers served, the esteem enhancement motivations and the reasons tapping understanding proved valuable. Volunteers who enlisted with the AIDS organization to fill voids in their own lives and to understand AIDS better remained active longer than volunteers who joined in attempts to fulfill other psychological motivations and functions.

Thus continuing volunteers could be distinguished from quitters not so much by their community concern and humanitarian values, as one might expect, but by their more "selfish" desires to feel good about themselves and to learn about AIDS. These selfish reasons, as noted previously, are also characteristic of volunteers active in non-AIDS causes (Omoto & Snyder, 1989b). Taken together, these findings suggest that volunteer organizations might profit from attending to the psychological benefits that volunteers themselves derive from their work as one key to promoting their continued service as volunteers. The good (and perhaps romantic) intentions related to humanitarian concern may not be strong enough to sustain volunteers who are faced with the tough realities of working with PWAs.

Summary

These studies of AIDS volunteerism have revealed no simple answers to the questions of who volunteers to help PWAs and why these individuals engage in their helpful acts. AIDS volunteers cannot easily and conveniently be characterized in terms of demographic characteristics or personality traits, nor are their reasons for volunteering marked by a single theme. AIDS volunteerism is perceived quite differently from other types of volunteer work and this perception is even held by people who are known to possess Samaritan tendencies. Consistent with a functional approach, the reasons that AIDS volunteers report for going through training and doing volunteer work indicate a diversity of underlying motivations. There is at least one common thread woven throughout these studies, however; namely that humanitarian and value-based concerns seem to figure prominently in people's initial decisions to pursue AIDS-related volunteer work. Importantly, though, a 1-year follow-up of actual volunteers revealed that these motivations are relatively unimportant in accounting for continuing volunteer service, at least as compared to more personal and selfish reasons. Although these results are only preliminary, they nevertheless seem to have clear and important implications for AIDS organizations attempting to recruit new volunteers most effectively and to structure their subsequent training and work experience.

References

Arno, P.S. (1988). The nonprofit sector's response to the AIDS epidemic: Community based services in San Francisco. *American Journal of Public Health, 76,* 1325–1330.

Batson, C.D. (1990). How social an animal? The human capacity for caring. *American Psychologist, 45,* 336–346.

Clary, E.G., & Snyder, M. (1991). A functional analysis of altruism and prosocial behavior: The case of volunteerism. In M.S. Clark (Ed.), *Review of personality and social psychology* (Vol 12, pp. 119–148). Newbury Park, CA: Sage

Dumont, J.A. (1989), Volunteer visitors for patients with AIDS, *Journal of Volunteer Administration, 8,* 3–8.

Fineberg, H.V. (1989). The social dimensions of AIDS. In J. Piel (Ed.), *The science of AIDS: Readings from* Scientific American (pp. 111–121). San Francisco: Freeman.

Herek, G.M., & Glunt, E.K. (1988). An epidemic of stigma: Public reaction to AIDS. *American Psychologist, 43,* 886–891.

HIV: Longer life before AIDS begins. (1990, March 18). *San Francisco Examiner,* p. A5.

Independent Sector. (1988). *Giving and volunteering in the United States: Findings from a national survey.* Washington, DC: Author.

Katz, D. (1960). The functional approach to the study of attitudes. *Public Opinion Quarterly, 24,* 163–204.

Latané, B., & Darley, J.M. (1970). *The unresponsive bystander: Why doesn't he help?* New York: Appleton Century Crofts.

Lewin, K. (1951). *Field theory in social science* (D. Cartright, Ed.). New York: Harper & Row.

Lopez, D., & Getzel, G.S. (1987). Strategies for volunteers caring for persons with AIDS. *Social Casework, 68,* 47–53.

Lui, K., Darrow, W., & Rutherford, G.W. (1988). A model-based estimate of the mean incubation period for AIDS in homosexual men. *Science, 240,* 1333–1335.

Mark, M.M., & Bryant, F.B. (1984). Potential pitfalls of a more applied social psychology: Review and recommendations. *Basic and Applied Social Psychology, 5,* 231–253.

Morgan, W.M., & Curran, J.W. (1986). Acquired immunodeficiency syndrome: Current and future trends. *Public Health Reports, 101,* 459–465.

Morin, S.F. (1988). AIDS: The challenge to psychology. *American Psychologist, 43,* 838–842.

Noble experiment: Volunteers' distress cripples huge effort to provide AIDS care. (1990, March 12), *Wall Street Journal,* p. A1.

Omoto, A.M., & Snyder, M. (1989a). [AIDS volunteers' narrative accounts of their experiences]. Unpublished raw data

Omoto, A.M., & Snyder, M. (1989a, May). *Volunteering to work with people with cancer or AIDS: Differences between me and you.* Paper presented at the meeting of the Midwestern Psychological Association, Chicago, IL.

Omoto, A.M., & Snyder, M. (1990). Basic research in action: Volunteerism and society's response to AIDS. *Personality and Social Psychology Bulletin, 16,* 152–165.

Smith, M.B., Bruner, J.S., & White, R.W. (1950). *Opinions and personality.* New York: John Wiley.

Snyder, M., & DeBono, D.G. (1987). A functional approach to attitudes and persuasion. In

M.P. Zanna, J.M. Olson, & C.P. Herman (Eds.), *Social influence: The Ontario symposium* (Vol. 5, pp. 107–125). Hillsdale, NJ: Lawrence Erlbaum.

Snyder, M., & DeBono, D.G. (1989). Understanding the functions of attitudes: Lessons from personality and social behavior. In A.R. Pratkanis, S.J. Breckler, & A. G. Greenwald (Eds.), *Attitude structure and function* (pp. 339–359). Hillsdale, NJ: Lawrence Erlbaum.

Volunteering drops as AIDS cases rise. (1990, June 20). *San Jose Mercury News,* p. 1A.

Wicker, A.W. (1989). Substantive theorizing. *American Journal of Community Psychology,* *17,* 531–547.

Williams, M.J. (1988). Gay men as "buddies" to persons living with AIDS and ARC. *Smith College Studies in Social Work, 59,* 38–52.

Wills, T.A. (1981). Downward comparison principles in social psychology. *Psychological Bulletin, 90,* 245–271.

8

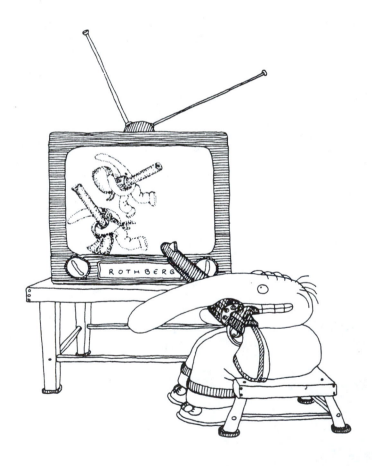

Aggression: The Nature and Sources of Harm

Violence seems to be a part of our lives. It is impossible to read the newspaper or watch television without running head on into it. Alongside the debate over whether a violent instinct exists among humans, psychologists and others have asked how we can control, reduce, or even eliminate aggressive behavior.

Edward Donnerstein is a Professor in the Department of Communication at the University of California at Santa Barbara. He is widely recognized as a leading expert in mass media violence, especially sexual violence. He has testified at numerous governmental hearings and has recently published *The Question of Pornography* (with Daniel Linz and Steven Penrod) and *Big World, Small Screen* (with several colleagues).

Our conversation covered a number of topics from America's violent nature to issues of the media. Prof. Donnerstein points out ways that social psychologists can become involved in reducing violence and offers an optimistic view that we can have a significant impact.

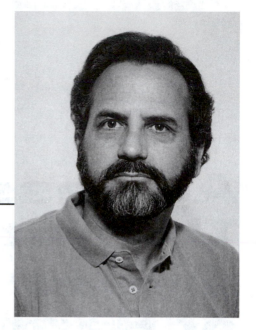

A CONVERSATION WITH
EDWARD DONNERSTEIN

University of California
at Santa Barbara

Krupat: *Human beings seem to be pretty aggressive creatures. Do we have aggressive instincts, do we learn it, or just how does aggression come about?*

Donnerstein: This is an issue where there are a lot of differing opinions. I serve on the American Psychological Association's Commission on Violence and Youth, and our report will be issued sometime in the near future. We take the position that there might be some hardwired, biological possibilities, but even if that is the case there are very strong cultural and societal factors influencing aggression. For instance, you could take the position that males are more aggressive than females, yet we can certainly find cultures where it's just the opposite. My feeling is that societal norms and pressures interact with many of these other biologically based factors. By taking the position that the environment plays a very strong role, I think there's a more optimistic outlook. Obviously, if aggression is learned, it can be unlearned.

Krupat: *When I first asked the question, I was asking about people in general. How about the United States in particular. Why is this such a violent society?*

Donnerstein: People have argued that, if you look at the history of this country and how we were founded, there is a sense that violence is acceptable. It's interesting, in my own area of research on the mass media, that in the U.S. violence is highly acceptable yet sexual material is not—whereas it is just the opposite in most other places on the globe. When I go to international film conferences, people from other societies ask what is it about America that makes us produce these sorts of things. I am against censorship, but when our movies go to other countries they do cut a lot of the violence out. They are really appalled by it, and they have this fear of coming here, which might be justified unfortunately. Of course I can point to places in Europe and the Middle East that are just as violent in some ways. But on a day-to-day basis, we have a culture that is very accepting.

Krupat: *Are there other factors?*

Donnerstein: Certainly the availability of firearms plays a strong role. Where the United States is more violent than other places is in terms of homicides and aggravated assaults, and I think the availability of guns increases this substantially. There are also issues of poverty, discrimination, and racism which very much reinforce societal norms that violence is acceptable in this particular culture. But we are not unique. You don't have to look very far to see some of these things played out all over the world.

Krupat: *Let's go back then and start with young children. To the extent we believe that violence is learned, how exactly is it communicated? How does a one-year-old get enrolled in Violence 101?*

Donnerstein: Obviously, it can be communicated by parents. There is a whole body of literature suggesting that children who are abused have a very good chance to become abusers themselves. A recent report from the National Academy of Sciences argues that the best predictor of adult aggressive behavior is being a victim as a child. Another factor is witnessing violence in the family, which seems to be a very good predictor, as well as witnessing violence within the community. There is a lot of research going on in the inner city in terms of how the daily viewing and experience of violence can have an effect on a general callousness toward violence.

Krupat: *If violence is to be learned, does it have to happen early?*

Donnerstein: The general feeling now is that socialization, working with hardwired tendencies, is really going to take its effect in childhood. Beyond that, the chances of becoming a violent individual are fairly remote because the processes that have been developing from early on are now fairly stable. Again, the best predictor of adult aggressive behavior seems to be childhood aggressive behavior.

Krupat: *To move into the area of media as an influence, many students say to me, "I watched Saturday morning cartoons, I've seen violent movies, and I'm not violent."*

Donnerstein: For whatever reasons, certain kids are predisposed to some form of aggression. Those children search out this kind of material or find the material reinforcing their value system. These are kids who tend to be having trouble in school or are already having run-ins. So it's a perpetual cycle. For most of us it just isn't having that effect. We can watch a lot of violence and have no problem. Psychologists are still trying to answer questions such as which children are most susceptible and what the underlying processes are.

Krupat: *Well, what are some of the mechanisms that account for the apparent link between violent media and violence in real life?*

Donnerstein: There are a number of potential processes. One argument is that violence in the media teaches children certain scripts about how one deals with conflict in interpersonal relations. So that process is initially taking place. You could also talk about desensitization, which makes you less aroused to violence so it becomes a little easier to perpetuate violence. Another process would be simple learning or imitation where certain individuals who are predisposed come to model or imitate aggressive acts. So if we look at all of the research together, there's a general feeling that there's a sort of a desensitization that creates a callousness, there is a reinforcing of values and behaviors which children are learning, and there's some sort of direct imitation. Although direct imitation is really for those individuals who are very much predisposed to aggressive behavior to start with.

Krupat: *You mentioned desensitization briefly. That seems like a very important mechanism. Could you elaborate on that some more?*

Donnerstein: What we tend to find is initially when people view violent or sexually violent material, not pornographic but just R rated material, desensitization occurs. You become less bothered by what you see, less aroused, less concerned, less upset—a classic type of habituation. There's also a change in your perceptions of violence. You tend to see less violence in the material with the passage of time. An important finding is that exposure to this type of material can actually change your perceptions of real victims of violence. For instance, in some of our research we have people act as jurors in a mock rape trial, and a couple of days later they see an actual victim of rape. We actually find in some of these studies less empathy or sympathy towards the rape victim. They see less pain and suffering on the part of the victim. It is not that these people are going to go out and commit violent acts, but they just aren't bothered by what they're seeing. We are really concerned about children who are growing up with a steady diet of witnessing violence in the media, or in the home, or in the neighborhood. It makes it that much easier to be violent because you're not as aroused or as sympathetic, and you cannot easily empathize with your victim. I think all of these can really make for a very lethal type of combination.

Krupat: *I can hear a Hollywood producer responding by saying, "But you are blaming everything wrong with society on my movies."*

Donnerstein: No, not all. Our position would be: Look, violence is a part of society. It is not that violence shouldn't be presented at all; it's how and the context in which it is presented. There is a big difference between the movies *Platoon* and *Rambo* in terms of how war and the Vietnam War is presented. Nobody sees *Platoon* and says, "Let's go back there." *Rambo* is just the opposite. You can present violence without glamorizing it, without glorifying it, without making it gratuitous and excessive. Nobody is suggesting regulation or censorship. Not at all. I just wish they would stop and think, "What are the messages you are sending about violence?" And some of these can be very, very subtle messages.

Krupat: *And I assume these messages can especially have an effect on young children.*

Donnerstein: And on those who are predisposed. Think for the moment about violent films such as *Batman.* It was R rated, but it was obviously directed at an incredibly young audience. MacDonald's was giving away cups, and every promo was made for young kids. In terms of how the violence was portrayed, it was exactly the kind that creates problems. It was excessive and gratuitous, it was performed by heroes as part of a fantasy, there were no consequences, and it was used to solve conflict. It had everything that is wrong about violence mixed up in it.

Krupat: *Is there something good to be said for media violence? For instance, what's become of the idea of catharsis, the notion that viewing violence can drain off your own aggressions?*

Donnerstein: That hopefully has died, although it is still brought up by the movie industry. There are many myths about violence, and one of those is that catharsis is an effective process. That's fine, except there is no empirical evidence for it at all. There are other myths, for example, that violence has always been in literature and entertainment throughout history. People will cite Shakespeare and things of that nature, but they forget that the violence was always onstage, whereas today it is obviously right in front of you and quite graphic and high tech, which produces a much different effect.

Krupat: *It sounds to me like what we have here is a vicious cycle. How do you turn it around? How can we go about reducing violence?*

Donnerstein: My feeling is that we need very early intervention. There should be media literacy, violence courses, conflict resolution courses, intervention programs at a very early age. Very young children have to learn that there are alternatives to deal with conflict other than violence. That's only one step, dealing with the individual. Other issues have to be dealt with—political issues, economic issues, educational issues all have to be part of the solution if people really want to accomplish something. There's the drug problem and large disparities in terms of equal opportunity among individuals, and all sorts of social problems. Teaching conflict resolution is great, but it's not going to do much when those kids go back to their neighborhood where there are drive-by shootings. I think we've got to deal with the issues on many levels.

Krupat: *As a social psychologist, how do you feel about entering a world that likely goes well beyond your early training?*

Donnerstein: I see myself much more as an applied social psychologist than ever before. I have an interest not only in laboratory findings, but in the policy implications of our findings and the use and misuse of social science data. I have a much stronger feel now for the need for social psychologists to have input into the policy arena, the legal arena, and into the industry to make their findings known for society as a whole. We should be asking ourselves how can we take what we know to turn it around, to mitigate the effects of violent media? This means that we have an obligation to work effectively on a real multidisciplinary level, not only with our colleagues in many fields, but also with the industry that produces the material we are interested in.

Krupat: *Would you consider yourself at all optimistic about the future in this area?*

Donnerstein: Oh yes, I always am. When I give talks on violence prevention and media literacy, people sometimes say "You're a bit naive to think educational interventions will work." That is fine, but I believe there is a lot of excitement out there for social psychologists. And I am optimistic that we can do something about it if we realize that we're going to have to act on a very applied level with many types of groups— environmental groups, industry groups, and academicians in an interdisciplinary, multifaceted way. That is new and that is exciting, and it does make me optimistic in terms of being able to deal with the question of violence.

The Man Who Counts the Killings

In this article from the *Atlantic Monthly* Scott Stossel tells us about the pioneering work of George Gerbner concerning violence on television. Citing research conducted by Gerbner's Cultural Indicators project, Stossel notes that the average American child will have watched over 8,000 murders and 100,000 assorted violent acts on television before ever making it to kindergarten. Stossel details the problems that violent television can bring, the manner in which it desensitizes children to pain and suffering and makes them think that violence is acceptable and normal. Yet Stossel also presents some of the rebuttal of those who would defend television. In reading this article, you are invited to reflect on your own experiences, the attitudes of your parents toward your television viewing, and the often-violent nature of today's society. How strong do you believe the links are? What can or should be done about violence in television and media in general?

After the Second World War, in the course of which he has seen enough violence, suffering, and pain to harden even the softest sensibility, and during which he has personally identified and arrested the fascist Hungarian Prime Minister, who is subsequently executed, a brooding Hungarian poet travels with his wife to America. He earns a Ph.D. from the University of Southern California, in the process writing the first-ever master's thesis on the subject of education and television, and begins a long career in academia studying the effects of television on its viewers. In 1964 he becomes the dean of the newly founded Annenberg School of Communication, at the University of Pennsylvania, where he builds a curriculum and a faculty from scratch. In 1989, after twenty-five years as dean, George Gerbner retires.

Television, Gerbner believes, is modern-day religion. It presents a coherent vision of the world. And this vision of the world, he says, is violent, mean, repressive, dangerous—and inaccurate. Television programming is the toxic by-product of market forces run amok. Television has the capacity to be a culturally enriching force, but, Gerbner warns, today it breeds what fear and resentment mixed with economic frustration can lead to—the undermining of democracy.

Is Gerbner tilting at windmills? Is he just a mediaphobe with a quixotic message? Or is he a lonely voice of insight, telling us things that are hard to comprehend but that we need to hear if we are to remain free from repression? Right or wrong, is his crusade at bottom a futile one? Do we need to change television programming, and if so, how can we do it? After all, network executives say, viewers are simply getting what they want.

VIOLENCE AND TELEVISION: A HISTORY

In 1977 Ronny Zamora, a fifteen-year-old, shot and killed the eighty-two-year-old woman who lived next door to him in Florida. Not guilty, pleaded his lawyer, Ellis Rubin, by reason of the boy's having watched too much television. Suffering from what Rubin called "television intoxication," he could no longer tell right from wrong. "If you judge Ronny Zamora guilty," Rubin argued, "television will be an accessory." The jury demurred: Ronny was convicted of first-degree murder.

Although few anti-television activists would agree that excessive television viewing can exculpate a murderer, a huge body of evidence—including 3,000 studies before 1971 alone—suggests a strong connection between television watching and aggression. "There is no longer any serious debate about whether violence in the media is a legitimate problem," Reed Hundt, the chairman of the Federal Communications Commission, said in a speech last year. "Science and commonsense judgments of parents agree. As stated in a year-long effort, funded by the cable-TV industry . . . 'there are substantial risks of harmful effects from viewing violence throughout the television environment.'"

The study cited by Hundt reveals nothing new. Researchers have been churning out studies indicating links between television violence and real-life violence for as long as television has been a prominent feature of American culture. Just a few examples demonstrate the range of the investigations.

A 1956 study compared the behavior of twelve four-year-olds who watched a Woody Woodpecker cartoon containing many violent episodes with that of twelve other four-year-olds who watched "The Little Red Hen," a nonviolent cartoon. The Woody watchers were much more likely than the Hen watchers to hit other children, break toys, and be generally destructive during playtime.

In 1960 Leonard Eron, a professor of psychology at the University of Michigan's Institute for Social Research, studied third-graders in Columbia County in semi-rural New York. He observed that the more violent television these eight-year-olds watched at home, the more aggressive they were in school. Eron returned to Columbia County in 1971, when the children from his sample were nineteen. He found that the boys who had watched a lot of violent television when they were eight were more likely to get in trouble with the law when older. Eron returned to Columbia County a third time in 1982, when his subjects were thirty. He discovered that those who had watched the most television violence at age eight inflicted more violent punishments on their children, were convicted of more serous crimes, and were reported more aggressive by their spouses than those who had watched less violent television. In 1993, at a conference of the National Council for Families & Television, Eron estimated that 10 percent of the violence in the United States can be attributed to television.

Although Eron's study did not make a special effort to control for other potentially violent-inducing variables, other longitudinal studies have done so. For example, in 1971 Monroe Lefkowitz published "Television Violence and Child Aggression: A Follow-up Study," which confirmed that the more violence an eight-year-old boy watched, the more aggressive his behavior would be at age eighteen. Lefkowitz controlled for other possible variables directly implicating media violence as an instigator of violent behavior.

Shouldn't the weight of thousands of such studies be sufficient to persuade broadcasters, required by law since the 1930s to serve the public interest, to change the content of television programming? Especially when polls—such as one conducted by *U.S. News & World Report* last year—indicate that 90 percent of Americans think that violent television shows hurt the country? We don't want to become a nation of Ronny Zamoras, do we?

Periods of increasing popular agitation about the effects of television on children (usually inspired by a rising crime rate or by a sensational story like Ronny Zamora's) lead to spasms of political posturing. Studies are commissioned. Imminent legislative or regulatory action is threatened. The broadcast industry filibusters. Within a few months the politicians turn their attention to something new, and the broadcasting industry slips quietly away, barely chastened.

"A TELEGENIC LITTLE GIZMO"

The latest burst of activity around the issue of television violence, culminating in the legislating of the V-chip, can be traced to a night in the mid-1980s when a weary Senator Paul Simon, of Illinois, lying in his motel bed, flipped on the television and saw, in graphic detail, a man being sliced in half with a chain saw—a victim, Simon's staff later surmised, of Colombian drug dealers in *Scarface*. Appalled that there was nothing to prevent a child from witnessing such grisliness, Simon urged the passage of a law reducing gore on television.

The result, the 1990 Television Violence Act, was a compromise between the broadcasting industry and those who, like Simon, wanted somehow to reduce the violence on shows that children might be watching. Ordinarily, antitrust laws prohibit broadcast networks from collaborating, but Simon's proposal gave the networks a three-year exemption from the laws so that they could jointly work out a policy to curb violence. Though Simon hailed the announcement of the networks (except Fox), in December of 1992, a set of guidelines governing television violence, this basically toothless bit of legislation had little effect until it was about to expire, at which point network executives promised that they would place parental advisories at the beginning of violent programs ("Due to violent content, parental discretion is advised"). When the act expired, in December of 1993, television was as violent as ever.

Meanwhile in Canada, the invention of a Vancouver engineer had come to the attention of Keith Spicer, then the chairman of the Canadian Radio–Television and Telecommunications Commission (Canada's FCC equivalent). This invention—in Spicer's words, a "sexy telegenic little gizmo that fulfills the fantasy of a magic wand" and could solve the problem of television violence without censorship—was the V-chip, the basic rationale for which is by now generally known. Using the chip, which receives encoded information about each show as part of the broadcast transmission, parents can program their television to block out shows that have been coded as violent or sexually explicit. Spicer championed the V-chip and ultimately got a law passed mandating its use in all new television sets sold in Canada.

2,605 VIOLENT ACTS A DAY

In 1968 President Johnson's National Commission on the Causes and Prevention of Violence appointed Gerbner, who had already been studying violence in the media at the Annenberg School, to analyze the content of television shows. Thus began the Cultural Indicators project, the longest-running continuous media-research undertaking in the world. Gerbner and his team presented findings about both the quantity of violence on prime-time television—that is, how many violent acts are committed each night—and the quality. In analyzing these acts Gerbner's team asked questions like: Was it serious or funny? Was it the only method of conflict resolution offered? Were realistic repercussions of violence shown? Who committed most of it? Who suffered the most because of it? The quantity of violence on television was stunning; no less significant to Gerbner, though, were the ways in which this violence was portrayed. But in the first instance of what has since become a frustrating pattern for him, the mainstream media seized on the quantity and ignored his findings about the quality of television violence.

The media continue to be fixated on the amount of violence the Cultural Indicators project finds, because the numbers are staggering. Today someone settling down to watch television is likely to witness a veritable carnival of violent behavior. On average there are more than five violent scenes in an hour of prime time, and five murders a night. There are twenty-five violent acts an hour in Saturday-morning cartoons—the programs most watched by children, usually without any supervision. And that's only network television. A survey by the Center for Media and Public Affairs that looked at all programming—including cable—in Washington, D.C., on April 7, 1994, tallied 2,605 acts of violence that day, the majority occurring in the early morning, when kids were most likely to be watching. By the reckoning of the Cultural Indicators project, the average American child will have witnessed more than 8,000 murders and 100,000 other violent acts on television by the time he or she leaves elementary school. Another study, published in the Journal of the American Medical Association in 1992, found that the typical American child spends twenty-seven hours a week watching television and will witness 40,000 murders and 200,000 other violent acts by the age of eighteen. Ellis Rubin's defense of Ronny Zamora begins to sound plausible.

Of course, there is blood in fairy tales, gore in mythology, murder in Shakespeare, lurid crimes in tabloids, and battles and wars in textbooks. Such representations of violence are legitimate cultural expressions. But the historically defined, individually crafted, and selectively used symbolic violence of heroism, cruelty, or authentic tragedy has been replaced by the violence with happy endings produced on the dramatic assembly line.

The Cultural Indicators project has since 1968 amassed a database of reports on the recurring features of television programming. One of the basic premises of Gerbner's cultivation analysis is that television violence is not simple acts but rather "a complex social scenario of power and victimization." What matters is not so much the raw fact that a violent act is committed but who does what to whom. Gerbner is as insistent about this as he is about anything, repeating it in all his writings and speeches. "What is the message of violence?" he asks me rhetorically over tea in his office at the University of Pennsylvania, a cozy, windowless rectangle filled with books, pictures, and objects d'art. "Who can get away with what against whom?" He leans forward intently, as though confiding something, although he has already said this to me several other times, during several other conversations. His eagerness to make me understand is palpable. "The media keep focusing on the amount of violence. But concentrating on that reinforces the message of violence. It concentrates on the law-and-order aspect of violence. Harping on this all the time makes people more fearful—which is the purpose of violence to begin with."

"THE MEAN WORLD SYNDROME"

So what, exactly, has nearly thirty years of cultivation analysis shown? Among other things, the following:

- For every white male victim of violence there are seventeen white female victims.
- For every white male victim there are twenty-two minority female victims.
- For every ten female aggressors there are sixteen female victims.
- Minority women are twice as likely to be victims as they are to be aggressors.
- Villains are disproportionately male, lower-class, young, and Latino or foreign.

What is the significance of all this? First, the sheer quantity of violence on television encourages the idea that aggressive behavior is normal. Viewers become desensitized. The mind, as Gerbner puts it, becomes "militarized." This leads to what Gerbner calls "the Mean World Syndrome." Because television depicts the world as worse than it is (at least for white suburbanites), we become fearful and anxious—and more willing to depend on authorities, strong measures, grated communities, and other proto-police-state accoutrements. Discounting the dramatic increase in violent crime in the real world, Gerbner believes, for example, that the Mean World Syndrome is an important reason that the majority of Americans now support capital punishment, whereas they did not thirty years ago. "Growing up in a violence-laden culture breeds aggressiveness in some and desensitization, insecurity, mistrust, and anger in most," he writes. "Punitive and vindictive action against dark forces in a mean world is made to look appealing, especially when presented as quick, decisive, and enhancing our sense of control and security."

The more violence one sees on television, the more one feels threatened by violence. Studies have shown direct correlations between the quantity of television watched and general fearfulness about the world: heavy viewers believe the world to be much more dangerous than do light viewers. Thus heavy viewers tend to favor more law-and-order measures: capital punishment, three-strikes prison sentencing, the building of new prisons, and so forth. And the fact that most of the heavy viewers are in low-income, low-education families means that the most disenfranchised in our society—and, it should be said, the people more exposed to real violence—are making themselves even more so by placing their fate in the hands of an increasingly martial state. Politicians exploit this violence-cultivated sensibility by couching their favored policies in militaristic terms: the War on Crime, for example, or the War on Drugs. "We are headed in the direction of an upsurge in neofascism in a very entertaining and very amusing disguise," Gerbner told a lecture audience in Toronto two years ago.

The first time I talked to Gerbner after reading his writings, I asked him if this wasn't all a bit Big Brotherish. "TV images are complex," he told me. "The disempowering effects of television lead to neofascism. That kind of thing is waiting in the wings. Nazi Germany came on the heels of a basic sense of insecurity and powerlessness like we have here now. I don't want to oversimplify, but that is the direction we might be heading."

Violence, Gerbner says, is all about power. The violence on television serves as a lesson of power that puts people in their place. Members of minority groups grow up feeling that they're more vulnerable than others. Television cultivates this view. But, I counter, minorities are more vulnerable. They are victims more often than middle-class white Americans are. Improving the depiction of minorities on television will not change this social fact. Gerbner strives to clarify: "Television doesn't 'cause' anything. We're wary of saying television 'causes' this or that. Instead we say television 'contributes' to this or that. The extent of contribution varies. But it's there."

Elsewhere Gerbner is less circumspect. "The violence we see on the screen and read about in our press bears little relationship either in volume or in type, especially in its consequences, to violence in real life," he has written. "This sleight of hand robs us of the tragic sense of life necessary for compassion." No doubt a victim of the Mean World Syndrome myself, I was surprised to learn that Gerbner is absolutely right, at least about the volume of violence. Scary and crime-ridden though the world is these days (violent crime has more than doubled over the past thirty years; an American is six times as likely to be the victim of assault with a weapon as he or she would have been in 1960), prime-time television presents a world in which crime rates are a hundred times worse.

THE NEW RELIGION

"Whoever tells most of the stories to most of the people most of the time has effectively assumed the cultural role of parent and school," Gerbner says, ". . . teaching us most of what we know in common about life and society." In fact, by the time children reach school age, they will have spent more hours in front of the television than they will ever spend in college classrooms. Television, in short, has become a cultural force equaled in history only by organized religion. Only religion has had this power to transmit the same messages about reality to every social group, creating a common culture.

Most people do not have to wait for, plan for, go out to, or seek out television, for the TV is on more than seven hours a day in the average American home. It comes to you directly. It has become a member of the family, telling its stories patiently, compellingly, untiringly. We choose to read *The New York Times,* or Dickens, or an entomology text. We choose to listen to Bach or Bartok, or at least to a classical station or a rock station or a jazz station. But we just watch TV—turn it on, see what's on. And in Gerbner's view it is an upper-middle-class conceit to say "Just turn off the television"—in most homes there is nothing as compelling as television at any time of the day or night.

It is significant that this viewing is nonselective. It's why Gerbner believes that the Cultural Indicators project methodology—looking at television's overall patterns rather than at the effects of specific shows—is the best approach. It is long-range exposure to television, rather than a specific violent act or a specific episode of a specific show, that cultivates fixed conceptions about life in viewers.

Nor is the so-called hard news, even when held distinct from infotainment shows like Hard Copy and A Current Affair, exempt from the disproportionate violence and misrepresentations on television in general. The old news saw, "If it bleeds, it leads" usually prevails. Watch your local newscast tonight: it is not unlikely that the majority of news stories will be about crime or disaster—and it may well be that all six stories will be from outside your state, especially if you live far from any major metropolis. Fires and shootings are much cheaper and easier to cover than politics or community events. Violent news also generates higher ratings, and since the standards for television news are set by market researchers, what we get is lots of conformity, lots of violence. As the actor and director Edward James Olmos has pointedly observed, "For every half hour of TV news, you have twenty-three minutes of programming and seven minutes of commercials. And in that twenty-three minutes, if it weren't for the weather and the sports, you would not have any positive news. As for putting in even six minutes of hope, of pride, of dignity—it doesn't sell." The author and radio personality Garrison Keillor puts it even more pointedly: "It's a bloody as Shakespeare but without the intelligence and the poetry. If you watch television news you know less about the world than if you drank gin out of a bottle."

The strength of television's influence on our understanding of the world should not be underestimated. "Television's Impact on Ethnic and Racial Images," a study sponsored by the American Jewish Committee's Institute for American Pluralism and other groups, found that ethnic and racial images on television powerfully shape the way adolescents perceive ethnicity and race in the real world. "In dealing with socially relevant topics like racial and ethnic relations," the study said, "TV not only entertains, it conveys values and messages that people may absorb unwittingly—particularly young people." Among viewers watching more than four hours each

Aggression: The Nature and Sources of Harm | **289**

day, 25 percent said that television showed "what life is really like" and 40 percent said they learned about the world.

IS I DREAM OF JEANNIE VIOLENT?

Gerbner's methodology draws fire mostly for its supposed insufficient emphasis on context. For years he has been ridiculed for a single example he cited as part of a routine Cultural Indicators project profile: network executives have never ceased to bring up the *I Dream of Jeannie* episode from 1968 that Gerbner deemed excessively violent. ("It had a really violent dream sequence," Gerbner says.) Frustrated by incidents like this one (more recently the project classified the Laugh-in twenty-fifth-anniversary special as very violent owing to pratfalls and slapstick), Gerbner will no longer willingly discuss the content of individual shows, insisting that it is the overall pattern that matters most.

In 1983 ABC published a critique, "A Research Perspective on Television and Violence," that took particular issue with Gerbner's findings. Gerbner's inclusion of accidents, slapstick comedy, acts of nature, and cartoons within his definition of violence, the study said, "results in tallies that distort the amount of realistic violence." Though ABC's critique was dismissed by academic researchers as self-serving, an ABC vice-president, Christine Hikawa, reflected the sentiment prevailing among broadcasters at the National Council for Families & Television Conference in 1993 when she said, "When researchers equate Tom and Jerry with I Spit on Your Grave, their credibility goes right out the window."

Most people, I think, would agree with Hikawa. A cartoon is surely more appropriate for and less damaging to young viewers than a verisimilitudinous movie like *Silence of the Lambs*. Road Runner's depredations against Wile E. Coyote lack the visceral effect of the gorier violence committed by, say, the serial killer in the 1995 movie *Seven*, in which the rabidity is clearly meant to be disturbing.

But a cartoon's lack of brute visceral impact, Gerbner says, is precisely what makes it so insidious. "Violence in our studies is overt, physical demonstration of power that hurts or kills. Whether it is done in a so-called serious way or a so-called humorous way has no functional significance." He continues, "Humor is a sugar coating that makes the pill of violence go down much more easily—so it gets integrated into one's framework of knowledge." "Pratfalls are dangerous," Gerbner told me when I asked how his studies could implicate my beloved Three Stooges. "To make pain seem painless is sugarcoating power, sugarcoating the message of power. People don't understand that humor can be very violent and very cruel."

"SWIFT, PAINLESS, EFFECTIVE"

When George Plimpton recently asked why, if television causes violence in the streets, television comedy doesn't cause comedy in the streets, he was making a commonsense observation: we don't directly replicate in our lives most of what we see on TV. But Gerbner doesn't say that we do. The reason that even apparently innocuous comedy can be so dangerous, he says, is that it reinforces viewers' perceptions of how the world works. No, comedy doesn't cause comedy in the streets. But TV violence indirectly contributes to our understanding that there is violence in the streets, typically wrought by a stronger entity against a weaker one. "Humorous stories are easier to digest," Gerbner says, "easier to absorb. But basically they are all messages of power. Messages of who can get away with what against whom."

Gerbner has coined a term that describes most of the screen violence we see. "We are dealing with the formula-driven mass production of violence for entertainment—what I call 'happy violence.' It is swift, painless, effective . . . and always leads to a happy ending." Happy violence appears both in cartoons and in action movies like *True Lies* and *Die Hard,* wherein all problems can be solved by violence and violence has no serious consequences. Movies, it should be noted, are an important part of the constant violent fare on television and in the culture in general. They must become more and more graphic if they are to penetrate our violence-hardened sensibilities. Gerbner points out that body counts always rise in action sequels: the first *Die Hard* movie had eighteen deaths, and the second had 264; the first *Robocop* movie had thirty-two deaths, and the second had eighty-one; and the three *Godfather* movies piled up twelve, eighteen, and fifty-three corpses respectively. "Escalating the body count," he has written, "seems to be one way to get attention from a public punch-drunk on global mayhem." What, Gerbner asks, does this cultivate in our kids, in society? "We live in a world that is erected by the stories we tell . . . and most of the stories are from television. These stories say this is how life works. These are the people who win; these are the people who lose; these are the kinds of people who are villains. It's a highly stereotypic world day after day. It doesn't matter whether it's serious or humorous. The main difference is that cartoons can go further. There is no more serious business for a culture or a society than the stories you tell your children."

Television, in Gerbner's view, is by no means inherently bad. It does much that is good. For many people who would otherwise be just plain bored, television represents an enrichment of cultural horizons. It has gone a long way toward diminishing isolation and parochialism and has given us cultural capital to hold in common. No modern state can govern without television; it is the social cement that religion once was, holding disparate groups and subgroups together. But, Gerbner firmly believes, so potent is television's power to inform and control, so strong is its power to teach us who gets away with what against whom, that a democratic people that cedes controls of television to a nonelected few will not remain a democratic people for long. The more one contemplates the pervasiveness of stereotypical patterns in television, the more one perceives the inaccurate picture of reality it cultivates in viewers—and the more one inclines toward a charitable understanding of Gerbner's fears about fascism.

Richard E. Nisbett

Violence and U.S. Regional Culture

In this article, Richard Nisbett takes an interesting and unusual approach to the study of violence by comparing regional records of homicides and violent crimes in the Southern and Northern regions of the United States. Nisbett reports that Southerners are no more in favor of violence in general, but are more likely to endorse violence for protection and as a response to insults. Consistent with this, rates of homicide are particularly higher in the South when they are argument-related. Nisbett suggests that these differences derive from a "culture of honor" that resulted from the herding society of the early South, but also notes that the values consistent with this kind of violent behavior seem to have sustained themselves rather than disappeared.

Throughout the history of the United States, Southerners have been regarded—by Northerners, by travelers from Europe, and by themselves—as being more violent than Northerners. The *Encyclopedia of Southern Culture* devotes 39 pages to the topic of violence, beginning with the sentence "Violence has been associated with the South since the time of the American Revolution" (Gastil, 1989, p. 1473). The subsequent pages are replete with accounts of feuds, duels, lynchings, and bushwhackings—events that are held to have been relatively commonplace in the South and relatively rare in the North. Less lethal forms of violence are also reputed to have characterized the South. Autobiographies of Southerners, more than of Northerners, report severe beatings by parents (Fischer, 1989, p. 689). Pastimes that seem inconceivable on a New England village green or a Middle Atlantic town square were commonplace in the old South. For example, there was a sport called "purring," in which two opponents grasped each other firmly by the shoulders and began kicking each other in the shins at the starting signal. The loser was the man who released his grip first (McWhiney, 1988, p. 154).

Assuming the accuracy of the historical evidence, why should there be such strong regional differences in preference for violence? Historians, anthropologists, and other social scientists have offered five different explanations.

One explanation calls on the temperature difference between North and South.

There is a reliable relationship between temperature and violence; homicides (Anderson, 1989) and other violent acts, such as injuries from mis-thrown baseball pitches (Reifman, Larrick, & Fein, 1991), are more common in hot weather than in cooler weather.

A second explanation is poverty. The South is poorer than the rest of the country, and poverty is associated with crimes of all kinds, including crimes of violence. Hence, greater Southern rates of violence might be attributable to greater poverty (Blau & Blau, 1982).

A third explanation, and one of the oldest, attributes Southern violence to the institution of slavery. Tocqueville (1835/1969) traveled down the Ohio River and contrasted the industrious farmers on the Ohio side with the boisterous layabouts he found on the Kentucky side. He noted that the institution of slavery made it both unnecessary and demeaning for the Whites to work and that the resulting idleness allowed them to turn to exciting, dangerous pastimes.

A fourth explanation is that the violence of the Whites was the result of imitating the violence of African Americans (Cash, 1941). The violence of that group might be due to an originally violent culture or a reaction to ill treatment at the hands of Whites, but whatever its cause, Whites may have been unconsciously mimicking it (see Hackney, 1969).

HERDING ECONOMIES AND THE CULTURE OF HONOR

A fifth explanation, and the one that I argue for, is that the South is heir to a culture, deriving ultimately from economic determinants, in which violence is a natural and integral part. New England and the Middle Atlantic states were settled by sober Puritans, Quakers, and Dutch farmer–artisans. In their advanced agricultural economy, the most effective stance was one of quiet, cooperative citizenship with each individual being capable of uniting for the common good. In contrast, the South was settled initially by swashbuckling cavaliers of noble and landed gentry status, who took their values not from the tilling of the soil and the requirements of civic responsibility but from the knightly, medieval standards of manly honor and virtue. The major subsequent wave of immigration, and a much larger and ultimately more influential one, was from the borderlands of Scotland and Ireland (Fischer, 1989; McWhitney, 1988). These Celtic peoples had long had an economy based on herding, primarily pig herding. At the time of the Puritan migrations, they were "isolated from and hostile to their English neighbors, and they remained tribal, pastoral and warlike" (McWhiney, 1988, p. xxiv). Upon arrival in America, during the 17th and 18th centuries, they moved inland from the northeast coast (usually from the entry port of Philadelphia) to the southern and western frontiers, especially to the hill country regions. There they continued and even intensified the hunting and herding practices at the base of their economy.

Herding, even when carried out in less isolated circumstances than the American frontier, predisposes people to a violent stance toward their fellows (Lowie, 1954; Peristiany, 1965). This is so because pastoralists are extraordinarily vulnerable economically. Their livelihoods can be lost in an instant by the theft of their herds. To reduce the likelihood of this occurring, pastoralists cultivate a posture of extreme vigilance toward any act that might be perceived as threatening in any way, and respond with sufficient force to frighten the offender and the community into recognizing that they are not to be trifled with. In writing of the Mediterranean herding culture, similar in many ways to traditional Celtic cultures of Europe and the American South, Campbell (1965) described the task confronting young shepherds:

> The critical moment in the development of the young shepherd's reputation is his first quarrel. Quarrels are necessarily public. They may occur in the coffee shop, the village square, or most frequently on a grazing boundary where a curse or a stone aimed at one of his straying sheep by another shepherd is an insult which inevitably requires a violent response. . . . It is the critical nature of these first important tests of his manliness that makes the self-regard (*egoismos*) of the young shepherd so extremely sensitive. It is not only the reality of an obvious insult which provokes him to action, but even the finest of allusions on which it is possible to place some unflattering construction. (p. 148)

Young White Southern men were taught to create a similar impression of themselves as being ferocious in defense of their reputations.

> From an early age, small boys were taught to think much of their own honor, and to be active in its defense. Honor in this society meant a pride of manhood in masculine courage, physical strength and warrior virtue. Male children were trained to defend their honor without a moment's hesitation—lashing out against their challenges with savage violence. . . . These backcountry child ways were . . . transplanted from the borders of North Britain, where they were yet another cultural adaptation to the endemic violence of that region. . . . This system of child rearing flourished in its new American environment. (Fischer, 1989, p. 690)

The socialization of Andrew Jackson, the first U.S. president raised in a herding region (the hills of Tennessee), was very much in this culture-of-honor tradition. In advice to the young Jackson, his mother made it clear how he was to deal with insults: "Never tell a lie, nor take what is not yours, nor sue anybody for slander or assault and battery. Always settle them cases yourself." (McWhitney, 1988, p. 169) Jackson, a true representative of his culture, was involved in more than 100 violent quarrels in his lifetime, including one in which he killed a political opponent.

Southern society seems to have retained aspects of the culture of honor even in this century, resulting in very different views about violence there than are common in the rest of the country. Hodding Carter, a Mississippi journalist, reported that in the 1930s he served on a jury in a homicide case. The accused was an irritable man who lived next to a gas station. Day after day, the workers at the station made jokes at the man's expense until one morning the man emptied his shotgun into the crowd, maiming one of the jokers, wounding another, and killing an innocent customer. Carter was the only juror for conviction. As one of the 11 jurors voting for acquittal put it, "He ain't guilty. *He wouldn't of been much of a man if he hadn't shot them fellows*" (Carter, 1950, p. 50). Brearley (1934) wrote that in much of the South of his time it was impossible to obtain a conviction for murder if the perpetrator had (a) been insulted and (b) had warned the victim of his intention to kill if the insult were not retracted or compensated. Lundsgraade (1977) has maintained that the same pattern holds in modern Houston, Texas. And until the 1970s, Texas law held that there was no crime if a man killed his wife's lover caught *in flagrante delicto* (Reed, 1981).

REGIONAL DIFFERENCES IN HOMICIDE

There is abundant historical and anecdotal evidence supporting the view that the South is more violent and other such evidence linking this violence of the herder–warrior culture of honor. What is the status of statistical evidence of the sort likely to convince a social scientist? Most research to date has focused on homicide, both because of its obvious importance and because excellent, relatively error-free data are available. It is a simple matter to determine whether homicide rates are higher in one region than another, and in fact most investigators find that they are higher in the South. Linking this difference to the nature of traditional Southern White culture has proved to be a matter of great dispute. Some investigators (e.g., Blau & Blau, 1982) have maintained that Southern homicide rates are no higher than the South is poorer, has greater income inequality, and has more African Americans—three factors associated with higher homicide rates. However, the elimination of differences among regions through statistical adjustment obscures potentially important differences among regions.

It seems to make sense to examine the rates for Whites separately, at each city size separately, and see whether the rates are different between North and South. This is what Gregory Polly, Sylvia Lang, and I did (Nisbett, Polly, & Lang, 1993). We looked at both male offender rates and victim rates, because they have different sources of error. Offender rates could be wrong about the race of some of the perpetrators because the wrong person was arrested. Victim data would rarely be wrong about the race of the victim, but in a small fraction of cases the perpetrator is not of the same race as the victim (Hackney, 1969). We examined White, non-Hispanic offender and victim data for small cities (10,000–50,000 inhabitants) medium sized cities (50,000–200,000 inhabitants), and large cities (more than 200,000 inhabitants) for the period 1976–1983. We included in our analysis every variable found by any investigation we have read to be significantly associated with homicide rates in the United States, including an index of poverty, an index of income inequality (the "Gini" index; U.S. Bureau of the Census, 1983), population density and percentage of the population who are males between the ages of 15 and 29. We followed the recommendation of Gastil (1971) and used a continuous variable of degree of "Southernness" of the state in which the offense occurred. This variable reflects the fact that some non-Southern states, including several Western and southern Midwest states, were settled primarily by Southerners. In fact, in the mid-to-late 19th century, the great majority of the residents of some non-Southern states, such as Oklahoma and Arizona, had been born in the South. Gastil's scheme assigns a score to each state reflective of the proportion of the population descended from Southerners.

We may examine first the data just for cities with 90% or more residents who are White and non-Hispanic. This means that population density, poverty, and income inequality data are derived primarily from the White population. There are no cities of more than 200,000 people having 90% or more White non-Hispanic populations, but there are significant numbers of smaller cities like that in our sample to make an analysis meaningful. The only variables that predict homicide rates consistently across both measures and both city sizes are poverty and Southernness. Although poverty is an important predictor of homicide, Southernness is also important and remains important even when poverty differences among regions are taken into account.

The regional differences are really quite large in absolute terms. For the smaller cities, the ratio of homicides in the South to homicides in New England, the least Southern region, is about three to one. For the medium-size cities, the ratio is more than two to one. It is important to note that the rates for Southern regions are higher than for comparable, more Northern regions even when one takes into account poverty differences between regions. For example, the small cities of the plains region of Texas having the lowest poverty rates produce much higher homicide rates than the small cities of the plains region of Nebraska having the highest poverty rates (and substantially higher than the poverty rates of the low-poverty-rate Texas cities).

Essentially the same picture can be found by examining the White homicide rates for cities of all kinds, including those with high non-White and Hispanic populations. Again, the ratio of White homicides for a random sample of all small cities is three times higher for the South than for New England, and twice as high for medium-size cities. For cities of more than 200,000, however, the regional difference is very slight.

The pattern of greater regional differences for smaller cities has two important implications. First, it shows that the South is not uniform with respect to homicide. It is the smaller communities of the South—and West—that have elevated homicide rates. This pattern suggests that the phenomenon is primarily rural in nature, consistent with the historical argument about the importance of type of agricultural economy in producing the cultural differences in the first place. Second, it indicates that temperature differences between regions are not the basis of regional differences in homicide, because regional temperature differences are as great for large cities as for small ones.

REGIONAL DIFFERENCES IN ATTITUDES TOWARD VIOLENCE

Of course, the argument to this point is what sociologists call a merely *residual* one. Southernness may be correlated with something not yet measured that no one would want to call culture. It would be good to have some positive indication that there are regional differences in attitudes or other psychological variables between North and South that could plausibly explain the homicide differences. As many investigators have pointed out, there just are not that many documented differences between Southerners and non-Southerners in attitudes toward violence (e.g., Reed, 1981).

(It is customary, though, to find Southerners more in favor of whatever war the United States is fighting at the time of the survey, more approving of spanking as a discipline technique for children, and more opposed to gun control.)

Dov Cohen and I (in press) have recently begun a review of the major national surveys that have covered topics of violence and have conducted our own survey of White men in the most rural counties of the South and the western portion of the Midwest. The national surveys include the National Opinion Research Council (NORC, Davis & Smith, 1989) items of the past 20 years that have dealt with questions of interpersonal violence and the classic study by Blumenthal, Kahn, Andrews, and Head (1972) on American males' attitudes toward violence. I report the data for White men only from each of these surveys.

The NORC and Blumenthal et al. (1972) data sets contained numerous questions about violence in the abstract, but few produced regional differences. For example, respondents from different regions proved equally willing to endorse items such as, "An eye for an eye and a tooth for a tooth is a good rule for living"; "Many people only learn through violence"; and "When someone does wrong, he should be paid back for it." Although there were a few abstract questions for which Southerners were more inclined to endorse violence (e.g., "It is often necessary to use violence to prevent violence"), there were just as many for which Southerners were less inclined to endorse violence (e.g., "When a person harms you, you should turn the other cheek and forgive him"). Even when the questions were made more concrete, specifying the settings or participants, Southerners were not necessarily more likely than Northerners to endorse violence. For example, Southerners were no more likely to agree that police may sometimes have to beat suspects or that it might be right for a man to punch another adult male.

Despite these results, Cohen and Nisbett (in press) found three specific categories of survey items that differentiate Southerners from non-Southerners—items that relate to self-protection, to the proper response to an insult, and to the role of violence in the socialization of children.

Attitudes Toward Violence for Self-Protection

The protection items show a difference relating both to protection of property and to the protection of human life, including one's own. For example, when asked whether a man has the right to kill to defend his home, 36% of White Southern men agreed a great deal, compared with 18% of non-Southern White men. (There is a North Carolina proverb saying that "Every man is a sheriff on his own hearth.") Southern men were also more likely to agree that "a man has the right to kill a person to defend his family" (80% vs. 67%). Similarly, Southern men were more likely to say that police should shoot, or even shoot to kill, to protect against rioters, whether the rioters are Black, gangs of hoodlums, or students (all examples are from Blumenthal et al., 1972).

In our survey of rural counties, we found White Southern men to be twice as likely to report having guns for purposes of protection as rural Midwestern White men, although they were no more likely to report owning them. It seems not to be a stretch to explain both the customary Southern opposition to gun control and the customary Southern endorsement of the war of the moment in terms of the greater importance of protection. If protection of life and property by violent means is a necessity, then ownership of guns is required, and gun control imperils self-protection. Wars are usually defended (at least in this century) in terms of the need for self-protection, which might be expected to appeal to Southerners.

Attitudes Toward Violence in Response to Insults

The second major difference we find has to do with the appropriate response to insults. A pair of NORC questions presented in Table 8.1 is revealing. Respondents were asked if they thought it could ever be right for an adult male to punch another male and whether it could ever be right for a man to hit a drunk who bumped into the man and his wife. Although there were no regional differences in approval of the notion that it could ever be right for a man to punch another adult male, there were differences when it was specified that the other man was a drunk who bumped into the man and his wife, a situation that many would regard as an insult. Cohen and Nisbett (in press) included the insult item in their survey of rural respondents and found similar results. Other concrete scenarios, which did not involve insults, pro-

TABLE 8.1 Percentage Endorsing 1990 NORC Questions on Violence as a Function of Region

| Region | NORC national data[a] | | Cohen & Nisbett rural country survey[b] |
	Ever approve of a man punching adult male	Approve of hitting a drunk who bumped into a man and his wife	Approve of hitting a drunk who bumped into a man and his wife
New England	73	7	—
Middle Atlantic	68	7	—
Midwest	69	8	6
Pacific	73	8	—
Mountain	72	10	—
Southwest	70	14	—
South	73	15	16

Note: NORC = National Opinion Research Council.

[a]Davis & Smith, 1989.

[b]"Self-Protection and the Culture of Honor" by D. Cohen and R. E. Nisbett, in press. *Personality and Social Psychology Bulletin.*

duced no regional differences in endorsement of a man punching another man, either in the NORC data or in Cohen and Nisbett's data.

Cohen and Nisbett (in press) presented their subjects with a series of scenarios in which an insult occurs and asked them whether a violent response—either fighting or shooting the person who does the insulting—would be justified, extremely justified, or not at all justified. For example, they described a situation in which "Fred fights an acquaintance because that person looks over Fred's girlfriend and starts talking to her in a suggestive way" and another situation in which "Fred shoots another person because that person sexually assaults Fred's 16-year-old daughter." In addition, they asked those subjects who felt that the violence would be justified whether they thought that the insulted person "would not be much of a man" if he failed to respond violently.

White Southern men were more likely than White Midwestern men both to feel that the violent response to the insult is extremely justified (12% vs. 6%) and to say that a failure to respond violently would indicate that the insulted person was not much of a man (19% vs. 12%). It is important to note that these results cannot be explained by differences in either educational or economic status, both of which were nearly identical for the Northern and Southern samples.

Socialization for Violence

The third major area in which Southern attitudes differ from Northern ones has to do with socialization for violence. Anthropologists point out that an adult male cannot be expected to respond with violence to insults and to be prepared to defend himself and his family and property with violence when threatened unless he has a long-time familiarity with violence. Thus, his own youthful infractions may have been dealt with violently—by spankings or beatings—and he may have been encouraged to respond with violence, from an early age, to the insults of his peers (e.g., Cambell, 1965; Lowie, 1954; Peristiany, 1965).

Cohen and Nisbett (in press) have found that these patterns of socialization for violence are characteristic of modern Southern White men. They asked their subjects whether they thought spankings in general were justified and whether they thought that a spanking for a specific infraction, such as shoplifting, was justified. About 49% of their Southern subjects strongly agreed that spanking was an appropriate discipline policy, whereas only 31% of their Midwestern subjects thought so. Similarly, 67% of their Southern subjects thought spanking was appropriate for shoplifting, whereas only 45% of their Northern subjects thought so. These differences are comparable to others reported in the literature on regional differences in attitudes toward spanking.

Cohen and Nisbett (in press) also presented their subjects with two scenarios in which a young child was bullied. Respondents were asked to imagine that a 10-year-old boy named James is confronted with "a boy a year younger who picks a fight with him. James tries to talk the other boy out of fighting, but it doesn't work. The boy gives James a black eye and bloody nose in front of a crowd of other children." They were also asked to imagine that "every day another boy pushes James down and steals his lunch money. One time, James tries to talk to the other boy to get him to quit. But the other boy still continues to bully and steal from him every day." Subjects were asked what they thought most fathers would expect James to do—"take a stand and fight the other boy" or avoid fighting. For both questions, Southern respondents were more likely than Northern respondents to think that most fathers would expect fighting (39% vs. 25%).

Thus, there appears to remain today a difference between Southern and Northern White men in attitudes toward children and violence. More Southern than Northern respondents believe in spanking as a means of discipline, and more Southerners than Northerners believe that fathers would expect their bullied child to fight.

REGIONAL DIFFERENCES IN BEHAVIORAL RESPONSES TO INSULTS

If Northern and Southern cultures differ so much in the meaning and importance they attach to insults, then it ought to be possible to show that Southerners have different reactions to insults than do Northerners—for example, that they respond to insults with more anger, that they see more aggressiveness and hostility in their environment, or that insults prime violent imagery. Norbert Schwarz, Brian Bowdle, and I decided to examine these possibilities in the laboratory (Bowdle, Nisbett, & Schwartz, 1993). This is a tricky business if one wishes to avoid damaging people's sense of well-being or making them feel quite unhappy, but we believe we have hit on a way of insulting people in the laboratory with little risk of such damage.

Male out-of-state undergraduate students at the University of Michigan were screened for their permanent addresses and randomly called and asked to participate (for $5) in a study in which they would be performing a variety of cognitive tasks under time pressure. Subjects filled out a brief questionnaire on arrival and were asked to take it to a table at the end of a long, narrow hall. On the way to the table, they had to crowd past a male undergraduate confederate working at an open file cabinet. The confederate was required to close the file cabinet and press himself against it to allow the subject room to pass. When the subject returned a few seconds later, the confederate, who had just reopened the file drawer, slammed it shut, pushed his shoulder against the shoulder of the subject, and said, loudly enough to be clearly heard by the subject, "Asshole." The confederate then quickly entered a room with a locked door at the end of the hall. (The locked door was a needed precaution. One angry subject actually pursued the confederate and rattled the door knob.) Two confederates were posted at opposite ends of the narrow hall to observe the subject's reaction and record their impressions of the anger, amusement, and other emotions expressed by the subject. (The confederate near the locked door was prepared to intervene to announce that the provocation was part of the experiment if this had been necessary, but it never was.)

Upon their return to the laboratory, subjects were presented with two apperception tasks allowing for assessment of their level of hostility. They were asked to complete words from a series of letters including a blank, for example, _ight, gu_, _ill. Each letter series could be completed to form words with hostile connotations (e.g., fight, gun, kill) or nonhostile ones (e.g., light, gum, hill). Immediately following that task, subjects were asked to rate a series of photographs of male faces for the degree to which they expressed several emotions, including anger. Finally, subjects were asked to provide completions for three different written scenarios. Although two of the scenarios were intended to be neutral, the third involved a clear insult to the protagonist. In this scenario, which takes place at a party, a man's fiancee tells him that an acquaintance, who knows them to be engaged, has made two clear passes at her during the course of the evening. Following the collection of some background data, subjects were gently debriefed, including an apology by the experimenter for the deception and an explanation of the reasons for it and a reconciliation session with the confederate.

The various assessment procedures in the experiment allows us to compare the emotional response of Southerners and Northerners to an insult. We can determine whether such a provocation differentially causes Southerners versus Northerners to see hostility in pictures of faces, to complete word fragments in a manner reflective of violence, or to provide aggressive completions to the scenarios.

The results concerning the subjects' immediate emotional response to the insult were quite clear. We subtracted the observer's ratings to subjects' amusement from their ratings of subjects' anger. The reaction patterns were remarkably different for the two groups of subjects. For 65% of the Northern subjects, but only 15% of Southern subjects, the amusement ratings were higher than the anger ratings.

It seems equally clear, however, that the insult did not cause Southern subjects to spend the rest of their time in the experiment in a state of hostility or paranoia. Their word fragment completions did not yield more hostile words than those of either noninsulted Southerners or Northerners, whether insulted or not. Nor did the insulted Southerners see more anger (or fear, or any of the other emotions rated) in the male faces they saw. Nor did they offer more violent completions to the two neutral scenarios. However, in reacting to the third scenario, involving affront and sexual challenge, the insulted Southerners were far more likely to respond with violent imagery. Seventy-five percent of insulted Southerners completed the affront scenario with events in which the protagonist physically injured, or threatened to injure, his antagonist, whereas this was true for only 25% of Southerners who were not insulted—a highly significant difference. Northerners were unaffected by the manipulation, being equally likely to conclude the senarios with violence whether insulted or not.

In summary, the results indicate that Southerners are more sensitive to a given provocation, one interpretable as an insult, than are Northerners—in two respects. First, the provocation makes them angrier. It seems not to be something they can brush off as easily as Northerners can. Secondly, it seems to prime violent responses to subsequently encountered insult stimuli. The implications of these results seem clear. Southerners, by virtue of the emotional meaning that the insult has for them, are more likely to display anger in certain situations in which escalation is dangerous and are more susceptible to considering violent responses in those situations.

ARGUMENTS AND REGIONAL DIFFERENCES IN HOMICIDE

Much of the evidence presented above suggests that it might only be certain types of homicide, and not homicide in general, that should be more common in the South. Situations in which an affront occurs should be disproportionately likely to trigger violent responses. There is little reason to expect the rates of other kinds of homicide, such as those occurring in the context of robbery or burglary, to be elevated. To examine this possibility, I compared the rates for homicide committed in the context of another felony with the rates for homicide that seemed likely to be argument-related (e.g., lovers' triangles, barroom quarrels, and acquaintance homicide).

It may be seen in Table 8.2 that White male homicide rates in small cities are much higher in the South and Southwest than in other areas for argument-related cases but not for felony-related cases. In larger cities, the homicide rates again are higher in the South and Southwest for argument-related cases, but they are actually smaller for felony-related cases.

REGIONAL DIFFERENCES IN VIOLENCE: PAST, PRESENT, AND FUTURE

The evidence suggests several conclusions, with more clarity than one expects for historical and cultural questions.

1. There is a marked difference in White homicide rates between regions of the United States, such that homicide is more common in the South and in regions of the country initially settled by Southerners.

2. There is solid negative evidence against a temperature interpretation of the difference in homicide rates. Regional differences are larger for smaller towns and

TABLE 8.2 White Male Homicide Rates for Felony-Related and Argument-Related Murders as a Function of Region and City Size

	City size	
Homicide type	Less than 200,000	200,000 or more
Felony-related murders		
South & Southwest	1.16	2.25
Other regions	.88	3.22
Argument-related murders		
South & Southwest	4.77	7.66
Other regions	2.13	6.51

Note: Data are adapted from *Uniform Crime Reports United States: Supplementary Homicide Reports 1976–1983* by J. A. Fox and G. L. Pierce, 1987, Boston Northeastern University, Center for Applied Research.

more rural areas than for large cities, although regional differences in temperature are obviously just as great in the small-population towns and counties. In addition, the warmest areas of the South have the lowest homicide rates.

3. There is also good evidence against two of the traditional cultural interpretations of Southern violence. Appealing to a history of slavery to explain current regional differences in violence seems doomed because the regions of the South that had the highest concentrations of slaves in the past are those with the lowest homicide rates today. Similarly, imitation of African-American violence seems an implausible explanation, because the counties with small African-American populations have the highest White homicide rates.

4. Although differences in poverty are associated with higher homicide rates, regional differences in homicide are by no means completely explained by poverty, because Southernness remains a predictor of homicide even when poverty differences between regions are taken into account; and because in microregions of North and South that are highly comparable from the standpoint of ecology, population density, economy, and other variables, the richest Southern towns have higher homicide rates than even the poorest Northern towns.

5. There is positive evidence of cultural differences between North and South in attitudes toward violence and in responses to insults. These differences are not explainable as a consequence of Southern poverty. The behavioral data were obtained from college students, and the attitudinal differences were found for rural samples that did not differ in income.

6. The most theoretically interesting but inherently hardest to establish proposition is that the South has a culture of honor with historical roots that underlies its preferences for violence. Southerners do not endorse violence in the abstract more than do Northerners, nor do they endorse violence in all specific forms of circumstances. Rather, they are more likely to endorse violence as an appropriate response to insults, as a means of self-protection, and as a socialization tool in training children. This is the characteristic cultural pattern of herding societies the world over. Consistent with the culture-of-honor interpretation, it is argument-related and not felony-related homicide that is more common in the South.

Finally, it should be noted that what is referred to as Southern violence, in the historical and anthropological literature, as well as in this article for purposes of brevity, is actually a much more complicated regional phenomenon. It is the rural counties and smaller towns of the South and West, especially those with a herding economy, that have elevated homicide rates.

This localized pattern of violence may indicate something about the future and the likelihood that regional differences will persist. Already, the biggest urban regions of the South and West show only a trace of the elevation in White homicide rates found in other population units. This may be due in part to the manifest irrelevance of the culture of honor to the conditions of urban life, and it may be due in part to the admixture of Northern culture to these centers in the form of immigration from other regions of the country. A purely material interpretation of the Southern attitude toward violence indicates that it will not persist. It is already long since an anachronism. Few people today live in any realistic danger of having their entire livelihood taken irrevocably away from them by outlaws, not even current American pastoralists.

On the other hand, the material interpretation of the culture of honor may not be a complete explanation for its existence. Certain cultural stances may take on a life of their own because they are embedded in a matrix of behavioral patterns that sustains them. If individuals believe that they must own and even carry weapons for protection, and if they respond to insults with sufficient anger to occasionally cause them to use those weapons, this will tend to affect the entire local community. Its members may respond with heightened consciousness of the need for protection, more vigilance concerning threats, and a consequent greater likelihood of violence.

There is another sense in which the culture of honor might turn out to be self-sustaining or even capable of expanding into mainstream culture. The culture is a variant of warrior culture the world over, and its independent invention countless times (Gilmore, 1990), combined with the regularities in its themes having to do with glorification of masculine attributes, suggests that it may be a particularly alluring stance that may be capable of becoming functionally autonomous. Many observers (e.g., Naipaul, 1989; Shattuck, 1989) have noted that contemporary Southern backcountry culture, including music, dress, and social stance, is spreading beyond its original geographical confines and becoming a part of the fabric of rural, and even urban, working-class America. Perhaps for the young males who adopt it, this culture provides a romantic veneer to everyday existence. If so, it is distinctly possible that the violence characteristic of this culture is also spreading beyond its confines. An understanding of the culture and its darker side would thus remain important for the foreseeable future.

References

Anderson, C. A. (1989). Temperature and aggression: Ubiquitous effects of heat occurrence of human violence. *Psychological Bulletin, 106,* 74–96.

Baron, L., & Straus, M. A. (1988). Cultural and economic sources of homicide in the United States. *The Sociological Quarterly, 29,* 371–390.

Blau, J. R., & Blau, P. M. (1982). The cost of inequality: Metropolitan structure and violent crime. *American Sociological Review, 47,* 114–129.

Blumenthal, M. D., Kahn, R. L., Andrews, F. M., & Head, K. B. (1972). *Justifying violence: Attitudes of American men.* Ann Arbor, MI: Institute for Social Research.

Bowdle, B., Nisbett, R. E., & Schwarz, N. (1993). *Regional differences in responses to insults.* Unpublished manuscript, University of Michigan.

Brearley, H. C. (1934). The pattern of violence. In W. T. Couch (Ed.), *Culture in the south* (221–238). Chapel Hill: University of North Carolina Press.

Campbell, J. K. (1965). Honour and the devil. In J. G. Peristitiany (Ed.), *Honour and shame: The values of Mediterranean society* (pp. 112–175). London: Weidenfeld & Nicolson.

Carter, H. (1950). *Southern legacy.* Baton Rouge: Louisiana State University Press.

Cash, Wilbur J. (1941). *The mind of the South.* New York: Knopf.

Cohen, D., & Nisbett, R. E. (in press). Self-protection, insults and the culture of honor: Explaining southern homicide. *Personality and Social Psychology Bulletin.*

Davis, J. A., & Smith, T. W. (1989). *General social surveys, 1972–1990*. Storrs, CT: National Opinion Research Center.

Fischer, D. H. (1989). *Albion's seed: Four British folkways in America*. New York: Oxford University Press.

Gastil, R. D. (1971). Homicide and a regional culture of violence. *American Sociological Review, 36*, 416–427.

Gastil, R. D. (1989). Violence, crime and punishment. In C. R. Wilson & W. Ferris (Eds.), *Encyclopedia of Southern culture* (pp. 1473–1476). Chapel Hill: University of North Carolina Press.

Gilmore, D. D. (1990). *Manhood in the making: Cultural concepts of masculinity*. New Haven, CT: Yale University Press.

Hackney, S. (1969). Southern violence. *The American Historical Review, 74*, 906–925.

Lowie, R. H. (1954). *Indians of the plain*. New York: McGraw-Hill.

Lundsgraade, H. P. (1977). *Murder in space city: A cultural history*. New York: Oxford University Press.

McWhiney, G. (1988). *Cracker culture: Celtic ways in the old South*. Tuscaloosa: University of Alabama Press.

Naipaul, V. S. (1989). *A turn in the South*. New York: Knopf.

Nisbett, R. E., Polly, G., & Lang, S. (1993). *Homicide and regional U.S. culture*. Unpublished manuscript, University of Michigan.

Peristiany, J. G. (Ed.). (1965). *Honour and shame: The values of Mediterranean society*. London: Weidenfeld & Nicolson.

Reifman, A. S., Larrick, R. P., & Fein, S. (1991). Temper and temperature on the diamond: The heat-aggression relationship in major league baseball. *Personality and Social Psychology Bulletin, 17*, 580–585.

Shattuck, R. (1989, March 30). The reddening of America. *New York Review of Books*, pp. 3–5.

Tocqueville, A. de. (1969). *Democracy in America* (J. P. Mayer, Ed., G. Lawrence, Trans.). Garden City, NY: University of Chicago Press. (Original work published 1835)

U.S. Bureau of the Census. (1983). *Characteristics of the U.S. population: Vol. 1*. Washington, DC: U.S. Government Printing Office.

Alan S. Reifman
Richard P. Larrick
Steven Fein

Temper and Temperature on the Diamond: The Heat-Aggression Relationship in Major League Baseball

Social psychologists have long been interested in the relationship between temperature and aggression, and conflicting data exist as to whether aggression continues to climb as the thermometer does. Although much of the research has focused on crime and urban riots, the authors here take an unusual look at this issue by considering the relationship between heat and the number of times pitchers hit batters in major league baseball. Using records from the 1986–88 baseball seasons, the authors are able to rule out several alternative interpretations of their data and conclude that there is a direct and positive relationship between temper and temperature on the baseball diamond.

Mark Twain, among others, observed that everybody talks about the weather. One aspect of weather that people have talked about for centuries is its effect on human behavior. Probably the most discussed idea regarding the effects of weather on people's behavior is the idea that very hot weather is associated with aggression and violence. This idea has been expressed many times, from the classic works of the theater, such as Shakespeare's *Romeo and Juliet,* to contemporary film, such as Spike Lee's *Do the Right Thing.* Indeed, the metaphors of anger and aggression, such as "hot under the collar," "steamed," and "blood boiling," are replete with imagery of heat.

This long-standing idea that heat and aggression are related has recently inspired a growing body of research that aims to test this hypothesis scientifically and to determine how and why they are related. During the last two decades numerous studies—both correlational and experimental—have found that aggressive behavior increases as a function of increasing ambient temperatures (for a review, see Anderson, 1989). Although the basic heat-aggression relationship appears well established, research on this problem continues today on several fronts. One important issue concerns the range of domains to which the relationship can be extended. Anderson (1987) has stated that only through the cumulation of results using different operationalizations and different social contexts can the authenticity of a heat-aggression relationship be confirmed. Thus far, however, most of the field/archival studies on this topic have examined crime statistics as the measure of aggression (e.g., Anderson, 1987), although other domains have begun to be explored, such as horn honking among drivers (Baron, 1976; Kenrick & MacFarlane, 1984). One domain in which the heat-aggression relationship has not been investigated is that of sports. This is an important domain because much of our leisure time is spent participating in or watching others engage in sports and, depending on the nature of the sport, there is often the opportunity for aggression and even violence to manifest itself during the course of a game. An examination of the heat-aggression relationship in sports should be valuable both because of the ubiquity of sports in our culture and because the measures of aggression therein would not be associated with extraneous factors (e.g., socioeconomic variables, number of people outdoors) that plague much of the archival research, nor would they be as trivial as some of the measures of aggression used in field and laboratory research. The present authors were especially interested in examining the heat-aggression relationship in the sport of baseball. Baseball offers the advantages of typically being played outdoors and in the summertime. Furthermore, it is a game in which much of what occurs on the field is easily quantified. Indeed, major league baseball fans are notorious for their love of baseball statistics.

A second issue with which research on heat and aggression is concerned is how heat and aggression are related. Specifically, what is the shape of the relation? Several shapes have been suggested, including a straight linear function, a J-shaped function, an inverted-U-shaped function, and an M-shaped function (Anderson, 1989). Because major league baseball is played from midspring to midfall, games are played in a great variety of temperatures. Although games are rarely played in uncomfortably cold temperatures, they are played in temperatures that are as hot as the weather ever gets in most places in the United States and Canada. Therefore, data from major league baseball games offer a good naturalistic test of some of the theories concerning the shape of the heat-aggression relationship.

Although we are aware of no previous research that has investigated the issue of heat and aggression in sports, some research has been conducted on other variables affecting aggression in sports. For example, Frank and Gilovich (1988) found that professional football and ice hockey teams with black uniforms received more penalties over a period of several years than teams with nonblack uniforms. It may be interesting to note that Dick Butkus, one of professional football's most aggressive linebackers of all time, responded to this finding by saying, "All I know was that we wore dark in the hot weather, dark colors attract heat, and it was uncomfortable" (Boxer, 1989, p. 56).

In the present study aggression was operationalized as the number of times major league baseball pitchers hit batters with pitched balls. In recent years, batters being hit by pitches has been a serious and highly publicized problem in baseball. Baseball players and analysts have suggested numerous causes, such as pitchers' frustration and need to intimidate hitters (Hersch, 1987; Lopresti, 1987). A goal of the present research was to determine whether heat, independent of these factors, may be a significant factor that has been largely overlooked by the baseball community. Specifically, using the individual baseball game as the unit of analysis, we examined whether the number of hit batters was related to ambient temperature in a large sample of major league games.

Because factors other than ambient temperature might contribute to the rate of batters being hit by pitches, the most plausible of these were incorporated into the analyses as control variables. Partly on the basis of the speculations of baseball players and experts about the causes of batters being hit by pitches (e.g., Hersch, 1987; Lopresti, 1987), the following potential predictors of the number of batters hit by pitches during a game were recorded for each game: the total number of walks, the total number of wild pitches, the total number of passed balls, the total number of errors, the total number of home runs, and the attendance. The number of walks and wild pitches in a game may serve as an index of pitcher inaccuracy or wildness and thus may correlate with the number of batters hit by pitches. Errors are a measure of inaccuracy or wildness displayed by all the players on the team in fielding and throwing. Passed balls may serve as an index either of pitcher wildness or of inaccuracy displayed by the catcher. Home runs are likely to covary with the number of batters hit by a pitch in a game for two reasons that have frequently been cited by baseball analysts. One is that allowing home runs is a source of frustration for pitchers and they may vent their frustrations by hitting batters. A second reason is strategic. After allowing a home run, pitchers need to reclaim their authority on the mound by intimidating the hitters and preventing them from taking their best swings. Finally, attendance was used as an index of the importance or intensity of a game. It was thought that the more important a game, the more aggressively it would be played, perhaps leading to an increased number of hit batters. Because temperature and perceived importance of a game are likely to covary (games played in August have both higher temperatures and higher perceived importance than games played in April), this control variable is particularly important.

Concerning the shape of the heat-aggression relationship, the existing literature would suggest a priori hypotheses of both linearity and curvilinearity. The latter would arise if aggression increased with temperature up to a point but then declined owing to debilitation or to the opportunity to escape the hot environment rather than aggressing. Other curvilinear functions besides this inverted-U might also be possible (for a discussion of these issues, see Anderson, 1989).

METHOD

Microfilm issues of major daily newspapers were consulted to obtain data on weather and major league baseball games. Random samples of games were taken from three major league baseball seasons: 1986, 1987, and 1988. The 1986 sample included every 10th game played during the season ($n = 215$ games). Every 7th game during the season was included for the 1987 ($n = 304$) and 1988 ($n = 307$) samples. For each game sampled, the number of players hit by a pitch (HBP) was recorded. Within the same newspaper issue, the high temperature (°F) in the home city the day of the game was also recorded. The numbers of walks, wild pitches, passed balls, errors, home runs, and fans in attendance in each game were recorded as control variables.

RESULTS

To test the primary prediction that the number of HBPs in a game increases with temperature, a Pearson product-movement correlation between temperature and HBPs was calculated for all the games in our sample from the 1986, 1987, and 1988 seasons. As predicted, this correlation was positive and significant. To determine whether this relationship would be maintained with the potentially confounding variables described above controlled for, we regressed HBP on temperature, walks, wild pitches, passed balls, errors, home runs, and attendance. Supporting our prediction, temperature was positively and significantly related to HBP when the alternative variables were partialed out.

The results of the multiple regression indicate that the temperature-HBP relationship is not mediated by pitcher wildness (as measured by walks, wild pitches, and passed balls). An additional way of understanding this point is to examine the correlations between the measures of pitcher wildness and HBP and between pitcher wildness and temperature. If temperature produces wildness (e.g., resulting from fatigue or a pitcher's slippery hand), and if wildness mediates the temperatures-HBP relationship, then one would expect that (a) temperature would be positively correlated with pitcher wildness and (b) pitcher wildness would be positively correlated with HBP. However, temperature is *negatively* correlated with the measures of wildness. Thus, heat does not lead to greater pitcher wildness, and the alternative explanation that wildness mediates the temperature-HBP relationship is rendered less plausible.

The Temperature-HBP Relationship in Each of the Home Parks

Although the analyses reported above discredit several potentially trivializing mediators of the temperature-HBP relationship, a final alternative explanation that must be ruled out is that this relationship was produced spuriously by incidental differences in the tendency to throw HBPs among the various teams. This alternative explanation arises in part because the 26 home parks of the teams are located in regions that vary greatly in climate. It is possible that the relationship reported between temperature and HBPs could be due simply to the fact that the teams that throw the most HBPs just happen to play in warmer climates and the teams that throw the fewest happen to play in colder climates, for reasons that have nothing to do with temperature.

To examine this issue, we calculated Pearson product-moment correlations between total number of HBPs and temperature for all the games played at each of the

23 home parks that are not doomed. These results indicate that batters were not significantly more likely to be hit in one home park than in another.

Replication of the Relationship in the 1962 Season

The analyses reported thus far concern data from games played during the 1986, 1987, and 1988 season. We also collected temperature and HBP data for the 1962 season, using the same sampling procedure as was used for the 1987 and 1988 seasons. We collected these additional data for two reasons. First, this would allow us to examine the generalizability of the temperature-HBP relationship across different periods of time. Second, by looking at a season in which the personnel and the personalities of the teams, and even several of the teams themselves, were very different than among the 26 teams in the 1986–1988 seasons, this would provide an additional test of the alternative explanation that the relationship we found was produced by incidental differences among the pitchers who pitched for the 26 teams between 1986 and 1988.

The Pearson product-moment correlation between temperature and HBP for the 1962 games was positive and marginally significant. As can be seen in Table 8.3, the correlation for the 1962 season was similar in magnitude to the correlations found for the 1986, 1987, and 1988 seasons. The consistency of these correlations supports the generalizability of the relationship between temperature and HBP. In addition, it further reduces the plausibility of the idea that incidental differences among the pitchers on the 26 teams during 1986–1988 could have produced the temperature-HBP relationship found for those seasons.

The Shape of the Temperature-HBP Relationship

One of the issues that has been important in the heat-aggression literature is the shape of the function that relates heat to aggression. In order for the reader to examine the shape of the relationship between temperature and HBP, we have displayed in Figure 8.1 the mean numbers of HBPs in games from our 1986–1988 sample that were played at four levels of temperature.

The shape of the relationship between temperature and HBP was analyzed by applying a set of orthogonal polynomial contrasts to the average number of HBPs in

TABLE 8.3 Correlations Between Temperature and Number of Players Hit by a Pitch (HBP) for Individual Seasons

	1986	1987	1988	1962
Correlations between	.11	.09	.11	.10
temperature and HBP (*n*)	(215)	(304)	(307)	(228)

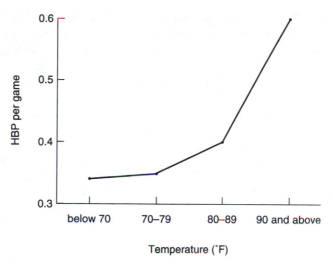

FIGURE 8.1

Mean number of players hit by a pitch (HBPs) in games played below 70°F ($n = 176$), between 70°F and 79°F ($n = 315$), between 80°F and 89°F ($n = 224$), and at 90°F and above ($n = 111$).

games played at the four levels of temperature. These results are most consistent with a linear, rather than a curvilinear, relationship between temperature and HBP.

DISCUSSION

The results of the present study revealed that mean hit-by-pitch levels rose linearly with temperature. Regression analyses revealed that this relationship remained positive and significant when several variables that have nothing to do with aggression but could plausibly mediate a temperature-HBP relationship were partialed out. Indeed, because the measures of pitcher wildness and inaccuracy were negatively correlated with temperature, the measures of pitcher wildness apparently suppressed, rather than confounded, the temperature-HBP relationship.

Moreover, the results of a series of correlations between temperature and HBPs calculated for each of the nondomed home stadiums and of an analysis looking for significant differences among the mean numbers of HBPs thrown at the various home parks suggest that the observed temperature-HBP relationship was not produced spuriously by incidental differences among the teams. Further discrediting this alternative explanation was the finding of a similar temperature-HBP relationship in the 1962 season, a season featuring none of the players—and not all of the teams—who were included in the 1986–1988 samples. Though not reported in the Results section, one final piece of evidence arguing against the alternative explanation is that only 50% of the pitchers who pitched in the major leagues for all three seasons, 1986–1988, played for the same team throughout (MacLean, 1989). Indeed, this figure underestimates the turnover rate because it does not take into account the rookies who entered and the players who retired from the leagues at various points during the three seasons.

This study provides further evidence for the existence of a relationship between heat and aggression, and it extends our knowledge of this relationship to the domain of sports. In addition, the results of this study lend some support to the idea that the shape of the heat-aggression relationship is linear. Of course, no major league baseball games are played in extremely cold temperatures, and few are played in temperatures that exceed 100°F. Therefore, the data from our study cannot allow us to rule out the possibility that heat and aggression are related in a nonlinear fashion at temperatures more extreme than in our range. It should be noted, however, that our sample does accurately represent the range of temperatures present in the summer months in most of the United States and southern Canada.

Heat-aggression effects have usually been explained in terms of the major theories of aggression, such as excitation-transfer/misattribution and cognitive neoassociation (for this type of discussion, see Anderson, 1989). A recently proposed theory of emotion also offers an interesting insight into the possible mechanisms underlying the heat-aggression relationship. In their vascular theory of emotional efference, Zajonc, Murphy, and Inglehart (1989) suggest that brain temperature—which is partially regulated by a venous structure in the nose—and temperature-related neurochemistry may underlie heat-aggression effects. Proposed mechanisms such as these are clearly far away from our level of data collection. They do, however, represent useful hypotheses about the nature of the relationship of temperature to negative affect and aggression, as well as suggest possible interventions to reduce aggression in naturalistic settings such as sports.

In addition to their theoretical implications, the results have practical significance. Although the magnitude of the correlation is rather small, the slope of the temperature-HBP function is fairly steep in the higher temperatures. In fact, there is approximately a two-thirds greater chance of a batter's being hit in a game played when the temperature is in the nineties or above than in a game played when the temperature is in the seventies or below. Considering that during the course of one full baseball season 2,106 major league baseball games are played, numerous batters will suffer the consequences of the relationship between heat and aggression. Given the potential for serious injury whenever a batter gets hit with a pitch traveling approximately 90 miles per hour, any statistical relationship found between heat and batters being hit must be regarded as noteworthy.

These results suggest that the current trends in major league baseball of a greater number of night games and a greater number of domed stadiums, trends that have aroused the ire of many a baseball purist, may prove to save some careers or even lives. Although the authors do not call for the abolishment of summer day games in nondomed stadiums, we do suggest that baseball; players should take care to keep cool during games played in hot weather. Indeed, the many nonprofessional athletes who flock to the recreational fields and courts as the weather gets warm every spring and summer should also be careful of rising temperatures and tempers.

It may be that talking about weather, and specifically about what effects it can have on human behavior, can save many from pain and remorse.

References

Anderson, C. A. (1987). Temperature and aggression: Effects on quarterly, yearly, and city rates of violent and nonviolent crime. *Journal of Personality and Social Psychology, 52,* 1161–1173.

Anderson, C. A. (1989). Temperature and aggression: Ubiquitous effects of heat on occurrence of human violence. *Psychological Bulletin, 106,* 74–96.

Baron, R. A. (1976). The reduction of human aggression: A field study of the influence of incompatible reactions. *Journal of Applied Social Psychology, 6,* 260–274.

Boxer, S. (1989, April 17). Dark forces. *Sports Illustrated,* pp. 52–56.

Frank, M. G., & Gilovich, T. (1988). The dark side of self- and social perception: Black uniforms and aggression in professional sports. *Journal of Personality and Social Psychology, 54,* 74–85.

Hersch, H. (1987, July 20). It's war out there! *Sports Illustrated,* pp/ 14–17.

Kenrick, D. T., & MacFarlane, S. W. (1984). Ambient temperature and horn-honking: A field study of the heat/aggression relationship. *Environment and Behavior, 18,* 179–191.

Lopresti, M. (1987, July 30). Homer-stung pitchers fight back. *USA Today,* pp. C1–C2.

MacLean, N. (Ed.). (1989). *Who's who in baseball.* New York: Who's Who in Baseball Magazine Co.

Zajonc, R. B., Murphy, S. T., & Inglehart, M. (1989). Feeling and facial efference: Implications of the vascular theory of emotion. *Psychological Review, 96,* 395–416.

9

Stereotypes and Prejudice: Devaluing Others

Prejudice and group stereotypes affect the ways in which we see people and groups, the ways in which we evaluate people, and the manner in which people who hold stereotypes deal with one another. In spite of a great deal of interest and study, few people have offered important new perspectives in this area that both derive from theory and have significant consequences.

The work of Claude Steele, Professor of Psychology and Chairman of the Department of Psychology at Stanford University, offers us that unique combination of scholarship and social impact. Throughout his career, he has been interested in the ways that people cope with threats to their self-images. In our conversation, Professor Steele notes that people can be affected by stereotypes without actually internalizing them. Introducing the concept of stereotype threat, he explains that people sometimes protect their self-esteem by *disidentifying* with the domain in which they are stereotyped. He applies this specifically to the manner in which African Americans have related to achievement in school, and how women deal with achievement in math. Professor Steele's theorizing and research are noteworthy in that they have clear implications about the way in which teachers and schools should and should not relate to their pupils in areas related to stereotypes.

A CONVERSATION WITH
CLAUDE STEELE

Krupat: *It's been said that stereotypes label people so that all we see is color or gender, not the person. Do people who are stereotyped feel disturbed or threatened by this? And what could they do to avoid this?*

Steele: Let me respond with a story from Brent Staples' autobiography, *Parallel Time*. He's a Black editorialist for *The New York Times*, and describes going to graduate school in Psychology at University of Chicago. Walking down the streets of urban Hyde Park, he realized that he was making whites uncomfortable. They probably saw him through the lens of a stereotype as a potentially menacing Black male. He would get followed in stores and hotels, and people would look at him strangely. So he learned a particular tactic to handle this: As he walked down the street he would whistle Vivaldi.

Krupat: *I've never tried that, but I guess I have also never been in a situation where I felt subject to those kind of stares either.*

Steele: That is what stereotype threat is, realizing that he is being seen or could be seen this way. It's making him tense and the people around him are getting tense, so he punctures the stereotype by doing this a-stereotypical thing. And then people don't see him through the lens of the stereotype. They relax and he relaxes, and interactions go along quite normally.

Krupat: *To what extent is this story about the way others see him or is* *it about how he sees himself? Just what is the impact of being born into a minority group on a person's self-image?*

Steele: That's a good launching point to talk about the work I have been doing because I think that it has evolved into a certain position on that question that is interesting. Not that it's anything more than a working hypothesis at this point, but it's somewhat different than the traditional way to look at it. The standard understanding of that experience, being born into a negatively stereotyped or stigmatized group, is that after a time of being exposed to the negative stereotypes in society the person would internalize them. And once internalization has taken place, it could undermine the person's self-esteem or confidence in certain tasks. A number of people have launched that point of view, from Freud's "identification with the oppressor" to a variety of theories in the thirties and forties, sometime called self-hatred theories, that were usually applied to the experience of being Jewish or being Black.

Krupat: *That sounds like the way I have heard psychologists describe that experience to me. What has led you to think differently about this?*

Steele: That story changed in the late 80's when a number of findings and ideas came to the fore which challenged that. For instance, Jenny Crocker and Brenda Major, in a paper on stigma and stigmatization, proposed that when you look at the self-esteem literature comparing groups, you simply don't find a detriment in self-esteem for groups that are negatively stereotyped or stigmatized. And isn't that a puzzle in light of this other idea?

Krupat: *What was their explanation for this?*

Steele: Crocker and Major had the idea that being stigmatized may actually give you certain tools for protecting your self-esteem. You might blame your negative outcomes on the existence of prejudice. You might decide to compare your outcomes with other people who are similarly stereotyped as opposed to comparing yourself to the society at large, and so on. And these things might enable you, even though your group is negatively stereotyped, to not internalize the message. To me it suggests that there are probably a set of defenses that help protect self-esteem from the threat of being negatively stereotyped in society. And one of them—and this is where our work enters this story—is the possibility of *disidentifying* with the domain where one is specifically negatively stereotyped.

Krupat: *So let me see if I follow. What I'm hearing you say is that rather than a general internalization of a negative message about the whole self, it is specific to areas or domains that the stereotype is applied to?*

Steele: Yes, the threat is very specific to certain domains, although even in those domains I doubt that much internalization goes on. Let me give you an example. African-Americans might feel this threat in academic domains, in school, because of the nature of negative stereotypes in American society about their academic abilities. If you were a woman, the stereotype threat you might encounter would be in advanced math. Not necessarily in high school math, but advanced math where stereotyping becomes applicable and can threaten women. And I would maybe go one step farther. We find that the effects of stereotype threat on standardized test performance is strongest for the strongest of students in those groups, the ones with the best preparation. They're the ones for whom this extra threat of possibly being seen stereotypically becomes something to worry about. And it can distract and disrupt their performance. For students who don't care as much about the domain, it's just much less important.

Krupat: *Which argues that for people who are already good at or oriented toward achievement in that area, it's kind of a double whammy.*

Steele: That's right. Let's say a woman has been really good in math throughout her life. Now she's a junior in college taking some advanced course on Riemann surfaces. But if she's the only woman in there and she's experiencing a lot of stereotype threat, she might start to feel really fatigued. To protect her self-esteem she begins to disidentify with the domain, and she becomes a psychology major.

Krupat: *Is this really likely?*

Steele: We see lots of women do this en route from the natural sciences into something more comfortable. And after that process has taken place, after she's disidentified with the troubling math domain and reidentified with something else, then she says, "I was no good at math anyway." And it looks like she has an internalized belief about her math ability, but I think the more primary process is the process of disidentification.

Krupat: *Whereas you are saying that this sort of belief is more a sort of rationalization, merely a justification of her behavior?*

Steele: Yes that's right. So if internalization happens, I think it's an after-effect of a person ceasing to care about the domain. If we go back to that survey data which shows that negatively stereotyped groups have positive self-esteem, it's because they often disidentify with the domains in which those stereotypes apply.

Krupat: *If the threat of being stereotyped leads Black children to disidentify with school or women to stay away from math, what can be done to help? What can we do to correct this situation?*

Steele: I think that there's probably a right way and a wrong way, a more effective and less effective way of rendering that kind of help. Take, for example, programs that emphasize remediation as a goal. The risk there is that that will strengthen the stereotype and the threat one feels about being seen through its lens.

Krupat: *But why would providing remedial help strengthen the stereotype? Why should it make things worse rather than better?*

Steele: Remedial help can signal that the institution offering the help actually believes the stereotype, that in singling out this group the school or the university views them stereotypically. It's giving the sub-text message that the help is tied to being Black. That really worsens the stereotype threat they're normally under, it magnifies the meaning of every failure they have. So help of this kind could backfire.

Krupat: *If this sort of approach could do more harm than good, I assume there must be alternatives, a set of do's as well as don't's.*

Steele: Yes, the essence of it would be that you approach the student by a combination of offering real challenge, at the same time expressing a conviction in their potential to meet the challenge. This principle was developed in research by Geoff Cohen in conjunction with Lee Ross and myself. For negatively stereotyped groups, it may be helpful to say explicitly, "This is challenging work, but we believe you have the potential to meet that challenge." That tells them that the school isn't viewing them through the lens of the stereotype. Imagine a fourth grade teacher in a Toledo suburb who has just had ten new Black kids from across town show up in her classroom.

Krupat: *I assume she needs some advice that is simple but will work, something that would apply to all the students in her classroom.*

Steele: That has been one of our missions, to boil some of the lessons down into simple principles. We've been trying to identify a single technique that would work for stereotype-threatened students, and not harm, or maybe even help those who are not stereotype-threatened. And what we've been able to come up with is to offer a combination of challenging work—regardless of where they are, what level they're at, they can be challenged—along with affirmations of their potential to meet the challenge. That second part may be the somewhat awkward part for the teacher because it seems extra. But for the minority student, it's necessary. Challenge them and affirm their potential.

Krupat: *And you have evidence that this works?*

Steele: We have studies here at Stanford where Geoff has tried this out. Affirming the potential of the average white Stanford student is a little awkward because it's something they presume they have. So for these students, that doesn't seem to have much consequence. But it has a big effect on minority students.

Krupat: *That is impressive. To realize that the principle applies to fourth grade students in Toledo and to sophomores at Stanford suggests that the idea is pretty powerful. But let me change our focus just a bit. Since you are dealing with issues that have important practical implications in the real world, this might argue that you should be spending your time fighting with school boards and politicians, or at the least testing your ideas out there beyond the laboratory, out in the field. But I know that you are also seriously concerned with developing theory and testing that in the laboratory. How have you been able to maintain this kind of dual orientation?*

Steele: We have tried to do both, to go back and forth between the lab and the field. In the lab you can test some of the pure logic of the theory or the argument. In the field, you can't test the pure logic as well, but you can find out how important the process that you're thinking about is in relation to the other things that drive the phenomenon. So going back and forth between those two informs us in those two ways. We can test the central logic in the lab, and we can see what's important in the real world setting by doing the field research. They complement each other.

Krupat: *How about an example.*

Steele: Sure. Working in the laboratory, it became clear to us that it wasn't the students that had internalized doubts or low expectations that were showing our stereotyped threat effect. It was the stronger students. And I am not sure when we would have realized this if we were just working in the field. So looking at the thing in a sort of petri dish, the purity of a laboratory situation, can bring to light things that are hard to see in the much more complex buzz of a field experiment.

Krupat: *What would you say is your goal in doing this? How much of it is conceptual, to advance issues from a theoretical point of view, and how much of your efforts are aimed at making a difference in the real world?*

Steele: I really say equal amounts of both. I could be deluding myself, but we really are theoretically oriented in a serious way, and that is maybe not typical of some people who do research in the field on a problem like this.

Krupat: *How about people who would criticize you saying that testing* *theory is okay, but doesn't that sort of activity distract you from making a difference in the real world?*

Steele: I think the answer to that goes back to Kurt Lewin, the founder of our field, who said that there's nothing as practical as a good theory.

Krupat: *Then would you call yourself optimistic about the implications of your research and what it has to contribute to our understanding of the effects of race and gender on people's self-images?*

Steele: I think so. Chris Edley, who is a lawyer who advises the President on affirmative action policy, opens his talks by saying that affirmative action in matters of race is not rocket science; it's much harder. And I've come to appreciate that. For us to make progress on these issues, we're going to have to do more than just be guided by broad ideological and value positions, which is the way we tend to reflexively respond to these issues. We also have to understand the specifics involved, the social psychology of these situations. And I feel very optimistic about that.

The Nature of Prejudice: What Is the Problem?

Originally published in 1954, Gordon Allport's classic book, *The Nature of Prejudice,* was one of the first sources of clear, scientific thinking about this topic. This selection, which was taken from that book, points out that prejudice involves prejudgment and generalization, two processes that are common and not *necessarily* bad. However, when the generalization is faulty and inflexible and when a person is judged just because of his or her membership in a group, then we are dealing with prejudice. While prejudice involves beliefs, Allport notes that discrimination involves unfair treatment and represents the acting out of prejudice.

The word *prejudice,* derived from the Latin noun *praejudicium,* has, like most words, undergone a change of meaning since classical times. There are three stages in the transformation.

1. To the ancients, *praejudicium* meant a *precedent*—a judgment based on previous decisions and experiences.
2. Later, the term, in English, acquired the meaning of a judgment formed before due examination and consideration of the facts—a premature or hasty judgment.
3. Finally the term acquired also its present emotional flavor of favorableness or unfavorableness that accompanies such a prior and unsupported judgment.

Perhaps the briefest of all definitions of prejudice is: *thinking ill of others without sufficient warrant.* This crisp phrasing contains the two essential ingredients of all definitions—reference to unfounded judgment and to a feeling-tone. It is, however, too brief for complete clarity.

In the first place, it refers only to *negative* prejudice. People may be prejudiced in favor of others; they may think *well* of them without sufficient warrant. The wording offered by the New English Dictionary recognizes positive as well as negative prejudice:

> A feeling, favorable or unfavorable, toward a person or thing, prior to, or not based on, actual experience.

While it is important to bear in mind that biases may be *pro* as well as *con,* it is none the less true that *ethnic* prejudice is mostly negative. A group of students was asked to describe their attitudes toward ethnic groups. No suggestion was made that might lead them toward negative reports. Even so, they reported eight times as many antagonistic attitudes as favorable attitudes. In this volume, accordingly, we shall be concerned chiefly with prejudice *against,* not with prejudice *in favor of,* ethnic groups.

The phrase "thinking ill of others" is obviously an elliptical expression that must be understood to include feelings of scorn or dislike, of fear and aversion, as well as various forms of antipathetic conduct: such as talking against people, discriminating against them, or attacking them with violence.

Similarly, we need to expand the phrase "without sufficient warrant." A judgment is unwarranted whenever it lacks basis in fact. A wit defined prejudice as "being down on something you're not up on."

It is not easy to say how much fact is required in order to justify a judgment. A prejudiced person will almost certainly claim that he has sufficient warrant for his views. He will tell of bitter experiences he has had with refugees, Catholics, or Orientals. But, in most cases, it is evident that his facts are scanty and strained. He resorts to a selective sorting of his own few memories, mixes them up with hearsay, and overgeneralizes. No one can possibly know *all* refugees, Catholics, or Orientals. Hence any negative judgment of these groups *as a whole* is, strictly speaking, an instance of thinking ill without sufficient warrant.

Sometimes, the ill-thinker has no first-hand experience on which to base his judgment. A few years ago most Americans thought exceedingly ill of Turks—but very few had ever seen a Turk nor did they know any person who had seen one. Their warrant lay exclusively in what they had heard of the Armenian massacres and of the legendary crusades. On such evidence they presumed to condemn all members of a nation.

Ordinarily, prejudice manifests itself in dealing with individual members of rejected groups. But in avoiding a Negro neighbor, or in answering "Mr. Greenberg's" application for a room, we frame our action to accord with our categorical generalization of the group as a whole. We pay little or no attention to individual differences, and overlook the important fact that Negro X, our neighbor, is not Negro Y whom we dislike for good and sufficient reason; that Mr. Greenberg, who may be a fine gentleman, is not Mr. Bloom, whom we have good reason to dislike.

So common is this process that we might define prejudice as:

an avertive or hostile attitude toward a person who belongs to a group, simply because he belongs to that group, and is therefore presumed to have the objectionable qualities ascribed to the group.

This definition stresses the fact that while ethnic prejudice in daily life is ordinarily a matter of dealing with individual people it also entails an unwarranted idea concerning a group as a whole.

Returning to the question of "sufficient warrant," we must grant that few if any human judgments are based on absolute certainty. We can be reasonably, but not absolutely, sure that the sun will rise tomorrow, and that death and taxes will finally overtake us. The sufficient warrant for any judgment is always a matter of probabilities. Ordinarily our judgments of natural happenings are based on firmer and higher probabilities than our judgments of people. Only rarely do our categorical judgments of nations or ethnic groups have a foundation in high probability.

Take the hostile view of Nazi leaders held by most Americans during World War II. Was it prejudiced? The answer is No, because there was abundant available evidence regarding the evil policies and practices accepted as the official code of the party. True, there may have been good individuals in the party who at heart rejected the abominable program; but the probability was so high that the Nazi group constituted an actual menace to world peace and to humane values that a realistic and justified conflict resulted. The high probability of danger removes an antagonism from the domain of prejudice into that of realistic social conflict.

In the case of gangsters, our antagonism is not a matter of prejudice, for the evidence of their antisocial conduct is conclusive. But soon the line becomes hard to draw. How about an ex-convict? It is notoriously difficult for an ex-convict to obtain a steady job where he can be self-supporting and self-respecting. Employers naturally are suspicious if they know the man's past record. But often they are more suspicious than the facts warrant. If they looked further they might find evidence that the man who stands before them is genuinely reformed, or even that he was unjustly accused in the first place. To shut the door merely because a man has a criminal record has *some* probability in its favor, for many prisoners are never reformed; but there is also an element of unwarranted prejudgment involved. We have here a true borderline instance.

We can never hope to draw a hard and fast line between "sufficient" and "insufficient" warrant. For this reason we cannot always be sure whether we are dealing with a case of prejudice or nonprejudice. Yet no one will deny that often we form judgments on the basis of scant, even nonexistent, probabilities.

Overcategorization is perhaps the commonest trick of the human mind. Given a thimbleful of facts we rush to make generalizations as large as a tub. One young boy developed the idea that all Norwegians were giants because he was impressed by the gigantic stature of Ymir in the sagas, and for years was fearful lest he meet a living Norwegian. A certain man happened to know three Englishmen personally and proceed to declare that the whole English race had the common attributes that he observed in these three.

There is a natural basis for this tendency. Life is so short, and the demands upon us for practical adjustments so great, that we cannot let our ignorance detain us in our daily transactions. We have to decide whether objects are good or bad by classes. We cannot weigh each object in the world by itself. Rough and ready rubrics, however coarse and broad, have to suffice.

Not every overblown generalization is a prejudice. Some are simply *misconceptions,* wherein we organize wrong information. One child had the idea that all people living in Minneapolis were "monopolists." And from his father he had learned that monopolists were evil folk. When in later years he discovered the confusion, his dislike of dwellers in Minneapolis vanished.

Here we have the test to help us distinguish between ordinary errors of prejudgment and prejudice. If a person is capable of rectifying his erroneous judgments in th light of new evidence he is not prejudiced. *Prejudgments become prejudices only if they are not reversible when exposed to new knowledge.* A prejudice, unlike a simple misconception, is actively resistant to all evidence that would unseat it. We tend to grow emotional when a prejudice is threatened with contradiction. Thus the difference between ordinary prejudgments and prejudice is that one can discuss and rectify a prejudgment without emotional resistance.

Taking these various considerations into account, we may now attempt a final definition of negative ethnic prejudice—one that will serve us throughout this book. Each phrase in the definition represents a considerable condensation of the points we have been discussing:

> Ethnic prejudice is an antipathy based upon a faulty and inflexible generalization. It may be felt or expressed. It may be directed toward a group as a whole, or toward an individual because he is a member of that group.

The net effect of prejudice, thus defined, is to place the object of prejudice at some disadvantage not merited by his own misconduct.

ACTING OUT PREJUDICE

What people actually do in relation to groups they dislike is not always directly related to what they think or feel about them. Two employers, for example, may dislike Jews to an equal degree. One may keep his feelings to himself and may hire Jews on the same basis as any workers—perhaps because he wants to gain goodwill for his factory or store in the Jewish community. The other may translate his dislike into his employment policy, and refuse to hire Jews. Both men are prejudiced, but only one of them practices *discrimination.* As a rule, discrimination has more immediate and serious social consequences than has prejudice.

It is true that any negative attitude tends somehow, somewhere, to express itself in action. Few people keep their antipathies entirely to themselves. The more intense the attitude, the more likely it is to result in vigorously hostile action.

We may venture to distinguish certain degrees of negative action from the least energetic to the most.

1. *Antilocution.* Most people who have prejudices talk about them. With like-minded friends, occasionally with strangers, they may express their antagonism freely. But many people never go beyond this mild degree of antipathetic action.
2. *Avoidance.* If the prejudice is more intense, it leads the individual to avoid members of the disliked group, even perhaps at the cost of considerable inconvenience. In this case, the bearer of prejudice does not directly inflict harm upon the group he dislikes. He takes the burden of accommodation and withdrawal entirely upon himself.
3. *Discrimination.* Here the prejudiced person makes detrimental distinctions

of the active sort. He undertakes to exclude all members of the group in question from certain types of employment, from residential housing, political rights, educational or recreational opportunities, churches, hospitals, or from some other social privileges. Segregation is an institutionalized form of discrimination, enforced legally or by common custom.

4. *Physical attack.* Under conditions of heightened emotion, prejudice may lead to acts of violence or semiviolence. An unwanted Negro family may be forcibly ejected from a neighborhood, or so severely threatened that it leaves in fear. Gravestones in Jewish cemeteries may be desecrated. The Northside's Italian gang may lie in wait for the Southside's Irish gang.

5. *Extermination.* Lynchings, pogroms, massacres, and the Hitlerian program of genocide mark the ultimate degree of violent expression of prejudice.

This five-point scale is not mathematically constructed, but it serves to call attention to the enormous range of activities that may issue from prejudiced attitudes and beliefs. While many people would never move from antilocution to avoidance; or from avoidance to active discrimination, or higher on the scale, still it is true that activity on one level makes transition to a more intense level easier. It was Hitler's antilocution that led Germans to avoid their Jewish neighbors and erstwhile friends. This preparation made it easier to enact the Nürnberg laws of discrimination which, in turn, made the subsequent burning of synagogues and street attacks upon Jews seem natural. The final step in the macabre progression was the ovens at Auschwitz.

From the point of view of social consequences, much "polite prejudice" is harmless enough—being confined to idle chatter. But unfortunately, the fateful progression is, in this century, growing in frequency. The resulting disruption in the human family is menacing. And as the peoples of the earth grow ever more interdependent, they can tolerate less well the mounting friction.

Race and the Schooling of Black Americans

Claude Steele's article from the *Atlantic Monthly* is a perceptive and troubling analysis of why black children are more likely than their white counterparts to fail in school. Steel notes the subtle and not-so-subtle ways that lead young blacks to "disidentify" with school, to resist measuring themselves against the values and goals of the classroom. He advocates the concept of "wise schooling," in which teachers and classmates see value and promise in black children rather than the opposite. Although he does not refer directly to them, note how Steele's analysis fits very well with modern social psychological theories about the development and maintenance of self-esteem.

My former university offered minority students a faculty mentor to help shepherd them into college life. As soon as I learned of the program, I volunteered to be a mentor, but by then the school year was nearly over. Undaunted, the program's eager staff matched me with a student on their waiting list—an appealing nineteen-year-old black woman from Detroit, the same age as my daughter. We met finally in a campus lunch spot just about two weeks before the close of her freshman year. I realized quickly that I was too late. I have heard that the best way to diagnose someone's depression is to note how depressed you feel when you leave the person. When our lunch was over, I felt as gray as the snowbanks that often lined the path back to my office. My lunchtime companion was a statistic brought to life, a living example of one of the most disturbing facts of racial life in America today: the failure of so many black Americans to thrive in school. Before I could lift a hand to help this student, she had decided to do what 70 percent of all black Americans at four-year colleges do at some point in their academic careers—drop out.

I sense a certain caving-in of hope in America that problems of race can be solved. Since the sixties, when race relations held promise for the dawning of a new era, the issue has become one whose persistence causes "problem fatigue"—resignation to an unwanted condition of life.

This fatigue, I suspect, deadens us to the deepening crisis in the education of black Americans. One can enter any desegregated school in America, from grammar school to high school to graduate or professional school, and meet a persistent reality: blacks and whites in largely separate worlds. And if one asks a few questions or looks at a few records, another reality emerges: these worlds are not equal, either in the education taking place there or in the achievement of the students who occupy them.

As a social scientist, I know that the crisis has enough possible causes to give anyone problem fatigue. But at a personal level, perhaps because of my experience as a black in American schools, or perhaps just as the hunch of a myopic psychologist, I have long suspected a particular culprit—a culprit that can undermine black achievement as effectively as a lock on a schoolhouse door. The culprit I see is *stigma,* the endemic devaluation many blacks face in our society and schools. This status is its own condition of life, different from class, money, culture. It is capable, in the words of the late sociologist Erving Goffman, of "breaking the claim" that one's human attributes have on people. I believe that its connection to school achievement among black Americans has been vastly unappreciated.

This is a troublesome argument, touching as it does on a still unhealed part of American race relations. But it leads us to a heartening principle: if blacks are made less racially vulnerable in school, they can overcome even substantial obstacles. Before the good news, though, I must at least sketch in the bad: the worsening crisis in the education of black Americans.

Despite their socioeconomic disadvantages as a group, blacks begin school with test scores that are fairly close to the test scores of whites their age. The longer they stay in school, however, the more they fall behind; for example, by the sixth grade blacks in many school districts are two full grade levels behind whites in achievement. This pattern holds true in the middle class nearly as much as in the lower class. The record does not improve in high school. In 1980, for example, 25,500 minority students, largely black and Hispanic, entered high school in Chicago, Four years later only 9,500 graduated, and of those only 2,000 could read at grade level. The situation in other cities is comparable.

Even for blacks who make it to college, the problem doesn't go away. As I noted, 70 percent of all black students who enroll in four-year colleges drop out at some point, as compared with 45 percent of whites. At any given time nearly as many black males are incarcerated as are in college in this country. And the grades of black college students average half a letter below those of their white classmates. At one prestigious university I recently studied, only 18 percent of the graduating black students had grade averages of B or above, as compared with 64 percent of the whites. This pattern is the rule, not the exception, in even the most elite American colleges. Tragically, low grades can render a degree essentially "terminal" in the sense that they preclude further schooling.

Blacks in graduate and professional schools face a similarly worsening or stagnating fate. For example, from 1977 to 1990, though the number of Ph.D.s awarded to other minorities increased and the number awarded to whites stayed roughly the same, the number awarded to American blacks dropped from 1,116 to 828. And blacks needed more time to get those degrees.

Standing ready is a familiar set of explanations. First is societal disadvantage. Black Americans have had, and continue to have, more than their share: a history of slavery, segregation, and job ceilings; continued lack of economic opportunity; poor schools; and the related problems of broken families, drug-infested communities, and social isolation. Any of these factors—alone, in combination, or through accumulated effects—can undermine school achievement. Some analysts point also to black American culture, suggesting that, hampered by disadvantage, it doesn't sustain the values and expectations critical to education, or that it fosters learning orientations ill suited to school achievement, or that it even "opposes" mainstream achievement. These are the chestnuts, and I had always thought them adequate. Then several facts emerged that just didn't seem to fit.

For one thing, the achievement deficits occur even when black students suffer no major financial disadvantage—among middle-class students on wealthy college campuses and in graduate school among black students receiving substantial financial aid. For another thing, survey after survey shows that even poor black Americans value education highly, often more than whites. Also, as I will demonstrate, several programs have improved black school achievement without addressing culturally specific learning orientations or doing anything to remedy socioeconomic disadvantage.

Neither is the problem fully explained, as one might assume, by deficits in skill or preparation which blacks might suffer because of background disadvantages. I first doubted that such a connection existed when I saw flunk-out rates for black and white students at a large, prestigious university. Two observations surprised me. First, for both blacks and whites the level of preparation, as measured by Scholastic Aptitude Test scores, didn't make much difference in who flunked out; low scores (with combined verbal and quantitative SATs of 800) were no more likely to flunk out than high scores (with combined SATs of 1,200 to 1,500). The second observation was racial: whereas only two percent to 11 percent of the whites flunked out, 18 percent to 33 percent of the blacks flunked out, even at the highest levels of preparation (combined SATs of 1,400). Dinesh D'Souza has argued recently that college affirmative-action programs cause failure and high dropout rates among black students by recruiting them to levels of college work for which they are inadequately prepared. That was clearly not the case at this school; black students flunked out in large numbers even with preparation well above average.

And, sadly, this proved the rule, not the exception. From elementary school to graduate school, something depresses black achievement *at every level of preparation, even the highest.* Generally, of course, the better prepared achieve better than the less prepared, and this is about as true for blacks as for whites. But given any level of school preparation (as measured by tests and earlier grades), blacks somehow achieve less in subsequent schooling than whites (that is, have poorer grades, have lower graduation rates, and take longer to graduate), no matter how strong that preparation is. Put differently, the same achievement level requires better preparation for blacks than for whites—far better: among students with a C+ average at the university I just described, the mean American College Testing Program (ACT) score for blacks was at the 98th percentile, while for whites it was at only the 34th percentile. This pattern has been documented so broadly across so many regions of the country, and by so many investigations (literally hundreds), that it is virtually a social law in this society—as well as a racial tragedy.

Clearly, something is missing from our understanding of black underachievement. Disadvantage contributes, yet blacks underachieve even when they have ample resources, strongly value education, and are prepared better than adequately in terms of knowledge and skills. Something else has to be involved. That something else could be of just modest importance—a barrier that simply adds its effect to that of other disadvantages—or it could be pivotal, such that were it corrected, other disadvantages would lose their effect.

That something else, I believe, has to do with the process of identifying with school. I offer a personal example:

I remember conducting experiments with my research adviser early in graduate school and awaiting the results with only modest interest. I struggled to meet deadlines. The research enterprise—the core of what one does as a social psychologist—just wasn't *me* yet. I was in school for other reasons—I wanted an advanced degree, I was vaguely ambitious for intellectual work, and being in graduate school made my parents proud of me. But as time passed, I began to like the work. I also began to grasp the value system that gave it meaning, and the faculty treated me as if they thought I might even be able to do it. Gradually I began to think of myself as a social psychologist. With this change in self-concept came a new accountability; my self-esteem was affected now by what I did as a social psychologist, something that hadn't been true before. This added a new motivation to my work; self-respect, not just parental respect, was on the line. I noticed changes in myself. I worked without deadlines. I bored friends with applications of arcane theory to their daily lives. I went to conventions. I lived and died over how experiments came out.

Before this transition one might have said that I was handicapped by my black working-class background and lack of motivation. After the transition the same observer might say that even though my background was working-class, I had special advantages: achievement-oriented parents, a small and attentive college. But these facts alone would miss the importance of the identification process I had experienced: the change in self-definition and in the activities on which I based my self-esteem. They would also miss a simple condition necessary for me to make this identification: treatment as a valued person with good prospects.

I believe that the "something else" at the root of black achievement problems is the failure of American schooling to meet this simple condition for many of its black students. Doing well in school requires a belief that school achievement can be a promising basis of self-esteem, and that belief needs constant reaffirmation even for advantaged students. Tragically, I believe, the lives of black Americans are still haunted by a specter that threatens this belief and the identification that derived from it at every level of schooling.

THE SPECTER OF STIGMA AND RACIAL VULNERABILITY

I have a good friend, the mother of three, who spends considerable time in the public school classrooms of Seattle, where she lives. In her son's third-grade room, managed by a teacher of unimpeachable good will and competence, she noticed over many visits that the extraordinary art work of a small black boy named Jerome was ignored—or, more accurately perhaps, its significance was ignored. As a genuine art talent has a way of doing—even in the third grade—his stood out. Yet the teacher seemed hardly to notice. Moreover, Jerome's reputation, as it was passed along from one grade to the next, included only the slightest mention of his talent. Now, of course, being ignored like this could happen to anyone—such is the overload in our public schools. But my friend couldn't help wondering how the school would have responded to this talent had the artist been one of her own, middle-class white children.

Terms like "prejudice" and "racism" often miss the full scope of racial devaluation in our society, implying as they do that racial devaluation comes primarily from the strongly prejudiced, not from "good people" like Jerome's teacher. But the prevalence of racists—deplorable through racism is—misses the full extent of Jerome's burden, perhaps even the most profound part.

He faces a devaluation that grows out of our images of society and the way those images catalogue people. The catalogue need never be taught. It is implied by all we see around us: the kinds of people revered in advertising (consider the unrelenting racial advocacy of Ralph Lauren ads) and movies (black women are rarely seen as romantic partners, for example); media discussions of whether a black can be President; invitation lists to junior high school birthday parties; school curricula; literary and musical canons. These details create an image of society in which black Americans simply do not fare well. When I was a kid, we captured it with the saying "If you're white you're right, if you're yellow you're mellow, if you're brown stick around, but if you're black get back."

In ways that require no fueling from strong prejudice or stereotypes, these images expand the devaluation of black Americans. They act as mental standards against which information about blacks is evaluated: that which fits these images we accept; that which contradicts them we suspect. Had Jerome had a reading problem, which fits these images, it might have been accepted as characteristic more readily than his extraordinary art work, which contradicts them.

These images do something else as well, something especially pernicious in the classroom. They set up a jeopardy of double devaluation for blacks, a jeopardy that does not apply to whites. Like anyone, blacks risk devaluation for a particular incompetence, such as failed test or a flubbed pronunciation. But they further risk that such performances will confirm the broader, racial inferiority they are suspected of. Thus, from the first grade through graduate school, blacks have the extra fear that in the eyes of those around them their full humanity could fall with a poor answer or a mistaken stroke of the pen.

Moreover, because these images are conditioned in all of us, collectively held, they can spawn racial devaluation in all of us, not just in the strongly prejudiced. They can do this even in blacks themselves: a majority of black children recently tested said they like and prefer to play with white rather than black dolls—almost fifty years after Kenneth and Mamie Clark, conducting similar experiments, documented identical findings and so paved the way for *Brown v. Topeka Board of*

Education. Thus Jerome's devaluation can come from a circle of people in his world far greater than the expressly prejudiced—a circle that apparently includes his teacher.

In ways often too subtle to be conscious but sometimes overt, I believe, blacks remain devalued in American schools, where, for example, a recent national survey shows that through high school they are still more than twice as likely as white children to receive corporal punishment, be suspended from school, or be labeled mentally retarded.

Tragically, such devaluation can seem inescapable. Sooner or later it forces on its victims two painful realizations. The first is that society is preconditioned to see the worst in them. Black students quickly learn that acceptance, if it is to be won at all, will be hard-won. The second is that even if a black student achieves exoneration in one setting—with the teacher and fellow students in one classroom, or at one level of schooling, for example—this approval will have to be rewon in the next classroom, at the next level of schooling. Of course, individual characteristics that enhance one's value in society—skills, class status, appearance, and success—can diminish the racial devaluation one faces. And sometimes the effort to prove oneself fuels achievement. But few from any group could hope to sustain so daunting and everlasting a struggle. Thus, I am afraid, too many black students are left hopeless and deeply vulnerable in America's classrooms.

"DISIDENTIFYING" WITH SCHOOL

I believe that in significant part the crisis in black Americans' education stems from the power of this vulnerability to undercut identification with schooling, either before it happens or after it has bloomed.

Jerome is an example of the first kind. At precisely the time when he would need to see school as a viable source of self-esteem, his teachers fail to appreciate his best work. The devalued status of his race devalues him and his work in the classroom. Unable to entrust his sense of himself to this place, he resists measuring himself against its values and goals. He languishes there, held by the law, perhaps even by his parents, but not allowing achievement to affect his view of himself. This psychic alienation—the act of not caring—makes him less vulnerable to the specter of devaluation that haunts him. Bruce Hare, an educational researcher, has documented this process among fifth-grade boys in several schools in Champaign, Illinois. He found that although the black boys had considerably lower achievement-test scores than their white classmates, their overall self-esteem was just as high. This stunning imperviousness to poor academic performance was accomplished, he found, by their deemphasizing school achievement as a basis of self-esteem and giving preference to peer-group relations—a domain in which their esteem prospects were better. They went where they had to go to feel good about themselves.

But recall the young reader whose mentor I was. She had already identified with school, and wanted to be a doctor. How can racial vulnerability break so developed an achievement identity? To see, let us follow her steps onto campus: Her recruitment and admission stress her minority status perhaps more strongly than it has been stressed at any other time in her life. She is offered academic and social support services, further implying that she is "at risk" (even though, contrary to common belief, the vast majority of black college students are admitted with qualifications well above the threshold for whites). Once on campus, she enters a socially circumscribed world in which blacks—still largely separate from whites—have lower status; this is reinforced by sidelining of minority material and interests in the curriculum and in university life. And she can sense that everywhere in this new world her skin color places her under suspicion of intellectual inferiority. All of this gives her the double vulnerability I spoke of: she risks confirming a particular incompetence, at chemistry or a foreign language, for example; but she also risks confirming the racial inferiority she is suspect of—a judgment that can feel as close at hand as a mispronounced word or an ungrammatical sentence. In reaction, usually to some modest setback, she withdraws, hiding her troubles from instructors, counselors, even other students. Quickly, I believe, a psychic defense takes over. She *disidentifies* with achievement; she changes her self-conception, her outlook and values, so that achievement is no longer so important to her self-esteem. She may continue to feel pressure to stay in school—from her parents, even from the potential advantages of a college degree. But now she is psychologically insulated from her academic life, like a disinterested visitor, cool, unperturbed. But, like a pain-killing drug, disidentification undoes her future as it relieves her vulnerability.

The prevalence of this syndrome among black college students has been documented extensively, especially on predominantly white campuses. Summarizing this work, Jacqueline Fleming, a psychologist, writes, "The fact that black students must matriculate in an atmosphere that feels hostile arouses defensive reactions that interfere with intellectual performance. . . . They display academic demotivation and think less of their abilities. They profess losses of energy." Among a sample of blacks on one predominantly white campus, Richard Nisbett and Andrew Reaves, both psychologists, and I found that attitudes related to disidentification were more strongly predictive of grades than even academic preparation (that is, SATs and high school grades).

To make matters worse, once disidentification occurs in a school, it can spread like the common cold. Blacks who identify and try to achieve embarrass the strategy by valuing the very thing the strategy denies the value of. Thus pressure to make it a group norm can evolve quickly and become fierce. Defectors are called "oreos" or "incognegroes." One's identity as an authentic black is held hostage, made incompatible with school identification. For black students, then, pressure to disidentify with school can come from the already demoralized as well as from racial vulnerability in the setting.

Stigmatization of the sort suffered by black Americans is probably also a barrier to the school achievement of other groups in our society, such as lower-class whites, Hispanics, and women in male-dominated fields. For example, at a large midwestern university I studied women who matched men's achievement in the liberal arts, where they suffer no marked stigma, but underachieved compared with men (get lower grades than men with the same ACT scores) in engineering and premedical programs, where they, like blacks across the board, are more vulnerable to suspicions to inferiority.

"WISE" SCHOOLING

"When they approach me they see . . . everything and anything except me. . . .
[This] invisibility occurs because of a peculiar disposition of the eyes. . . ."
Ralph Ellison, *Invisible Man*

Erving Goffman, borrowing from gays of the 1950s, used the term "wise" to describe people who don't themselves bear the stigma of a given group but who are accepted by the group. These are people in whose eyes the full humanity of the stigmatized is visible, people in whose eyes they feel less vulnerable. If racial vulnerability undermines black school achievement, as I have argued, then this achievement should improve significantly if schooling is made "wise"—that is, made to see value and promise in black students and to act accordingly.

And yet, although racial vulnerability at school may undermine black achievement, so many other factors seem to contribute—from the debilitations of poverty to the alleged dysfunctions of black American culture—that one might expect "wiseness" in the classroom to be of little help. Fortunately, we have considerable evidence to the contrary. Wise schooling may indeed be the missing key to the schoolhouse door.

In the mid-seventies black students in Philip Uri Treisman's early calculus courses at the University of California at Berkeley consistently fell to the bottom of every class. To help, Treisman developed the Mathematics Workshop Program, which, in a surprisingly short time, reversed their fortunes, causing them to outperform their white and Asian counterparts. And although it is only a freshman program, black students who take it graduate at a rate comparable to the Berkeley average. Its central technique is group study of calculus concepts. But it is also wise; it does things that allay the racial vulnerabilities of these students. Stressing their potential to learn, it recruits them to a challenging "honors" workshop tied to their first calculus course. Building on their skills, the workshop gives difficult work, often beyond course content, to students with even modest preparation (some of their math SATs dip to the 300s). Working together, students soon understand that everyone knows something and nobody knows everything, and learning is speeded through shared understanding. The wisdom of these tactics is their subtext message: "You are valued in this program because of your academic potential—regardless of your current skill level. You have no more to fear than the next person, and since the work is difficult, success is a credit to your ability, and a setback is a reflection only of the challenge." The black students' double vulnerability around failure—the fear that they lack ability, and the dread that they will be devalued—is thus reduced. They can relax and achieve. The movie *Stand and Deliver* depicts Jamie Escalante using the same techniques of assurance and challenge to inspire advanced calculus performance in East Los Angeles Chicano high schoolers. And, explaining Xavier University's extraordinary success in producing black medical students, a spokesman said recently, "What doesn't work is saying, 'You need remedial work.' What does work is saying, 'You may be somewhat behind at this time but you're a talented person. We're going to help you advance at an accelerated rate.'"

The work of James Comer, a child psychiatrist at Yale, suggests that wiseness can minimize even the barriers of poverty. Over a fifteen-year period he transformed the two worst elementary schools in New Haven, Connecticut, into the third and fifth best in the city's thirty-three-school system without any change in the type of students—largely poor and black. His guiding belief is that learning requires a strongly accepting relationship between teacher and student. "After all," he notes, "what is the difference between a scribble and a letter of the alphabet to a child? The only reason the letter is meaningful, and worth learning and remembering, is because a *meaningful* other wants him or her to learn and remember it." To build these relationships, Comer focuses on the over-all school climate, shaping it not so much to transmit specific skills or to achieve order per se, or even to improve achievement, as to establish a valuing and optimistic atmosphere in which a child can—to use his term—"identify" with learning. Responsibility for this lies with a team of ten to fifteen members, headed by the principal and made up of teachers, parents, school staff, and child-development experts (for example, psychologists or special-education teachers). The team develops a plan of specifics: teacher training, parent workshops, coordination of information about students. But at base I believe it tries to ensure that the students—vulnerable on so many counts—get treated essentially like middle-class students, with conviction about their value and promise. As this happens, their vulnerability diminishes, and with it the companion defenses of disidentification and misconduct. They achieve, and apparently identify, as their achievement gains persist into high school. Comer's genius, I believe, is to have recognized the importance of these vulnerabilities as barriers to *intellectual* development, and the corollary that schools hoping to educate such students must learn first how to make them feel valued.

These are not isolated successes. Comparable results were observed, for example, in a Comer-type program in Maryland's Prince Georges County, in the Stanford economist Henry Levin's accelerated-schools program, and in Harlem's Central Park East Elementary School, under the principalship of Deborah Meier. And research involving hundreds of programs and schools points to the same conclusion: black achievement is consistently linked to conditions of schooling that reduce racial vulnerability. These include relatively harmonious race relations among students, a commitment by teachers and schools to seeing minority-group members achieve, the instructional goal that students at all levels of preparation achieve, desegregation at the classroom as well as the school level, and a de-emphasis on ability tracking.

That erasing stigma improves black achievement is perhaps the strongest evidence that stigma is what depresses it in the first place. This is no happy realization. But it lets in a ray of hope: whatever other factors also depress black achievement—poverty, social isolation, poor preparation—they may be substantially overcome in a schooling atmosphere that reduces racial and other vulnerabilities, not through unrelenting niceness or ferocious regimentation but a wiseness, by *seeing* value and acting on it.

WHAT MAKES SCHOOLING UNWISE

But if wise schooling is so attainable, why is racial vulnerability the rule, not the exception, in American schooling?

One factor is the basic assimilationist offer that schools make to blacks: You can be valued and rewarded in school (and society), the schools say to these students, but you must first master the culture and ways of the American mainstream, and since that mainstream (as it is represented) is essentially white, this means you must give up many particulars of being black—styles of speech and appearance, value priorities, preferences—at least in mainstream settings. This is asking a lot. But it has been the "color-blind" offer to every immigrant and minority group in our nation's history, the core of the melting-pot ideal, and so I think it strikes most of us as fair. Yet non-immigrant minorities like blacks and Native Americans have always been here, and thus are entitled, more than new immigrants, to participate in the defining images of the society projected in school. More important, their exclusion from these images denies their contributive history and presence in society. Thus, whereas immigrants can tilt toward assimilation in pursuit of the opportunities for which they came, American blacks may find it harder to assimilate. For them, the offer of acceptance in return for assimilation carries a primal insult: it asks them to join in something that has made them invisible.

Now, I must be clear. This is not a criticism of Western civilization. My concern is an omission of image-work. In his incisive essay "What America Would Be Like Without Blacks," Ralph Ellison showed black influence on American speech and language, the themes of our finest literature, and our most defining ideals of personal freedom and democracy. In *The World They Made Together,* Mechal Sobel described how African and European influences shaped the early American South in everything from housing design and land use to religious expression. The fact is that blacks are not outside the American mainstream but, in Ellison's words, have always been "one of its major tributaries." Yet if one relied on what is taught in America's schools, one would never know this. There blacks have fallen victim to a collective self-deception, a society's allowing itself to assimilate like mad from its constituent groups while representing itself to itself as if the assimilation had never happened, as if progress and good were almost exclusively Western and white. A prime influence of American society on world culture is the music of black Americans, shaping art forms from rock-and-roll to modern dance. Yet in American schools, from kindergarten through graduate school, these essentially black influences have barely peripheral status, are largely outside the canon. Thus it is not what is taught but what is *not* taught, what teachers and professors have never learned the value of, that reinforces a fundamental unwiseness in American schooling, and keeps black disidentification on full boil.

Deep in the psyche of American educators is a presumption that black students need academic remediation, or extra time with elemental curricula to overcome background deficits. This orientation guides many efforts to close the achievement gap—from grammar school tutoring to college academic-support programs—but I fear it can be unwise. Bruno Bettelheim and Karen Zelan's article "Why Children Don't Like to Read" comes to mind: apparently to satisfy the changing sensibilities of local school boards over this century, many books that children like were dropped from school reading lists; when children's reading scores also dropped, the approved texts were replaced by simpler books; and when reading scores dropped again, these were replaced by even simpler books, until eventually the children could hardly read at all, not because the material was too difficult but because they were bored stiff. So it goes, I suspect, with a great many of these remediation efforts. Moreover, because so many such programs target blacks primarily, they virtually equate black identity with substandard intellectual status, amplifying racial vulnerability. They can even undermine students' ability to gain confidence from their achievement, by sharing credit for their successes while implying that their failures stem from inadequacies beyond the reach of remediation.

The psychologist Lisa Brown and I recently uncovered evidence of just how damaging this orientation may be. At a large, prestigious university we found that whereas the grades of black graduates of the 1950s improved during the students' college years until they virtually matched the school average, those of blacks who graduated in the 1980s (we chose only those with above-average entry credentials, to correct for more-liberal admissions policies in that decade) worsened, ending up considerably below the school average. The 1950s graduates faced outward discrimination in everything from housing to the classroom, whereas the 1980s graduates were supported by a phalanx of help programs. Many things may contribute to this pattern. The Jackie Robinson, "pioneer" spirit of the 1950s blacks surely helped them endure. And in a pre-affirmative-action era, they may have been seen as intellectually more deserving. But one cannot ignore the distinctive fate of the 1980s blacks: a remedial orientation put their abilities under suspicion, deflected their ambitions, distanced them from their successes, and painted them with their failures. Black students on today's campuses may experience far less overt prejudice than their 1950s counterparts but, ironically, may be more racially vulnerable.

THE ELEMENTS OF WISENESS

For too many black students school is simply the place where, more concertedly, persistently, and authoritatively than anywhere else in society, they learn how little valued they are.

Clearly, no simple recipe can fix this, but I believe we now understand the basics of a corrective approach. Schooling must focus more on reducing the vulnerabilities that block identification with achievement. I believe that four conditions, like the legs of a stool, are fundamental.

- If what is meaningful and important to a teacher is to become meaningful and important to a student, the student must feel valued by the teacher for his or her potential as a person. Among the more fortunate in society, this relationship is often taken for granted. But it is precisely the relationship that race can still undermine in American society. As Comer, Escalante, and Treisman have shown, when one's students bear race and class vulnerabilities, building this relationship is the first order of business—at all levels of schooling. No tactic of instruction, no matter how ingenious, can succeed without it.
- The challenge and the promise of personal fulfillment, not remediation (under whatever guise), should guide the education of these students. Their present

skills should be taken into account, and they should be moved along at a pace that is demanding but doesn't defeat them. Their ambitions should never be scaled down but should instead be guided to inspiring goals even when extraordinary dedication is called for. Frustration will be less crippling than alienation. Here psychology is everything: remediation defeats, challenge strengthens—affirming their potential, crediting them with their achievements, inspiring them.

But the first condition, I believe, cannot work without the second, and vice versa. A valuing teacher-student relationship goes nowhere without challenge, and challenge will always be resisted outside a valuing relationship. (Again, I must be careful about something: in criticizing remediation I am not opposing affirmative-action recruitment in the schools. The success of this policy, like that of school integration before it, depends, I believe, on the tactics of implementation. Where students are valued and challenged, they generally succeed.)

- Racial integration is a generally useful element in this design, if not a necessity. Segregation, whatever its purpose, draws out group differences and makes people feel more vulnerable when they inevitably cross group lines to compete in the larger society. This vulnerability, I fear, can override confidence gained in segregated schooling unless that confidence is based on strongly competitive skills and knowledge—something that segregated schooling, plagued by shortages of resources and access, has difficulty producing.

- The particulars of black life and culture—art, literature, political and social perspective, music—must be presented in the mainstream curriculum of American schooling, not consigned to special days, weeks, or even months of the year, or to special-topic courses and programs aimed essentially at blacks. Such channeling carries the disturbing message that the material is not of general value. And this does two terrible things: it wastes the power of this material to alter our images of the American mainstream—continuing to frustrate black identification with it—and it excuses in whites and others a huge ignorance of their own society. The true test of democracy, Ralph Ellison has said, is "the inclusion—not assimilation—of the black man."

Finally, if I might be allowed a word specifically to black parents, one issue is even more immediate: our children may drop out of school before the first committee meets to accelerate the curriculum. Thus, although we, along with all Americans, must strive constantly for wise schooling, I believe we cannot wait for it. We cannot yet forget our essentially heroic challenge: to foster in our children a sense of hope and entitlement to mainstream American life and schooling.

H. Andrew Sagar
Janet Ward Schofield

Racial and Behavioral Cues in Black and White Children's Perceptions of Ambiguously Aggressive Acts

Sagar and Schofield studied the effect of stereotypes on our perceptions by presenting black and white sixth graders with ambiguous situations that are likely to happen in school (such as two students bumping into one another, or one requesting food from another). As they predicted, both black and white children rated these behaviors as more mean and more threatening when the perpetrator was black than white. In addition, though both groups were subject to this effect, the white children were more likely to read threat into those situations where no physical contact was involved. Given the inherent unfairness of this, you might consider how it would be possible to overcome this tendency and see each person's actions, threatening or not, independent of his or her race.

A recent study by Duncal (1976) suggests that perceptions of an ambiguously aggressive act can be influenced to a remarkable degree by the race of the actor. White male college students coded behaviors observed in what they thought was a live dyadic interaction on a television monitor. The ambiguous shove that concluded the increasingly heated argument on the monitor was coded as violent behavior by 35 of the 48 persons who saw a black actor shove another person. Of the 48 students who saw a presumably identical act by a white actor, only 6 used the violent behavior code. Duncan argued that because of stereotypes associating blacks with violence, the violent behavior category is cognitively more accessible to subjects viewing a black perpetrator than to those viewing a white one.

Duncan's (1976) study raises at least three important questions, the first of which is methodological: Were the stimulus tapes completely comparable so that the subjects' differential responses can be attributed solely to racial cues rather than to subtle differences in the behavior of the black and white actors? Second, assuming the manipulation to be valid, is the phenomenon Duncan demonstrated unique to whites, or might black subjects have responded in a similar fashion? Finally, is the violent black stereotype applied selectively to blacks who engage in potentially confirmatory behavior, or does it bias perceptions even of those blacks whose behavior is clearly nonconfirmatory?

Since the methodological question poses a potentially serious threat to Duncan's (1976) findings, we will discuss it first. Duncan sought to make the taped interactions used in his research conceptually, rather than literally, identical to each other. Although this strategy probably made the tapes realistic, it leaves open the question of whether the subjects' differential responses to blacks and whites were based on visual race cues, as Duncan contended, or on variations in the verbal and behavioral styles of the actors.

The experimental realism achieved in Duncan's scenario may have been high; nevertheless, confidence in the experiment's conclusions would be greatly increased if similar results could be obtained with stimuli whose precise comparability could be more clearly documented.

A second question, raised by the fact that all of Duncan's subjects were white, is whether the biased perception of blacks' behavior revealed by that study is unique to whites. It is easy to assume that the tendency to code the black actor's behavior as violent represents a motivated response to a negatively valued outgroup. Cooper and Fazio (1979), for example, argued that observers often deem it safer to infer the worst about out-group members than to risk a premature lowering of their cognitive guard. Negative characterizations of outgroup members may also reflect a desire for the relative enhancement of the ingroup. For example, Howard and Rothbart (1980) found that subjects who believed that their group assignment implied something fundamental about their psychological characteristics associated more negative and fewer positive statements with the experimentally created outgroup than with their own group. Either of these motives might be expected to contribute to symmetrical responses by black and white subjects, with each group inferring greater violence on the part of the other.

In contrast, a considerable body of research in desegregated schools indicates that both black and white students tend to link blacks with concepts of threat, aggression, and violence, although the link appears generally stronger in the minds of whites (Clement, Eisenhart, & Harding, 1979; Patchen, Hoffmann, & Davidson, 1976; Scherer & Slawski, 1979; Schofield, in press). These shared perceptions may well derive in part from observation of actual behavioral differences between members of the two groups, which are commonly characterized by unequal socioeconomic and academic status within the same school. In addition, Hamilton and Gifford (1976) have demonstrated that a cognitive bias, such as illusory correlation (Chapman, 1967), can produce discrepant impressions of different groups apart from any motivational or objective considerations. Also, Tversky and Kahneman (1974) have demonstrated several other cognitive biases that, by logical extension, might be expected to affect blacks' and whites' perceptions of social groups in similar ways. In the absence of overriding ingroup-enhancement motives, then, blacks and whites exposed to similar behavioral evidence should process it via the same cognitive shortcuts, with shared stereotypic beliefs as the expected result.

We hypothesized that, like Duncan's white college population, the preadolescent white children participating in the present study would consider ambiguously aggressive behaviors to be more mean and threatening (and less playful and friendly) when these behaviors were attributed to a black rather than to a white peer. Furthermore, the literature on black and white children's racial beliefs, as well as our own extensive observations in the school from which our subjects were selected, led us to hypothesize, somewhat more tentatively, that a similar pattern of responses would be evidenced by black children.

One final question derives from Duncan's use of the concept of category accessibility to explain his results. Stereotypes, often by definition, are generally assumed to affect impressions of all members of the stereotyped group (Brigham, 1971). In contrast, Bruner's (1957) discussion of category accessibility raises the possibility that the violent-black stereotype may bias trait attributions to persons who engage in stereotype-relevant behavior without influencing responses to those who do not. That is, a black person performing an ambiguously aggressive action may be more readily categorized as violent and therefore be considered a more violent person than an identically behaving white; in contrast, a clearly nonaggressive black may not be considered any more violent than his or her white counterpart because nothing in his or her behavior brings the violent-black stereotype to mind. Such a response pattern, if found, would help to explain how persons who are convinced that they judge each black person as an individual might nevertheless overestimate the physical aggressiveness of blacks as a group.

It is of course possible that the association of blacks with threat and violence influences the perception of all black stimulus persons. If such be the case, even those black persons whose observed behavior is clearly nonaggressive should be considered to have a somewhat less nonviolent disposition than identically behaving white persons. The Duncan study, in focusing solely on the shove and its perpetrator, did not address this issue. We assumed that ratings of individuals' personal characteristics relating to threat and violence, such as the extent to which they are mean, rude, unfriendly, and so forth, would be influenced primarily by whether they were the initiator or the target of the ambiguously aggressive act. A more interesting prediction, flowing from the work on category accessibility, was that black initiators would be judged even more negatively than white initiators because of the ready availability of relevant black stereotypes, whereas the passive black and passive white targets of these acts would be judged similar to each other.

Although we expected both black and white subjects' ratings of behaviors to be influenced by racial cues, we also anticipated that the two subject groups would respond differently to the behaviors per se, independently of racial cues. The work by Triandis and his colleagues on subjective culture (Triandis, 1976; Triandis, Vassiliou, Vassiliou, Tanaka, & Shanmugam, 1972) provides a clear basis for anticipating different interpretations of specific behaviors by black and white subjects. This work has shown that persons from different culture groups (including, occasionally, black and white Americans) often make different causal attributions for the same behavior, with interpersonal misunderstanding as the result. For example, if physically assertive actions are both more common and more functional in the black ghetto than in the surrounding middle-class areas, as Maruyama (cited in Triandis, 1976) has concluded, then ghetto residents might have higher thresholds for perceiving such actions (or those who perform them) negatively, independently of the actor's race. Thus, we predicted that the predominantly lower socioeconomic status (SES) black students in our sample would consider the stimulus behaviors as intrinsically less mean and threatening (and more playful and friendly) than would the predominantly middle-to-upper SES white students, regardless of the actor's race.

In summary, the research reported here constitutes a conceptual replication of the Duncan study in its attempt to explore, with a different population and more precisely equivalent stimuli, the influence of racial cues on the interpretation of ambiguously aggressive acts. It goes beyond that study, not only in varying the behavior of both white and black stimulus persons but also in comparing the responses of white and black observers.

METHOD

The Research Site

The study was conducted in an urban north-eastern middle school with approximately a 2:1 black–white student ratio. The school had been interracial through the 3 years of its existence but drew its students from neighborhoods characterized by a high degree of residential segregation. As is typical of desegregated public schools in the United States, black students as a group were characterized by lower average socioeconomic status and academic achievement than their white counterparts. Nearly 3 years of extensive observation in the school had revealed virtually no overt racial conflict, and examples of positive interracial interaction were numerous. (See Schofield & Sagar, 1979, for a fuller account of the school and its social climate.)

This generally positive picture was balanced by interview data in which both black and white students reported that white students were more likely to be intimidated by their black peers than vice versa. (Schofield, in press; Patchen & Davidson, 1974, and Scherer & Slawski, 1979, found a similar pattern among high school students.) Respondents in these interviews rarely reported specific incidences of serious intimidation, however, and the proper interpretation of those incidents that were described was often unclear. It was precisely the ambiguity of such events that gave racial cues an opportunity to significantly influence their interpretation.

Subjects

From the school's male sixth-grade population, 40 white and 40 black students were selected randomly, within race categories. Of those originally selected, 1 white and 2 blacks classified by the school administration as learning disabled were replaced because of possible difficulties in following the experimental instructions. Parental permission for the students' participation was sought with a success rate of 88% for white students and 78% for black students. Most failures to obtain permission reflected an inability to reach the parents rather than direct refusals. When permission was not obtained, alternates were selected randomly from the same population.

Stimulus Materials

Each subject was provided with oral descriptions and artist's renditions of four different dyadic interactions determined by prior observation and/or student interviews to be fairly common in the school and subject to different interpretations as to their benign or threatening nature. The depicted interactions were bumping in the hallway, requesting food from another student, poking a student in the classroom, and using another's pencil without asking. Verbal descriptions of the four interactions were identical across subjects. Two of these descriptions follow in full:

> Donald had just sat down in the cafeteria with his lunch when Anthony came up to him and said, "Hey, can I have your cake?" Donald didn't know Anthony very well, but he let him have his cake, even though it was a kind he usually ate himself.

> Mark was sitting at his desk, working on his social studies assignment, when David started poking him in the back with the eraser end of his pencil. Mark just kept on working. David kept poking him for a while, and then he finally stopped.

The descriptions were read directly to each child, rather than recorded, to maintain attention and to make the session more natural. The experimenters were trained to read the accounts in comparable tones.

Four different sets of pictorial stimuli were used, with each experimenter's subjects assigned randomly, in equal numbers, to each set. Each set depicted the same four interaction types, with each interaction type involving a different one of the four possible black/white racial permutations of actors and targets. Across stimulus sets, each interaction type was shown with all four racial permutations. Table 9.1 illustrates that makeup of the stimulus sets. The order of presentation of interaction types within each set was randomized independently for each student.

TABLE 9.1 Assignment of Pictorial Stimuli to Stimulus Sets

Stimulus set	Interaction Type			
	Bumps	Asks for cake	Pokes	Takes pencil
1	WW	WB	BB	BW
2	BW	BB	WB	WW
3	BB	BW	WW	WB
4	WB	WW	BW	BB

Note: B means black; W means white. Within each cell, the first letter stands for race of the actor; the second stands for race of the target.

The portrayal of various combinations of black and white boys in different situations was natural in this particular school setting, given the interracial student body and the increasing use of curriculum materials that routinely portray both blacks and whites. None of the children indicated that they were aware of the experiment's concern with the race factor in response to a postexperimental question on this matter.

To ensure complete comparability of detail in the four pictorial versions of each interaction, pictures were photocopied from original line drawings depicting two white males. Racial identities were changed as necessary, prior to duplication, by redrawing the hair and noses and, in a few cases, slightly softening prominent chins. Because of their importance as expressive features, eyes and mouths were left unchanged, as were all other details. The resulting pictures were colored with pencils to increase visual interest and to make actors' and targets' racial identities unambiguous. Faces and arms were colored either with a brown or "flesh" pencil.

All pictured students were male and were drawn to appear about the same age as the subjects themselves. Familiar furniture and background details helped support the experimenter's assertion that the depicted interactions had been observed in the subjects' own school.

Procedure

Each student met individually in a private conference room in the school building with an adult male experimenter of the student's own race. (Two black and two white experimenters participated in the study.) The experimenter referred to the ongoing observational study of the school, explaining that the researchers occasionally saw incidents that they had difficulty interpreting and suggesting that the subject might be able to help. The experimenter then instructed the subject in the use of the 7-point semantic differential-type scale and summarized the procedure to follow.

The set of pictures that the subject was to see and the order in which he was to see them were randomly assigned ahead of time. The pictures were displayed on a small stand, which prevented the experimenter from seeing them and thus kept him blind to the race of the interactants. The race manipulation was therefore purely visual, as would have been the case if the subjects had directly observed an actual interaction.

Following the pictorial and oral presentation of each dyadic interaction, the subject rated how well each of several adjectives (playful, friendly, mean, and threatening) described the actor's behavior. They then rated the probable personal characteristics of both actor and target on identical sets of semantic differential scales that covered dimensions believed relevant to the depicted behaviors (e.g., thoughtless–considerate, strong–weak, threatening–harmless).

Results

The significant main effect of race permutations on the summed mean/threatening scales, was found to reflect, as expected, a tendency for subjects to rate the behaviors of black actors more mean/threatening than identical behaviors by white actors.

TABLE 9.2 Mean Ratings of Both White and Black Actors' Behaviors by Both White and Black Subjects

Subject group[a]	Actor race	Rating Scale	
		Mean/ threatening	Playful/ friendly
White	White	8.28	6.43
	Black	8.99	6.24
Black	White	7.38	7.19
	Black	8.40	6.74

Note: Means are based on sums of paired 7-point scales indicating how well the given adjective described the behaviors, from 1 (not at all) to 7 (exactly)

[a]$n = 40$ for each group.

Race permutations did not affect the playful/friendly ratings. No statistically significant main effects or interactions were found for target race, indicating that target race did not measurably influence judgments of the actors' behaviors.

The lack of any statistical interaction between race of subject and race permutations, suggests, as had been tentatively predicted, that the ratings reflect a general bias among this male student population, rather than a uniquely white response. The means in Table 9.2 reveal the similar pattern of response by black and by white subjects. The black actors' behaviors were rated more mean/threatening than those of the white actors by black subjects, as well as by white subjects.

Both black and white subjects' mean ratings of the various behaviors, collapsed across race permutations, are shown in Table 9.3 As predicted in the subjective culture hypothesis, both requesting food and taking a pencil were rated more mean/threatening, and less playful/friendly, by white than by black subjects. Racial differences in rating the bumping and poking behaviors were not significant. Thus,

TABLE 9.3 Black Subjects' and White Subjects' Mean Ratings of Four Ambiguous Behaviors Collapsed Across Dyad Race

Rating scale	Subject race[a]	Behavior			
		Bumps	Requests food	Pokes	Takes pencil
Mean/threatening	White	9.98	7.85	8.13	8.58
	Black	9.60	6.10	9.18	6.71
Playful/friendly	White	4.73	7.01	8.15	5.45
	Black	5.66	8.28	7.31	6.65

Note: Means are based on sums of paired 7-point scales indicating how well the given adjective described the behaviors, from 1 (not at all) to 7 (exactly)

[a]$n = 40$ for each group.

TABLE 9.4 Mean Trait Ratings of White and Black Actors and Targets

		Rating Scale	
Role	Race	Strong/weak[a]	Threatening/harmless[b]
Actor	White	4.48	4.35
	Black	4.91	4.60
Target	White	3.90	2.31
	Black	4.53	2.69

Note: Means were based on 7-point scales ranging from 1 to 7. Each cell represents two ratings by each of 80 subjects.

[a]Higher values indicate greater strength.

[b]Higher values indicate greater threat.

the expected main effect for race of subject was not significant on either the mean/threatening or playful/friendly scales summed across behavior types. Instead, race of subject interacted with behaviors on both scales, respectively, due to the fact that our predictions of a race main effect were borne out for only two of the four behaviors. Interestingly, the behaviors whose ratings conformed to our expectations were the two that involved no direct physical contact.

Despite the evidence of a tendency to judge an ambiguous *behavior* more negatively when it was performed by a black as compared to a white, the subjects' ratings of the pictured blacks' and whites' *personalities* were heavily influenced by the depicted behavior and the stimulus person's role (actor or target), as we expected. Black and white subjects agreed that the actors were ruder, meaner, more thoughtless, playful, threatening, unfriendly, and less likable than targets, regardless of race permutations. There were only two exceptions to this pattern of general agreement between black and white children about the characteristics of the actors and targets: White students assumed that actors were stronger than targets, and that targets were more fearful than actors, whereas black students did not.

We had predicted that actors' personality ratings on dimensions related to threat and violence would also be influenced by their race, whereas no such race effect was predicted for ratings of targets. The results suggest that race generally had relatively little impact on the personality ratings of either actors or targets. Only two of the scales showed a race effect (see Table 9.4). Black actors were rated stronger than white actors, and black targets were rated stronger than white targets. Black actors were only marginally more threatening than white actors, but white targets were considered even less threatening (i.e., more harmless) than the equally passive black targets.

Discussion

Duncan's experiment and the present study, with their complementary methodological strengths, together provide clear evidence that even relatively innocuous acts by black males are likely to be considered more threatening than the same behaviors by white males. This tendency to perceive threat in blacks' behaviors appears to be all too generalizable to a number of situations and populations in this country. It occurred in Duncan's study in which white college students saw one confederate give another a light shove in the context of a rather heated discussion. It appeared again in this study as sixth-grade students judged four different interaction types that involved no direct suggestion of anger and, in two cases, no physical contact whatsoever. Most notably, in this study behavior ratings by black students reflected the same antiblack bias as those by white students.

The similarly biased responses of the black and the white students suggest that such biases should not be regarded as ego-motivated reactions to an outgroup. Some might argue that the black subjects had simply internalized the antiblack attitudes of the dominant white culture, as suggested by the early doll-choice studies (Kluger, 1976); but, without rejecting that argument completely, we suspect that the convergence between the two groups in this biracial school reflects a complex interaction between actual behavioral differences and apparently universal cognitive processes. For example, the tendency to overestimate the difference between the distributions of an observable characteristic in two different populations (Allport, 1954; Eiser & Stroebe, 1972/ Tajfel & Wilkes, 1963) would be expected to apply to black and to white observers alike.

The fact that our subjects attributed no more negative traits to black than to white actors, although unexpected, may simply indicate that the technique of rating behaviors provides the more sensitive measure of subtle stereotyping tendencies. It may be that as overt antiblack prejudice has become socially more undesirable, Americans have learned to describe black persons with caution but have not yet recognized reactions to specific behaviors as potential indicators of prejudice. The symbolic racism scale (McConahay & Hough, 1976), which often detects antiblack feeling among persons who do not appear prejudiced on more traditional scales, may be effective in part because many of its items give respondents the opportunity to disapprove of the alleged behavior, rather than the personal characteristics, of black Americans as a group.

Despite the apparent generalizability of the tendency to interpret actions by a black person as more violent or threatening than the same actions performed by a white person, it should be emphasized that the phenomenon has thus far been demonstrated only in the case of males observing interactions between males. A similar study employing female subjects and stimuli might well produce a similar, or even stronger, pattern of results because of the disproportionate emphasis placed on the value of feminine daintiness and vulnerability in white, as opposed to black, culture (Clement, Eisenhart, Harding, & Livesay, Note 1). Research designed to explore this issue would be worthwhile.

The expected tendency of the white subjects in this study to read more threat into the ambiguous behaviors than black subjects was confirmed only in the case of the behaviors that involved no physical contact but did involve one person acting to obtain a material good from another. Staple's (1976) assertion that black culture tends to consider property a collective asset may be relevant here: The black subjects appear to have considered these two behaviors to be at least marginally legitimate. The white subjects, in contrast, may have assumed that the actors would not have initiated such seemingly inappropriate acts, had they not been prepared to back them up with physical force. This reasoning is supported by the fact that the white subjects assumed actors were stronger and less fearful than their targets, whereas the black subjects did not.

It should be apparent that none of the tendencies noted here can be linked with race per se. The black students participating in the study were, on the average, clearly of lower socioeconomic status than the whites, as is the case in most desegregated schools and indeed in the United States as a whole. If such differences did not exist and the background of the black and the white students in the school had been equivalent, the indicated cultural differences might well not have appeared and the stereotype that gave rise to the biased behavior ratings might not have been so much in evidence. But in the existing social order, the stereotype is all too real. To activate it, the person engaging in an ambiguous behavior need only be black.

Reference Note

1. Clement, D. C., Eisenhart, M., Harding, J. R., & Livesay, J. M. *The emerging order: An ethnography of a southern desegregated school.* Chapel Hill: University of North Carolina, Anthropology Department, October 1977.

References

Allport, G. W. *The nature of prejudice.* Cambridge, MA: Addison-Wesley, 1954.

Brigham, J. C. Ethnic stereotypes. *Psychological Bulletin,* 1971, *76,* 15–38.

Bruner, J. S. On perceptual readiness. *Psychological Review,* 1957, *64,* 123–151.

Chapman, L. J. Illusory correlation in observational report. *Journal of Verbal Learning and verbal Behavior,* 1967, *6,* 151–155.

Clement, D. C., Eisenhart, M., & Harding, J. R. The veneer of harmony: Social race relations in a southern desegregated school. In R. C. Rist (Ed.), *Desegregated schools: Appraisals of an American experiment.* New York: Academic Press, 1979.

Cooper, J., & Fazio, R. H. The formation and persistence of attitudes that support intergroup conflict. In W. G. Austin & S. Worchel (Eds.), *The social psychology of intergroup relations.* Monterey, CA: Brooks/Cole, 1979.

Duncan, B. L. Differential social perception and attribution of intergroup violence: Testing the lower limits of stereotyping of blacks. *Journal of Personality and Social Psychology,* 1976, *34,* 590–598.

Dutton, D. G. Tokenism, reverse discrimination and egalitarianism in interracial behavior. *Journal of Social Issues,* 1976, *32*(2), 93–107.

Eiser, J. R., & Stroebe, W. *Categorization and social judgment.* New York: Academic Press, 1972.

Hamilton, D. L., & Gifford, R. K. Illusory correlation in interpersonal perception: A cognitive basis of stereotypic judgments. *Journal of Experimental Social Psychology,* 1976, *12,* 392–407.

Howard, J. W., & Rothbart, M. Social categorization and memory for ingroup and outgroup behavior. *Judgment of Personality and Social Psychology,* 1980, *38,* 301–310.

Kirk, R. E. *Experimental design: Procedures for the behavioral sciences.* Monterey, CA: Brooks/Cole, 1968.

Kluger, R. *Simple justice: The history of Brown v. Board of Education and Black America's struggle for equality.* New York: Knopf, 1976.

McConahay, J. B., & Hough, J. C., Jr. Symbolic racism. *Journal of Social Issues,* 1976, *32*(2), 23–45.

Patchen, M., & Davidson, J. D. *Patterns and determinants of interracial interaction in the Indianapolis public high schools: Final report.* West Lafayette, IN: Purdue University, 1974. (ERIC Document Reproduction Service No. ED 095 252).

Patchen, M., Hoffmann, G., & Davison, J. Interracial perceptions among high school students. *Sociometry,* 1976, *39*(4), 341–354.

Scherer, J., & Slawski, E. J. Color, class, and social control in an urban desegregated school. In R. C. Rist (Ed.), *Desegregated schools: Appraisals of an American experiment.* New York: Academic Press, 1979.

Schofield, J. W. Complementary and conflicting identities: Images and interaction in an interracial school. In S. Asher & J. Gottman (Eds.), *The development of friendship.* Cambridge, England: Cambridge University Press, in press.

Schofield, J. W., & Sagar, H. A. The social context of learning in an interracial school. In R. C. Rist (Ed.), *Desegregated schools: Appraisals of an American experiment.* New York: Academic Press, 1979.

Staples, R. *Introduction to black sociology.* New York: McGraw-Hill, 1976.

Tajfel, H., & Wilkes, A. L. Classification and quantitative judgment. *British Journal of Psychology,* 1963, *54,* 101–114.

Triandis, H. C. (Ed.), *Variations in black and white perceptions of the social environment.* Urbana, IL: University of Illinois Press, 1976.

Triandis, H. C., Vassiliou, V., Vassiliou, G., Tanaka, Y., & Shanmugam, A. (Eds.), *The analysis of subjective culture.* New York: Wiley, 1972.

Tversky, A., & Kahneman, D. Judgment under uncertainty: Heuristics and biases. *Science,* 1974, *185,* 1124–1131.

10

Applied Social Psychology: Health and the Law

In recent years, social psychologists have branched out in a wide range of directions. Businesses are guided by the principles of group dynamics as developed in social psychological laboratories, juries are selected based on social psychological research, dormitories are designed in consultation with social psychologists, and physicians are trained to relate to patients using basic principles of social interaction.

Andrew Baum is Professor of Medical Psychology at the Uniformed Services University of the Health Sciences in Bethesda, Maryland. He is the editor of the *Journal of Applied Social Psychology* and associate editor of *Health Psychology*. After gaining a reputation as a leading researcher in environment psychology, he made the transition into health psychology through his research on stress-provoking events, such as the Three Mile Island nuclear reactor incident. In our conversation Prof. Baum considers the unique contributions that social psychologists can make and lays out a whole series of issues for social psychology to address.

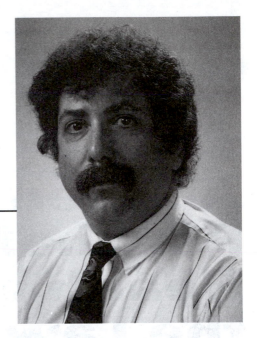

A CONVERSATION WITH
ANDREW BAUM
Uniformed Services University
of the Health Sciences

Krupat: *The topic of applied social psychology seems to come up a great deal. What is applied social psychology, and what does it deal with?*

Baum: Social psychology has many different focuses. Applied social psychology is the use of basic social psychological theories and findings to investigate and solve social issues and problems of society. The best current example that I can think of is in the struggle against the AIDS virus. Given that this disease has no cure as far as we know, there is no vaccine that effectively prevents one from becoming infected, the most important tools that we have in combating the disease are techniques that really involve social influence and persuasion. If we can convince people not to do certain things that encourage the spread of the virus and give them social skills and techniques to avoid infection, we may be able to halt its progress and minimize lives lost.

Krupat: *Why are social psychologists involved in applied research? What kinds of unique contributions can we make?*

Baum: Social psychology has two important aspects that are particularly useful in this effort. One is that the body of knowledge and the areas of investigation that social psychologists are interested in are basic and central to our interactions in our daily lives. Social psychologists have staked out a domain of behavior that is central to almost everything that goes on in human life. The second and perhaps more important thing is that social psychologists use unique methodologies in understanding the problems that they study. Because of the nature of the phenomena that they are studying, social psychologists are forced to use laboratory studies and field studies, as well as a host of imaginative techniques. I think that the combination of this unique focus on content and this unusual methodological approach makes social psychology particularly important in applications to social problems.

Krupat: *How does this research translate into action?*

Baum: Intervention is one of the goals of a lot of research that goes on within social psychology. Let's consider the AIDS virus in relation to college students. One goal is to come up with an intervention, something that we can deliver to college students that will make it easier for them to avoid becoming infected with the virus. So a social psychologist might do research on the best persuasion techniques that seem to create long-term behavior change or at least create intentions to change behavior. Then they might focus on providing social skills that will make people more successful in avoiding infection. The work would build toward creating an intervention, which in this case might be a training program or an educational program, and an evaluation of the intervention.

Krupat: *Are we doing much more applied psychology now than we ever were, or are there cycles in the history of the field?*

Baum: Right now I think that we are doing a lot of applied work, but to some extent this does come in cycles, which are a product of the demands of the world that we live in. An early period of very active application of social psychology occurred during World War II, and this was a function of the demands created by the war. Another surge in applied work occurred in the late sixties through the mid-seventies, when the society we were living in was in turmoil, when environmental issues were suddenly of great concern, and a number of changes in the society demanded new knowledge and new application. Currently, there is a combination of forces, one of which is again a demand on science to try to answer some of the questions that people have been unable to answer in other ways. In general, I think the distinctions between basic and applied psychology have become less clear, and I see the whole field moving a bit toward the applied dimension.

Krupat: *Which I assume you think is a good direction?*

Baum: I think it's a good direction as long as it doesn't go too far toward the other extreme.

Krupat: *I agree. What do you think of the feelings expressed by some critics that social psychology runs in fads, that areas such as health psychology are popular now, but soon we will move on. How would you respond to that?*

Baum: I really don't see social psychology in the guise of an ambulance chaser. Health is going to be an important issue for a long time, whether or not social psychologists are contributing to the effort to prevent and heal disease. Back in the middle and late eighties, there was concern in organized psychology that most researchers were not particularly interested in the AIDS problem, when in fact we were getting messages from the Surgeon General and others that understanding behavior change and social influence was absolutely vital to the solution of the AIDS problem. And yet as a group, psychologists seemed somewhat reluctant to become involved. A series of meetings took place, and I wrote a paper with one of my students for the *American Psychologist,* attempting to show psychologists some of the things that we needed to do and all that could be done. Today there is greater interest in HIV disease and AIDS. I'm certainly not suggesting that the article or even the meetings had much to do with this increased interest, but people didn't suddenly wake up one day and say, "Gee, that's a hot area. Let's get involved in it." It took some coaxing and some cautious examination of the potential of social psychological research in this area. I think that, if you look carefully at the history of application in social psychology, you'll see that it is really not a matter of going after hot topics, but rather of the right people finding the right matches between what they do and the kinds of problems that need solutions.

Krupat: *When social psychologists get involved in these issues, they often end up working with physicians and lawyers or architects. How has that collaboration gone?*

Baum: It has been very exciting. My experience has been that psychologists are uniquely trained to be able to interact across these different disciplinary lines. I have found instances where I have been in a group of biomedical scientists who have less in common with each other than I have in common with each of them. Part of that has to do with the nature of what psychologists study. There is a certain inescapability of mental and behavioral processes in almost all of these issues, so that a virologist might be studying only a small piece of a problem, whereas the psychologist may be involved in almost all of it. And that has led in my experience to psychologists becoming very central in these clusters of interdisciplinary scientists.

Krupat: *Are there cases where you have found that others have been skeptical of your contributions?*

Baum: Sure. There's a certain skepticism that is built in whenever other people are dealing with a discipline that describes something that's very common to everyone. Part of what social psychologists have to deal with is the perception that a lot of what we do has a certain common sense quality to it, and that people find it difficult to take social psychology seriously at times. There is also a skepticism that's not just unique to psychology, but is more globally applied to scientists in general. A lot of lawyers, for example, approach these collaborations with a sense that we are "ivory tower" scientists. They are not as familiar with scientists who are out there in the real world getting their hands dirty with the kinds of problems that we work on.

Krupat: *But don't lawyers sometimes wonder how a psychologist can be telling them how to present evidence? Or don't physicians question what psychologists can tell them about clinical reasoning?*

Baum: There is some of that, although my experience has been that, if they have figured out that they need the expertise, they are likely to be open to the advice. Lawyers and physicians who ask for help usually have a positive attitude toward the kind of contribution that can be made before they go ahead and ask.

Krupat: *Do we have to wait until people ask?*

Baum: We shouldn't. But frequently that's the way that things get started. Certainly we shouldn't have needed to be asked to become involved with HIV disease and heart disease, but in many cases we did.

Krupat: *You are based in a medical school. Most social psychologists are still in standard psychology departments, but others are now in law schools and business schools. Some are completely outside of academia. What advantages or disadvantages for the field or the individual lie in having these different kinds of affiliations?*

Baum: Where you are located affects who you interact with on a daily basis and what kinds of cross-fertilizations are likely to occur. In a medical school environment, there are few other social scientists, and almost everyone else is a natural or life scientist. What you get in your daily interactions is very different from what you would get if you were in a liberal arts college where there are lots of other psychologists as well as sociologists, political scientists, and economists. I'm not sure that this is good or bad, just different. The point is, the interactions and collaborations differ, and these affect the directions that research and theory may take. I find that the interactions I have in the medical school setting are essential to my continued growth and have influenced my research. I miss a lot of the other kinds of interaction, but I try to make up for that by maintaining a network of colleagues that I talk with. I think that the overall proliferation of psychology into these different areas is good for the science of psychology in that it provides us with new opportunities by virtue of contacting different kinds of people and researchers. And it also broadens the base of the field so that now we are not just an academic discipline with its roots exclusively in psychology departments.

Krupat: *I agree with you. But how about extending even further and talking about social psychologists in ad agencies, government positions, and all sorts of nonacademic settings?*

Baum: I haven't had a lot of experience with ad agencies, but I do know it is good for government agencies to have a lot of different types of people in them. When there are enough people with different kinds of perspectives to keep each other "honest," it discourages narrow thinking or even a groupthink type of phenomenon. My guess is that in most of the nonacademic settings it is not only good for the field, but it is good for the product as well. It provides a different perspective on what things should be done and how things might be done.

Krupat: *Within health psychology, which is the field that you have been involved in, what kinds of specific issues and problems have social psychologists become involved in?*

Baum: We can start with stress research, which is ubiquitous because stress is involved in almost all health processes and it has a large social component. Consider things such as social support, which is one of the very basic buffers of stress. There is also the study of coping and how we deal with stressful events. Perceived control, which is derived directly from basic research in social psychology, has proven important not just in response to environmental stressors, but also in things like preparation for surgery. There are also areas such as compliance with medical regimens—how do you get patients to do what their health care professionals prescribe for them? If you've got a high-risk individual who needs to go for hypertensive screening every year or if you have someone who needs to go on a diet to lose weight, how do you go about convincing them, making sure that they understand and remember what they are supposed to do, and seeing to it that they actually do this? The compliance problem is enormous; about 50 percent of all people on antihypertensive medication drop out by about a year after they begin their treatment. And that is going to affect their health and the outcome of therapy that is being prescribed. So that's another area where I think social psychologists have very specific essential expertise. There are also disease-specific areas. There is research on heart disease, much of which has social and personality psychological components, and cancer research is becoming more and more influenced by psychological and social psychological constructs. The AIDS epidemic, of course, also requires this kind of work. There is also smoking, health promotion, diet, eating behaviors, exercise, and managing chronic illness. I could go on and on.

Krupat: *I ask half seriously how these fields ever existed without us.*

Baum: It's really a good question. And the answer to it is that they did, and they are better now because the information we are providing them is being incorporated. I can tell you from personal experience that major institutions investigating health and disease, such as comprehensive cancer centers all across the country, have added biobehavioral or psychosocial units to help not only in patient care but also in the basic and applied research they are doing.

Krupat: *I hear you saying that, while social psychology, especially as it relates to health care, has arrived only recently, it has assumed a highly important place. So what is the future like?*

Baum: The future is difficult to predict now because of all of the changes that are going on around us in health care reform. Sometimes it feels as if the ground we are standing on is moving as we speak. I see the psychological and social psychological study of health as continuing to grow, particularly as we see major diseases and major health problems in our society being problems of lifestyle or diseases that are influenced by behavioral variables. As long as cancer, heart disease, HIV disease, and others like them are primary problems that we have to deal with, and as long as people are people and we have difficulties with compliance and other health behaviors, I can't imagine that we won't have behavioral research directed toward these problems.

Shelley E. Taylor
Gayle A. Dakof

Social Support
and the Cancer Patient

If you have ever been under stress, had a major illness, or experienced a personal loss, you know how important it is to have people around on whom you felt you could lean. In this article, Shelley Taylor and Gayle Dakof look at the role of social support in
the case of women who have been diagnosed with breast cancer.
Although a label such as cancer sometimes is so threatening that
friends or family avoid the person, they found that the majority of
women felt that their social support network was adequate if not
outstanding. Nonetheless, about one fifth of these women did express concerns, and several questioned whether their families
truly understood their experiences. The authors report that support definitely helped women to adjust to their condition, but that
a given type of behavior was seen as helpful by one person but
not so helpful by another. For instance, some women said that
they valued "just being there" from their spouses, whereas other
women felt that was not useful unless it was accompanied by expressions of concern and love. When you have needed it, what
kind of support have you found most useful?

Over the last two decades, research has examined the possibility that social and
emotional ties, otherwise known as social support, can foster good psychological
and physical health. *Social support* has been defined as "an interpersonal transaction
involving one of the following: (1) emotional concern (liking, loving, empathy), (2)
instrumental aid (goods or services), (3) information (about the environment), or (4)
appraisal (information relevant to self-evaluation) (House, 1981, p. 39). Social support can come from family members, such as a spouse, partner, or child; from
friends or professional caregivers; from social and community ties, such as clubs or
religious organizations; or from groups especially organized to provide social support (i.e., social support groups, such as Alcoholics Anonymous).

The research to date clearly indicates that social support can reduce the psychological impact of stressful events (e.g., Billings & Moos, 1982; Kaplan, Robbins, &
Martin, 1983; Lin, Simeone, Ensel, & Kuo, 1979; Williams, Ware, & Donald,

1981). The influence of social support on physical health is somewhat less clear. Some studies have indicated that individuals with high levels of social support are less likely to develop serious illnesses (e.g., Berkman & Syme, 1979; Jackson, 1956; Nuckolls, Cassell, & Kaplan, 1972; for a review, see Wallston, Alagna, DeVellis, & DeVellis, 1983). Other studies have failed to find lower levels of illness among individuals with high levels of social support (Wallston et al., 1983). However, the evidence consistently suggests a relationship between social support and prospects for recovery. People who are already ill seem to recover more quickly if they have high levels of social support (Chambers & Reiser, 1953; Cobb, 1976; Dimond, 1979; Robertson & Suinn, 1968; for reviews, see DiMatteo & Hays, 1981, and Wallston et al., 1983).

How social support may enable people to cope with stressful events has been a particular research focus. Two hypotheses have been explored. One, termed the *direct effects hypothesis,* maintains that social support is beneficial during nonstressful times as well as stressful times. The other, termed the *buffering hypothesis,* maintains that the health and mental health benefits of social support are chiefly evident during periods of high stress. According to the buffering hypothesis, social support acts as a resource and reserve that blunts the effects of stress or enables an individual to cope with high levels of stress more effectively. There is research evidence to support both hypotheses, and they are not mutually exclusive (for a review, see Cohen & Wills, 1985).

SOCIAL SUPPORT AND CANCER

The occurrence of cancer is a highly stressful event that is receiving increasing research attention as its incidence rises. At the present time, nearly one out of every three individuals will develop at least one malignancy in his or her lifetime (American Cancer Society, 1986). Because cancer is an ongoing stressor that continually requires physical and psychological adjustments even in the best of cases, it is a chronically stressful event. Patients with active cancers face potential physical deterioration and the debilitating effects of certain treatment such as chemotherapy or radiation therapy. Even patients whose cancers are in remission may have physical disabilities to manage as well as ongoing concerns about whether or not the cancer will recur (Dunkel-Schetter, 1984). Social support is a potential resource to help cancer patients deal with these fears and ambiguities (Bloom, 1982; Carey, 1974).

As is true for other stressful events, research suggests that social support is psychologically beneficial for cancer patients. Numerous studies have suggested a positive relationship between emotional support from family members and degree of physical and psychological adjustment to cancer (Bloom, 1982; Carey, 1974).

Thus there is clear evidence that social support can be helpful to cancer patients. However, there is also some suggestion that cancer may threaten the availability of social support. Work by Wortman and Dunkel-Schetter (1979), Dunkel-Schetter and Wortman (1982), and Silver and Wortman (1980) has suggested that sometimes victims, such as cancer patients, do not receive either enough social support or enough appropriate social support. These authors have suggested that cancer patients can be inadvertently victimized by their families and friends. Cancer creates two conflicting reactions in significant others: first, feelings of fear and aversion to cancer, and second, beliefs that appropriate behavior toward cancer patients requires maintaining a cheerful, optimistic facade. The conflict between these reactions may produce ambivalence toward the patient and anxiety about interacting with him or her. Consequently, significant others may physically avoid the patient or may avoid open communication about the disease. These discrepancies in behavior (i.e., positive verbal but negative nonverbal behavior) can lead a cancer patient to feel rejected or abandoned by loved ones.

Research evidence concerning this so-called victimization hypothesis is mixed. On the one hand, the available research suggests that the majority of cancer patients perceive the degree of social support that they receive as adequate or outstanding (Dunkel-Schetter, 1984; see Lichtman & Taylor, 1986, for a review). On the other hand, cancer patients sometimes report guarded communications from family members (Cobb, 1976; Gordon et al., 1980; Klagsbrun, 1971; Lichtman & Taylor, 1986; Wellisch, Jamison, & Pasnau, 1978). Peters-Golden (1982) found that breast cancer patients reported that social support was often not available to them, and when it was, it was sometimes inappropriate (see also Wortman, 1984). In extreme cases, a patient may even be blamed for his or her cancer (Abrams & Finesinger, 1953; Giacquinta, 1977; Vettese, 1976).

In this chapter, we will review a program of research that we have undertaken with our associates over the past eight years. The interest of the senior author in this problem was initially sparked by a cancer conference, which posed the question: What does your discipline tell us about how to define and meet the needs of the cancer patient? In putting together a talk on the contributions of social psychology to an understanding of cancer, she was struck, first, by the wealth of social psychological findings that were potentially applicable to defining and meeting the cancer patient's needs, and second, by the total absence of direct research on this problem area in social psychology. Consequently, the potential to make a contribution was one impetus for conducting this research. A second impetus for both authors was a growing feeling that basic social psychological processes such as interpersonal interaction, causal attributions, or beliefs in personal control cannot be fruitfully studied in the laboratory alone. Without input from real-world situations, the theories concerning these variables fail to incorporate real-world contingencies that may greatly modify the meaning and consequent effects of these very important variables.

In presenting our program of research, we will concentrate on two major issues: Do cancer patients experience social support or lack of support from their significant others following the cancer experience? When problems with social support from significant others emerge, what is the nature of those problems?

SOCIAL SUPPORT FOLLOWING CANCER: EMPIRICAL EVIDENCE

In our first study of social support (Lichtman & Taylor, 1986; Lichtman, Taylor, & Wood, in press), we conducted interviews with 78 breast cancer patients. Patients were recruited through a three-physician private oncology practice in Los Angeles. The sample ranged in age from 29 to 78, with a median age of 53. Overall, 71% were married, 19% were divorced, separated, or never married, and 10% were widowed. A total of 49% of the sample was employed either full-time or part-time. The sample was largely middle and upper-middle class, with the median level of education being one year of college. All but two of the women in the sample had had their breast cancer treated surgically either by lumpectomy (31%) or by mastectomy (67%). Some 31% had good prognoses, and 69% had fair to poor prognoses.

Each patient was interviewed by a trained psychological interviewer who followed a structured set of questions. The interviews typically lasted approximately an hour and a half and covered: basic demographic data; details about the woman's cancer experience; questions regarding attributions for cancer and beliefs about the ability to control the cancer; life changes experienced since cancer; perceptions of marital, family, and social relationships following cancer; perceptions of own adjustment; the amount of information the respondent had about cancer and how she had acquired it; and social comparisons made with respect to cancer.

In the section concerning social support, the patient was asked first to rate separately the degree of support she had received from her spouse or partner, if relevant, from other family members, and from her friends. Then she was asked to identify and describe any particular relationships in which she had experienced a lack of support when she was expecting it. She was also asked whether or not people treated her any differently after the cancer, and if so, who and in what way. She next rated the openness and honesty of communication between herself and other people. The patient was asked if her social life had changed in any respect, and if so, how. Next she was asked if she was spending more, the same, or less time with her friends, with her immediate family, and with her extended family. In the section dealing with the relations between the patient and her spouse or partner, the patient was asked to rate her degree of satisfaction with the relationship prior to the cancer and her current satisfaction. Next she was asked how open and honest communication was between them. Patients were also asked how much they had been able to share their concerns with the significant other.

Overall, the amount of social support reported by these women was high; 75% rated the amount of support received from their spouse as "a great deal," which was the highest level; 77% reported a great deal of support from other family members; and 81% reported a great deal of support from friends. When asked how open and honest communications with other people were after the cancer, 80% of the sample rated them in the two highest categories, with only 7% in the two lowest categories. Generally, then, respondents reported a high level of social support and ability to communicate with their significant others following cancer. However, we caution against generalizing too far from this sample since it was female, heavily middle to upper-middle class, and had a cancer site typified by a generally favorable prognosis.

To address further the social support experiences associated with cancer, we conducted a questionnaire survey of Southern California cancer patients (Taylor, Falke, Shoptaw, & Lichtman, 1986; Taylor, Falke, Mazel, & Hilsberg, in press). Because a portion of the research addressed the cancer support-group experience, we attempted to recruit approximately half of our respondents from cancer support groups and half from general cancer practices. To recruit those who had attended cancer support groups, we obtained lists of Southern California area support groups, contacted the group leaders, and obtained mailing lists of the group members. To recruit cancer patients who had not attended support groups, we selected Southern California oncologists randomly from the University of California Cancer Center lists. Physicians were sent a contact letter that was followed by phone calls to obtain mailing lists of patients.

In all, we contacted 1,068 potentially eligible individuals. The final sample of 668 individuals represents a response rate of 72.5%. Respondents ranged in age from 21 to 89 with a median age of 58. The sample was disproportionately female (78% of the sample), and Caucasian (93%). Subjects with all types of cancers participated n the study, and as would be expected, there were high percentages of patients with breast, gastrointestinal, and lymphatic cancers.

On the whole, the results from the study were consistent with the previous study, suggesting that cancer patients report positive, socially supportive experiences following cancer. A full 86% indicated that their spouses had been very helpful or helpful in addressing the needs that cancer brought on; 80% indicated that other family members had been very helpful or helpful; and 81% indicated that friends had been very helpful or helpful. Moreover, these reports did not vary systematically by sex, socioeconomic status, site of cancer, or prognosis.

However, in response to the question, "Do you wish you could talk more freely or openly about your cancer with family or friends?", 55% indicated they wished very much or somewhat that they could do so. A substantial minority (36%) also endorsed the statement, "Sometimes I feel that my family members don't really understand what I am going through."

To summarize, then, if we look at these data in the context of the Wortman and Dunkel-Schetter (1979) hypothesis that cancer patients are inadvertently victimized by their families and friends, we might conclude that the weak version but not the strong version of their hypothesis is supported. That is, generally, cancer patients do not report a high level of difficulties with social support following cancer. However, a minority (approximately 20%) are at least somewhat dissatisfied with their social support, and a substantial number report some concerns over whether or not their families truly understand their experiences.

Social Support and Adjustment

In our research, we also examined whether social support was associated with positive adjustment, as previous work has found. In the interview study of breast cancer patients, we employed multiple measures of psychological adjustment: the patient's self-rating of psychological adjustment on a 5-point scale; the oncologist's rating of the patient's adjustment using the Global Adjustment to Illness Scale (GAIS—a standardized 100-point measure that has been used previously with cancer patients); the interviewer's rating of the patient on the GAIS; the spouse or partner's rating of the patient's adjustment on the 5-point scale; the patient's self-rating of the patient's adjustment on a 5-point scale; the patient's self-ratings of anxiety and depression, and two objective measures of psychological adjustment, the Index of Well-Being developed by Campbell, Converse, and Rogers (1976), and the Profile of Mood States (POMS—McNair, Lorr, & Droppleman, 1971).

When we correlated perceived social support from family and friends with psychological adjustment, the results were significant in both studies (Falke, 1987; Lichtman, Taylor, & Wood, in press). Depending upon the particular measure of support used, the correlations in both studies typically centered around .30. For example, in the breast cancer study, women were better adjusted who perceived supportiveness from their families, as were women who reported that they could share concerns with their husbands, who reported open and honest communications with their husbands, or who reported open and honest communications with others around them. Patients who said that their social life had increased since the cancer showed better adjustment than those who had reported a decrease.

It is important to note that in examining these correlational relationships, it is not possible to make a definitive statement regarding the causal direction. It is possible that people who are well-adjusted to their cancer either make more effective use of the social support that is available to them, or profit from social support by not driving it away. Maladjusted cancer patients may drive off people who could otherwise provide them with support support. On the other hand, it is also possible that more social support helps to produce better patient adjustment.

PROBLEMS IN SOCIAL SUPPORT

When cancer patients do experience problems of social support, what is the nature of these problems? Our initial study of 78 breast cancer patients addressed this issue. Although relatively few individuals in that sample reported rejection by family and friends, 42% of the sample indicated that they had been surprised by at least one occurrence of rejection or isolation by a particular person. This lack of support came from the patient's mother in 26% of the cases, a close friend in 23% of the cases, a casual friend in 21% of the cases, and the spouse in 32% of the cases (Lichtman & Taylor, 1986; Lichtman, Taylor, & Wood, in press).

The problems that cancer patients typically experienced with their mothers were either withdrawal or oversolicitousness. For example, one woman, representative of several, stated about her mother:

> She won't even discuss the cancer with me; she pretends it never happened.

In contrast, other women reported incidents like the following:

> My mother drove me nuts. She would wake me up from a sleep to make sure I was O.K. She scared the hell out of me.

With respect to friends, typically our patient sample did not experience rejection from them, and in fact patients often grew closer to their female friends following breast cancer. However, it was not uncommon for a patient to report that one particular friend cut off all contact and communication following the cancer episode. For example,

> I had one friend who wouldn't talk to me. Couldn't even face me. They had an effect on how I now look at people.

A similar incident:

> I had one girlfriend who had just had a baby. After I finished radiation therapy, we had gotten together. We went over to her house and she kept the baby away from me. It was real strange. When we left, I said to my husband, "You know Sue thinks I am contagious," and that was the last we ever heard from them.

A full third of the women we interviewed in the breast cancer study indicated that, despite general satisfaction with the support they received from their spouses following the cancer episode, a particular persistent communication difficulty occurred between themselves and their spouses. Typically, the form of this communication difficulty was that patients indicated a need for more opportunities to express freely their fears and anxieties about cancer recurrence and death, whereas their spouses expressed the belief that talking about it would be maladaptive to the patient's adjustment and might even lead to a recurrence.

Contributing to this difficulty was an apparent difference in temporal perspective about the cancer. The patients felt that the cancer was still an ongoing threat, and they needed to express their fears several months or even years later. Family members, on the other hand, sometimes expressed the thought that the cancer was a crisis that had been successfully resolved, and so did not require further discussion after the crisis period had ended.

One woman still close to the breast cancer episode spoke about her husband's attitude.

> It's five years before they consider you are cured. Well, for his peace of mind as far as he is concerned, it's over and done with. The issue is closed. He doesn't want to talk about it.

As the husband put it:

> We never talked about death. That was my private concern and I didn't want to let on about that either. You must say "O.K. you had the operation. It's over and done with, let's get back on the track." So I never talked about it.

This particular communication difficulty, namely that victims wanted to talk about the incident and significant others avoided communication about it, appears to be a typical problem for victims other than cancer patients as well. In Silver and Wortman's (1980) analysis of undesirable life events, they observed that victims dealing with a variety of losses, including the death of a spouse or child, often needed to air their feelings about the event months or even years later. However, family and friends often discouraged these efforts on the grounds that it was time for the patient to put the incident to rest. Silver and Wortman suggested that nonvictims may have incorrect ideas about how quickly people can overcome victimizing events. Nonvictims may believe that victims can voluntarily control their negative thoughts and emotions when this may not be the case.

Overall, one can ask the question, Who is right? Should patients put the incident behind them or should significant others be more open to communication about the issue? That question cannot be answered definitively. However, in our breast cancer data set (Lichtman, Taylor, & Wood, in press), we found that couples who shared their realistic thoughts, such as worries about recurrence or death, and those who appeared to be more sensitive to each other's emotions and thoughts had higher marital adjustment. Moreover, patients' self-reports that communications with a spouse were open and honest were positively correlated with patients' emotional adjustment. These results tentatively suggest that it may be better for patients to air their grievances and concerns than for them to follow what appear to be frequent wishes of spouses and family members that the concerns be put out of mind and kept covered up.

SOCIALLY SUPPORTIVE AND UNSUPPORTIVE TRANSACTIONS

To this point, we have focused primarily on relatively global reports of social support and lack of it. However, there are several lines of work in the social support literature suggesting that a more fine-grained approach to social support is appropriate. The first is a general caution raised by social support researchers (Barrera, 1981; Dunkel-Schetter, Folkman, & Lazarus, in press; Wortman, 1984) that the field must focus on specific social support transactions and not merely on measures of the perceived availability of social support. That is, to appreciate fully what kinds of actions, information, and comments are helpful from others, researchers need to look at specific instances of social support efforts.

Another reason for focusing on specific social support transactions stems from the fact that not all kinds of social support may be equally beneficial from the same individuals (Brown & Harris, 1978; Gottlieb, 1981; Hirsch, 1980; Shinn, Lehmann, & Wong, 1984). Researchers have suggested that if social support efforts come from the wrong person, or if the wrong kind of support is offered, it may actually exacerbate stress (Cohen & McKay, 1983; Suls, 1982; Wortman, 1984). In her study of cancer patients, Dunkel-Schetter 91984) found evidence for this position. She asked cancer patients to describe the most helpful and most unhelpful things anyone had done since their cancer diagnoses. When possible, responses were coded into four categories: emotional support, instrumental support, informational support, and appraisal support. Her respondents indicated that family, medical caregivers, and, to a lesser extent, friends were all extremely helpful in providing social support during the cancer episode. However, different types of support were reported to be helpful from different individuals. Overall, instances of emotional support were perceived as most helpful by 81% of respondents. Informational support, that is the provision of specific information to the cancer patient by another person, was perceived as extremely helpful by 41% of respondents. Providing direct aid and giving patients appraisal support were much less frequently perceived as extremely helpful, each by 6% of respondents.

More interesting were the patterns of which kinds of support were desirable from whom. Somewhat surprisingly, emotional support was perceived as helpful regardless of whether it came from family, friends, or medical personnel. In fact, the lack of emotional support from physicians and other medical caregivers was commonly perceived as unhelpful. In contrast, information and advice were perceived as helpful when they came from medical caregivers, but were often perceived as unhelpful if they came from family and friends. Clearly, then, when one considers adequacy of social support for cancer patients, one must examine not only the overall amount of support an individual receives, but who is providing what kind of support.

A Recent Study

To address this issue, we selected a subset of individuals from the larger interview study we had conducted on social support (Taylor et al., 1986). Respondents were selected from the larger sample on the basis of gender (equal representation of men and women), age (between 30 and 70), prognosis (split on good and fair/poor prognosis), and whether or not the individual had participated in a cancer support group. All sites of cancer were included.

A total of 55 people, 30 women and 25 men, with a median age of 54 participated in the interview study. In all, 83% (N = 47) were married, and 84% had children; 31 (56%) were employed, mostly in white collar or professional jobs, and the median yearly family income was between $40,000 and $49,000. Some 93% had completed high school, and 29% were college graduates. Overall, 44% were Protestant, 25% were Jewish, 13% were Catholic, and 18% indicated either another or no religious affiliation.

All participants had first had their cancer diagnosed or had sustained a recurrence (whichever was most recent) within the previous six years ($M = 3.2$ years, $SD = 1.7$); 11 study participants (20%) were receiving treatment for their cancer at the time of the interview. Using medical chart materials, an independent oncologist rated prognosis on a five-point scale ranging from 1 (very guarded or grave prognosis) to 5 (probable cure). Overall, 36 patients had cancers that were rated 4 or 5 (in remission), and the remainder ($N = 19$) had prognostic ratings of 1, 2, or 3 (active cancers).

A total of 27% had never attended a support group, 22% had attended only briefly, and 50% had at one time been regular attendees. Only 10 patients (18%), however, were regularly attending support group meetings at the time of the interview.

Each study participant was asked about the social support or nonsupport received from each of seven sources: spouse, other family members, friends, casual acquaintances, other cancer patients, physicians, and nurses. The specific questions were: (1) In the time since your diagnosis, what is the most helpful thing that (support target) has said or done to help you with your cancer? and (2) In the time since your diagnosis, what has your (support target) said or done that you experienced as most annoying, or that upset you, made you angry, or just somehow rubbed you the wrong way?

Some Results

The most commonly reported helpful and annoying or upsetting actions provided by each of the seven potential social support providers were as follows. From the *spouse,* three behaviors were mentioned as most helpful. They included physical presence (just being there) (35%), expressions of concern and love (33%), and a calm acceptance of the participant's illness and its consequences (30%). The following quote about a patient's husband illustrates two codes, physical presence and expression of concern and love:

> He was always there beside me, even when I was throwing up from the chemotherapy. He still loved me even when I lost my hair.

Other helpful actions from spouses were the provision of practical assistance (20%) and expression of optimism about the patient's prognosis or ability to live successfully with the cancer (20%). (The total exceeds 100% because several respondents indicated more than one helpful action.)

The most annoying behaviors that patients reported from their spouses included being critical of how the patient was handling the cancer (20%), minimizing the impact of the cancer (13%), and expressing too much worry and pessimism about the illness (13%). One woman described how her husband was critical of her:

> I might be okay for months, and then all of a sudden, and I still don't know why, I'll feel insecure and depressed. He gets angry at my inability to mentally tolerate these things. so, of course, I get angry at him cause I say to myself, "You don't know what it's like."

Overall, 39% of the married respondents could not think of an unsupportive spousal act.

In response to the question inquiring about the helpful social support provided by *other family members,* 68% of respondents with children reported about a helpful example of support provided by their children. Most commonly, helpful experiences centered on three behaviors: expressions of concern and affection (40%), mere presence (29%), and practical assistance such as providing transportation, preparing meals, and providing postsurgical care (24%).

In response to the question about asking family behaviors that were most upsetting, the two most frequently mentioned acts were family members minimizing the seriousness of the cancer (18%), or criticizing the patient's response to the cancer (13%).

From *friends,* the most helpful efforts at support were showing love and concern (30%), providing practical assistance (24%), and calmly accepting the illness (23%). In the following quote, a patient describes how his friends' calm acceptance of his cancer was helpful:

> I faced and my friends faced it. They just accepted it. So I had cancer, and you

know it was no big deal. Because that's the way I wanted it. I didn't want no big deal, crying the blues and all that kind of stuff.

With respect to unhelpful or upsetting behaviors, 17% (33% of respondents who had any complaints about their friends) reported that the most annoying or up-setting thing a friend did was to avoid social contact with them. This pattern reflects the same problem reported by the breast cancer patients. As in the study, the finding presented here does not denote social rejection from friends generally, but that re-spondents were often bothered by a particular friend who withdrew from them. In addition to concern over being avoided, 13% of respondents were upset by friends who were overtly pessimistic about their cancer or cancer in general.

Respondents' views of what was helpful and unhelpful from *acquaintances* were, on certain dimensions, similar to what they said about friends. For example, being concerned (16%) and calm (14%) were helpful and being pessimistic (20%) was experienced as unhelpful. But they also had very different experiences with these two groups of people. Practical assistance was more frequently helpful from friends, but infrequently mentioned with respect to acquaintances (only 7%). Social avoidance was the single most frequently mentioned complaint about friends, but only rarely mentioned for acquaintances (4%). The two most frequently mentioned examples of nonsupport from acquaintances were their pessimism about cancer (20%), and rude or inappropriate remarks about the illness (13%). Examples of re-sponses that were coded as rude and inappropriate include comments about the pa-tient's hair (e.g., "Your hair has grown in all grey"), physical damage resulting from surgery (e.g., "How can you still feel like a woman?"), and other miscellaneous rude remarks (e.g., "I thought you had died!"). In some cases, the acquaintances' inap-propriate or pessimistic comments stemmed from the fact that they did not know that the person with whom they were speaking was a cancer patient. In other cases, acquaintances seemed simply not to know how to act or what to say, and as a result said or did the wrong thing.

With respect to *other people who had or have had cancer,* the most frequently reported helpful behavior was their ability to offer the special kind of understand-ing that one gets from sharing a similar experience (27%), as the following quote illustrates:

> I don't have to say much to another breast cancer patient for her to understand. The most common one is what happens a week to a few days prior to getting a check-up. All you got to do is say, "My check-up is in three days," and they know what that experience is like. It's almost like a club. When you get hypersensitive to an unusual symptom or feeling, you only have to say a few words and they understand.

The provision of useful information about cancer and its treatment (25%), and acting as a good role model (21%) were also common helpful behaviors offered by others with cancer. The single most unsupportive thing that others with cancer did was to deal with their own cancer in a way that the respondent thought was self-destructive or foolish (23%) such as being pessimistic or continuing to smoke.

Concerning health care professionals, respondents indicated that the most helpful things provided by *physicians* were medical information (38%), effective medical care (27%), and expressions of optimism about the prognosis or the patient's ability to live with the cancer (27%). As examples of nonsupportive physician behaviors, respondents reported that not giving sufficient medical information (25%), and failure to express concern and empathy (16%) were the most unhelpful things their physicians did. From *nurses,* the most helpful behaviors were being concerned and empathetic (24%), being generally pleasant and kind (18%), providing practical assistance (i.e., nursing care—18%), and providing information (16%). As for unsupportive actions, 20% mentioned technical incompetence, 14% mentioned minimizing the impact of the illness, and 11% reported that being unconcerned with the patient as a person were the most annoying or upsetting acts.

In outlining general trends regarding helpful actions, it is evident that to a greater or lesser extent, concern and empathy—the warm aspects of interpersonal relationships—were perceived as helpful from all sources. These results are consistent with Dunkel-Schetter's (1984) findings. Emotional support was most important from close others (spouse, family, and friends), but it was clearly important from medical personnel as well. With the exception of this dimension, however, there seemed to be considerable specificity in the socially supportive actions that were experienced as helpful by different providers. Intimates' most helpful actions included love and concern, physical presence, calm acceptance of the disease, and to a lesser extent, practical assistance. Other people with cancer provided information about the disease, the special understanding that comes from being a similar other, and a good role model. Medical personnel provided capable medical care, medical information, and optimism.

It is notable that very few respondents reported that being permitted to express the full range of their emotions (ventilation) was a helpful function with regard to the cancer. This missing finding was unexpected. It is commonly assumed, both by professionals and layman, that "getting concerns off your chest" is beneficial, yet very few respondents mentioned this as a socially supportive function.

Patients generally reported different unhelpful efforts from different categories of people. From the spouse, being critical of how the patient was handling the illness was the most frequently cited unhelpful experience. These incidents often appeared to be misfired efforts at social support in that, based on the examples reported, spouses were apparently attempting to provide useful feedback, which was experienced by the patients as critical.

Regarding friends, the most common complaint was that at least one friend avoided social contact with them, and this appears to be a fairly robust finding. As for acquaintances, pessimism and rude remarks about cancer were experienced as most upsetting. Finally, respondents reported that the most unhelpful acts experienced from health care professionals involved their failure to provide information, human concern, or technically competent medical care.

As noted earlier, social support researchers have been alert to the possibility that different types of social support may be valuable from different individuals in a social network, and our data largely support that caution. However, a parallel point suggested by these data should also be noted, namely that different kinds of social support may be valuable for different individuals undergoing the same stressful event. Our data suggest relatively little consensus about what types of behaviors are seen as supportive and unsupportive from particular targets in the social support network. For example, one individual may consider the spouse just being there to be a sign of support, whereas another individual may experience the spouse's presence as supportive only if it is accompanied by expressions of concern and love. Similarly, one individual may find the physician's medical attention to the cancer to be sufficiently helpful, whereas another individual may feel a need for emotional support as well.

It should be noted that there were relatively few instances in which a behavior seen as helpful by one individual was seen as unhelpful by another. For example, no respondent suggested that expressions of emotional concern from a medical caregiver were unhelpful. On the other hand, consensus regarding supportive and unsupportive behaviors was never greater than 35%, indicating that there is clear variability in what is seen as helpful or unhelpful from the same target. These findings suggest that, while medical caregivers, family and friends, and others in a cancer patient's network can be appraised of the kinds of actions that are typically perceived as supportive and unsupportive by cancer patients, they must also be alert to the fact that there are considerable individual differences in these preferences. Thus recommendations regarding supportive or unsupportive behaviors should be tempered with knowledge about particular patients and their preferences for certain kinds of actions.

References

Abrams, R. D., & Finesinger, J. E. (1953). Guilt reactions in patients with cancer. *Cancer, 6,* 474–482.

American Cancer Society. (1986). *Cancer facts and figures 1986.* New York: Author.

Barrera, M. (1981). Social support in the adjustment of pregnant adolescents: assessment issues. In B. Gottlieb (Ed.), *Social networks of social support* (pp. 69–96). Beverly Hills, CA: Sage.

Berkman, L. F., & Syme, S. L. (1979). Social networks, host resistance, and mortality: A nine-year follow-up study of Alameda County residents. *American Journal of Epidemiology, 109,* 186–204.

Billings, A. A., & Moos, R. H. (1982). Social support and functioning among community and clinical groups: A panel model. *Journal of Behavioral Medicine, 5,* 295–312.

Bloom, J. R. (1982). Social support, accommodation to stress, and adjustment to breast cancer. *Social Science and Medicine, 16,* 1329–1338.

Brown, G. W., & Harris, T. (1978). *Social origins of depression.* London: Tavistock.

Campbell, A., Converse, P. E., & Rogers, W. L. (1976). *The quality of American life: Perceptions, evaluations, and satisfactions.* New York: Russell Sage.

Carey, R. C. (1974). Emotional adjustment in terminal patients: A quantitative approach. *Journal of Counseling Psychology, 21,* 433–439.

Chambers, W. N., & Reiser, M. F. (1953). Emotional stress in the precipitation of congestive heart failure. *Medicine, 15,* 38–60.

Cobb, S. (1976). Social support as a moderator of life stress. *Psychosomatic Medicine, 38,* 300–314.

Cohen, S., & McKay, G. (1983). Interpersonal relationships as buffers of the impact of psychosocial stress on health. In A. Baum, S. E. Taylor, & J. E. Singer (Eds.), *Handbook of psychology and health* (Vol. 4, pp. 253–267). Hillsdale, NJ: Lawrence Erlbaum.

Cohen, S., & Wills, T. A. (1985). Stress, social support, and the buffering hypothesis. *Psychological Bulletin, 98,* 310–357.

DiMatteo, M. R., & Hays, R. (1981). Social support and serious illness. In B. H. Gottlieb (Ed.), *Social networks and social support in community mental health* (pp. 117–147). Beverly Hills, CA: Sage.

Dimond, M. (1979). Social support and adaptation to chronic illness: The case of maintenance hemodialysis. *Research in Nursing and Health, 2,* 101–108.

Dunkel-Schetter, C. (1984). Social support and cancer. Findings based on patient interviews and their implications. *Journal of Social Issues, 40*(4), 77–98.

Dunkel-Schetter, C., & Wortman, C. B. (1982). The interactional dynamics of cancer: Problems in social relationships and their impact on the patient. In H. S. Friedman & M. R. Di Matteo (Eds.), *Interpersonal issues in health care* (pp. 69–100). New York: Academic Press.

Dunkel-Schetter, C., Folkman, S., & Lazarus, R. S. (in press). Correlates of social support receipt. *Journal of Personality and Social Psychology.*

Giaquinta, B. (1977). Helping families face the crisis of cancer. *American Journal of Nursing, 77,* 1585–1588.

Gottlieb, B. H. (1981). Preventive interventions involving social networks and social support. In B. H. Gottlieb (Ed.), *Social networks and social support* (pp. 201–232). Beverly Hills, CA: Sage.

Hirsch, B. J. (1980). Natural support systems and coping with major life changes. *American Journal of Community Psychology, 8,* 159–179.

House, T. A. (1981). *Work stress and social support.* Reading, MA: Addison-Wesley.

Jackson, J. K. (1956). The problem of alcoholic tuberculous patients. In P. F. Sparer (Ed.), *Personality stress and tuberculosis* (pp. 504–538). New York: International Universities Press.

Kaplan, B. H., Robbins, C., & Martin, S. S. (1983). Antecedents of psychological stress in young adults: Self-rejection, deprivation of social support, and life events. *Journal of Health and Social Behavior, 24,* 230–244.

Lichtman, R. R., & Taylor, S. E. (1986). Close relationships and the female cancer patient. In B. L. Andersen (Ed.), *Women with cancer: Psychological perspectives.* New York: Springer-Verlag.

Lichtman, R. R., Taylor, S. E., & Wood, J. V. (in press). Social support and marital adjustment after breast cancer. *Journal of Psychosocial Oncology.*

Lin, N., Simeone, R. S., Ensel, W. T., & Kuo, W. (1979). Social support, stressful life events, and illness: A model and an empirical test. *Journal of Health and Social Behavior, 20,* 108–119.

McNair, D. M., Lorr, M., & Droppleman, L. F. (1971). *EITS manual for the profile of mood states.* San Diego, CA: Educational and Industrial Testing Service.

Nuckolls, K. B., Cassel, J. C., & Kaplan, B. H. (1972). Psychosocial assets, life crisis, and the progress of pregnancy. *American Journal of Epidemiology, 95,* 431.

Peters-Golden, H. (1982). Breast cancer: Varied perceptions of social support in the illness experience. *Social Science and Medicine, 16,* 483–491.

Robertson, E. K., & Suinn, R. M. (1968). The determination of rate of progress of stroke patients through empathy measures of patient and family. *Journal of Psychomatic Research, 12,* 189–191.

Shinn, M., Lehmann, S., & Wong, N. W. (1984). Social interaction and social support. *Journal of Social Issues, 40*(4), 55–76.

Silver, R. L., & Wortman, C. B. (1980). Coping with undesirable life events. In J. Garber & M.E.P. Seligman (Eds.), *Human helplessness: Theory and application* (pp. 279–340). New York: Academic Press.

Suls, J. (1982). Social Support, interpersonal relations, and health: Benefits and liabilities. In G. S. Saunders & J. Suls (Eds.), *Social psychology of health and illness* (pp. 255–277). Hillsdale, NJ: Lawrence Erlbaum.

Taylor, S. E., Falke, R. L., Mazel, R. M., & Hilsberg, B. L. (in press). Sources of satisfaction and dissatisfaction among members of cancer support groups. In B. Gottlieb (Ed.), *Creating support groups: Formats, processes, and effects.* Beverly Hills, CA: Sage.

Taylor, S. E., Falke, R. L., Shoptaw, S. J., & Lichtman, R. R. (1986). Social support, support groups, and the cancer patient. *Journal of Consulting and Clinical Psychology, 54,* 608–615.

Vettese, J. M. (1976). Problems of the patient confronting the diagnosis of cancer. In J. W. Cullen, B. H. Fox, & R. N. Isom (Eds.), *Cancer: The behavioral dimensions* (pp. 275–282). New York: Raven.

Wallston, B. S., Alagna, S. W., DeVellis, B. M., & DeVellis, R. F. (1983). Social support and physical health. *Health Psychology, 2,* 367–391.

Williams, A. W., Ware, J. E., Jr., & Donald, C. A. (1981). A model of mental health, life events, and social supports applicable to general populations. *Journal of Health and Social Behavior, 22,* 324–336.

Wortman, C. B. (1984). Social support and the cancer patient. *Cancer, 53* (Suppl. 10), 2339–2360.

Wortman, C. B., & Dunkel-Schetter, C. (1979). Interpersonal relationships and cancer: A theoretical analysis. *Journal of Social Issues, 35*(1), 120–155.

Larry Bernard
Edward Krupat

The Patient–Practitioner Relationship

In this article, Bernard and I take a basic understanding of social relationships and apply this to the medical realm in discussing the patient–practitioner relationship. For instance, just as in any relationship, there must be open communication and good information sharing. We review the different kinds of relationships that doctors and patients form, asking if one kind or another is the best. In general, research has indicated that patients are most satisfied when they are treated with warmth and respect and as a whole people, not just medical conditions. Ask yourself how satisfied you are with your primary physician. What are some of the things he or she does that make you most or least pleased?

Modern medicine has progressed to a point beyond the imagination of early health practitioners. Technological advances and medical breakthroughs have given the physician an ability to diagnose and treat that would have been considered science fiction only years ago. Yet, in spite of these great discoveries—or in part because of them—all is not well with modern medicine. For all of the growth we have witnessed on the technical side of medicine, the interpersonal side, involving the human element of care, has not kept pace. In fact, several observers, including doctors, have asked whether this aspect of medical care has suffered with the advent of modern technological and bureaucratic medicine.

THE ART AND SCIENCE OF MEDICINE

The idea of treating the body by attending to the spirit has always caused tension in medicine. Although the philosopher Descartes expounded on the duality of body and mind, early physicians relied heavily on their interpersonal skills. In fact, sometimes they could offer little more than compassion, hope, and an effective bedside manner. The early Greek Hippocrates, known as the father of medicine, once wrote that it is possible that a patient "may recover his health through his contentment with the goodness of his physician."

In modern health care, the general practitioner and the small town doctor who minister to all of a family's problems, physical as well as personal, are quickly disappearing. Increasingly, patients are being seen in large medical complexes by teams of highly specialized practitioners who diagnose via computer and treat using the latest technology. As a result, the technical quality of care has improved, but patients often report that "something is missing" in their relationship with their physician. As stated by one concerned physician, "Increasingly, people feel that their doctors do not or cannot listen, and are too caught up in struggles for money, status, knowledge, and power. . . . The patient and doctor no longer know and appreciate each other as people, working toward a common goal." (Roter & Hall, 1992)

This discussion underlines the distinction between the *art* and the *science* of medicine (Bloom, 1963; DiMattero, 1979), between the tasks of *caring* versus *curing*. Yet, health psychologists feel strongly that the interpersonal and technical sides of medicine cannot be separated, and that a health professional must combine both in order to provide effective treatment. In referring to the perspective of health psychologists, Friedman and DiMatteo (1979) have stated:

> They are not merely saying that the physician should smile, as did the old family physician, while prescribing a particular treatment regimen. Nor are they saying that modern physicians should remember that the patient is a person with feelings, and should be treated as such as a matter of civility. Rather, they are proposing that interpersonal relations are a part of the basic process of healing. . . . Ignoring these factors is not an error of ethics or courtesy; it is a scientific error (p. 4).

THE NATURE OF THE PATIENT–PRACTITIONER RELATIONSHIP

It is curious that the term "relationship" has been used to describe what goes on between a physician and a patient. Some people have preferred to use the more neutral term "encounter" (Anderson & Helm, 1979) or the term "health transaction" (Stone, 1979) to capture its more business-oriented or problem-centered side. The concept of relationship does fit, however, because it captures the essential elements of what goes on in all relationships: Two people come together and enter into an agreement to engage in some form of exchange with the purpose of accomplishing one or more goals. When a patient and practitioner enter into a relationship, their goals may be well defined or vague, mutually agreed upon or not, and the interaction may differ in terms of its length, commitment, or intensity. Still, a bond is formed between the two participants about a key issue for them both, the patient's health (Krupat, 1983).

The Szasz-Hollender Models

In a classic paper, Szasz and Hollender (1956) have described three different types or models of patient–practitioner relationship. In the first, the model of activity–passivity, a great asymmetry of power exists, almost like the relationship between a parent and a very young child. The doctor is in complete control, and the patient is passive, little more than a work object to whom things are done. The treatment of the patient is almost totally determined by the physician and takes place independent of any preferences or contributions of the patient. Clinically, this might be appropriate in cases of acute trauma where the patient is bleeding, or when the patient is anesthetized or in a coma.

The second model, guidance-cooperation, underlies much of modern medical practice, especially in the treatment of acute illness. In this model, the patient's thoughts, feelings, and desires are made known, yet they still only serve as background for the choice of the physician. The patient has a problem and seeks answers from a knowledgeable health professional, readily willing to cooperate with the solution generated. An asymmetry of power still exists, but in contrast to the activity–passivity model, it is closer to that between a parent and adolescent.

The third model is mutual participation. This relationship is characterized by mutual respect, information sharing, and a decision-making process in which both participants have equal input. This is the sort of adult-to-adult partnership more likely found in the treatment of chronic disease, and it is often advocated by those who have taken a more activist stance.

The Consumer Model

Although it is difficult to estimate how common each of these models has become, there has been a clear trend away from patient passivity. The old authority relationship in which absolute trust was placed in the physician is slowly but surely eroding, and in its place, we see one in which the physician's automatic right to govern is being challenged and the patient's rights to participate and decide are being demanded (Haug & Lavin, 1983). Conceptualizing these models somewhat differently, Roter and Hall (1992) have included a consumerist model, which was not even considered by Szasz and Hollender when they were writing in the 1950s (see Table 10.1).

The consumerist model goes one step beyond the mutual participation model in reversing the balance of power between patient and practitioner. It envisions a health care relationship in which the practitioner is more of a skilled consultant who responds to the directives and needs of an informed and increasingly skeptical health care consumer. The consumerist model has been embraced by many but criticized by others for going too far. Its critics argue that those who take this orientation may underutilize the health professional's skills and expertise, placing themselves in a position of conflict and lack of trust (Steward & Roter, 1989).

TABLE 10.1 Types of Doctor–Patient Relationships

Patient Control	Physician Control	
	Low	High
Low	Default	Paternalism
High	Consumerist	Mutuality

Patient Satisfaction

At the heart of the discussion of patient–practitioner relations are two basic questions: To what extent are people satisfied with the medical care that they receive? And what aspects or elements are they most satisfied and dissatisfied with? These questions have been difficult to answer for several reasons. First, different studies of satisfaction have defined and measured satisfaction in unique ways, making cross-study comparisons difficult. Second, the degree of satisfaction found differs somewhat depending on how specifically the question is asked. The more specific the question ("How satisfied are you with your last visit with your doctor?" versus "Are you satisfied with the health care system?"), the more satisfied people report that they are (Hall & Dornan, 1998a). Third, the level of satisfaction reported depends on whom is asked, and when (Ross, Wheaton, & Duff, 1981).

Recently, Judith Hall, Debra Roter, and their colleagues (Hall & Dornan, 1990; 1988a, 1988b; Hall, Roter & Katz, 1988) have applied the method of meta-analysis, a statistical technique that allows the results of many different studies to be combined and compared, to summarize the results of more than 200 satisfaction studies. Overall, they found very high levels of satisfaction, averaging 81% and ranging from a high of 99% to a low of 43% (Hall & Dorman, 1988a).

Satisfaction has been divided into many different categories (Ware & Hays, 1988; Ware, Davies-Avery, & Stewart, 1978; Pascoe, 1983). In Table 10.2, we present the 10 specific aspects of care evaluated by Hall and Dorman, ranked according to patient satisfaction. In spite of concerns about the interpersonal skills of physicians, humaneness is the factor with which patients are most satisfied, followed closely by the competence of physicians and the outcome of care. In the bottom half, we find two types of issues. The first involves the patient's relationship to the sys-

TABLE 10.2 Overall Ranking of Satisfaction With 10 Specific Aspects of Medical Care Based on 107 Studies

Aspects	Rank
Humaneness	1
Competence	2
Outcome	3
Facilities	4
Continuity of care	5
Access	6
Informativeness	7
Cost	8
Bureaucracy	9
Attention to psychosocial problems	10

Source: Hall, J. A., & Dornan, M. C., (1988b).

tem, as represented by concerns over cost, access to care, and bureaucracy. The second deals with the amount of information patients receive, and whether they are treated by their doctors as something more than a narrowly defined medical problem.

DOCTOR–PATIENT COMMUNICATION

Patients seem to be least satisfied with the degree to which doctors address their psychosocial concerns, treating them as whole people within the border context of their lives. For instance, a study of 75 women who were receiving radiotherapy following a mastectomy showed that one third developed sexual problems and one quarter showed signs of clinical depression within a year of their operations. However, none of the sexual problems were identified by their physicians, and only half of the depressed women were identified and treated for this problem (McGuire et al., 1978). It is easy to see how these psychological and sexual problems might be missed if we assume that the physicians were taking a disease-centered approach. When physicians define the problem narrowly according to the biomedical model, they may look no further than the malignancy and miss other important aspects or consequences of the illness experience that are not technically a part of the physical ailment.

Information Sharing

Information giving, which is the single variable that best predicts satisfaction, ranked 8 out of the 10 dimensions measured (Hall, Roter, & Katz, 1988). During a typical visit, doctors and patients do not spend a great deal of time together, an average of 16.5 minutes according to research by Howard Waitzkin (1984). Of that time, 1 minute and 18 seconds, less than 10%, involves information given by doctor to patient. Still, when asked how much time they had spent giving information, on the average the doctors responded almost 9 minutes, overestimating by a factor of almost 7. And when asked how much information their patients wanted, the physicians underestimated the amount desired in 65% of the cases.

Although it might be easy to blame doctors for this lack of information giving, patients typically ask no more than 3 or 4 questions per visit (Roter, 1984), and question-time ranges from 0 to 97 seconds, averaging an unbelievably low 8 seconds (Waitzkin, 1984). Still, patients report that they would like more information about their diagnosis, the prognosis for recovery, and the origins of their condition (Kindelan & Kent, 1987), as well as more complete disclosure about the risks of procedures and medications (Faden et al., 1981; Keown, Slovic, & Lichtenstein, 1984).

Information and power. To explain the lack of time allotted to information giving and question asking, a broad range of possibilities exist. Several noted researchers (Waitzkin, 1985; Waitzkin & Stoeckle, 1976; Freidson, 1970) believe that doctors avoid giving information and leave patients in a state of uncertainty to preserve power, that the doctor–patient relationship is a "micropolitical situation" in which the doctor withholds information to maintain dominance and patients seek it to challenge that dominance. Yet, to the extent that the doctor and patient are in a "struggle" over information, much of the evidence suggests that patients do not put up much of a fight. Many patients hesitate to ask for information, clarification, or additional information for fear of appearing ignorant, while others fear that they are taking time from more pressing requirements of the doctor or other more needy patients (Tuckett et al., 1985).

Although some doctors may withhold information to maintain power, the patient's desire for information is not necessarily accompanied by a desire to challenge the physician's right to make decisions (Beisecker & Beisecker, 1990). When technical knowledge is needed for decision making, people are generally willing to let the person with more expertise do so. However, when a choice must be made between equally effective treatments, in this case patients want some control over the decision (Kaplan, 1991; Pitts et al., 1991).

Patient characteristics. Another explanation for the lack of information exchange between patient and provider focuses on the characteristics of the patient (Clark, Potter, & McKinlay, 1991). In general, patients who are white, older, or female, as well as those with greater education and from the middle and upper classes, are given more time, ask more questions, and get more explanations. The more serious the diagnosis and the longer the doctor and patient have known each other, the greater the exchange of information as well (Hall, Roter, & Katz, 1988; Waitzkin, 1985). These findings suggest that physicians probably spend more time with people with whom they are most comfortable, and they dispense more or less information according to how much they believe patients want or can benefit from it. However, these assessments may often be inaccurate when they are based on stereotypes about race, sex, and class.

Quality of Doctor–Patient Communication

More than the mere *quantity* of information conveyed, what can we say about the *quality* of doctor–patient communication? In a classic study, Barbara Korsch and her colleagues (Korsch, Gozzi, & Francis, 1968) tape recorded 800 pediatric visits in a hospital outpatient clinic and then conducted follow-up interviews with the mothers. The communication tone of the visits was generally very technical and narrowly focused—that is to say, disease centered. The mothers reported that their emotional concerns were rarely addressed, and approximately one quarter did not have the opportunity to express the single most important problem on their minds. Twenty percent felt they were not given a clear explanation of what was wrong with their child, and almost half were unsure of what had caused their child's illness. Although these interactions involved white American, middle-class physicians with patients who were predominantly poor and black, similar findings have been reported in a wide variety of settings and with different patient populations in different countries (Ben-Sira, 1985; Clark, Potter, & McKinlay, 1991; Pendleton & Bochner, 1980).

Even when information is conveyed from doctor to patient, it is not always understood. In another classic study, Bonnie Svarstad (1976) observed patients at a neighborhood health center reputed to be one of the best of its kind. She found that more than three out of four times the physicians failed to give explicit instructions about how prescribed drugs should be taken, and when they did, the instructions were often ambiguous. In fact, more than half of the patients interviewed misunderstood the very purpose for which they were taking their medications. Some of the patients who had received prescriptions to control their blood pressure reported that the drug was meant to treat symptoms as diverse as asthma, palpitations, and lower back pain. Even more notably, Svarstad reported that many times she herself could not understand the directions offered to the patients. Even for something as basic as naming a condition, Hadlow and Pitts (1991) report that patients often misunderstand a range of terms such as "eating disorder," "migraine," and "stroke."

Medical jargon. Some of the failure of communication between patient and practitioner can be traced to the use of medical jargon. Defined as the specialized or technical language of a trade, jargon allows doctors to speak to one another in a strange dialect that is all their own. Pediatrician Perri Klass (1987), telling of her experience in learning this new language, offers one such example:

> "Mrs. Tolstoy is your basic L.L.L. in N.A.D. admitted for a soft rule-out M.I.," the intern announces. I scribble that on my patient list. In other words Mrs. Tolstoy is a Little Old lady in No Apparent Distress who is in the hospital to make sure she hasn't had a heart attack (rule out myocardial infarction). And we think it's unlikely that she has had a heart attack (a soft rule-out). (p. 73)

Physicians even use terms that laypeople cannot understand even when there are simpler ways of saying things. They might say, "He had a pneumonectomy" instead of, "He had a lung removed." At other times they may communicate almost completely in numbers, noting that "his PO_2 is 45; pCO_2, 40; and pH 7.4" (Johnson, 1980). After a while, "doctor talk" becomes so natural that physicians forget when they are speaking it.

Jargon serves several purposes for health professionals. It allows them to communicate with one another in a fast, efficient manner and creates a sense of professional spirit and identification among people who are working under daily stress. Jargon helps to distance health professionals from the strong emotions that come with their work, yet it can distance them from their patients as well. When patients hear their doctors talking to one another about them in technical language, or when they are offered explanations in terms that they cannot understand, it makes them feel left out and leaves them frustrated.

Waitzkin (1984) has recommended that the communication ability of physicians be assessed according to how often physicians use *multilevel explanations* and *nondiscrepant responses*. Multilevel explanations offer a technical explanation accompanied by an explanation in everyday terms. In this way the physician educates the patient in the jargon, while at the same time offering understandable information. Nondiscrepant responses are answers given by physicians at the same level of technicality as the question asked by the patient. By giving complex answers to complex questions (and vice versa), physicians indicate that they have listened carefully, and they offer useful information by speaking in a language that matches the patient's level of sophistication.

Nonverbal communication. In addition to the content of verbal communication, we have become increasingly aware of the importance of nonverbal communication. The messages that gestures, tone of voice, posture, and facial expressions convey can be every bit as important as those communicated by words. Physician behaviors that express a warm social climate such as sitting close, maintaining eye contact, leaning forward, and nodding in response to patient comments are associated with patient satisfaction (Hall, Roter, & Katz, 1988). In addition, physicians who have greater nonverbal sensitivity both in their ability to decide patients' emotions and to express their own feelings have more satisfied patients (DiMatteo, Hays, & Prince, 1986; DiMatteo et al., 1980; Friedman, 1982).

In sum, what do patients want from their doctors? A simple answer is difficult because patients differ according to their orientations, values, and needs. Some desire an active, involved relationship while others are satisfied to remain passive (Haug & Lavin, 1983; Krantz, Baum, & Weideman, 1980; Woodward & Wallston, 1987). However, we can make some generalizations that hold for a large part of the populace. People want to be treated with warmth and respect, to be given good technical care but related to as "whole people," not just as medical conditions. When they begin to interact with a physician in what is known as the history section of a medical encounter, they want the opportunity to express their concerns in their own words. And at the end, in the conclusion section, they want to be provided with information and have the chance to engage in feedback exchanges that build a partnership between doctor and patient (Stiles et al., 1979a, 1979b).

IMPROVING DOCTOR–PATIENT RELATIONS

Doctor–patient communication and patient satisfaction are not just topics of academic interest. Dissatisfied patients are more likely to shop around for doctors, to change health plans, to fail to follow medical advice, and even to sue (Kaplan & Ware, 1989). Conversely, greater patient involvement and satisfaction have been directly associated with better patient health outcomes (Greenfield, Kaplan, & Ware, 1985; Greenfield et al., 1988).

Several programs to improve satisfaction and communication have been initiated. One focus has been on the training of physicians. Medical schools such as those at Harvard, the University of New Mexico, and McMaster in Canada have been leaders in integrating the behavioral sciences into medical study and in highlighting the teaching of communication skills (Nooman, Schmidt, & Ezzat, 1990; Tosteson, 1990). At Long Beach Memorial Medical Center in California, residents are actually required to spend time as hospital patients to truly appreciate the patient's perspective.

Programs working with practicing physicians have also been effective. At the

Johns Hopkins Hospital, a series of tutorial sessions were set up for physicians using the Health Belief Model as a guide for interviewing. The doctors were asked to inquire about patients' attitudes, beliefs and perceptions concerning their condition rather than focusing on physical signs and complications. After a single session, the physicians in this program were found to spend more time on patient teaching and to generate greater patient knowledge than physicians who did not receive this training (Inui, Yourtee, & Williamson, 1976). Bertakis (1977) encouraged physicians to end their medical sessions by having patients repeat information in their own words, clarifying anything that was confusing or adding relevant information that was omitted. When questioned later on, patients were not only more satisfied, but recalled 20% more information than a control group.

Other programs have focused on the patient rather than on the physician. Roter (1984) encouraged patients to identify questions they would like answered during their visit. She reported that this intervention increased question asking compared to a control group, although on the average patients did not end up asking as many questions as they initially intended. More recently, Thompson, Nanni, & Schwankovsky (1990) had one group of women write down questions to ask their doctor before a visit. A second group received a brief note from their doctor encouraging question asking, and a third (control) received no special treatment. The researchers found that both intervention groups were more likely to ask what was on their minds, felt more in control, and were also more satisfied with their visits.

Using a more comprehensive approach, Greenfield, Kaplan, & Ware (1985) reviewed patients' medical records with them, went over methods of treatment, and coached them in how to discuss and negotiate with their doctors. Patients who received this 20-minute coaching session were significantly more active and assertive with their doctors, received more information, and indicated that they liked taking a more active role. Most important, they reported fewer physical limitations during the 8 weeks following the study.

Programs such as these, which involve only small investments of time on the part of patients and doctors, have been quite successful and are likely to grow in the future. They acknowledge that every encounter between a doctor and patient represents a therapeutic opportunity, and that technical skill and knowledge must be accompanied by equal amounts of caring and communication. As we incorporate this into everyday practice, the doctor–patient relationship will improve, and so will medical care.

References

Anderson, W. T., & Helm, D. T. (1979). The physician-patient encounter. A process of reality negotiation. In E. G. Jaco (Ed.), *Patients, physicians, and illness* (3rd ed.). New York: Free Press.

Balint, M., Hung, J., Joyce, D., Marinker, M., and Woodcock, J. (1970). *Treatment or diagnosis: A study of repeat prescription in general practice.* Toronto: J. B. Lippincott.

Beisecker, A. E., and Beisecker, T. D. (1990). Patient information–seeking behaviors when communicating with doctors. *Medical Care, 28,* 19–28.

Ben-Sira, Z. (1985). Primary medical care and coping with stress and disease: The inclination of primary care practitioners to demonstrate affective behavior. *Social Science and Medicine, 21,* 485–498.

Bertakis, K. D. (1977). The communication of information from physician to patient: A method for increasing patient retention and satisfaction. *Journal of Family Practice, 5,* 217–222.

Bloom, J. R. (1982). Social support, accommodation to stress, and adjustment to breast cancer. *Social Science and Medicine, 16,* 1329–1338.

Byrne, P. S., & Long, B. E. L. (1976). *Doctors talking to patients.* London: Royal College of General Practitioners.

Clark, J. A., Potter, D. A., & McKinlay, J. B. (1991). Bringing social structure back into clinical decision-making. *Social Science and Medicine, 32,* 853–866.

DiMatteo, M. R. (1979). A social psychological analysis of physician-patient rapport: Toward a science of the art of medicine. *Journal of Social Issues, 35,* 12–33.

DiMatteo, M. R., Hays, R. D., & Prince, L. M. (1986). Relationship of physicians' nonverbal skill to patient satisfaction, appointment non-compliance, and physician workload. *Health Psychology, 5,* 581–594.

DiMatteo, M. R., Taranta, A., Friedman, H. S., & Prince, L. M. (1980). Predicting patient satisfaction from physicians' nonverbal communication skills. *Medical Care, 18,* 376–387.

Faden, R. R., Becker, C., Lewis, C., Freeman, J., & Faden, A. I. (1981). Disclosure of information to patients in medical care. *Medical Care, 19,* 718–733.

Freidson, E. (1970). *Profession of medicine. A study in the sociology of applied knowledge.* New York: Dodd, Mead.

Friedman, H. S. (1982). Nonverbal communication in medical interaction. In H. S. Friedman & M. R. DiMatteo (Eds.), *Interpersonal issues in health care.* New York: Academic Press.

Friedman, H. S. & DiMatteo, M. R. (1979). Health care as an interpersonal process. *Journal of Social Issues, 35,* 1–11.

Greenfield, S., Kaplan, S. H., & Ware, J. E., Jr. (1985). Expanding patient involvement in care: Effects on patient outcomes. *Annals of Internal Medicine, 102,* 520–528.

Greenfield, S., Kaplan, S. H., Ware, J. E., Jr., Yano, E. M., & Frank, H. J. (1988). Patient participation in medical care: Effects on blood sugar control and quality of life in diabetes. *Journal of General Internal Medicine, 3,* 448–457.

Hadlow, J. & Pitts, M. (1991). The understanding of common health terms by doctors, nurses, and patients. *Social Science and Medicine, 32,* 193–196.

Hall, J. A., & Dorman, M. C. (1988a). Meta-analysis of satisfaction with medical care: Description of research done in and analysis of overall satisfaction levels. *Social Science and Medicine, 26,* 637–644.

Hall, J. A., & Dorman, M. C. (1988b). What patients like about their medical care and how often they are asked: A meta-analysis of the satisfaction literature. *Social Science and Medicine, 27,* 935–939.

Hall, J. A., & Dorman, M. C. (1990). Patient sociodemographic characteristics as predictors of satisfaction with medical care: A meta-analysis. *Social Science and Medicine, 30,* 811–818.

Hall, J. A., Roter, D. L., & Katz, N. R. (1988). Meta-analysis of correlates of provider behavior in medical encounters. *Medical Care, 26,* 657–675.

Haug, M. R., & Lavin, B. (1983). *Consumerism in medicine: Challenging physician authority.* Beverly Hills, CA: Sage.

Henbest, R. J. & Stewart, M. (1990). Patient-centeredness in the consultation. 2: Does it really make a difference? *Family Practice, 7,* 28–33.

Inui, T. S., Yourtee, E. L., & Williamson, J. W. (1976). Improved outcomes in hypertension after physician tutorials: A controlled trial. *Annals of Internal Medicine, 84,* 646–651.

Johnson, D. (1980). Doctor talk. In L. Michaels & C. Ricks (Eds.), *The state of the language.* Berkeley, CA: University of California.

Kaplan, R. M. (1991). Health-related quality of life in patient decision-making. *Journal of Social Issues, 47,* 69–90.

Kaplan, S. H., & Ware, J. E., Jr. (1989). The patient's role in health care and quality assessment. In N. Goldfield & D. B. Nash (Eds.), *Providing quality care.* Philadelphia: American College of Physicians.

Keown, C., Slovic, P., & Lichtenstein, S. (1984). Attitudes of physicians, pharmacists, and laypersons toward seriousness and need for disclosure of prescription drug side effects. *Health Psychology, 3,* 1–2.

Kindelan, K., & Kent, G. (1987). Concordance between patients' information preferences and general practitioners' perceptions. *Psychology and Health, 1,* 399–409.

Klass, P. A. (1987). *Not an entirely benign procedure.* New York: Signet.

Korsch, B. M., Gozzi, E. K., & Francis, V. (1968). Gaps in doctor–patient communication. 1. Doctor-patient interaction and patient satisfaction. *Pediatrics, 42,* 855–871.

Krantz, D. S., Baum, A., & Weideman, M. V. (1980). Assessment of preferences for self-treatment and information in health care. *Journal of Personality and Social Psychology, 39,* 977–990.

Krupat, E. (1983). The doctor-patient relationship: A social psychological analysis. In R. F. Kidd & M. J. Saks (Eds.), *Advances in Applied Social Psychology* (Vol. 2). Hillsdale, NJ: Erlbaum.

Levenstein, J. H., Brown, J. B., Weston, W. W., Stewart, M., McCracken, E. C., & McWhinney, I. (1989). Patient-centered clinical interviewing. In M. Steward & D. Roter (Eds.), *Communicating with medical patients.* Beverly Hills, CA: Sage.

Maguire, G. P., Lee, E. G., Barington, D. J., Kuchemann, C. S., Crabtree, R. J., & Cornell, C. E. (1978). Psychiatric morbidity in the first year after mastectomy. *British Medical Journal, 1,* 963–965.

Mishler, E. G. (1984). *The discourse of medicine: Dialectics of medical interviews.* Norwood, NJ: Ablex.

Nooman, Z. M., Schmidt, H. G., & Ezzat, E. S. (1990). *Innovation in medical education: An evaluation of its present status.* New York: Springer-Verlag.

Pascoe, G. C. (1983). Patient satisfaction in primary health care: A literature review and analysis. *Evaluation and Program Planning, 6,* 185–210.

Pendleton, D., & Bochner, S. (1980). The communication of medical information as a function of patients' social class. *Social Science and Medicine, 14A,* 669–673.

Pitts, J. S., Schwankovsky, L., Thompson, S. C., Cruzen, D. E., Everett, J., & Freedman, D. (1991, August). *Do people want to make medical decisions?* Paper presented at the annual meeting of the American Psychological Association, San Francisco.

Ross, L. E., Wheaton, B., & Duff, R. S. (1981). Client satisfaction and the organization of medical practice: Why time counts. *Journal of Health and Social Behavior, 22,* 243–255.

Roter, D. L. (1984). Patient question asking in physician-patient interaction. *Health Psychology, 3,* 395–410.

Roter, D. L., & Hall, J. A. (1992). *Doctors talking with patients—patients talking with doctors.* Westport, CT: Auburn House.

Stewart, M., & Roter, D. (1989). Introduction. In M. Stewart & D. Roter (Eds.), *Communicating with medical patients.* Beverly Hills, CA: Sage.

Stiles, W. B., Putnam, S. M., James, S. A., & Wolf, M. H. (1979a). Dimensions of patient and physician roles in medical screening interviews. *Social Science and Medicine, 13A,* 335–341.

Stiles, W. B., Putnam, S. M., Wolf, M. H., & James, S. A. (1979b). Interaction exchange structure and patient satisfaction with medical interviews. *Medical Care, 17,* 667–681.

Stone, G. C. (1979). Health and the health system: A historical overview and conceptual framework. In G. C. Stone, F. Cohen, & N. E. Adler (Eds.), *Health psychology—A handbook* (pp. 1–17). San Francisco: Jossey-Bass.

Svarstad, B. (1976). Physician-patient communication and patient conformity with medical advice. In D. Mechanic (Ed.), *The growth of bureaucratic medicine.* New York: Wiley.

Szasz, T. S., & Hollender, M. H. (1956). The basic models of the doctor-patient relationship. *Archives of Internal Medicine, 35,* 156–184.

Thompson, S. C., Nanni, C., & Schwankovsky, L. (1990). Patient-oriented interventions to improve communication in a medical visit. *Health Psychology, 9,* 390–404.

Tosteson, D. C. (1990). New pathways in general medical education. *New England Journal of Medicine, 322,* 234–238.

Tuckett, H. D., Boulton, M., Olson, C., & Williams, A. (1985). *Meetings between experts: An approach to sharing ideas in medical consultations.* London: Tavistock.

Waitzkin, H. (1984). Doctor-patient communication. *Journal of American Medical Association, 252,* 2441–2446.

Waitzkin, H. (1985). Information giving in medical care. *Journal of Health and Social Behavior, 26,* 81–101.

Waitzkin, H., & Stoeckle, J. D. (1976). Information control and the micropolitics of health care: Summary of an ongoing research project. *Social Science and Medicine, 10,* 263–276.

Ware, J. E., Jr., Davies-Avery, A., & Stewart, A. L. (1978). The measurement and meaning of patient satisfaction. *Health and Medical Care Services Review, 1,* 2–15.

Ware, J. E., Jr., & Hayes, R. D. (1988). Methods for measuring patient satisfaction with specific medical encounters. *Medical Care, 26,* 393–402.

Weston, W. W., Brown, J. B., & Stewart, M. (1989). Patient-centered interviewing. Part I: Understanding patients' experiences. *Canadian Family Physicians, 35,* 147–151.

Elizabeth F. Loftus
John C. Palmer

Reconstruction of Automobile Destruction: An Example of the Interaction Between Language and Memory

The article by Loftus and Palmer represents a simple demonstration of the way in which the reconstruction of an event in memory can be biased. Its findings are so clear and implications so strong that it is one of the most cited pieces of research in the area of eyewitness testimony. Loftus and Palmer showed students films of auto accidents and then asked them how fast the cars were going at the time. By using verbs such as "collided" or "smashed" versus "bumped" or "hit," they were able to affect the speed that people reported, and, even though there was *no* broken glass in the film, a week later those who were asked about the cars that "smashed" were more likely to recall having seen glass at the scene.

How accurately do we remember the details of a complex event, like a traffic accident, that has happened in our presence? More specifically, how well do we do when asked to estimate some numerical quantity such as how long the accident took, how fast the cars were traveling, or how much time elapsed between the sounding of a horn and the moment of collision?

It is well documented that most people are markedly inaccurate in reporting such numerical details as time, speed, and distance (Bird, 1927; Whipple, 1909). For example, most people have difficulty estimating the duration of an event, with some research indicating that the tendency is to overestimate the duration of events which are complex (Block, 1974; Marshall, 1969; Ornstein, 1969). The judgment of speed is especially difficult, and practically every automobile accident results in huge variations from one witness to another as to how fast a vehicle was actually traveling (Gardner, 1933). In one test administered to Air Force personnel who knew in advance that they would be questioned about the speed of a moving automobile, estimates ranged from 10 to 50 mph. The car they watched was actually going only 12 mph (Marshall, 1969, p. 23).

Given the inaccuracies in estimates of speed, it seems likely that there are variables which are potentially powerful in terms of influencing these estimates. The present research was conducted to investigate one such variable, namely, the phrasing of the question used to elicit the speed judgment. Some questions are clearly more suggestive than others. This fact of life has resulted in the legal concept of a leading question and in legal rules indicating when leading questions are allowed (*Supreme Court Reporter,* 1973). A leading question is simply one that, either by its form or content, suggests to the witness what answer is desired or leads him to the desired answer.

In the present study, subjects were shown films of traffic accidents and then they answered questions about the accident. The subjects were interrogated about the speed of the vehicles in one of several ways. For example, some subjects were asked, "About how fast were the cars going when they hit each other?" while others were asked, "About how fast were the cars going when they smashed into each other?" As Fillmore (1971) and Bransford and McCarrell (in press) have noted, *hit* and *smashed* may involve specification of differential rates of movement. Furthermore, the two verbs may also involve differential specification of the likely consequences of the events to which they are referring. The impact of the accident is apparently gentler for *hit* than for *smashed.*

EXPERIMENT I

Method

Forty-five students participated in groups of various sizes. Seven films were shown, each depicting a traffic accident. These films were segments from longer driver's education films borrowed from the Evergreen Safety Council and the Seattle Police Department. The length of the film segments ranged from 5 to 30 sec. Following each film, the subjects received a questionnaire asking them first to, "give an account of the accident you have just seen," and then to answer a series of specific questions about the accident. The critical question was the one that interrogated the subject about the speed of the vehicles involved in the collision. Nine subjects were asked, "About how fast were the cars going when they hit each other?" Equal numbers of the remaining subjects were interrogated with the verbs *smashed, collided, bumped,* and *contacted* in place of *hit.* The entire experiment lasted about an hour and a half. A different ordering of the films was presented to each group of subjects.

Results

Table 10.3 presents the mean speed estimates for the various verbs. Some information about the accuracy of subjects' estimates can be obtained from our data. Four of the seven films were staged crashes; the original purpose of these films was to illustrate what can happen to human beings when cars collide at various speeds. One collision took place at 20 mph, one at 30, and two at 40. The mean estimates of speed for these four films were: 37.7, 36.2, 39.7, and 36.1 mph, respectively. In agreement

TABLE 10.3 Speed Estimates for the Verbs Used in Experiment 1

Verb	Mean Speed Estimate
Smashed	40.8
Collided	39.3
Bumped	38.1
Hit	34.0
Contacted	31.8

with previous work, people are not very good at judging how fast a vehicle was actually traveling.

Discussion

The results of this experiment indicate that the form of a question (in this case, changes in a single word) can markedly and systematically affect a witness's answer to that question. The actual speed of the vehicles controlled little variance in subject reporting, while the phrasing of the question controlled considerable variance.

Two interpretations of this finding are possible. First, it is possible that the differential speed estimates result merely from response-bias factors. A subject is uncertain whether to say 30 mph or 40 mph, for example, and the verb *smashed* biases his response toward the higher estimate. A second interpretation is that the question form causes a change in the subject's memory representation of the accident. The verb *smashed* may change a subject's memory such that he "sees" the accident as being more severe than it actually was. If this is the case, we might expect subjects to "remember" other details that did not actually occur, but are commensurate with an accident occurring at high speeds. The second experiment was designed to provide additional insights into the origin in the differential speed estimates.

EXPERIMENT II

Method

One hundred and fifty students participated in this experiment, in groups of various sizes. A film depicting a multiple car accident was shown, followed by a questionnaire. The film lasted less than 1 min; the accident in the film lasted 4 sec. At the end of the film, the subjects received a questionnaire asking them first to describe the accident in their own words, and then to answer a series of questions about the accident. The critical question was the one that interrogated the subject about the speed of the vehicles. Fifty subjects were asked, "About how fast were the cars going when they smashed into each other?" Fifty subjects were asked, "About how fast were the cars going when they hit each other?" Fifty subjects were not interrogated about vehicular speed.

One week later, the subjects returned and without viewing the film again they

TABLE 10.4 Distribution of "Yes" and "No" Responses to the Question, "Did You See Any Broken Glass?"

	Verb Condition		
Response	Smashed	Hit	Control
Yes	16	7	6
No	34	43	44

answered a series of questions about the accident. The critical question here was, "Did you see any broken glass?" which the subjects answered by checking "yes" and "no." This question was embedded in a list totalling 10 questions, and it appeared in a random position in the list. There was no broken glass in the accident, but, since broken glass is commensurate with accidents occurring at high speed, we expected that the subjects who had been asked the *smashed* question might more often say "yes" to this critical question.

Results

The mean estimate of speed for subjects interrogated with *smashed* was 10.46 mph; with *hit* the estimate was 8.00 mph. Table 10.4 presents the distribution of "yes" and "no" responses for the *smashed, hit,* and control subjects. The probability of saying "yes" to the question about broken glass is .32 when the verb *smashed* is used, and .14 with *hit.* Thus *smashed* leads both to more "yes" responses and to higher speed estimates. It appears to be the case that the effect of the verb is mediated at least in part by the speed estimate. The question now arises: Is *smashed* doing anything else besides increasing the estimate of speed? To answer this, the function relating P(Y) to speed estimate was calculated separately for *smashed* and *hit.* If the speed estimate is the only way in which effect of verb is mediated, then for a given speed estimate, P(Y) should be independent of the verbs. Table 10.5 shows that this is not the case. P(Y) is lower for *hit* than for *smashed;* the difference between the two verbs ranges from .3 for estimates of 1–5 mph to .18 for estimates of 6–10 mph. The average difference between the two curves is about .12.

TABLE 10.5 Probability of Saying "Yes" to, "Did You See Any Broken Glass?" Conditionalized on Speed Estimates

	Speed Estimate (mph)			
Verb condition	1–5	6–10	11–15	16–20
Smashed	.09	.27	.41	.62
Hit	.06	.09	.25	.50

DISCUSSION

To reiterate, we have first of all provided an additional demonstration of something that has been known for some time, namely, that the way a question is asked can enormously influence the answer that is given. In this instance, the question, "About how fast were the cars going when they smashed into each other?" led to higher estimates of speed than the same question asked with the verb *smashed* replaced by *hit*. Furthermore, this seemingly small change had consequences for how questions are answered a week after the original event occurred.

As a framework for discussing these results, we would like to propose that two kinds of information go into one's memory for some complex occurrence. The first is information gleaned during the perception of the original event; the second is external information supplied after the fact. Over time, information from these two sources may be integrated in such a way that we are unable to tell from which source some specific detail is recalled. All we have is one "memory."

Discussing the present experiments in these terms, we propose that the subject first forms some representation of the accident he has witnessed. The experimenter then, while asking, "About how fast were the cars going when they smashed into each other?" supplies a piece of external information, namely, that the cars did indeed smash into each other. When these two pieces of information are integrated, the subject has a memory of an accident that was more severe than in fact it was. Since broken glass is commensurate with a severe accident, the subject is more likely to think that broken glass was present.

There is some connection between the present work and earlier work on the influence of verbal labels on memory for visually presented form stimuli. A classic study in psychology showed that when subjects were asked to reproduce a visually presented form, their drawings tend to err in the direction of a more familiar object suggested by a verbal label initially associated with the to-be-remembered form (Carmichael, Hogan, & Walter, 1932). More recently, Daniel (1972) showed that recognition memory, as well as reproductive memory, was similarly affected by verbal labels, and he concluded that the verbal label causes a shift in the memory strength of forms which are better representatives of the label.

When the experimenter asks the subject, "About how fast were the cars going when they smashed into each other?" he is effectively labeling the accident a smash. Extrapolating the conclusions of Daniel to this situation, it is natural to conclude that the label, smash, causes a shift in the memory representation of the accident in the direction of being more similar to a representation suggested by the verbal label.

References

Bird, C. The influence of the press upon the accuracy of report. *Journal of Abnormal and Social Psychology,* 1927, 22, 123–129.

Block, R. A. Memory and the experience of duration in retrospect. *Memory & Cognition,* 1974, 2, 153–160.

Bransford, J. D., & McCarrell, N. S. A sketch of a cognitive approach to comprehension: Some thoughts about understanding what it means to comprehend. In D. Palermo &

W. Weimer (Eds.), *Cognition and the symbolic processes.* Washington, DC: V. H. Winston & Co., in press.

Carmichael, L., Hogan, H. P., & Walter, A. A. An experimental study of the effect of language on the reproduction of visually perceived form. *Journal of Experimental Psychology,* 1932, 15, 73–86.

Clark, H. H. The language-as-fixed-effect fallacy: A critique of language statistics in psychological research. *Journal of Verbal Learning and Verbal Behavior,* 1973, 12, 335–359.

Daniel, T. C. Nature of the effect of verbal labels on recognition memory for form. *Journal of Experimental Psychology,* 1972, 96, 152–157.

Fillmore, C. J. Types of lexical information. In D. D. Steinberg and L. A. Jakobovits (Eds.), *Semantics: An interdisciplinary reader in philosophy, linguistics, and psychology.* Cambridge: Cambridge University Press, 1971.

Gardner, D. S. The perception and memory of witnesses. *Cornell Law Quarterly,* 1933, 8, 391–409.

Marshall, J. *Law and psychology in conflict.* New York: Anchor Books, 1969.

Whipple, G. M. The observer as reporter. A survey of the psychology of testimony. *Psychological Bulletin,* 1909, 6, 153–170.

Supreme Court Reported, 1973, 3: Rules of Evidence for United States Courts and Magistrates.

Saul M. Kassin
Lawrence S. Wrightsman

The American Jury on Trial: Inside the Jury Room

This selection by Kassin and Wrightsman is about jury deliberations, but it is just as much about the social psychology of social
influence and group behavior. Noting that opinions can differ
widely in a jury, the authors utilize basic theory and research to explain some of the reasons behind the acceptance of influence and
allow us to understand better who accepts influence from whom.
The "sounds of deliberation" that they discuss follow directly from
the principles of conflict resolution and illustrate how these same
concepts can describe the stages that any groups, whether families
or warring nations, might follow in trying to come to a reasonable
resolution.

It is often said that the distinctive power of the system is that the jury functions as a
group. Is it? How do jurors carrying different opinions manage to converge on a single verdict? Indeed, what does transpire behind the closed doors of the jury room?
We will see that although the jury meets in total privacy, the courts have articulated
a clear vision of what the dynamics of deliberation should look like. Basically, there
are three components to this ideal.

The first component is one of independence and equality. No juror's vote
counts for more than any other juror's vote. A 12-person jury should thus consist of
12 *independent* and *equal* individuals, each contributing his or her own personal
opinion to the final outcome. The courts attempt to foster this ideal in a number of
ways. For example, judges instruct jurors to refrain from discussing the trial with
each other until they retire for their deliberations. In this way, each juror develops
his or her own unique perspective on the case, uncontaminated by others' views.
This ensures not only the independence of individual members but also the diversity
of the group as a whole.

Unlike other task-oriented groups, the jury's role is ideally structured to advance the cause of equal participation. The cardinal rule of jury decision making is
that verdicts be based only on the evidence introduced in open court. By limiting the
task as such, jurors are discouraged from basing their arguments on private or outside sources of knowledge. Because they experience the same trial, and because

they are provided with identical information, jurors are placed on an equal footing. To further promote equality, the courts often exclude from service people who are expected to exert a disproportionate amount of influence over other jurors. Lawyers or others who are particularly knowledgeable about trial-relevant subjects are thus excluded despite their otherwise welcome expertise. Several years ago, Edmund G. Brown, then Governor of California, was among those picked at random from a pool of 219 prospective jurors in Sacramento. At least publicly, nobody questioned his impartiality. But wouldn't his presence on the panel overwhelm other jurors? Despite the voir dire, the defense lawyer asked a prospective juror, "Would you hesitate to disagree with him in deliberation?" she replied, "No, I've disagreed with him before." In the end, Brown was seated on the jury and elected foreperson.

The second component of the deliberation ideal is an openness to informational influence. Once inside the jury room, jurors have a duty to interact and discuss the case. They should share information, exchange views, and debate the evidence. Thus, when an Indianapolis juror locked herself in the ladies' room after 20 hours of deliberation and refused to talk after having been called a "big mouth," the judge was forced to declare a mistrial. Two essential characteristics of an ideal jury follow from the requirement of deliberation. One is that jurors maintain an open mind, that each juror withhold judgment until "an impartial consideration of the evidence *with his fellow jurors*." Openmindedness is such an important aspect of an ideal deliberation that if a juror dies before a verdict is announced, then the jury cannot return a verdict even if all the remaining jurors indicate that the deceased had agreed with their decision. The reasoning behind this rule is that "the jurors individually and collectively have the right to change their minds prior to the reception of the verdict."

The second is that consensus should be achieved through an exchange of information. Jurors should scrutinize their own views, be receptive to others', and allow themselves to be persuaded by rational argument. One juror advances a proposition; the others either accept it, challenge it, or modify it on publicly defensible grounds. As the Supreme Court put it almost a century ago, "The very object of the jury system is to secure unanimity by a comparison of views, and by arguments among the jurors themselves. . . . It cannot be that each juror should go to the jury-room with a blind determination that the verdict shall represent his opinion of the case at that moment; or that he should close his ears to the arguments of men who are equally honest and intelligent as himself."

The third component of the deliberation ideal follows from the second. Although juries should strive for a consensus of opinion, it should *not* be achieved through heavy-handed normative pressure. Obviously, jurors who dissent from the majority position should not be beaten, bullied, or harangued into submission. Indeed "no juror should surrender his honest conviction as to the weight or effect of the evidence solely because of the opinion of his fellow jurors, or for the mere purpose of returning a verdict." The reason for discouraging juries from securing unanimity through social pressure is simple. Jurors are expected and, in fact, instructed to vote with their conscience. If they change their minds because they are genuinely persuaded by new information, fine. But if they comply with the majority just to avoid being rejected or to escape an unpleasant experience, then their final vote will not reflect their true beliefs. In the Supreme Court's words, "the verdict must be the verdict of each individual juror, and not a mere acquiescence in the conclusion of his fellows."

A Social-Psychological Analysis

It is rare for all jurors to agree on a verdict at the outset of their deliberations. For that reason, the process of deliberation is, by and large, a study in persuasion and social influence. With that in mind, the legal system is clear in its prescriptions for how its juries should manage the inevitable tension between minority and majority viewpoints; between individual expression and independence on the one hand, and the collective need for consensus, on the other. How should jurors influence and be influenced? What kinds of pressure comport with the ideals of deliberation? Before evaluating the extent to which juries meet the courts' standards, let us look at the psychology of group influence.

In a now classic series of experiments, social psychologist Solomon Asch confronted people with the following awkward situation. Subjects were scheduled in small groups to participate in a study of visual discrimination. Upon their arrival, they were seated around a table and instructed that they would be making a series of simple judgments. Presented with a single vertical line on one board and three lines of varying length on another, subjects were asked to decide which of the three comparison lines was the same as the standard. Because the task was straightforward, the experimenter remarked, he would save time by having subjects announce their judgments out loud in order of their seating position. Actually, there was only one real subject in the group—the others were "confederates" posing as subjects but working for the experimenter. The first two judgments passed uneventfully. The discriminations were simple and all subjects agreed on the correct answer. Then on 12 of the next 16 trials, the first confederate gave what clearly seemed to be the wrong answer. The next four did the same. With all eyes on the subject, how does he respond? Much to Asch's surprise, subjects conformed with the incorrect majority 37 percent of the time. Only when they had an ally, or even another member who dissented from both their own and others' judgments, were subjects able to resist the pressure to conform.

Asch's study raised important questions, the first being, why did people conform as often as they did? By interviewing his subjects, Asch discovered that they followed the majority for different reasons. Some claimed they actually agreed with what the majority had reported; others became uncertain of their own perceptions; still others maintained their original beliefs but went along anyway. Shortly after Asch's initial demonstration, social psychologists Morton Deutsch and Harold Gerard repeated the experiment with one significant modification. In one condition, subjects were separated by partitions and prevented from communicating with one another. And instead of publicly announcing their answers, they indicated their judgments by pressing a button. Do people still conform, even when protected by their anonymity within the group? The answer is, yes and no. Deutsch and Gerard found that subjects who participated in this anonymous condition were less likely to follow the incorrect majority than those who were in the face-to-face situation created by Asch. But they were still more likely to make incorrect judgments than a group of subjects who completed the line-judgment task alone.

Deutsch and Gerard concluded from this study that people are influenced by others for two distinct reasons—informational and normative. Through *informational* social influence, people conform because they want to be correct in their judgments and expect that when others agree with each other, they must be right. Thus in Asch's visual discrimination task, it is natural for subjects to assume that ten eyes are better than two. Through *normative* social influence, however, people conform because they fear the negative consequences of appearing deviant. Wanting to be accepted and well liked, they avoid behaving in ways that make them stick out like a sore thumb. And for good reason. Decision-making groups often reject, ridicule, and punish individuals who frustrate a common goal by adhering to a deviant position.

The distinction between normative and informational social influence is critical not just for an understanding of why people conform, but because it produces two very different types of conformity: public compliance and private acceptance. The term *public compliance* refers to a superficial change in behavior. Often, people will publicly vote with the majority, even though privately they continue to disagree. "To get along, go along," as they say. In contrast, as the term *private acceptance* indicates, there are times when people are genuinely persuaded by others' opinions. In these instances, they change not only their overt behavior, but their minds as well. Obviously, public compliance is a weaker and less stable outcome of social influence than private acceptance. The individual who complies without truly sharing the group's views is likely to revert to his or her own real attitude as soon as the promise of reward or threat of punishment are no longer in effect (for example, when he or she is not being observed).

The social psychology of group influence provides a framework and, as we will see, an empirical literature with which we can evaluate the ideals of jury deliberation. As the courts have long recognized, an ideal jury enters the jury room with diverse opinions and open minds. Through a vigorous exchange of viewpoints, a majority faction develops. It then strives toward unanimity through a process of informational influence until the final holdouts come to accept that position. In the ideal, then, a jury's final verdict reflects each individual's vote of conscience. In contrast to this information–acceptance model, there is what might be called the normative–compliance model of deliberation. It is characterized by the use of heavy-handed social pressure that leads dissenters to publicly support the jury's verdict while privately harboring reservations. As the poet Ferlinghetti put it, "Just because you have silenced a man does not mean you have changed his mind." In this less-than-ideal model, the jury completes its task unanimous in vote but not in conscience.

There are important reasons to protect individual jurors from the kinds of normative pressure that would force merely their compliance. To begin with, justice itself is undermined when a jury renders a verdict not supported even by its own membership. Criminal defendants should not be convicted by juries that are plagued by a reasonable doubt within its membership. There is also danger that people's perceptions of justice are undermined as well by deliberations that follow a normative–compliance model. How much faith in the legal system can a juror have after voting against his or her conscience? The following case illustrates the point.

In 1981 a Miami jury deliberated for more than six hours on whether four defendants had paid undercover agents $220,000 for 15 pounds of cocaine. At one point the jurors reported they were deadlocked, so the judged asked that they try further to reach agreement. Three hours later they returned with verdicts: three convictions and an acquittal. When the judge began polling them in open court as to whether they agreed in conscience with their decisions, the very first juror said, "no." The judge sent them back to the jury room. A few minutes later, they returned with the same verdicts. Polled again, the first juror agreed, but juror #5 said, "No, it's not my verdict." Again, the judge sent them back. This time, they returned and confirmed the verdicts. But one of the defense lawyers said, "We noticed juror #11 kick the back of juror #5's chair when it was her turn." Polled separately, jurors 1 and 5 both repudiated their verdicts. Sent back a fourth time, the jurors deliberated half an hour more, returned with the same verdicts, and stood by them. Then when the trial had ended, jurors 1 and 5 approached two of the defendants and apologized for their convictions. According to their report, two jurors insisted on concluding that night because they had vacation plans. One of them swung at another juror, and four who initially had voted for acquittal were "brow-beaten into submission."

Now that we have a clear image of the informational–acceptance and normative–compliance models of deliberation, we should add that they rarely appear in their pure form. Most decision-making groups achieve a consensus of opinion through a combination of forces. Juries are no exception. As Kalven and Zeisel noted, the deliberation process "is an interesting combination of rational persuasion, sheer social pressure, and the psychological mechanism by which individual perceptions undergo change when exposed to group discussion." With that reality in mind, it is clear that the ideals of deliberation should be stated in relative terms. *A jury verdict meets the courts' standards if, following a vigorous exchange of information and a minimum of normative pressure, it accurately reflects each of the individual jurors' private beliefs.*

BEHIND CLOSED DOORS: WHO SAYS WHAT TO WHOM?

If only the walls of the jury room could talk, what would they say? By carefully observing mock jury deliberations, by interviewing actual jurors, and by analyzing trial verdict records, it is possible to piece together what transpires during deliberations. How is the foreperson elected? Who does the talking? What is said, and to whom is it said? How and when are votes taken? How do factions develop? These are among the many questions jury researchers have tried to answer.

Leaders, Participants, and Followers

Juries should consist of 12 independent and equal individuals, each contributing to the final outcome. Let us consider whether that is a realistic ideal. Many trial lawyers do not think so. Robert Duncan, an experienced Kansas City attorney, asserts that "most juries consist of one or two strong personalities with the rest more or less being followers. Thus, often the jury trial actually consists of a one or two person jury." Looking at the empirical literature, it is clear there is an element of truth to that observation. In virtually all kinds of small-group discussions, the rate of participation among individual members is very uneven—a few people do almost all the talking. Exactly the same pattern seems to characterize how juries function. In one study more than 800 people watched a reenactment of a murder trial and then participated in one of 69 mock juries. By video-taping the deliberations and then counting the number of statements contributed by each juror within each group, the experimenters were able to measure how equally the individuals had participated in their respective groups. The results of this analysis were clear. In each group a few jurors controlled the discussion, while the others spoke at a much lower rate. In fact, most groups included as many as three members who remained virtually silent through deliberations, speaking only to cast their votes. Add to that pattern the fact that the more a juror speaks, the more he or she is spoken to and the more persuasive he or she appears to the others, and it is apparent that dominance hierarchies develop in juries just as they do in other groups.

With juries stratifying into leaders, participants, and followers, it is natural to ask—what constitutes leadership on a jury, or any other kind of group for that matter? What kinds of people emerge as leaders, and under what circumstances? Social scientists have two ways of answering that general question. One is to focus on stable personal qualities that distinguish those in power from everyone else. The idea is that leaders are born, not made; that the history of nations and social movements is a history of great individuals; that to identify leaders, one must study their abilities, their character, their appeal, and their personality. The second approach is to focus on transient situational forces that propel certain individuals into positions of power and leadership. From this perspective, leadership is determined by current events, the needs and resources of a particular group, and the nature of the task that needs to be performed. A person who is prepared to lead in one situation may be ill equipped in another group at another time.

When it comes to small decision-making groups, everyday observation and empirical research have shown that leadership consists of two discrete components or—to put it differently—there are two types of leaders. In order to achieve a specific objective, groups need a *task-oriented leader,* one who takes charge, defines a substantive and procedural agenda, establishes a network of communication, and drives the group toward its destination. For the maintenance of interpersonal harmony, however, groups need a *socioemotional* leader, one who reduces tensions created by decision-making conflicts, provides emotional support to individual members, and helps to increase the cohesiveness and morale of the group as a whole. Both task and socioemotional roles are important. Within a group's life cycle, the relative needs for the two types of leadership change according to circumstances.

Turning to the jury, it is common for people to assume that the foreperson is the jury's leader. That is true only in a limited sense. The foreperson holds a position of responsibility that cannot be denied. Selected for the role by the judge, by random assignment, or by the jury itself, the foreperson announces the verdict in open court and acts as a liaison between the judge and jury. Although a leader in this formal sense, however, the foreperson is not necessarily the most influential juror in either a task-oriented or socioemotional sense.

Who are these forepersons and how are they selected? Research shows that juries spend little time at it. Forepersons are often chosen by acclamation and without dissent. People do not seem to seek the position actively. In fact, chances are the first juror who says, "What should we do about a foreman?" is immediately chosen. It is interesting that although the selection process is rather casual, its outcomes follow a predictable pattern. To begin with, the foreperson is, quite literally, a *foreman.* All sexist language aside, men are more likely to be selected than women. This finding was not particularly shocking when it appeared in the 1950s, at a time when traditional sex roles were intact. But the bias toward male forepersons continues even in today's era of greater equality for women. Apparently, people assume (erroneously, we might add) that men make better leaders than women. To illustrate how dramatic the difference is, a recent study of 179 trials held in San Diego revealed that although 50 percent of the jurors were female, 90 percent of the forepersons were male.

Other systematic patterns are evident too. For example, forepersons tend to be better educated and hold higher status jobs than the average juror. Those who have previous jury experience are also selected at a higher-than-expected rate. Then there is an interesting, less obvious selection bias. In 1961, jury researchers Fred Strodtbeck and L. H. Hook published a paper entitled "The social dimensions of a 12-man jury table." Looking at the most common geometrical layout, the rectangular table, they discovered that foreperson selections were predictable from where jurors were seated. Those who sat at the heads of the table were by far the most likely to be chosen, whereas those located in the middle were the least likely. Since it also turns out that jurors of higher status naturally tend to take more prominent seats, it appears that this dimension adds even further to the development of a dominance hierarchy within the jury.

Research has thus shown that although juries are casual about their choice of a foreperson, the selections follow systematic patterns. But research has also shown that it does not really matter who fills that role. To be sure, the foreperson is usually the most active member of the jury. Several of the Chicago Jury Project studies reported in the 1950s and 1960s found that, on the average, the foreperson accounts for approximately 25 percent of the statements made during deliberations. It turns out, however, that although forepersons carry a disproportionate amount of influence over the process of deliberation, they do not have the same kind of impact over its outcome. In one study, for example, forepersons contributed a great deal at first on primarily procedural matters (calling for votes or rereading judges' instructions), but then behaved like the more average participants as the deliberations progressed. Another study revealed that while forepersons raised organizational matters at five times the rate of other jurors, they were less likely to express an opinion concerning the verdict. This latter result suggests that it may be more accurate to think of the foreperson not as the jury's leader, but as a referee or moderator.

If the foreperson does not lead the jury to its verdict, who does? The answer to this question is simple. By and large, the same characteristics that are associated with foreperson selections are also related to opinion leadership: sex, employment status, jury experience, and seating position. Male and female jurors, for example, play very different roles in the jury room. Consistent with traditional sex roles, men assume a primarily task-oriented role, offering information and expressing opinions; women assume the more socioemotional role, agreeing with others' statements, offering support, and helping to reduce interpersonal tensions. Needless to say, male jurors are rated by their fellow panelists as more persuasive than their female counterparts.

Experienced and novice jurors are not equivalent in their levels of participation, either. When Dale Broeder interviewed jurors after their trials, he came across several experienced jurors who had taken on an air of expertise and tried to control the rest of the group. As an example, he described a woman who, immediately upon entering the jury room, cut paper ballots, explained that it was standard procedure to open with a secret vote, and "did everything but suggest that she be elected foreman." More controlled research with mock juries lends support to Broeder's observations. In one study, subjects who had previously served on a real jury talked more during deliberations than those who had not. These kinds of effects appear even when the subject's experience consists of having earlier participated in a mock jury. In this situation, the first author, in collaboration with Ralph Juhnke, found that new subjects reportedly participated less and made less persuasive comments than their more experienced peers. We also found that new subjects conformed to their groups more when they deliberated with others of experience than when they participated in fully inexperienced groups. Finally, consistent with the more situational theories of leadership, we suspect that individual jurors will lead or follow depending upon their suitability and expertise for a particular trial. In principle, all jurors are supposed to be created equal. In practice, however, this egalitarian ethic is seldom if ever realized. The fact of the matter is that dominance hierarchies develop that mirror the differences of status in the real world. Thus, despite the forces designed to place all jurors on an equal footing and neutralize individual differences, juries still consist in predictable ways of leaders, participants, and followers.

The Sounds of Deliberation

Imagine that you just sat through a full trial, having listened to several witnesses, lawyers, and the judge. You still have not communicated your thoughts and impressions to anyone else, nor do you know what the others on the panel are thinking. You may have formed some opinions, and you are probably filled with questions. Finally, the door of the jury room closes, and you find yourself with 11 strangers. Where do you begin? How do juries structure their discussions and what do they talk about? In short, what are the sounds of deliberation? Kalven and Zeisel offer the following colorful description:

> There is at first, in William James' phrase about the baby, the sense of buzzing, booming, confusion. After a while, we become accustomed to the quick, fluid movement of jury discussion and realize that the talk moves with remarkable flexibility. It

touches an issue, leaves it, and returns again. Even a casual inspection makes it evident that this is interesting and arresting human behavior. It is not a formal debate; nor, although it is mercurial and difficult to pick up, is it just excited talk.

Social psychologists interested in how groups solve problems describe the process through series of stages. According to this view, a group begins in an open ended, not very well defined *orientation* phrase. During these opening moments, the group defines its task and perhaps even a strategy for discussion. Questions are raised, issues are explored, and tentative views are expressed in general terms. Formally or informally, a vote is eventually taken. Differences of opinion are thus revealed, factions develop, and the group enters an *open conflict* phase. At this point, the discussion takes on a more focused, serious tone. With individuals taking sides in a debate, only points of disagreement are addressed. During this critical and often lengthy period, discussion is best characterized in social influence terms, with both informational and normative pressures operating. In most groups, a sizeable majority eventually emerges, and a mutually acceptable decision appears imminent. When that happens, the group enters a period of *conflict resolution and reconciliation.* If one or two individuals continue to hold out in the face of attempts to convert them through rational argument, then they become the targets of increasing pressures to conform. If and when unanimity is achieved, the group then goes through a period of reconciliation designed to heal the wounds of battle, express support and reassurance, and affirm its satisfaction with the final outcome.

Judges and lawyers are forever wondering about what jurors talk about in their deliberations. Do they stick like glue to the evidence, or do they allow themselves to wander onto topics prohibited by the judge? How much time do they spend talking about their own personal experiences? To answer these kinds of questions, sociologist Rita James Simon transcribed 10 mock-jury deliberations and then classified all statements made according to their content. She found that jurors spent most of their time talking about trial evidence and their reactions to that evidence. After that they were most likely to talk about procedures for deliberating, experiences from their daily lives, and the judge's instructions. For all categories, Simon found that jurors' statements were, for the most part, relevant, accurate, and helpful for reaching a verdict.

The problem with Simon's analysis is that it represents the deliberation process in static rather than dynamic terms. Do juries' discussions really sound the same in the opening and closing moments? Obviously not, according to the stage-like analysis described earlier. And what do juries do with their statements about evidence, instructions, procedure, and so on? Surely, the decision-making process does not consist of an unrelated string of sentences. More recent studies of jury deliberation are providing answers to these questions. In one study, psychologists Reid Hastie, Steven Penrod, and Nancy Pennington had more than 800 people participate in mock juries and deliberate until a verdict was reached. On the average, deliberations lasted for almost two hours. In order to monitor how discussions change from beginning to end, each deliberation was divided into five units of time. This analysis revealed a very consistent pattern about how juries operate.

As a first step, they spend a good deal of time exchanging views about the case facts and the credibility of the various witnesses. Then they struggle to make sense of the evidence by transforming it into a story of what probably happened. Storytelling, they found, is an important part of deliberation. Confronted with fragments of evidence, juries tend to reconstruct the events in question. As with other stories, what they usually come up with is a linked series of episodes that has a beginning, a middle, and an end. To construct these narratives, juries lean heavily on the evidence they find most compelling. Wanting to establish a coherent story, they might then fill in missing details, make inferences about the actors' goals, motives, and intentions, and reject evidence that is incompatible with their views.

As the deliberations progress, jurors become increasingly focused on the judge's instructions concerning the law, the requirements of proof, and the kinds of verdicts they could reach. They might argue about the differences between first and second degree murder, or about how to interpret the concept of an implied contract, or about how much doubt should be considered reasonable. In short, juries appear to shift, generally, from a concern for fact-finding (the "what happened" stage) to an application of the law (the "what do we do now?" stage).

The Drive Toward Unanimity

So far, the deliberation process sounds quite rational and orderly. Juries find facts, construct stories, and apply legal principles. But the jury does not speak with one voice. Indeed it is not a "collective mind" but a collection of individuals. Often, individual jurors express a legitimate disagreement with prevailing opinion. Others are ineloquent in their dissent, but just plain stubborn. How do juries ever achieve a consensus and, in the end, a unanimous verdict?

Before trying to answer that question, it is important that we first take the mystique out of popular, romanticized images of jury dynamics. To begin with, the majority almost always wins. Thus, to predict the outcome of deliberations with a fair degree of certainty, one need only know where the 12 individuals stand before they enter the jury room. Kalven and Zeisel found convincing support for this phenomenon in their research. Through posttrial interviews with jurors in 225 criminal juries, they were able to reconstruct how juries split on their very first vote. In all but 10 cases, there was at least a slight majority favoring a particular verdict. Out of these, only six juries reached a final decision that was not predictable from this initial breakdown. From that rather striking result, Kalven and Zeisel concluded that "the deliberation process might well be likened to what the developer does for an exposed film: It brings out the picture, but the outcome is predetermined. . . . The deliberation process, though rich in human interest and color appears not to be at the heart of jury decision making."

Though not a frequent occurrence, minorities sometimes manage to prevail. There are two rather distinct strategies that enable nonconformists to turn others around. One strategy, identified by Serge Moscovici and his colleagues, is to adopt right from the start a staunch, consistent, and unwavering position. Confronted with this self-confident opponent, those in the majority will sit up, take notice, and rethink their own positions. There is a second, very different strategy that can be taken. Based on the fact that dissent often breeds hostility, Edwin Hollander maintains that people who challenge the majority immediately, without having first earned the others' respect, run the risk of becoming alienated and powerless. Based on his own research, Hollander concludes that individual dissenters become influential by first conforming to the majority and establishing their credentials as accepted members of the group. Having accumulated enough "idiosyncrasy credits" (or brownie points), the individual is in a better position to exert influence.

Alternate Routes: Informational and Social Pressure

When jurors speak, what they say often conveys two messages. They provide information that could persuade others but, at the same time, they also reveal where they stand on the verdict. Suppose a juror says "I don't understand how the witness could have seen the defendant at 5:30, if his wife claims he returned home, which is almost half an hour away, at 5:45." A second juror then adds, "And how could the defendant have been on the street so early, anyway, when he was at work that day?" These statements contribute information *and* they indicate a preference, without a formal vote, for a not guilty verdict. If a third juror subsequently changes his vote from guilty to not-guilty, is that because he came to accept the position implied by the arguments, or is it because he came to realize that, like in Asch's situation, he held an unpopular opinion?

We turn to Kaplan's program of research for an answer. To test the relative effects of informational and normative influence processes, Kaplan developed an artificial but interesting method of "deliberation." Subjects read either a strong- or weak-evidence version of a manslaughter case and indicated whether they thought the defendant was guilty or not. In order to control the subsequent discussion, Kaplan had jurors, each seated in their own cubicles, communicate with each other by passing notes. Actually, all the original notes were intercepted and replaced with others written by the experimenter. Now imagine that you are a subject in this experiment and you believe the defendant is guilty. You write down your opinion, you write down the facts you used to form that opinion, and then you receive notes from other jurors who supposedly did the same. After reading all the notes, you find out that your colleagues either agree or disagree with your verdict. You also learn about facts that either support or refute that verdict. Finally, you are asked again for your judgment. What influences whether you adhere to or change your original position? How do you react if the facts you read about support your guilty verdict, but the other jurors favor an acquittal? Conversely, what if you were supported by others' opinions but not by the facts? Consistently, subjects were more responsive to new, substantive information than they were to the strictly normative pressures.

Research on other decision-making groups yields the same comforting conclusion: people change their minds and their votes according to information and rational argument. That does not mean, of course, that interpersonal forces are inoperative, especially in situations that involve truly important decisions. Kaplan and others are unwilling to close the door on the normative–compliance component of jury decision making. We would have to agree.

Informational and normative influences are not endpoints of a single continuum; they are two independent dimensions. The drive toward unanimity is not characterized by one or the other, but by both. With that in mind, we reiterate our working definition of the ideal deliberation as one in which the information influences are strong and the normative influences are weak. Some degree of social pressure is inevitable and perhaps even desirable. It is a fact of life not just on juries, but in the board room, the classroom, the social club, and the laboratory. The question is, how much pressure is too much? Opinions differ. We certainly part company with an Ohio judge who said, "When you get twelve people in one room, and they all have to reach one decision, things happen. I've known fist fights to break out in the jury room. Abuse that one juror gives to the other is not a reason to turn over a just verdict." A just verdict? How can a verdict be just when one or more jurors was coerced into the final vote? Consistent with a social-psychologist perspective, a simple rule applies: Normative influence exceeds an acceptable level whenever it leads people to vote against their true beliefs.

Research has shown that juries fulfill at least half of the deliberation ideal: they are responsive to informational influence. But then there is the other half. One cannot help but wonder about the pressures toward uniformity, and about jurors who appear to abandon their true convictions in order to avoid the role of being deviant. Stories can be found to illustrate both the more and less desirable versions of the deliberation process. Thus, following one trial in which the jury acquitted the defendant of rape and murder, several jurors expressed their pride and satisfaction with the way they had reached a verdict. As one participant put it, "It was not an easy decision to come to. I honestly think the verdict could have gone either way. And even if there was a little shouting, we all tried to listen to what other people are saying. There were shifts of opinion, but we tried not to pressure anyone."

In contrast, jurors sometimes succumb under the weight of inordinate pressure. Take as an example a 1986 trial of two New York City police officers charged with torturing a prisoner with an electric stun gun. Concluding two days of deliberation, a jury of seven women and five men announced a verdict of guilty. Afterwards, one of the jurors reported in an affidavit that she had agreed to the verdict only because she had been intimidated and abused for holding out. "When I argued that the defendants had to have engaged in 'knowing and intentional' conduct before they could be found guilty of any of the crimes charged, the foreman screamed at me words to the effect: 'How would you like a policeman to do this to you?' and, thereupon, he squeezed my left thigh. This physical touching put me in fear of further physical abuse, so I voted guilty on the first count that the jury took up for consideration."

As we have argued, isolated anecdotes and case studies do not provide an adequate basis for evaluating the jury system. Every story has its counterpart. What, then, is the incidence of undue normative pressure? How frequently do jurors exhibit public compliance without private acceptance? In one study, interviews with former jurors revealed that as many as 10 percent of those sampled admitted that they felt pressured into their verdict, and had lingering doubts even as the vote was announced. Since people are generally reluctant to admit their own weaknesses, this figure might even underestimate the problem.

Source Acknowledgments

Page 13, from Susan Fiske and Shelly Taylor, "Cognition in Social Psychology," *Social Cognition,* 2nd ed. Copyright © 1991. Reproduced with permission of the McGraw-Hill Companies.

Page 19, from Albert H. Hastorf and Hadley Cantril, "They Saw a Game—A Case Study," *Journal of Abnormal and Social Psychology,* Vol. 49. Copyright © 1954 by the American Psychological Association. Reprinted by permission.

Page 27, from Richard R. Lau and Dan Russell, "Attributions in the Sports Pages," *Journal of Personality and Social Psychology,* Vol. 39. Copyright © 1980 by the American Psychological Association. Reprinted by permission.

Page 46, from William B. Swann, Jr., J. Gregory Hixon, and Chris De La Ronde, "Embracing the Bitter "Truth": Negative Self-Concepts and Marital Commitment," *Psychological Science.* Copyright © 1992. Reprinted by permission of Blackwell Publishers.

Page 52, from David G. Myers and Jack Ridl, "Can We All Be Better Than Average?" *Psychology Today,* August 1979. Copyright © 1979 by Sussex Publishers, Inc. Reprinted with permission from *Psychology Today.*

Page 58, from Hazel Rose Markus and Shinobu Kitayama, "Culture and the Self: Implications for Cognition, Emotion and Motivation," *Psychological Review, 98.* Copyright © 1991 by the American Psychological Association. Reprinted by permission.

Page 84, from Robert Dialdini, "Social Proof: Monkey Me, Monkey Do," *Influence,* 3rd ed. Copyright © 1993. Reprinted by permission of Addison Wesley Educational Publishers, Inc.

Page 80, from Peter B. Smith and Michael Harris Bond, "Psychology Across Cultures: Conformity and Independence," excerpts from *Social Psychology Across Cultures.* Copyright © 1994 by Allyn & Bacon. Adapted by permission.

Page 84, from Philip Meyer, "If Hitler Asked You to Electrocute a Stranger, Would You?" *Esquire* magazine, February 1970. © Hearst Communications, Inc. By permission of Esquire magazine. Also, Esquire is a trademark of Hearst Magazines Property. All rights reserved.

Page 116, from Leon Festinger and James M. Carlsmith, "Cognition Consequences of Forced Compliance,"*Personality and Social Psychology Bulletin, 18.* Copyright © 1992 by the American Psychological Association. Reproduced by permission.

Page 125, from Richard E. Petty, John T. Cacioppo, and David Schumann, "Central and Peripheral Routes to Advertising Effectiveness: The Moderating Role of Involvement." From "Central Peripheral Routes to Advertising Effectiveness: The Moderating Role of Involvement," *Journal of Consumer Research, 10.* Copyright © 1983. Reprinted by permission of the University of Chicago Press.

Page 142, from Anthony Pratkanis and Elliot Aronson, "The Fear Appeal." *The Age of Propaganda.* Used with permission.

Page 156, from Wolfgang Stroebe, Michael Diehl, and Georgios Abakoumkin,"The Illusion of Group Effectivity," *Personality and Social Psychology Bulletin, 18.* Copyright © 1992. Reprinted by permission.

Page 168, from Stephen G. Harkins and Jeffrey M. Jackson, "The Role of Evaluation in Eliminating Social Loafing," *Personality and Social Psychology Bulletin.* Copyright © 1985 by the Society for Personality and Social Psychology, Inc. Reprinted by permission of Sage Publications, Inc.

Page 175, from Gregory Moorhead, Richard Ference and Chris Neck, "Group Decision Fiascoes Continue: Space Shuttle Challenger and a Revised Groupthink Framework," *Human Relations,* pp. 539–550. Copyright © 1991. Reprinted by permission of Plenum Publishing Corporation.

Page 194, from Caryl E. Rusbult, Dennis J. Johnson and Gregory D. Morrow, "Impact of Couple Patterns of Problem Solving on Distress and Nondistress in Dating Relationships." Copyright © 1986 by the American Psychological Association. Reprinted by permission.

Page 209, from Susan Sprecher, Quintin Sullivan, and Elaine Hatfield, "Mate Selection Preferences: Gender Differences Examined in a National Sample," *Journal of Personality and Social Psychology, 66.* Copyright © 1994 by the American Psychological Association. Reprinted by permission.

Page 221, from Robert J. Sternberg,"The Ingredients of Love." *The Triangle of Love.* Copyright © 1988. Reprinted by permission of Robert Sternberg.

Page 242, from Bibb Latané and John M. Darley, "Social Determinants of Bystander Intervention in Emergencies" (slightly abridged), *Altruism and Helping Behavior: Social Psychological Studies of Some Antededents and Consequences,* edited by J. Macaulay and L. Berkowitz. Copyright © 1970 by Academic Press. Reprinted by permission.

Page 254, from Samuel P. Oliner and Pearl M. Oliner, "The Altruistic Personality: Concern into Action," (abridged from chapter 8), *The Altruistic Personality: Rescuers of News in Nazi Europe.* Copyright © 1988. Reprinted with permission of The Free Press, a Division of Simon & Schuster.

Page 261, from Mark Snyder and Allen M. Omoto, "Who Volunteers and Why? The Psychology of AIDS Volunteerism," *Helping and Being Helped: Naturalistic Studies,* edited by S. Spacapan and S. Oskamp. Reprinted by permission of the authors.

Page 283, from Scott Stossel, "The Man Who Counts the Killings" (originally appeared in *Atlantic Monthly,* May 1997). Scott Stossel is executive editor of *The American Prospect* magazine. Reprinted by permission of the author.

Page 292, from Richard E. Nisbett, "Violence and U.S. Regional Culture," *American Psychologist, 48.* Copyright © 1993 by the American Psychological Association. Reprinted by permission.

Page 306, from Alan Reifman, Richard P. Larrick, and Steven Fein, "Temper and Temperature on the Diamond: The Heat-Aggression Relationship in Major League Baseball," *Personality and Social Psychology Bulletin.* Copyright © 1993 by the Society for Personality and Social Psychology, Inc. Reprinted by permission of Sage Publications, Inc.

Page 322, from Gordon Allport, "The Nature of Prejudice: What Is the Problem?" *The Nature of Prejudice,* pp. 6–9, 14 & 15. Copyright © 1979 by Addison Wesley Publishing Company, Inc. Reprinted by permission of Addison Wesley Longman.

Page 327, from Claude M. Steele, "Race and the Schooling of Black Americans," *Atlantic Monthly,* April 1992. Copyright © 1992. Reprinted by permission of the author.

Page 339, from H. Andrew Sagar and Janet Ward Schofield, "Racial and Behavioral Cues in Black and White Children's Perceptions of Ambiguously Aggressive Acts," *Journal of Personality and Social Psychology, 39.* Copyright © 1980 by the American Psychological Association. Reprinted by permission.

Page 358, from Shelley E. Taylor and Gayle A. Dakof, "Social Support and the Cancer Patient," *The Social Psychology of Health,* edited by S. Spacapan and S. Oskamp. Reprinted by permission of the authors.

Page 373, from Larry Bernard and Edward Krupat, "The Patient–Patient Relationship," *Health Psychology: Biopsychosocial Factors in Health and Illness.* Copyright © 1994 by Holt, Rinehart and Winston. Reprinted by permission of the publishers.

Page 385, from Elizabeth F. Loftus and John C. Palmer, "Reconstruction of Automobile Destruction: An Example of the Interaction Between Language and Memory," *Journal of Verbal Learning and Verbal Behavior,* 13, pp. 585–589. Copyright © 1974 by Academic Press, Inc.

Page 391, from Saul M. Kassin and Lawrence S. Wrightsman, "The American Jury on Trial: Inside the Jury Room," *The American Jury on Trial: Psychological Perspectives.* Reprinted by permission of Saul Kassin.

Index

Donnerstein, Edward, 277–282
Dorman, M. C., 376
D'Souza, Dinesh, 329
Duncan, B. L., 339–341
Duncan, Robert, 396
Dunkel-Schetter, C., 359–360, 362, 365, 369
Durkheim, Emile, 2–3

E

Earning potential of mate, gender differences in desire for, 210–219
Ecological self, 60–61
Edley, Chris, 321
Edwards, Jonathan, 142, 145
Elaboration Likelihood Model (ELM), 109, 111–113, 125, 128, 138
Ellison, Ralph, 334, 336
Emergencies, social determinants of bystander intervention in, 242–253
Empathic behavior, 238–240, 255–256, 259
Empty love, 229, 231
Encyclopedia of Southern Culture, 292
Eron, Leonard, 284
Escalante, Jamie, 334, 337
Evaluation, role in elimination of social loafing, 168–174
Exit, Voice and Loyalty: Response to Decline in Firms, Organizations and States (Hirschman), 190
Exit reaction, in relationships, 191–192, 195–206

F

Fatuous love, 229, 232–233
Fazio, R. H., 340
Fear tactics, 142–146
Feather, N. T., 28
Fein, Steven, 306–313
Feingold, A., 210
Ference, Richard, 175–184
Ferlinghetti, L., 394
Feshback, Seymour, 3
Festinger, Leon, 116–124
Feynman, Richard, 178
Fillmore, C. J., 386
Film violence, 279–280, 291
Fischhoff, Baruch, 54–55
Fishbein, Martin, 137

Fiske, Susan, 7–18
Fleming, Jacqueline, 333
Folkes, V. S., 35
Frager, R., 82
Frank, M. G., 307
Freud, Sigmund, 238
Friedman, H. S., 374
Friend, R., 80–81
Functional approach to volunteerism, 266–274

G

Gastil, R. D., 295
Geertz, C., 62, 65
Gender differences
  in mate selection preferences, 209–219
  in problem-solving responses in relationships, 202–205
Genovese, Kitty, 242–243, 248
Gerard, Harold, 393–394
Gerbner, George, 283–284, 286–291
Gifford, R. K., 340
Gilovich, T., 307
Goethe, Johann von, 87
Goffman, Erving, 328, 334
Gottman, J., 197, 203
Grajek, Susan, 224
Greenfield, S., 381
Greenwald, Anthony, 53
Groups, 149–184
  discrimination against, self-esteem and, 42–43
  groupthink, 175–184
  illusion of group effectivity, 156–166
  jury deliberation, 391–402
  social loafing and, 168–174
Groupthink, 175–184

H

Hadlow, J., 379
Hall, J. A., 375, 376
Hallowell, A. I., 60
Hamilton, D. L., 340
Hare, Bruce, 332
Harkins, Stephen G., 168–174
Harwood, R. L., 66
Hastie, Reid, 399
Hastorf, Albert H., 19–26
Hatfield, Elaine, 209–219, 225

Private acceptance, 394
Problem solving in dating couples, 194–206
Process gains and losses, 151

R

Public compliance, 394
Race
    children's perceptions of ambiguously
        aggressive acts and, 339–348
    gender differences in mate selection and,
        212–219
Rafferty, Y., 80–81
Reaves, Andrew, 333
Reciprocation, as influence mechanism,
    76–77
Reifman, Alan S., 306–313
Relationships, 187–233
    commitment in, 188–193
    mate selection preferences, 209–219
    problem solving in dating couples,
        194–206
    triangular theory of love, 221–233
*Report of the Presidential Commission on
    the Space Shuttle Accident,* 177–179,
    181, 182
Rescue behavior, 254–260
Reykowski, Janusz, 255
Rhetorical questions, 113–114
Rhine, Ramon, 128
Rogers, W. L., 363
Romantic love, 229, 231–232
Roosevelt, Franklin D., 144
Ross, Lee, 319, 320
Ross, M., 28, 35, 158, 164
Ross, Michael, 55
Roter, D. L., 375, 376, 381
Rothbart, M., 340
Rubin, Ellis, 284, 286
Rubin, Lillian, 224–225
Rubin, Z., 200
Rusbult, Caryl E., 187–206
Russell, Dan, 27–36
Ryan, Leo R., 92

S

Sagar, H. Andrew, 339–348
Sampson, E. E., 66
Scarcity, as influence mechanism, 77
Schlenker, Barry, 55

Schofield, Janet Ward, 339–348
Schroeder, Harry, 240
Schumann, David, 125–139
Schwankovsky, L, 381
Sears, David O., 127
Self, 39–67
    cultural differences and, 58–67
    defined, 40
    negative self-concept and marital
        commitment, 46–50
    self-serving bias, 52–57
Self-awareness, 43, 44
Self-consciousness, 43–44
Self-deception, 55
Self-disclosure, 225
Self-esteem, 40–43
    AIDS volunteerism and, 270–273
    fear arousal and, 144
    marital commitment and, 46–50
    stereotyping and, 317–318, 332–333
Self-protection, U.S. regional attitudes
    toward violence for, 297–298
Self-relevance, 113, 114
Self-serving bias, 52–57
Self-verification theory, 46–50
Severance, Laurence J., 128
Shaw, M., 158
Sherif, Carolyn W., 127
Sherif, Muzifer, 127
Shirer, William L., 96
Sicoly, F., 158, 164
Sicoly, Fiore, 55
Silver, R. L., 359–360, 364–365
Similarity, 84–95
Simon, J. G., 28
Simon, Paul, 285
Simon, Rita James, 399
"Sinners in the Hands of an Angry God"
    (Edwards), 142
Situationalism, 2
Smith, Peter B., 80–83
Snyder, Mark, 261–274
Sobel, Mechal, 336
Social cognition, 7–36
    attribution in sports pages, 27–36
    perceptions of social event case study,
        19–26
    perceptions of things *vs.* perceptions of
        people, 16–18